THE CATHOLIC UNIVERSITY OF AMERICA
CANON LAW STUDIES
No. 174

Dispensation From Vindicative Penalties

AN HISTORICAL CONSPECTUS AND COMMENTARY

BY THE

REV. JOSEPH JAMES CHRIST, M.A., S.T.L., J.C.L.
Priest of the Archdiocese of Chicago

A DISSERTATION

Submitted to the Faculty of the School of Canon Law of the Catholic University of America in Partial Fulfillment of the Requirements for the Degree of Doctor of Canon Law.

THE CATHOLIC UNIVERSITY OF AMERICA PRESS
WASHINGTON, D. C.
1943

Nihil Obstat:

LUDOVICUS MOTRY, S.T.D., J.C.D.,
Censor Deputatus.

Washingtonii, D. C., die 6 maii, 1943.

Imprimatur:

✠ SAMUEL A. STRITCH, D.D.
Archiepiscopus Chicagiensis.

Chicagiae, Illinois, die 6 maii, 1943.

Printed by
THE PAULIST PRESS
New York, N. Y.
61

TO

HIS EXCELLENCY

THE MOST REVEREND SAMUEL A. STRITCH, D.D.

ARCHBISHOP OF CHICAGO

TABLE OF CONTENTS

CHAPTER V

PART II

CANONICAL COMMENTARY

SECTION I

ORDINARY DISPENSATION FROM VINDICATIVE PENALTIES

CHAPTER VI

SECTION II

DISPENSATION FROM VINDICATIVE PENALTIES IN THE MORE URGENT CASES

CHAPTER VIII

CHAPTER X

FOREWORD

It has often been said that the justice and mercy of God permeate the penal legislation of His Church: justice in the penalties inflicted upon members who break the laws of His Church, and mercy in the leniency shown offenders who prove themselves worthy of mercy. It is to be expected that at times circumstances will arise in which the removal or mitigation of a penalty would be more conducive to the sanctification of an individual person or group of persons than would the rigorous application of the penalty. Thus it is that at times justice is tempered with mercy; and especially is this true in the exercise of dispensations from vindicative penalties.

The treatise which follows is a study of such a dispensation—the removal of a definite penalty inflicted by the Church upon members who break her laws. It treats of the dispensation from one type of penalty, the vindicative, which is by its nature punitive rather than medicinal. An attempt has been made to limit the study to penalties which are purely vindicative in nature, but, since this concept developed slowly through the centuries, it was necessary, especially in the first part of the historical synopsis, to treat of penalties which were only partially vindicative. However, these are treated summarily and only in so far as it was necessary for a complete understanding of the topic of this study.

Furthermore, special emphasis has been placed throughout on the discussion of the powers of bishops and priests to dispense from these penalties. The principles of papal dispensatory powers were established early in the Church and have remained stable; the powers of bishops and priests developed slowly and were determined clearly for the first time in the Code of Canon Law.

It is unfortunate that the legislator, in establishing the principles of canon 2290, saw fit to make reference to the prescriptions of canon 2254. For canonists have been content, in treating of canon 2290, to make the same reference, *servatis servandis,* without attempting to adapt or apply the principles stated therein. As a consequence, canon 2290 has until now merited little more than a paragraph or two in commentaries on the Code. As a matter of fact, this attitude of canonists is evidenced in the entire treatment of vindicative penalties. This undeserved neglect of the study of vindicative penalties is much to be regretted. True, a certain similarity between vindicative penalties and censures is present, but the differences, especially in regard to remission, are so great that vindicative penalties deserve special and thorough treatment. This work is an attempt at such a treatment.

It should be mentioned here that, as a result of this inadequate treatment of vindicative penalties by canonists, references are often made in this work to sources and writings which have a merely corroborative value, that is, references to opinions which authors hold in regard to censures but which by adaptation may be applied to vindicative penalties. Thus, frequently, the points established in the text are the writer's, while the footnotes are references to similar opinions held by canonists in regard to medicinal penalties.

The nature of canon 2290 has compelled the writer to adopt a disproportionate division of its treatment, for though each paragraph of this canon would seem to be entitled to separate treatment in a separate chapter, the great preponderance of material is to be found in canon 2290, § 1. The result is that the present consideration of these paragraphs is bound to suffer a noticeable lack of balance, with the last two chapters reduced to merely essential and peculiar elements and containing many cross references. But any other method of handling the overlapping material would have resulted in undesirable confusion.

A word must be said regarding the use of the term "vindicative penalty" instead of the more common "vindictive penalty." It is true that the word "vindictive" has the meaning of "punitive," and as such may well express the purpose of the Church in inflicting these penalties. But "vindictive," in its primary meaning,[1] connotes the idea of revenge and hate, an idea entirely foreign to the intention of the Church. The Church never punishes merely for the sake of the punishment; she intends always, even if merely as a secondary

[1] Both Webster's and Funk & Wagnalls' Dictionaries define the word "vindictive" as "having a revengeful spirit"; while "vindicative" is defined as "that which contributes to vindication."

motive, the correction of the individual.[2] As her primary purpose in inflicting these penalties, she intends the restoration of the social order, the triumph of justice, and the rehabilitation of public faith and tranquillity:[3] all of which are expressions of the idea of *vindication*. Of her it may be said, as St. Thomas says of God: "Deus enim non delectatur in poenis propter ipsas, sed delectatur in ordine suae iustitiae, quae hoc requirit." [4]

The writer wishes to express his sincere gratitude to His Excellency, the Most Reverend Samuel A. Stritch, Archbishop of Chicago, for the opportunity of graduate study in Canon Law, to the Reverend John J. O'Hearn for his keen interest and encouragement, to the members of the Faculty of the School of Canon Law of the Catholic University of America for their kind assistance and guidance in the preparation of this work, and to his family and friends, especially the student priests at the Catholic University of America, for their generous assistance.

[2] Cf. Cappello, *Tractatus Canonico-Moralis de Censuris iuxta Codicem Iuris Canonici* (3. ed., Taurinorum Augustae: Marietti, 1925), p. 3, note 6. (Hereafter cited as *De Censuris*.)

[3] Cf. Ottaviani, *Institutiones Iuris Publici Ecclesiastici* (2. ed., 2 vols., Typis Polyglottis Vaticanis, 1936), I, 132, 133. (Hereafter cited as *Institutiones*.)

[4] *Summa*, I^{a}, II^{ae}, qu. 87, a. 3, ad 3.

Part I

Historical Synopsis

CHAPTER I

PRELIMINARY NOTIONS

Article I. The Right of the Church to Inflict Penalties

The Church is a perfect and supreme society, established by Christ to lead men to heaven. She has, it is true, supreme legislative and judiciary power. But her mission, as instituted by Christ, would be entirely ineffective, unless there existed at the same time the right to coerce her contumacious members [1] by the infliction of both spiritual and temporal penalties. Like every society, the Church is an external organization, composed of human beings who have bodies as well as souls. She is, in fact, by the will of her divine Founder, a community, an association, of men, governed by men.[2]

Like every external organization, the Church must be governed by laws and regulations that will enable her to fulfill her mission and attain her end. The aim and purpose of the Church is the worship of God and the salvation of souls. Any action, therefore, on the part of her members which hinders her from carrying out her mission, and, consequently, whatever contravenes the regulations made by her concerning the worship of God and the sanctification of her children is punishable by her.[3] Thus, the "fundamentum et ratio" of the penalties of the Church, as of those of the civil power in regard to its end, is the fulfillment and attainment of her end and purpose.[4]

[1] Cf. Ottaviani, *Institutiones Iuris Publici Ecclesiastici,* I, 324.

[2] Cf. Soglia, *Institutiones Iuris Publici Ecclesiastici* (Parisiis, 1842), I, 137.

[3] Cf. Smith, *Elements of Ecclesiastical Law* (6. ed., 3 vols., New York, 1887), III, 7, 8.

[4] Cf. Hergenröther-Hollweck, *Katholisches Kirchenrecht* (Freiburg, 1905), p. 710.

It is not necessary here to enter upon the controversy as to what precisely is the primary purpose of the penalties of the Church. There are those who maintain that penalties are primarily corrective; there are others who state that they are principally reparative or punitive. It is enough here to state both opinions, and with Hergenröther, to establish this as the formula for canonical penalties: "Punitur ut corrigator et ne iterum peccetur." [5] In all her punishments, the Church always has a twofold object in view: the good of the offender and the common good of the Church.

Article II. Vindicative Penalties

The term *penalty (poena)* seems to have been derived from the Greek word, ποενή, whence comes its meaning of satisfaction or of a price by which an injury is compensated. [6] A penalty or punishment in general is an evil, a privation, a pain or suffering, whether of body or soul, inflicted for crime by a legitimate authority in order to preserve the social order.[7] When a person transgresses a law, he usually does so in order to satisfy his disorderly passion and to procure for himself some unlawful enjoyment. The lawgiver punishes him for his disobedience by depriving him of some lawful gratification, or by making him suffer some pain, either in his soul or in his body. Thus the illicit pleasure is atoned for and expiated by his privation and suffering.[8] From this it will be seen that punishment and guilt are correlatives. There can be no punishment where there is no willful crime. "Sine culpa, nisi subsit causa, non est aliquis puniendus." [9]

[5] Cf. Hergenröther-Hollweck, *op. cit.*, p. 711.

[6] Cf. Wernz, *Ius Decretalium* (6 vols., Romae et Prati, 1906-1913), VI, tit. IV, n. 71.

[7] Cf. Harquini. *Institutiones Iuris Publici Ecclesiastici* (Romae, 1862), n. 25; Schmalzgrueber, *Ius Ecclesiasticum Universum* (5 vols. in 12, Romae, 1843-1845), lib. V, tit. 37, n. 1 sq.

[8] Cf. Schmidt, *Thesaurus Iuris Ecclesiastici* (2 vols., Heidelbergae, 1779), tom. VII, cap. II, XXXVIII (hereafter cited as *Thesaurus*); Hinschius, *Das Kirchenrecht der Katholiken und Protestanten in Deutchland* (6 vols., Berlin, 1869-1897; Vols. I-IV, *System des katholischen Kirchenrechts*, Berlin, 1869-1888), IV, 747. (Hereafter cited as *Kirchenrecht*.)

[9] Reg. 23, R. J., in VI°. Cf. Reiffenstuel, *Ius Canonicum Universum* (5 vols. in 6, Parisiis, 1864-1870), lib. V, tit. 37, n. 2.

From the earliest ages of Christianity the Church exercised her own inherent right of punishing delinquent members.[10] Even in apostolic times, when among the faithful some were excluded from participation in ecclesiastical functions because of specified major offenses, one finds the basis of a definite penal system that was to develop gradually through the centuries of ecclesiastical history. The care of the religious and moral welfare of the faithful was placed, from the very beginning of the Church, in the hands of the apostles, and their successors, the bishops.[11]

However, in apostolic times no definite system of imposing penalties existed; the Church was as yet in her infancy and was unable to enact universal regulations which demanded the experience of centuries to perfect. In the first centuries one can not expect to find a fixed and exact terminology in the penal law of the Church. Terms and distinctions, common in the law today, were unknown then as such. In fact, during the period of the persecutions, that is, until the time of Constantine, precise laws were not often found.[12] It was only gradually with the gradual growth of disciplinary laws that precise terms developed and received universal acceptance in the Church.

Thus, the word *excommunication* in the beginning was employed to designate all ecclesiastical punishments and remedies.[13] It conveyed the broad meaning that the one penalized had been placed outside the communion to which his grade in the Church entitled him, either wholly or in part.[14] It was employed sometimes to designate expulsion from the Church, sometimes to signify merely the priva-

[10] Cf. Ottaviani, *Institutiones*, I, 323.

[11] Cf. I Cor. V, 2-4; II Thess. III, 14; Matt. XVIII, 15-17.

[12] Cf. Findlay, *Canonical Norms Governing the Deposition and Degradation of Clerics*, The Catholic University of America Canon Law Studies, n. 130 (Washington, D. C.: The Catholic University of America Press, 1941), p. 2.

[13] Cf. Hinschius, *Kirchenrecht*, V, p. 639; Hyland, *Excommunication, Its Nature, Historical Development and Effects*, The Catholic University of America Canon Law Studies, n. 49 (Washington, D. C.: The Catholic University of America Press, 1928), p. 19; (hereafter cited as *Excommunication*).

[14] Cf. Cappello, *Tractatus Canonico-Moralis de Censuris iuxta Codicem Iuris Canonici* (3. ed., Augustae Taurinorum: Marietti, 1933), p. 1, nota 1; Reiffenstuel, *Ius Canonicum Universum*, lib. V, tit. 39, n. 2.

tion of some right or rights belonging to the faithful, or to a certain class among them.[15] Then, as now, there were in the Church certain rights which were common to all members of the Church, such as the right to the reception of the sacraments, and to presence at Holy Mass and public prayers. There were other rights which were proper to the various grades among the clergy. Whoever, therefore, was deprived of all these rights, or of one or a number of them, might be designated by the general term "*excommunicated*," that is, placed outside the communion to which his position in the Christian society entitled him.[16] It was only in the twelfth and thirteenth centuries that the technical meaning of excommunication became definitely fixed, and that the term was used to designate exclusively one of the three penalties which were thereafter distinguished from all others by the name of censures.[17]

Furthermore, during the first six centuries it was not uncommon for the legislator to use the word *censure* to include also, with various distinctions, every kind of ecclesiastical punishment, namely, public penances, deposition, suspension, excommunication or interdict.[18] In fact, this loose use of the term *censure* continued, more or less, until the sixteenth century, when the definite concept of censure was fully evolved.[19]

Likewise, during these early centuries, the internal or penitential forum was not separated from the external or judicial forum.[20] The

[15] Cf. Gans, "Censure," *Catholic Encyclopedia*.

[16] Cf. I Council of Nicaea (325), c. 16—Mansi, *Sacrorum Conciliorum Nova et Amplissima Collectio* (53 vols. in 60, Paris, Arnhem, Leipzig, 1901-1927), II, 956 (this work will be referred to henceforth as Mansi); Berardi, *Commentaria in Ius Ecclesiasticum Universum* (2 vols., Mediolani, 1846), II, P. II, diss. 3, cap. 5.

[17] Cf. Ayrinhac-Lydon, *Penal Legislation in the New Code of Canon Law* (revised edition, New York, Cincinnati, Chicago, San Francisco: Benziger Brothers, 1936), n. 156.

[18] Wernz, *Ius Decretalium*, VI, n. 144; Moriarty, *Extraordinary Absolution from Censures*, The Catholic University of America Canon Law Studies, n. 113 (Washington, D. C.: The Catholic University of America Press, 1938), p. 5.

[19] Hinschius, *Kirchenrecht*, V, 641; Cappello, *De Censuris*, pp. 1, 2, nota 1; Richter, *Lehrbuch des katholischen und evangelischen Kirchenrechts* (8. ed., 1 vol. in 2, Leipzig, 1886), p. 774 (hereafter cited as *Kirchenrecht*).

[20] Cf. Morinus, *Commentarius Historicus de Disciplina in Administratione*

authorities of the Church did not often act against delinquent members except in the penitential and internal forum; and the punishment and penalties which were then inflicted were of necessity of the nature of penances, rather than penalties. The tribunal of penance, rather than a judicial, external tribunal, served as the means of punishing Christians who broke the laws of the Church.[21] Thus it was that most of the penalties inflicted by the Church upon laymen were penances, public penances; and this close connection, or rather union, of the penal law of the Church with her penitential discipline lasted until the disappearance of public penances, in the East at the beginning of the sixth century,[22] and in the West in the twelfth century.[23] Then, in the twelfth century, the external and judicial forum was definitely separated from the internal and penitential forum, and the penal law of the Church became distinct from her penitential law; [24] and in this distinct penal law the public ecclesiastical tribunal expanded and took the place of the tribunal of conscience.[25]

Just as vindicative penalties were so often bound up with the penitential discipline, likewise there was no sharp distinction between medicinal penalties and vindicative penalties as they exist today.[26] It seems that up to the sixth century all the penalties of the Church were largely vindicative in nature, for they served principally, even in their penitenial forms, to repair the social order which had been violated by the crime committed, since it was the public

Sacramenti Poenitentiae Tredecim Primis Saeculis in Ecclesia Occidentali, et huc usque in Orientali Observata (Parisiis, 1651), lib. L, cap. 9-10 (hereafter cited as *De Admin. Sacr. Poenit.;* Van Espen, *Tractatus Historico-Canonicus de Censuris Ecclesiasticis* (Lovanii, 1753), t. II, Pars III, tit. V, n. 1 (hereafter cited as *Tract. de Censuris*); Hinschius, *Kirchenrecht,* IV, 747.

[21] Cf. Van Espen, *Tract. de Censuris,* t. II, pars III, tit. XI, cap. I, nn, 2, 3; Hinschius, *Kirchenrecht,* IV, 747.

[22] Cf. Rauschen, *Eucharist and Penance in the First Six Centuries of the Church* (authorized translation from 2. German edition; translated from the German, St. Louis: Herder, 1913), p. 196; (hereafter cited as *Eucharist and Penance*).

[23] Cf. Morinus, *De Admin. Sacr. Poenit.,* L. VII, c. 7, n. 1; Rauschen, *op. cit.,* p. 213.

[24] Cf. Van Espen, *Tract. de Censuris,* t. II, pars III, tit. XI, cap. I, n. 3.

[25] Boudinhon, "Excommunication"—*Catholic Encyclopedia.*

[26] Cf. Hinschius, *Kirchenrecht,* IV, 748; V, 125.

aspect of the Church rather than the individual pursuits of her members that was stressed.[27] Some authors maintain that all the Church's penalties were purely vindicative in nature.[28] It is true that there were some penalties inflicted during these early centuries which were definitely vindicative, *v. g.*, deposition as a particular punishment for clerics guilty of grave crimes, consisting substantially in their perpetual removal from rank and office in the Church.[29] But most of these penalties seem to have combined both elements, punitive and medicinal, although the vindicative element seems to have predominated.[30] Thus, penalties which later became definitely medicinal in character, and exclusively so, were in the beginning vindicative penalties, with, however, some sort of medicinal character. Although they were inflicted with the primary purpose of restoring the violated social order, and were directed at the expiation of the crime,[31] the improvement of the sinner was not overlooked. Moreover, these early penalties, especially those of suspension, were usually imposed for a definite length of time,[32] and though the im-

[27] Cf. Rainer, *Suspension of Clerics,* The Catholic University of America Canon Law Studies, n. 111 (Washington, D. C.: The Catholic University of America Press, 1937), pp. 13, 14.

[28] Cf. Hinschius, *Kirchenrecht.* IV, 748, 756, 831; V, 127, 641; Meurer, "Die rechtliche Natur der Ponitenzen den katholischen Kirche in historischer Entwicklung,"—*Archiv fur katholisches Kirchenrecht* (Innsbruck, 1857-1861; Mainz, 1862—) XLIX (1883), 180-187 (hereafter cited as *AKKR*); Riegger, *De Poenitentiis et Poenis Ecclesiasticis* (4 vols., Vindobonae, 1772), p. 28; Roberti, *De Delictis et Poenis* (Romae, 1930), p. 248.

[29] Cf. I Letter of St. Clement to Corinthians, c. 44—*The Ante-Nicene Fathers* (Roberts and Donaldson, Editors, American reprint, 10 vols., New York, 1890), I, 17; Funk, *Patres Apostolici* (Tübingen, 1901), I, 108; Ottaviani, *Institutiones,* I, 328; Hefele, *A History of the Councils of the Church* (translated by W. Clarke, 2. ed., 5 vols., Edinburgh, 1883), I, 87.

[30] Cf. Cappello, *De Censuris,* p. 9.

[31] Cf. c. 35, X, *de sententia excommunicationis,* V, 39: "Cum publica auctoritate intersit ne crimina maneant impunita"; c. 8, X, *de officio iudicis ordinarii,* I, 31: ". . . Ad reprimandam malitiam perversorum poenae certae sunt in canonibus constitutae . . ."; Hinschius, *Kirchenrecht,* IV, p. 831.

[32] Cf. I Council of Rome (252)—Mansi, I, 866; Council of Epâon (517), c. 4: "Si Episcopus est, tribus mensibus se a communione suspendat duobus presbyter abstineat."—Mansi, VIII, 559; Council of Agde (506), c. 60: "Presbyter duobus mensibus se abstineat."—Mansi, VIII, 334.

provement of the sinner and his renunciation of his contumacy was intended, this was not placed as a necessary condition for the removal of the penalty. Thus, for example, canonical suspension was, until the fifth century,[33] or the sixth,[34] a purely vindicative penalty, inflicted for a definite length of time.[35] The medicinal suspension was the outgrowth of this vindicative penalty.[36] It is interesting to note the reason for this change as given by Hinschius: it happened that deprivation from office or the prohibition to exercise certain ecclesiastical rights proved somewhat inefficient at times, since after the lapse of the specified time the offender could again exercise his office and rights, even though his conduct did not improve. To deprive the culprit of his office and rights afresh demanded another penalty which would remain binding until contumacy ceased, or until sufficient guarantees were given to assure amendment in the future. This penalty was the medicinal suspension, the outgrowth of the vindicative penalty.[37]

Similarly, the interdict seems to have originally been a vindicative penalty.[38] Hinschius seems to have been of the opinion that the sole purpose of the interdict was punitive,[39] but this opinion is doubted by Krehbiel,[40] since quite often the offenders were obliged to perform long and severe penances even after the interdict was removed. However, the interdict also seems to have combined vindicative and medicinal elements.[41]

The major excommunication or *anathema* also combined both medicinal and vindicative elements,[42] although this has been dis-

[33] Cf. Hinschius, *Kirchenrecht,* IV, 756.

[34] Cf. Wernz, *Ius Decretalium,* VI, tit. VI, n. 203.

[35] Cf. Rainer, *Suspension of Clerics,* p. 14.

[36] Cf. Hinschius, *Kirchenrecht,* IV, 757.

[37] Cf. Hinschius, *Kirchenrecht,* IV, 757; cf. also Kahn, *Etude sur le délit et la peine en droit canonique* (Paris, 1898), p. 70.

[38] Cf. Conran, *The Interdict,* The Catholic University of America Canon Law Studies, n. 56 (Washington, D. C.: The Catholic University of America Press, 1930), p. 34.

[39] *Kirchenrecht,* IV, 747-749.

[40] *The Interdict* (Washington: American Historical Association, 1930), p. 11.

[41] Cf., e. g., c. 24, C. XI, q. 3.

[42] Cf. Probst, *Kirchliche Disciplin in den drei ersten christlichen Jahrhunderten* (Tübingen, 1873), p. 385; (hereafter cited as *Kirchliche Disciplin*).

puted by those who maintain that it was either purely vindicative[43] or entirely medicinal.[44]

The penalties of the early Church were exclusively of a *ferendae sententiae* character. The imposition of penalties immediately, *i. e.*, without preceding admonitions, was of a much later date, sometime after the seventh century. It is not necessary here to enter into a lengthy discussion on this point. Hinschius[45] and Boehmer[46] maintain that *latae sententiae* penalties did not exist. They base their claim principally on the words of Van Espen who contends that during the first ten centuries this type of penalty was unknown. He expresses serious doubt that even one instance of a *latae sententiae* penalty could be found in the *Decretum* of Gratian.[47] Schmidt[48] expresses a similar opinion.

However, although, as Van Espen points out, it is most difficult to find any citation among the canons of the early Church which contains the words "*ipso facto*" and similar terms, still the principle implied by those words is found in various councils. There is a clear *latae sententiae* penalty mentioned in the XIII Council of Toledo (683), wherein that Council declared that those who harbored fugitive clerics and monks were to consider themselves excommunicated and suspended, deprived of office as long as such remained under their protection.[49] Similar *latae sententiae* penalties are found in canon 75 of the IV Council of Toledo (633),[50] and also in the Council of Vernon (755).[51] From the wording of the

[43] Cf. Hinschius, *Kirchenrecht*, V, 127.

[44] Cf. Kober, *Der Kirchenbann nach den Grundsaetzen des canonischen Rechts* (Tübingen, 1863), pp. 23-26; (hereafter cited as *Der Kirchenbann*).

[45] *Kirchenrecht*, IV, 761.

[46] *Ius Ecclesiasticum Protestanticum* (5. ed., 5 vols., Magdeburgi, 1756), lib. III, cap. XLI, § 46; lib. V, cap. XXXIX, § 58.

[47] Cf. Van Espen, *Tract. de Censuris*, t. II, pars III, tit. XI, nn. 19, 20, 21.

[48] *Thesaurus*, VII, 176.

[49] Cf. canon 11: "Transgressor institutionis paternae tanto tempore excommunicatum et remotum se a suis officiis noverit esse, quanto eum qui fugiit sub sua potestate contigerit remorasse."—Mansi, XI, 1074.

[50] Cf. Hardouin, *Acta Conciliorum et Epistolae Decretales ac Constitutiones Summorum Pontificum* (12 vols., Parisiis, 1715), III, 593. (Hereafter this work will be cited as Hardouin); cf. also Mansi, X, 639.

[51] Canon 9: "Si quis presbyter ab episcopo suo degradatus fuerit, et ipse

two latter laws, Kober says it is evident that this penalty is not one that should follow merely upon the condemnation and sentence of the superior, but rather one to be incurred for even secret crimes of this nature.[52] Still earlier examples of seemingly *latae sententiae* vindicative penalties are those established in the I Council of Toledo (400), and especially in the XII Council of Toledo (681).[53] While not using the terminology that would be used at present, the canons certainly express the principle of the "*ipso facto*" incurred penalty.

Article III. Public Penance

The close connection between the penal law of the Church and her penitential discipline has been shown. The fact that most of the penalties of the early Church were public penances warrants a consideration of this institution. Now, it is not to be forgotten that there were penalties inflicted in the early Church which were not public penances, or necessarily connected with them. To say that all penalties were public penances, or inflicted as such would be absurd. Privation of office, deposition, and degradation, often expressed by the term *excommunication*,[54] certainly were distinct from

per contemptum postea aliquid de suo officio sine commeatu facere praesumpserit, et postea . . . excommunicatus fuerit; qui cum ipso communicaverit scienter sciat se esse excommunicatum. Similiter quicumque clericus, aut laicus, vel femina scienter incestum commiserit, et ab episcopo suo excommunicatus fuerit, si quis cum ipso communicaverit scienter, sciat se excommunicatum esse."—Hardouin, III, 1996; *Monumenta Germaniae Historica, Leges* (5 vols., I-IV edited by G. Pertz; V edited by Pertz-Waitz-Brunner, Hannoverae, 1835-1889), I, 25. (Hereafter this work will be cited as *MGH.*)

[52] *Der kirchenbann,* p. 54; cf. also Hollweck, *Die kirchlichen Strafgesetze* (Mainz, 1899), p. 87, nota 2.

[53] Cf. I Council of Toledo, canon 5: "Presbyter . . . si intra civitatem fuerat . . . et ad ecclesiam ad sacrificium quotidianum non venerit, clericus non habeature."—Mansi, X, 478. Cf. XII Council of Toledo, canon 5: "Quicumque . . . se a communione suspenderit, ab ipsa, qua se indicenter privabit gratia communionis anno uno repulsum se noverit. . . ."—Mansi, XI, 1033.

[54] Cf. I Council of Nicaea (325), canon 16, wherein clerics who refused to return to their own diocese were to be excommunicated. Balsamon and Zonares correctly explain this penalty as deposition.—Beveridge, *Synodicon sive Pandectae Canonum et Conciliorum* (2 vols., Oxonii, 1672), I, 77. Cf. also Findlay, *Canonical Norms Governing Deposition and Degradation of Clerics,* p. 2 ss.

public penances. Even in the first three centuries there existed these particular punishments for clerics guilty of grave crimes, consisting in their perpetual removal from rank and office in the Church.[55] Similarly, the major excommunication, or *anathema*, was never a public penance.[56]

And so, although not every excommunication or penalty inflicted by the Church was a public penance, every public penance was a form of excommunication.[57] This is evident from a consideration of the various privations suffered by the penitents in the various grades or "stations." These grades, at the time of the broadest development of the discipline of public penance, starting with the highest, were called *consistentia*,[58] *substratio*,[59] *auditio*,[60] and *fletus*.[61] The penitents in the station of *consistentia*, called *consistentes*, were deprived of the reception of the Eucharist and of the right to offer their gifts during Mass. Those in the *substratio*, the *substrati*, were denied the Eucharist and a part in the offering at Mass and, besides, had no part in the public prayers of the Church. The *audientes* were deprived of all the above privileges, of the prayers said by individual members of the laity and clergy over the kneeling *substrati*, and of attendance at Mass except at the first part. The *flentes*, or lowest grade of penitents, were subject to all the above mentioned privations and moreover were also forbidden to enter a church.[62] This type of excommunication is unknown today. A vestige of it is found in the minor excommunication, or deprivation of the passive use of

[55] Cf. Findlay, *loc. cit.*

[56] Cf. Morinus, *De Admin. Sacr. Poenit.*, L. V, c. 26, n. 18; L. IV, c. 2, n. 3; Van Espen, *Tract. de Censuris*, t. II, Pars III, tit. XI, I, n. 6; Hyland, *Excommunication*, pp. 22-25, 27-29.

[57] Cf. Devoti, *Institutiones Canonicae* (Namurci, 1835), lib. IV, t. II, tit. XVIII, § IV.

[58] Cf. Morinus, *De Admin. Sacr. Poenit.*, L. VI, cc. 17-18.

[59] Cf. Morinus, *op. cit.*, L. VI, cc. 6-8.

[60] Cf. Morinus, *op. cit.*, L. VI, cc. 3-5.

[61] Cf. Morinus, *op. cit.*, L. VI, c. 2.

[62] Cf. Rauschen, *Eucharist and Penance*, p. 202; Van Espen, *Ius Ecclesiasticum Universum* (Louvanii, 1753), II, 379; Morinus, *op. cit.*, L. VI, c. 25, n. 13; L. IV, c. 3, n. 10; Schmidt, *Thesaurus*, VII, 158, 159.

the sacraments,[63] mentioned before [64] and in the decretals of Gregory IX.[65] This minor excommunication disappeared with the publication of the Constitution *Apostolicae Sedis* by Pius IX in 1869.[66] Public penitents were still members of the Church, for their separation from the Church was only partial; the complete expulsion from the Church was the *anathema* or major excommunication which, as has been stated, in itself was never a public penance.

That public penance was a form of excommunication is clear from many sources. The penitential canons and the writings of the Fathers always referred to the grades of public penance as an excommunication, especially in the use of such expressions as *communione privetur*.[67] St. Augustine also testified to this: "Agunt etiam homines poenitentiam, si post Baptismum ita peccaverint, ut excommunicari et postea reconciliari mereantur; sicut in omnibus Ecclesiis illi qui proprie poenitentes appellantur." [68]

In the earlier centuries of the Church, when the term *excommunication* was used without qualification, it referred to these minor excommunications; only when the penalty was referred to as *anathema* or *mortal* excommunication was it understood to mean the major excommunication or total expulsion from the Church.[69] This practice remained until it was definitely decided in the decretals of Gregory IX that the major excommunication was intended when-

[63] Schmalzgrueber, *Ius Ecclesiasticum Universum*, lib. IV, tit. XXXIX, n. 211.

[64] Cf. Bernardus Papiensis, *Bernardi Papiensis Summa Decretalium* (ed. Ern. Laspeyres, Ratisbonae, 1860), lib. V, tit. 34, n. 2.

[65] Cf. c. 59, X, *de sententia excommunicationis*, V, 39; c. 2, X, *de exceptionibus*, II, 25; c. 10, X, *de clerico excommunicato*, V, 27.

[66] Cf. Smith, *Elements of Ecclesiastical Law*, III, 278; Putzer, *Commentarium in Facultates Apostolicas* (5. ed., New York, 1898), n. 1673.

[67] Cf. Chelodi, *Ius Poenale et Ordo Procedendi in Iudiciis Criminalibus iuxta Codicem Iuris Canonici* (4. ed., Tridenti: Libreria Moderna Editrice V. Dalpiaz, 1935), p. 3 (hereafter cited as *Ius Poenale*); Morinus, *De Admin. Sacr. Poenit.*, L. IV, cc. 2-7; Van Espen, *Ius Ecclesiasticum Universum*, II, 6.

[68] *Epist. 265* (ad Seleucinam), n. 7—Migne, *Patrologiae Cursus Completus, Series Latina* (221 vols., Parisiis, 1844-1855), XXXIII, 1088. (Hereafter this work will be cited as *MPL*).

[69] Cf. Moriarty, *The Extraordinary Absolution from Censures*, p. 8.

ever the unqualified word *excommunication* was used.[70] Even the privation of the Eucharist, which was common to all the grades of public penance, but was almost the only element of the highest grade, the *consistentia,* was a form of excommunication, although the very slightest.[71] Consequently, it is quite certain that the public penances were forms of excommunication, not of the major excommunication, but of the minor type.[72]

From this fact, that public penance was always an excommunication, it does not follow necessarily that it was also a censure, for, as has been shown, a clear distinction between medicinal and vindicative penalties simply did not exist then, and the concept of censure was far from any degree of full development. It would be absurd to contend that public penance was a pure censure,[73] as it would be to maintain, as some do, that it was entirely vindicative.[74] The fact is that it contained both elements. Its medicinal elements cannot be denied, in face of various testimonies. Thus, it is true that the contrition and humiliation shown by the penitent did affect his status in some cases.[75] Likewise, many Fathers referred to these penalties as *medicines.*[76]

Its vindicative nature is clear from its unusual duration, which varied as extending over a definite number of years or to the end

[70] C. 59, X, *de sententia excommunicationis,* V, 39. Cf. Gonzallez-Tellez, *Commentaria Perpetua In Singulos Textus Librorum Decretalium Gregorii IX* (5 vols. in 4, Lugduni, 1715), lib. V, tit. 39, cap. 59.

[71] Cf. Suarez, *Opera Omnia,* ed. Ludovicus Vives (26 vols., Parisiis, 1861), Vol. XXIII, *De Censuris in Communi,* disp. 24, sec. I, n. 6 (hereafter cited as *De Censuris*); Morinus, *De Admin. Sacr. Poenit.,* L. VI, cc. 17, 18.

[72] Cf. Richter, *Kirchenrecht,* pp. 776, 777; Phillips-Vering, *Compendium Iuris Ecclesiastici* (1. Latin version from 3. German edition, Ratisbonae, 1875), p. 366; Suarez, *op. cit.,* disp. 24, sec. I, n. 6.

[73] Cf. Moriarty, *Extraordinary Absolution from Censures,* p. 9.

[74] Cf. Meurer, "Die rechtliche Natur der Pönitenzen der katholischen Kirche in historischer Entwicklung"—*AKKR,* XLIX (1883), 180-187; Hinschius, *Kirchenrecht,* V, 126, nota 2.

[75] Cf. I Council of Nicaea (325), c. 12—Mansi, II, 956; Council of Ancyra (314), cc. 5, 7—Mansi, II, 523, 524.

[76] Cf. St. Augustine, *Sermo 351,* n. 10: ". . . Quamvis haec prohibitio [a communione] nondum sit mortalis, sed medicinalis. . . ."—*MPL,* XXXIX, 1546; Morinus, *De Admin. Sacr. Poenit.,* L. VII, c. 21, n. 7.

of the penitent's life. This is manifest in the penitential canons [77] and in the public penances in the penitential books.[78] The ecclesiastical superior was not obliged to pardon the penitent when he had shown signs of repentance, but it was left to the prudent judgment of the superior to shorten the length of time involved in the public penance: definite characteristics of vindicative penalties.[79] Then, too, especially after the time of Novatian, who lived in the third century, the absolution from sins was granted at the completion of the *substratio,* or second highest station of penance, so that those in the highest station, the *consistentes,* were already absolved from their sins, but were not yet allowed to receive the Eucharist; and this privation ceased only when they completed the *consistentia.*[80] This vindicative element remained throughout the centuries of the existence of the public penance, and is even referred to in the Council of Trent.[81]

Because of the vindicative nature of public penance, therefore, a study of the dispensation of vindicative penalties of necessity involves a consideration of the removal of these penances, as will be shown in the next chapter.

[77] Cf. Council of Elvira (306), c. 5—Mansi, II, 6; I Council of Nicaea (325), c. 12—Mansi, II, 956; Council of Ancyra (314), cc. 4-8, 19-24—Mansi, II, 523-528.

[78] Cf. Schmitz, *Die Bussbücher und die Bussdisciplin der Kirche* (Mainz, 1887), pp. 261, 490.

[79] Cf. Woywod, *A Practical Commentary on the Code of Canon Law* (4. ed., 2 vols., New York: Wagner, 1929), II, n. 2076 (hereafter cited as *A Practical Commentary*).

[80] Cf. Morinus, *De Admin. Sacr. Poenit.,* L. I, c. 10, n. 13; L. VI, c. 21, n. 1.

[81] Sess. XIV, cap. 8, *de poenitentia;* also sess. XXIV, de ref., cap. 6.

CHAPTER II

DISPENSATION FROM VINDICATIVE PENALTIES—FROM THE EARLIEST TIMES TO THE FOURTH CENTURY

Article I. The Vindicative Penalties

The penalties inflicted by the Church during this time were major excommunication, or total expulsion from the community of the faithful, complete expulsion from the Church,[1] public penance,[2] interdict,[3] and special penalties inflicted upon clerics who by their crimes had proved themselves unworthy of their sacred charge, suspension,[4] privation of revenues,[5] and deposition.[6] As has been shown, all these penalties were not purely vindicative, but most of them combined both medicinal and punitive elements. The vindicative element was prominent in the major excommunication and in the other forms of excommunication, namely, public penances and the interdict.[7] The privation of revenues and deposition were purely vindicative penalties.[8]

[1] Cf. Alterius, *De Censuris ecclesiasticis nempe de Excommunicatione, Suspensione et Interdicto cum Explicatione Bullae Coenae Dni.* (Romae, 1618), t. 1, lib. I, disp. III, cap. 3; Hyland, *Excommunication,* p. 16.

[2] Cf. Hinschius, *Kirchenrecht,* V, 128; Hollweck, *Die kirchlichen Strafgesetze,* § 22, nota 5; Probst, *Kirchliche Disciplin,* p. 385; Schmidt, *Thesaurus,* VII, 158, 159.

[3] Cf. Cappello, *De Censuris,* p. 142; Conran, *The Interdict,* p. 15; Smith, *Elements of Ecclesiastical Law,* III, n. 3330.

[4] Cf. *Apostolic Canons,* canon 5—Fulton, *Index Canonum* (New York, 1892), p. 83.

[5] Cf. Thomassinus, *Vetus et Nova Ecclesiae Disciplina circa Beneficia et Beneficiarios* (Moguntiaci, 1753), VII, 28 (hereafter cited as *Vetus et Nova Ecclesiae Disciplina*); Kober, *Die Suspension der Kirchendiener* (Tübingen, 1862), p. 21, nota 1.

[6] Cf. Chelodi, *Ius Poenale,* p. 55; Lega, *Praelectiones in Textum Iuris Canonici,* Vol. IV, *De Delictis et Poenis* (2. ed., Romae, 1910), p. 281 (hereafter cited as *De Delictis et Poenis*); Wernz-Vidal, *Ius Canonicum ad Normam Codicis Exactum* (7 tom. in 8 vol., Romae: Apud Aedes Universitatis Gregorianae, 1923-1938), VII, 351 (hereafter cited as *Ius Canonicum*).

[7] Cf. Conran, *The Interdict,* p. 15.

[8] Cf. Findlay, *Canonical Norms Governing the Deposition and Degradation of Clerics,* pp. 10, 117.

It may be noted that the only purely vindicative penalties imposed during this time were those involving clerics. This led some[9] to maintain that the Church in the beginning inflicted real penalties only upon her clerics, and not upon laymen, who were given only penances and purely medicinal punishments. As Hinschius points out,[10] this is not true. The major excommunication and the public penances were, if only in part, definitely vindicative in nature. It is true that crimes of laymen which did not pertain to the ecclesiastical tribunal were punished by the civil power; while clerics, who had the *privilegium fori*, were punished exclusively by the Church.[11] But it is clear that the Church in inflicting punishments upon her ministers as well as upon her other subjects, had the intention of using punitive, vindicative measures.

Article II. The Dispensation from Penalties

Because of the confusion of the internal, sacramental forum and the external or judicial forum and because of the lack of distinction between medicinal and vindicative penalties, it would seem that the principles of dispensation from penalties would likewise lack clarity and precision. And such was the case. The notion of dispensation was not clearly defined; it was used to designate every exception to a law of the Church, whether that exception was an abrogation of the law or a change in the law, an excuse from observing the law or the remission of a penalty inflicted by the law.[12]

The term "*dispensation*," though found occasionally during this time, was rarely used in the early ages of the Church. To signify dispensation, the words ordinarily used were *economia, indulgentia, venia, beneficium, temperamentum, misericordia, liberatio, relaxatio a summo iure, sapiens condescensio, medicinalis condescensio, de-*

[9] Cf. Hinschius, *Kirchenrecht*, IV, 747, 2.

[10] *Kirchenrecht*, IV, 447, 698.

[11] Cf. Wernz, *Ius Decretalium*, VI, 88.

[12] Cf. Stiegler, *Dispensation, Dispensationswesen und Dispensationsrecht im Kirchenrecht* (3 vols., Mainz, 1901), I, 24, 67-69 (hereafter cited as *Dispensation*); Brys, *De Dispensatione in Iure Canonico Praesertim apud Decretistas usque ad Medium Saeculum Decimum Quartum* (Brügis, 1925), pp. 15-19 (hereafter cited as *De Dispensatione*).

tractio rigori iuris.[13] Although these terms had a wide usage, in relation to purely vindicative penalties, such as deposition, their use was quite clear, as shall be seen. But in relation to those penalties which were only partially vindicative, many difficulties present themselves.

The major excommunication or anathema, complete saparation from the Church, was removed by the simple admission of the guilty person to the lowest grade of public penance.[14] By this "absolution"[15] the outcast from the Church was accepted as a member of the Church, in which he could gradually, by progressing through the various grades of penance, attain to full participation of membership.

Similarly, there was no special formulae of absolution from the minor excommunication of the public penances, but the penitent was released from the greater degree of separation from the communion of the faithful by a formal admission into a higher station of penance.[16] This formal and ritual admission to a higher station of penance took place either after the penitent has spent the allotted time in the various stations, or sooner, by a special discretionary act of the bishop, if the penitent gave evidence of repentance and sorrow.[17] It should be noted that public penance possessed a sacramental character; it was a constituent part, with confession and

[13] Cf. Pope Siricius (385), *Epist. ad Himerum*—Coustant. *Epistolae Romanorum Pontificum* (3 vols., Parisiis, 1721), I, 631—Jaffe, *Regesta Pontificum Romanorum ab condita Ecclesia ad annum post Christum natum MCXCVIII* (Editionem secundam correctam et auctam, auspiciis Gulielmi Wattenbach, curaverunt S. Loewenfeld, F. Kaltenbrunner, P. Ewald; Lipsiae, 1885-1888), JK, n. 255 (65). (Hereafter this work will be cited as JL, JK, JE, according to the editor of each particular section); Stiegler, *Dispensation,* I, 12, 13; Pyrrho, *Praxis Dispensationum Apostolicarum* (Coloniae Agrippinae, 1698), lib. I, cap. I; Brys, *De Dispensatione,* pp. 15, 16.

[14] Cf. Hollweck, *Die kirchlichen Strafgesetze,* 22, nota 5, b; Probst, *Kirchliche Disciplin,* pp. 406, 407; Morinus, *De Admin. Sacr. Poenit.,* L. I, c. 10, n. 13; Hinschius, *Kirchenrecht,* IV, 695.

[15] The term *absolution* was seldom used. Common terms were *reconciliatio, pax, communio, venia.*—Cf. Van Espen, *Tract. de Censuris,* L. VIII, c. I, n. 2; Morinus, *op. cit.,* L. VIII, c. I, n. 2.

[16] Cf. Morinus, *op. cit.,* L. VI, c. 5.

[17] Cf. I Council of Nicaea, canon 12—Mansi, II, 674; Devoti, *Institutiones Canonicae,* lib. II, tit. II, sec. IV, § LXXX.

absolution, of the sacrament of penance. There were two distinct absolutions given. The first, the *remissio peccatorum,* was granted immediately after the confession of sins, when a penance for a definite length of time was imposed. The second was the *remissio poenarum,*[18] granted when the penitent was again received into the communion of the Church.[19] The same minister who absolved from sins likewise absolved from the excommunication of public penance.[20] As in the case of major excommunication, the bishop together with his council of priests granted the absolution from the public penance, and sometimes delegated this power to his priests or even to laymen.[21]

The question arises here whether this "absolution" given for penalties which were at least partially vindicative in nature involved the notion of dispensation. There is no question here of the remission of purely vindicative penalties, such as deposition in the strict sense, absolutely distinct from absolution. There are some authors [22] who contend that the concept of dispensation was identified with that of absolution, and that the clear distinction between the two ideas developed much later. This is not true, although there does appear to be some confusion of the two ideas. There is the similarity and identity of terms used to designate the two concepts.[23] There is the lack of a definite formula of absolution from both major excommunication and public penance; and the many instances of mitigation in certain phases of penitential discipline, when exceptions were made, whereby, in spite of the practice of denying reconciliation to penitents except after a long penance, pardon was granted sooner,[24] seem to be dis-

[18] Cf. *Constitutiones Apostolicae,* I, II, c. 41—Migne, *Patrologiae Cursus Completus, Series Graeca* (161 vols., Parisiis, 1856-1866), I, 696. (Hereafter cited as *MPG.*

[19] Cf. Brys, *De Dispensatione,* p. 17.

[20] Cf. Van Espen, *Tract. de Censuris,* t. II, pars III, tit. XI, cap. 2.

[21] Cf. Schmidt, *Thesaurus,* VII, 167; Van Espen, *op. cit.,* t. II, pars III, tit. IV, nn. 1-4.

[22] Cf. Esmein, *Le mariage in droit canonique* (2. ed., 2 vols., Paris, 1935), II, 317; Cocchi, *Commentarium in Codicem Iuris Canonici ad Usum Scholarum* (5 vols. in 8, Taurinorum Augustae, 1922-1930), lib. V, *De Delictis et Poenis* (2. ed., Taurinorum Augustae, Marietti, 1928), n. 126.

[23] E. g., *venia,* as used indiscriminately for dispensation and absolution.

[24] Cf. St. Cyprian (210-258), *Epist. LIV—MPL,* IV, 348; *Epist. XX, XXI —MPL,* III, 791; *Corpus Scriptorum Ecclesiasticorum Latinorum* (Editum

pensations and are cited as such by most of the authors.[25] Even Brys, who argues for a clear distinction between the two concepts,[26] cites the letters of St. Cyprian as early examples of dispensations.[27] And so it seems that, although the concept of absolution was not identified with that of dispensation, and dispensations in the strict sense were given independently of absolution, in the absolution from penalties partially vindicative in nature there did exist a definite confusion of the ideas of absolution and dispensation.

For dispensations in the strict sense the pardon granted in cases of strictly vindicative penalties must be studied. It should be noted here that these dispensations occurred very rarely during this time, and the principles involved are very obscure.[28] Fuller development may be noted after the fourth century.

All who admit the existence of dispensations in these centuries [29] are unanimously of the opinion that bishops—each in his own territory—were the sole authors of dispensations.[30] The positive legislation of this time was limited to laws and regulations established by each bishop for his own territory, and was confined for the greater

consilio Academiae Litterarum Caesareae Vindobonensis, Vindobonae, 1866—), III, P. II (Recensit Gulielmus Hartel, 1871), 621.

25 Cf. Van Hove, *Commentarium Lovaniense in Codicem Iuris Canonici* (5 toms., Mechliniae—Romae: H. Dessain, 1928-1939), t. V, 299 (hereafter cited as *Commentarium Lovaniense in C. I. C.*); Morinus, *De Admin. Sacr. Poenit.*, L. IV, c. 25, n. 8; Hinschius, *Kirchenrecht*, IV, 748; Hefele, *Histoire des Conciles* (10 vols. in 19, Paris, 1907-1938), tom. I, pars I, p. 306; Batiffol, *Les Origines de la Penitence* (Paris, 1902), p. 63.

26 *De Dispensatione*, pp. 16-18. It is true that Brys presents here a distinction between dispensations *in the strict sense* and absolution; and that this dispensation in public penance was not such.

27 *De Dispensatione*, p. 13.

28 Cf. Thomassinus, *Vetus et Nova Ecclesiae Disciplina*, pars II, L. III, cap. XXIV, n. 3: ". . . iam naufragio temporum absorptum fuerat."; cf. Brys, *De Dispensatione*, pp. 23, 34, n. 3.

29 Among those who do not admit the existence of dispensations at this time but only absolutions are Cocchi (*Commentarium in Codicem Iuris Canonici*, I, n. 126), De Marca (*De Concordantia Sacerdotii et Imperii seu de Libertatibus Ecclesiae Gallicanae* [3 vols., Parisiis, 1641], lib. III, cap. 13; Esmein, *Le mariage in droit canonique*, t. II, p. 317.

30 Cf. Thomassinus, *op. cit.*, pars II, L. III, c. 24, n. 14; Van Espen, *Tract. de Censuris*, t. II, pars IV, c. 4, n. 7; Stiegler, *Dispensation*, I, 72-76.

part to regulations governing the penitential discipline, the qualifications of candidates for ordination, and the remission of ecclesiastical penalties.[31] In all these laws dispensations were granted by the bishop. He it was who remitted the penalties incurred by his clerics and subjects.[32] Just how far this power of the bishop extended is not clear, since there are no documents available; [33] but it seems that the bishops dispensed from penalties imposed by the general laws of the Church—in as far as such penal laws existed—whenever the public good demanded it.[34]

During these three centuries it seems that the Pope did not grant dispensations or relaxations of penalties outside of his own diocese at Rome.[35] And yet there were cases in which the Pope dispensed, in the interest of unity, from the vindicative penalty of deposition. Pope Cornelius (ca. 252) restored bishops and priests who had been deposed as a result of the Novatian schism: "Credimus autem fore, quinimmo pro certo iam confidimus, ceteros quoque qui in hoc errore sunt constituti in Ecclesiam brevi reversuros, cum auctores suos viderint nobiscum agere." [36] Similarly, there occurred another instance in which it seems that the Pope remitted a penalty of deposition inflicted upon two bishops, Basilides and Martial, who had been deposed by a council in Spain as *libellatici*.[37] With the restoration of peace these two bishops appealed to Rome, to Pope Stephen (254-257), who remitted the penalty and restored them to their sees. St. Cyprian objected to this procedure and convoked a council in Carthage in the year 258 to examine the case. The bishops assem-

[31] Cf. Stiegler, *Dispensation*, I, 14, 73.

[32] Cf. Thomassinus, *Vetus et Nova Ecclesiae Disciplina*, pars II, L. III, c. 24; cf. also St. Cyprian, *Epist.* [ad Antonianum]—*MPL*, IV, 230, 301.

[33] Cf. Van Hove, *Commentarium Lovaniense in C. I. C.*, I, p. 317; Brys, *De Dispensatione*, pp. 22, 34.

[34] Cf. Thomassinus, *op. cit.*, pars II, L. III, c. 24: ". . . ubi publica necessitas id iubeat nullo pontifici romano, nullo interveniente concilio provinciali. . . ."

[35] Cf. Brys, *De Dispensatione*, p. 31, Praenotanda.

[36] *Epist. VI* [ad Cyprianum], n. 3—*MPL*, III, 725; JK, n. 111 (13).

[37] *Libellatici* were those who privately and implicitly denied the Faith in producing fraudulently obtained certificates of apostacy, but avoided a public denial by bribery.

bled at Carthage approved the sentence of deposition passed by the Spanish synod and declared that "*libellatici* can indeed be admitted to penance but are correctly forbidden clerical ordination and the priestly dignity." [38]

This was but the expression of the mind of St. Cyprian, as shown in his letter to this council: "Such men (Basilides and Martial) strive in vain to claim for themselves the episcopate, since it is clear that men of this kind cannot rule over the Church of Christ nor may they offer sacrifices to God; especially since Cornelius also, our friend, a just and peaceful priest and moreover honored by God with martyrdom, long ago decreed with us and with all the bishops throughout the world, that men of this sort might indeed be admitted to the performance of penance, but were prohibited from the ordination of the clergy and from the priestly honor." [39]

This letter is significant in that it testifies to the admission of the clergy to public penance, and clearly shows the distinction between the partially vindicative penance and the purely vindicative deposition, which latter was perpetual. Repentance and fulfillment of the allotted time of public penance would restore the cleric to the peace of the Church, yet it would not qualify him to act in his office or to return to the clerical state. His return to the peace of the Church depended upon the absolution from his sins and from the public penance; his return to office or to his former state depended upon a dispensation, such as was granted by Pope Stephen.

[38] Cf. Baronius, *Annales Ecclesiastici* (36 vols., Vols. I-XXVIII, Barri Ducis, 1864-1875; Vols. XXIX-XXXVII, Parisiis, 1876-1883), III (ad annum 258), n. 1 ss; cf. also *MPL,* III, 1020.

[39] *Epist. ad Carthaginense Concilium—MPL,* III, 1031: ". . . frustra talis episcopatum sibi usurpare conantur, cum manifestum sit eiusmodi homines nec Deo sacrificia offerre debere, maxime cum iam pridem nobiscum et cum omnibus omnino episcopis in toto mundo constitutis etiam Cornelius collega nostra . . . decreverit, eiusmodi homines ad poenitentiam quidam agendam posse admitti, ab eiusmodi ordinatione autem cleri atque sacerdotali honore prohiberi."

CHAPTER III

FROM THE FOURTH CENTURY TO THE DECREE OF GRATIAN

ARTICLE I. THE VINDICATIVE PENALTIES

WITH the close of the period of persecution, at the beginning of the fourth century, a definite change occurred in the formation of penal laws, a change occasioned by the more peaceful circumstances of the existence of the Church. The bishops of the various territories or provinces were able to meet more easily in councils and to establish general laws which would govern these larger territories.[1] These provincial synods were held during the third century, but they became general only in the fourth century. At the same time laws established with papal authority became more numerous.[2]

The nature of the vindicative penalties of this time was explained by Pope Gregory the Great (590-604): "When evils which should be washed away in the tears of repentance are rather increased by excesses, then greater correction must be used on the delinquents, in order that they themselves may recognize, at least by the vindicative penalty, their great crime, and that the fear of ecclesiastical retribution may defer others from unlawful conduct." [3] Among the vindicative penalties thus established were major excommunication, privation of the Eucharist,[4] suspension,[5] interdict,[6] penal transfer from one place to another,[7] and deposition.[8]

[1] Cf. I Council of Nicaea, canons 5, 6—Mansi, II, 870; Thomassinus, *Vetus et Nova Ecclesiae Disciplina,* pars II, lib. III, cap. XXIV, n. 14.

[2] Cf. Reilly, *The General Norms of Dispensation,* The Catholic University of America, Canon Law Studies, n. 119 (Washington, D. C.: The Catholic University of America Press, 1939), pp. 12, 13.

[3] *Epist. 31* [ad Joannem Primae Iustinianae Illyrici Episcopum]—*MPL,* LXXVII, 1211; JE, 1164 (801).

[4] Cf. Hyland, *Excommunication,* pp. 19, 30.

[5] Cf. Rainer, *Suspension of Clerics,* pp. 13, 14.

[6] Cf. Conran, *The Interdict,* p. 24.

[7] Cf. Hinschius, *Kirchenrecht,* V, 126.

[8] Cf. Findlay, *Canonical Norms Governing the Deposition and Degradation of Clerics,* p. 22.

Among the corporal punishments were flagellation [9] and incarceration,[10] or seclusion in a monastery [11] Of course, the institute of public penance existed during this time, and the principles of its remission remained the same. However, the discipline of public penance for both public and occult grave sins ceased about the year 700.[12] About that time there began the practice of imposing public penance for public sins only, and private penance for occult sins, a practice universal in the western Church by the year 730.[13] The major excommunication, as during the previous centuries, was largely vindicative in nature. It did not become a censure in the strict sense until the twelfth century.[14]

Suspension remained a vindicative penalty until the sixth century; [15] and the interdict, although applied with greater frequency and inflicted upon entire districts, provinces and nations, remained the same until the eleventh century.[16] Deposition remained purely vindicative, perpetual in nature,[17] and was called "degradation." [18]

By the ninth century a new vindicative penalty had developed, that of *infamia iuris,* through the influence of Roman Law.[19] This

[9] Cf. St. Augustine, *De Civitate Dei,* I, tit. XIX, cap. 17; tit. XXI, cap. 11; Van Espen, *Ius Ecclesiasticum Universum,* t. II, pars III, tit. XI, cap. I, n. 38; Wernz, *Ius Decretalium,* VI, tit. V, n. 101; Devoti, *Institutiones Canonicae,* lib. IV, tit. XVII, nn. 1135, 1136.

[10] Cf. Wernz, *op. cit.,* VI, tit. V, n. 102; Van Espen, *op. cit.,* t. II, pars III, tit. XI, cap. I, n. 24.

[11] Cf. Wernz, *loc. cit.;* Van Espen, *loc. cit.*

[12] Cf. Morinus, *De Admin. Sacr. Poenit.,* L. LVI, c. 27, n. 1.

[13] Cf. Teetaert, *La Confession aux Laïques dans l'Eglise Latina depuis le VIIIe iusqu'au XIVe Siècle,* Universitas Catholica Lovaniensis, Dissertatio, Series II, Tomus 17 (1926), pp. 20, 21 (hereafter cited as *La Confession aux Laïques*); Schmidt, *Thesaurus,* VII, p. 158, 159, VI; Morinus, *De Admin. Sacr. Poenit.,* L. VII, c. 1, n. 1.

[14] Cf. Ayrinhac-Lydon, *Penal Legislation in the New Code of Canon Law,* n. 159.

[15] Cf. Wernz, *Ius Decretalium,* VI, tit. VI, n. 203.

[16] Cf. Kober, *Der Kirchenbann,* cap. XXI, n. 16.

[17] Cf. Findlay, *Canonical Norms Governing the Deposition and Degradation of Clerics,* pp. 16, 17.

[18] Cf. Council of Elvira (306), canon 20: "Si quis clericorum detectus fuerit usuras accipere, placuit eum degradari."—Hardouin, I, 252.

[19] Cf. Hinschius, *Kirchenrecht,* V, 41; Chelodi, *Ius Poenale,* p. 66.

penalty was further developed and clarified, however, during the eleventh and twelfth centuries.[20] Likewise, irregularities incurred through the commission of certain expressed crimes, whether occult or public, were sometimes considered as vindicative penalties.[21]

In the previous centuries the ecclesiastical penalties were exclusively of a *ferendae sententiae* character. During this period *latae sententiae* vindicative penalties appeared. The first indication which apparently points to such a *latae sententiae* vindicative penalty is found in the I Council of Toledo in the year 400; [22] and others are those of the XII Council of Toledo in 681 [23] and of the XIII Council of Toledo in 683. This latter council declared that those who harbored fugitive clerics and monks were to consider themselves excommunicated and deprived of their offices as long as such remained under their protection.[24] Many other such *latae sententiae* penalties appeared during the following centuries.[25]

Article II. The Dispensation from Penalties

As a result of the change in the establishment of penal laws, when these laws became more general in nature and were established by the provincial synods or with papal authority, the active subject of dispensation from these penalties changed. It was threefold: the bishops, the Pope, and the provincial synods.[26] Until the end

[20] Cf. c. 17, C. 6, q. 1; Hollweck, *Die kirchlichen Strafgesetze,* 78; Wernz, *Ius Decretalium,* II, n. 3.

[21] Cf. Glossa ad c. 6, D. 50; cc. 5, 6, 8, D. 50; c. 17, X, I, 11; Wernz, *Ius Decretalium,* II, tit. VII, n. 133; VI, tit. V, n. 107; Schmalzgrueber, *Ius Ecclesiasticum Universum,* lib. V, tit. 37, n. 66; Lega, *Praelectiones in Textum Iuris Canonici,* Vol. III, *De Delictis et Poenis,* n. 185 (hereafter will be cited as *De Delictis et Poenis*).

[22] C. 5: "Presbyter . . . si intra civitatem fuerat . . . et ad ecclesiam ad sacrificium quotidianum non venerit, clericus non habeatur"—Mansi, II, 403.

[23] C. 5—Mansi, II, 654.

[24] Canon 11: "Transgressor institutionis paternae tanto tempore excommunicatum et remotum se a suis officiis noverit esse, quanto eum qui fugiit sub sua potestate contigerit remorasse"—Mansi, XI, 1074.

[25] Cf. I Council of Vernon (755), canon 9—Mansi, XII, 582; cf. also Kober, *der Kirchenbann,* p. 54; Hollweck, *Die kirchlichen Strafgesetze,* p. 87.

[26] Cf. Hinschius, *Kirchenrecht,* III, 473-492; Sohm, *Das alt-katholische*

of the ninth century these three authorities granted dispensations from vindicative penalties more or less on an equal basis.[27]

The provincial synod granted relaxations of penalties enacted by the laws of the synod whenever a bishop would apply for such a dispensation.[28] The principle was established by canon 5 of the I Council of Nicaea, wherein it was decreed that "through the general assembly of all the bishops of the province such investigation may be undertaken, that everyone may know that those whose disobedience toward the bishop can be proved, are justly excommunicated (and will remain so) till it shall please the assembly of bishops to modify the sentence." [29] It did this in virtue of its legislative power.[30] Occasionally, too, the provincial synod dispensed from vindicative penalties inflicted by the general councils, though this practice was rare.[31] As to the penal laws established by individual bishops, the provincial synod seemed rather to exercise a right of vigilance and judgment over the dispensations granted or refused by bishops than to dispense directly from such penalties once inflicted. Thus, the Council of Antioch (314) stated that "if a priest or deacon has been deposed by his bishop, or if a bishop has been deposed by a synod, he should not presume to take his troubles to the emperor but betake himself to a higher synod." Thus the synod would rather grant dispensations on appeal. Deposed clerics who acted otherwise, the canon concluded, should not obtain any dispen-

Kirchenrecht und das Decretum Gratiani (Leipzig, 1892), I, 308; Brys, *De Dispensatione*, p. 34.

[27] This does not mean that the bishops and the synods had power equal to that of the Holy See, but that the lines of demarcation and the principles of that power were not well defined. Obviously the bishops were aware of the defect of their power in regard to certain vindicative penalties and applied to Rome for dispensations. Cf. Thomassinus, *Vetus et Nova Ecclesiae Disciplina*, Pars II, L. III, c. 24, n. 3; Phillips, *Kirchenrecht* (7 vols., Regensburg, 1845-1872), V, 163.

[28] Cf. Stiegler, *Dispensation*, I, 82.

[29] Cf. Mansi, II, 667; Translation from Schroeder, *Disciplinary Decrees of the General Councils* (St. Louis: Herder, 1937), p. 28.

[30] Freisen, *Geschichte des canonischen Eherechts bis zum Verfall der Glossenlitteratur* (Tübingen, 1888), p. 891.

[31] Cf. Hinschius, *Kirchenrecht*, III, 744.

sation or have any hope of regaining their rank in the future.[82]

The bishops granted dispensations from vindicative penalties enacted by their own diocesan laws, or inflicted by them whenever in their prudent judgment the circumstances demanded it, and also from those enacted by the provincial synods or general councils, when they had received delegation from the synods to do so.[83] However, very often bishops granted pardons and dispensations expressly denied to them by the synods or by the Pope.[84]

The Pope also granted dispensations from vindicative penalties inflicted by the law or by individual bishops. Pope Siricius in the year 385 granted by letter dispensations to certain priests deprived of the exercise of their office, and he termed these dispensations "misericordiam" and "veniam relaxatam." [85] In the same letter Siricius stated that incontinent clerics who had been deposed could never consider celebrating the holy mysteries: "nec umquam posse veneranda attractare mysteria." Then he added: "Because present examples (of incontinency) warn us to provide for the future that if any bishop, priest, or deacon . . . is found to be such hereafter, let him now understand that every avenue of pardon (dispensation) has been closed by us because it is necessary to cut off the wounded members that do not respond to medical treatment." [86] The principle here stated was that the vindicative penalty of deposition was a last resort and that its effects were final. As the Pope inferred, it was within his power to dispense from such a penalty, but necessity demanded that the power should not be used.[87] Innocent I in the

[82] Canon 12: ". . . huiusmodi nullam veniam habeat, neque locum affectionis suae, nec spem recipiendi gradus habeat in futurum"—Hardouin, I, 598.

[83] Cf. Council of Ancyra (314), canon 12—Mansi, II, 531; Synod of Carthage (412), canon 2; Brys, *De Dispensatione*, p. 36; Stiegler, *Dispensation*, I, 84.

[84] Cf. Stiegler, *op. cit.*, pp. 85-110.

[85] *Epist. I* [ad Himerum]—Coustant, *Epistolae Romanorum Pontificum*, I, p. 631; n. 11; *MPL*, XIII, 114; JK, n. 255 (65).

[86] *Ibid.*

[87] Cf. also Thomassinus, *Vetus et Nova Ecclesiae Disciplina*, Pars II, lib. I, c. LVI, n. 15, regarding the reasons for such severity.

year 414 likewise dispensed from a similar penalty in the case of priests who allowed themselves to be ordained by heretics.[38]

It should be noted here again that the concept of dispensation was not clearly defined during these centuries. The concept included dispensation in the strict sense, that is, the relaxation of a law in a special case, but it also included dispensation in the wide sense of the remission of penalties, whether already incurred *ipso facto* through the violation of a law, or inflicted by an ecclesiastical superior, or about to be inflicted. These two concepts were clearly distinguished by the later decretalists, as shall be shown; but before that time the term was used very loosely. Thus, when the term appeared in legislation, in the writings of Gratian, the Decretists and early Decretalists, or in the actual practice of this period, it was always understood in this wide sense. Consequently, the principles of dispensation from vindicative penalties must be drawn from the principles of general dispensation as they were understood at the time. These principles will be presented, not as particular norms of dispensation from vindicative penalties, but as general principles containing within themselves the norms of dispensation from such penalties.

At the end of the ninth century a marked change occurred in the matter of dispensations. Up to that time the Roman Pontiffs had granted dispensations in a more or less arbitrary manner; and both the provincial synods and the bishops granted dispensations from the general laws. It is true that in some matters the power of dispensation was reserved to the Holy See, and both the provincial synods and the bishops, with some exceptions,[39] acknowledged the need to apply to the Pope for certain dispensations.[40] Thus Pope Martin I in the year 649 delegated to John, Bishop of Philadelphia,[41]

[38] Cf. *Epist. ad Macedonenses*—Coustant, *Epistolae Romanorum Pontificum,* I, 835; JK, n. 303 (100).

[39] Thus, for example, both synods and bishops sometimes usurped the power of dispensing in matters which were expressly denied to them either by the synodal or papal law. Cf. Stiegler, *Dispensation,* I, 85-110; Brys, *De Dispensatione,* pp. 37, 41, n. 3.

[40] Cf. Stiegler, *op. cit.*, p. 85.

[41] Cf. Thiel, *Epistolae Romanorum Pontificum genuinae a S. Hilario usque ad Hormisdam* (Brunsbergae, 1868), I, 362.

and to the bishops of southern Italy and of Sicily[42] the power of dispensing from the penalties incurred by certain clerics of their dioceses. Likewise, the VIII General Council, held at Constantinople in 869, petitioned the Pope to dispense from the vindicative penalties incurred by certain lectors who had been ordained by the Patriarch Photius.[43]

But from the end of the ninth century the Popes expressly claimed the right to dispense from general laws,[44] and the general principle was established that the power of dispensation pertained to the legislator, and to others only when expressly granted to them.[45] Consequently, dispensations granted by papal authority increased. This change from the practice of previous centuries was brought about by the necessity of promoting unity in ecclesiastical discipline throughout the entire Church.[46]

It was not a sudden change, but a gradual one which finally was recognized and developed and propagated by the writers of the tenth, eleventh, and twelfth centuries and by the Popes. In the eighth century the Pope had frequently exercised his power of dispensing from vindicative penalties, especially in Germany where the authority of the Pope was greatly revered and where few provincial synods were held.[47] And during the ninth century there had been an increase in the number of petitions to Rome for dispensations which had been refused by the synods.[48] But in the tenth and eleventh centuries

[42] *Epist. 14* [ad Episcopos per Lucaniam et Brutios et Siciliam constitutos] —*MPL,* LXXVII, 159; cf. also c. I, D. IV; JE, 231.

[43] Cf. Hefele-Leclercq, *Histoire des Conciles,* IV, 535; Phillips, *Kirchenrecht,* V, 972.

[44] Pope Nicholas I (858-867) seems to have been the first to claim this right expressly: "Episcopo non licet iura aliena pervadere, nec in ullo a sacris canonibus deviare . . . sed ad Romam possunt quaedam accedere cuius auctoritate maior non est, et quae potest quaedam dispensatorie ordinare"—*MPL,* CXIC, 889; *MGH, Epistolae,* VI (edited by Ernestus Perels: Berolini, 1925), p. 637, n. 118.

[45] Cf. Van Hove, *Commentarium Lovaniense in C. I. C.,* I, Tom. V, n. 341.

[46] Cf. Thomassinus, *Vetus et Nova Ecclesiae Disciplina,* Pars II, L. III, c. 24, nn. 3-7.

[47] Cf. Hinschius, *Kirchenrecht,* III, 687.

[48] Cf. Thomassinus, *Vetus et Nova Ecclesiae Disciplina,* Pars II, L. III, c. 24, n. 3; Stiegler, *Dispensation,* I, 97, 98.

the Popes exercised this power more frequently still, chiefly to promote the reform begun by Gregory.[49] Because of the many violations of penal laws by bishops and priests and lower clerics, many dispensations were necessary, for, as Pope Gregory VII declared, hardly a cleric could be found who was not deprived of the exercise of his office, because of crimes against the laws of the Church.[50] The Popes, however, including Gregory VII, did not expressly claim an exclusive right to dispense from the general law.[51]

But it was in the tenth and eleventh centuries when the principles were clarified somewhat in canonical collections made both before and during the Gregorian Reform. Although some writers of this time, such as Hincmar of Rheims (+882)[52] and Burchard of Worms (+1025), the half-hearted reformer of episcopalistic tendency in his *Decretum*,[53] in establishing these principles, seemed to deny to the Pope the power to dispense from canons of the General Councils, others, like Abbo of Fleury (+1004), claimed for the legislator the exclusive right to dispense from such laws.[54]

The Gregorian Reform, with its insistence on the absolute supremacy and full independence of the Holy See, produced the systematic collections which vindicated the right of the Pope. Among the Gregorian collections, those of Cardinal Deusdedit (1087), Anselm of Lucca (1083), and Bishop Bonizo (1089-1095) particularly based this claim on ancient sources. Anselm especially was explicit in denying to the bishops the right of dispensing from general laws: "Nemo praesumere audeat temporare rigorem legis diurnae, vel praescriptionum S. Sedis." [55] Bernald of Constance (ca. 1054-1100) likewise showed that the Pope necessarily had the right to dispense from the general law inasmuch as the Roman Pontiff alone is the "auctor

[49] Cf. Brys, *De Dispensatione*, pp. 62, 63, for examples; also Stiegler, *Dispensation*, I, 150-154, 316.

[50] Cf. Thomassinus, *op. cit.*, Pars III, L. II, c. 13; Stiegler, *Dispensation*, p. 327.

[51] Cf. Brys, *De Dispensatione*, p. 66.

[52] *Epist. III* [ad Concilium Suessonense]—*MPL*, CXXVI, 50.

[53] *MPL*, CXL, 714.

[54] *MPL*, CXXXIX, 139, 481.

[55] Cf. *Anselmi Lucensis Collectio Canonum*, II, 33 (edited by Thaner, 2 vols., Innsbruck, 1906-1915), p. 111; Stiegler, *Dispensation*, I, 326.

canonum," [56] but he did not state that this was an exclusive right, nor did he determine the limits of episcopal power in this regard. Ivo of Chartres (ca. 1040-1116) held much the same view, but was not as explicit as Bernald of Constance, in consequence, it seems, of his dependence upon Burchard.[57]

As may be noted, these collectors either favored the reform begun and developed by the Popes or were somewhat opposed to it. Consequently, as they favored either the papal authority or that of the episcopacy, they limited or extended the right of bishops in granting dispensations from the general law. Cardinal Deusdedit (+ after 1097) did not touch upon this question of episcopal power. Anselm of Lucca (+1086) explicitly denied to bishops the power to dispense from any other than their own laws. Bernald maintained practically the same principle, although he did admit the power of bishops to dispense from general laws "maxime in legibus poenitentium, quod etiam canones illis concedunt," [58] thus seeming to necessitate for the exercise of such power delegation from the general canons. Ivo of Chartres, following the episcopalistic doctrine of Burchard, seemed to extend the power of bishops to dispense from the general law whenever they so desired.[59]

The bishops, too, in the exercise of the power of dispensation, either favored or opposed the reform measures which the Popes introduced to stabilize the papacy and to unify the disciplinary laws of the Church. Consequently, many bishops recognized this right of the Pope to dispense from all general laws; others recognized this power as an exclusive one which they did not possess; [60] while

[56] *De excommunicatis vitandis*, c. 59—*MGH*, *Libelli de Lite*, II (edited by Fredericus Thaner, Hannoverae, 1892), 141: "Ipsi (RR. Pontifices) enim sunt auctores canonum, et illa Sedes semper habuit hoc privilegium ut ligatum vel solutum sit quidquid ipsa ligaverit vel solverit."

[57] Cf. Stiegler, *Dispensation*, I, 322.

[58] *MGH*, *Libelli de Lite*, c. 59, t. II, 141.

[59] *MPL*, CLXI, 51.

[60] Cf. *Paschalis II Epist. LXXIV*—*MPL*, CLXIII, 93: "Amselmus: '. . . Peto ut per licentiam vestram possim quaedam, prout discretionem dabit mihi Deus, temporare. Quod petii a domno papa Urbano, et ipse posuit in mea deliberatione. . . .' "—JL, n. 5909 (4417).

others completely ignored this right of the Pope and freely dispensed from the general law.

The most common practice among the bishops seemed to be that of granting dispensations which were not reserved to the Holy See. They considered themselves as empowered to dispense when the right to do so was not expressly denied to them,[61] and Bernald of Constance indicated that this conviction was not entirely unfounded.[62]

[61] Cf. Stiegler, *Dispensation*, I, 145; Brys, *De Dispensatione*, pp. 45-60.

[62] *De excommunicatis vitandis*, c. 59: "Sed et alii episcopi etsi nullo modo, ut presul apostolicus, vel canones instituere vel iam institutos iudicare valeant, aliquando tamen pro modulo suo aliqua statuta temperant, et hoc maxime in legibus poenitentium, quod etiam ipsi canones concedunt. Nam Nicenum concilium (canon 12) episcopis concessisse legitur, ut digne poenitentes humanius tractent et canonicam severitatem in eis aliquatenus mitigent."—*MGH, Libelli de Lite*, II, 141.

CHAPTER IV

FROM THE DECREE OF GRATIAN TO THE COUNCIL OF TRENT

Article I. The Vindicative Penalties

The vindicative penalties inflicted by the Church during these centuries remained practically the same. The major excommunication was definitely recognized as a censure some time between 1198 and 1205, when Pope Innocent III declared that when the term "censure" was used, it was to be understood as referring to excommunication, suspension, and interdict,[1] although even then the concept of censure was not clearly defined.[2] The concept of excommunication as a medicinal rather than a vindicative penalty became clear and definite sometime before the sixth century.[3]

Due to various causes,[4] after the eleventh century the discipline of public penance began to relax very rapidly,[5] and by the twelfth century public penance disappeared entirely in the West.[6]

Latae sententiae penalties became more frequent during these centuries. Examples of such penalties are those established by Innocent II in canon 15 of the II General Council of the Lateran (1139),[7] by Gregory IX in the year 1230,[8] by Boniface VIII (1294-1303),[9] and by Clement V (1305-1314).[10]

[1] C. 20, X, *de verborum significatione*, V, 40.

[2] Cf. Wernz, *Ius Decretalium*, VI, 149; Hinschius, *Kirchenrecht*, V, 126, note 1.

[3] Cf. Hinschius, *op. cit.*, V, 641.

[4] Cf. Teetaert, *Confession aux Laïques*, pp. 22, 23.

[5] Cf. Morinus, *De Admin. Sacr. Poenit.*, L. X, c. 16, nn. 1, 2.

[6] Cf. Rauschen, *Eucharist and Penance*, p. 213.

[7] C. 29, C. XVII, q. 4.

[8] C. 2, X, *de solutionibus*, III, 23; c. 7, X, *de electione et electi potestate*, I, 6.

[9] C. 40, *de electione et electi potestate*, I, 6, in VI°; "Decernimus ut ii qui praemissa de caetero praesumpserint . . . eo ipso sint et tamdiu maneant ab officio et beneficiis quibuscumque suspensi . . ."; c. I, *de sententia et re iudicata*, II, 14, in VI°.

[10] C. I, *de haereticis*, V. 3, in Clem: "Quodsi odii, gratiae vel amoris, lucri

Article II. The Dispensation from Penalties

During these centuries the authorities granting dispensations from vindicative penalties remained the same: the Pope, the provincial synods, and the bishops. However, the principles became clarified, gradually, through the teachings of Gratian, of the Decretists and of the Decretalists.

Gratian, it is true, did not treat at length of dispensations from vindicative penalties as such. However, his teaching on such dispensations may be drawn from his treatment of dispensations in general. For Gratian, as those before him, did not clearly define dispensation, and used that term indiscriminately for any relaxation of the law,[11] of custom,[12] of precepts,[13] and of vindicative penalties.[14] Consequently he applied his norms of general dispensation to dispensations from vindicative penalties.[15]

The Pope had the power to dispense from the general law by virtue of his legislative power: "Romana Ecclesia canonibus auctoritatem praestat, ita tamen ut seipsam non subiaceat ipsis et licet Summis Pontificibus contra generalia decreta speciali beneficio concedere quod generali decreto prohibetur." [16] This power of the Pope was not an exclusive one,[17] although Gratian certainly favored that opinion and stated the principles which should logically lead to such an opinion.[18]

aut commodi temporalis obtentu contra iustitiam et conscientiam suam omiserint contra quemquam procedere, ubi fuerit procedendum super huiusmodi pravitate, aut obtentu eodem, pravitatem ipsam vel impedimentum officii sui alicui imponendo, eum super hoc praesumpserint quoque modo vexare: praeter alias poenas, pro qualitate culpae imponendas eisdem, episcopus aut superior suspensiones ab officio per triennium, alii vero excommunicationis sententias eo ipso incurrant"; also c. I, *de decimis, primitiis, et oblationibus,* III, 8, in Clem.

[11] Cf. Stiegler, "Dispensation"—*AKKR,* LXXVII (1897), p. 665.

[12] Dictum Gratiani post, c. I, D. XIV.

[13] Dictum Gratiani post, c. 23, C. I, q. 7.

[14] Dictum Gratiani, D. L, especially in relation to c. 27, where he proves that suspended clerics may, through a dispensation, exercise their offices.

[15] Cf. Freisen, *Geschichte des canonischen Eherechts bis zum Verfall der Glossenlitteratur,* p. 403; Brys, *De Dispensatione,* p. 74.

[16] Dictum Gratiani post, c. 16, C. XXV, q. 1.

[17] Cf. Sohm, *Kirchenrecht,* II, p. 101; Hinschius, *Kirchenrecht,* III, 746.

[18] Dictum Gratiani ante c. 10, D. XI.

Just as Gratian did not expressly claim an exclusive right of the Pope to dispense from the general law, so also he did not deny expressly that power to the bishops. Moreover, he did cite instances in which bishops dispensed from the general law.[19]

The Decretists, who applied themselves to a detailed study of the *Decretum* of Gratian, likewise used the term *dispensation* in its widest sense,[20] but they distinguished, in a general way, the notions of dispensation in the strict sense, and in the wide sense of a relaxation or remission of vindicative penalties.[21] Thus, Huguccio (1188) used the term in the strict sense of the relaxation of a law in a particular case,[22] and also in the wide sense "de relaxatione poenae" and "de mitigatione poenitentiae."[23] It may be noted here that the Decretists frequently used the term *dispensation* in this latter sense, thus confusing dispensation from vindicative penalties with "dispensations" from penances inflicted as satisfaction for sin,[24] even though they often defined vindicative penalties as *judicial* retribution for sin or *satisfaction* for crime[25] as distinguished from penance, which was understood as satisfaction for sin.[26] All the Decretists agreed that bishops and priests had the power to "dispense" or mitigate penances inflicted by bishops or priests according to the norms set down in the penitential books of the time.[27]

[19] C. 47, C. XVI, q. 1; c. 7, D. XXIV.

[20] Cf. Rufinus, ad c. 4, D. IV—*Die Summa Decretorum des Magister Rufinus* (edited by Singer, Paderborn, 1920), p. 14; ad C. XXV, q. 1—*ibid.*, p. 422.

[21] Cf. Bernardus Papiensis, *Summa Decretalium*, lib. V, tit. XXIV—*Bernardi Papiensis Summa Decretalium*, p. 271.

[22] *Summa*, ad dictum Gratiani ante c. 25, D. L.—MS. in the Paris National Library, n. 3892, fol. 59v, cited by Brys, *De Dispensatione*, p. 100.

[23] *Summa*, ad c. IV, D. IV—MS. in the Paris National Library, cited by Brys, *De Dispensatione*, p. 104, note 6.

[24] Cf. Huguccio, *Summa in Decretum*—cod. MS. in the Vatican Library, n. 2288, fol. 104v, col. 2, cited by Brys, *De Dispensatione*, p. 144.

[25] Cf. Bernardus Papiensis, *Summa Decretalium*, ad 1, tit. 33—*Bernardi Papiensis Summa Decretalium* (Laspeyres), p. 264.

[26] Bernardus Papiensis, *Summa Decretalium*—*Ibid.*, p. 269.

[27] Cf. Huguccio: ". . . Simplices vero sacerdotes sicut episcopi possunt dispensare et mitigare omnes canones penitentiales qui satisfactionem iniungunt pro peccato confesso in penitentia. . . . Simplices sacerdotes ultra hoc potesta-

But the Decretists certainly did not confuse the two notions of absolution from medicinal penalties and dispensation from vindicative penalties, as some of the Decretalists did later. Huguccio clearly explained the difference between these two pardons: in the case of medicinal penalties contrition sufficed as a requisite for absolution, but in the case of vindicative penalties, contrition was not sufficient as a cause for dispensation from such a penalty.[28]

It should also be noted that the Decretists, in speaking of dispensations from vindicative penalties, include in that category dispensations from penalties which had not yet been inflicted, that is, when the incurred penalty, through the mercy of the judge or ecclesiastical superior, was not inflicted. Thus the *Summa Coloniensis* (1169) declares: ". . . fit frequentissime dispensatio circa legum animadversiones, quia poenae molliendae sunt, non exasperandae. Est autem in iudiciis potestate mollire sententiam, et mitius iudicare quam leges."[29] And Sicardus of Cremona (1181) likewise joined the two notions: "[est dispensatio] quandoque poena infligenda non infligitur, quandoque inflicta remittitur, quandoque usurpatum conceditur, quandoque inhibitum confertur."[30] This moderation in the inflicting of vindicative penalties should not have been termed dispensation, as Pope Innocent IV (1243-1254) later observed, for the law itself allowed this moderation.[31]

tem dispensandi non habent."—*Summa in Decretum*—Cod. MS. in the Vatican Library, *ibid.*, col. 12, cited by Brys, *De Dispensatione*, p. 144, nota 5. Cf. also *Bernardi Papiensis Summa Decretalium* (Laspeyres), p. 205, ad tit. 2, L. II, 6: ". . . non ergo episcopus dispensare potest, nisi ubi ei permissum invenitur, ut in canonibus Poenitentialibus. . . ."

28 "Quod si haberet tantam (poenitentiam) quantam quis habere potest in hac vita, scilicet, ut si decederet statim intraret ad gloriam, ut fecit latro vel Stephanus, numquid deberet dispensandi cum eo? Non ob hoc: contritio enim cordis vel poenitentia non est causa dispensationis, licet facilius tunc dispensetur cum aliquo, arg. C. I, q. 7, Si quis; poenitentia enim etsi peccatum absorbeat, non tamen in pristinum statum restituit . . . ergo quantacumque sit contritio cordis non sufficit ad tollendam omnem poenam temporalem, licet sufficiat ad tollendam aeternam."—*Summa in Decretum*, ad c. 4, D. IV.

29 MS. Codex Bamberg., D. II, fol. 35, cited by Brys, *De Dispensatione*, p. 104.

30 *Summa in Decretum*—MS. Bamberg. Codex, D. II, fol. 150, cited by Brys, *De Dispensatione*, p. 121.

31 Cf. *Apparatus*, ad c. 15, *Dilectus*, X, *de temporibus ordinationum*, I, II:

All the Decretists claimed for the Pope the right to dispense from all vindicative penalties of the general law,[32] and the decrees of the councils and of the Popes claimed the same right, by the use of such expressions as "salva in omnibus auctoritate Romanae Ecclesiae" and "nisi auctoritas Sanctae Romanae Ecclesiae aliter imperavit." [33] This right of the Pope was due directly to his legislative power.[34]

The Decretists recognized the power of bishops to dispense from penal laws, *i. e.*, from *latae sententiae* vindicative penalties. All who wrote before the time of Huguccio (1210) acknowledged this power as one delegated *a iure* to the bishops, for they all expressly taught that bishops could dispense from such penalties only in cases where the canons had given them special faculties.[35]

"In poenis imponendas licet in eis qualitas personarum et honestas attendenda sit . . . et illis inspectis aliquando gravior aliquando minor poena imponenda sit, non tamen dicitur ibi dispensare, quia de iure communi inferuntur." Cf. also Ioannes Andreae, *In Sex Decretalium Libros Commentaria Novella* (6 vols. in 5, Venetiis, 1581), ad c. 15, X, I, II, n. 8 (hereafter cited as *Commentaria Novella*).

[32] Cf. Huguccio (*Summa in Decretum,* MS. Vat., n. 2288, fol. 140, col. 2): "In omnibus dispensalibus plenam potestatem habet apostolicus romanus interpretandi et dispensandi prout sapientissimo consilio suo decreverit, ut XXV, q. 1 *Sunt* quidem . . . ," cited by Brys, *De Dispensatione,* p. 144. Cf. also Rufinus, *Die Summa Decretorum des Magister Rufinus* (Singer), ad C. XXV, q. 1; p. 421; Sicardus of Cremona, *Summa in Decretum*—MS. Codex Bamberg., fol. 150, 203, cited by Brys, *De Dispensatione,* p. 141; Rolandus Bandinellus (Alexander III), *Die Summa Magistri Rolandi* (edited by Thaner, Innsbruck, 1874), p. 103.

[33] Cf. Rufinus, *Die Summa Decretorum des Magistri Rufinus* (Singer), p. 34.

[34] Cf. *Bernardi Papiensis Summa Decretalium* (Laspeyres), p. 205: "Solus autem ille dispensare potest, qui et constituere potest, ut Apostolicus et synodus. . . ."

[35] Cf. *Bernardi Papiensis Summa Decretalium* (Laspeyres), p. 205: ". . . non ergo episcopus dispensare potest, nisi ubi et permissum invenitur, ut in canonibus poenitentialibus, non autem in poenalibus, ut depositionis, quod intelligas, sententia lata." Cf. also Petrus Blesensis (*Opusculum de distinctionis in canonum interpretatione adhibendis, sive ut auctor voluit, speculum iuris canonici* [edited by Reimarus, Berlin, 1837], cap. XIX, p. 49 [cap. XI, in photostatic copy of MS. in Library of Congress, Washington, D. C.]): "Episcopis, qui non in plenitudinem potestatis sed in partem sollicitudinis sunt vocati, quandoque permittunt canones dispensare, ut canones poenitentiales et

However, Huguccio in his *Summa in Decretum* mentions the controversy which arose then regarding the interpretation of the decretal letter of Pope Alexander III (ca. 1179),[36] which granted bishops the right to dispense clerics from vindicative penalties inflicted for the crimes of adultery and for lesser crimes, after a certain degree of penance had been performed, but at the same time restricted the right of bishops to dispense in cases involving greater crimes. The Decretists certainly taught that bishops had no right whatsoever to dispense from vindicative penalties incurred through the so-called major or enormous crimes,[37] since this was clearly denied to them. But the controversy centered around the power of bishops to dispense from the penalties incurred through the minor or lesser crimes. Some, as Huguccio notes, held the opinion of the early Decretists and denied this right to the bishops except in cases in which power was expressly granted to them by law. Huguccio, however, held the opposite opinion: that bishops had this power except in cases in which the law expressly denied it to them.[38]

The Decretalists,[39] although they clarified the notion of dispen-

poenales; poenales diversi, qui nempe poenam suspensionis, vel degradationis, vel aliam poenam delinquentibus infligunt. Poenales tamen ab episcopis dispensari non debent, nisi ubi canones eis hoc specialiter indulgent. Ubi poenitentiales vero, dispensare episcopi . . . generaliter permittuntur." Cf. Huguccio: "Inferiores autem antistites et episcopi eatenus dispensare possunt quatenus eis a iure permittuntur"—*Summa in Decretum*—cod. MS. in the Vatican Library, *ibid.*, col. 2, cited by Brys, *De Dispensatione*, p. 145.

[36] C. 4, *At si clerici*, X, *de iudiciis*, II, I: "Si vero Episcopo de criminibus in iure confessi sunt, seu legitima probatione convicti, dummodo sint talia crimina propter quae suspensi debeant vel deponi, non immerito suspensi sunt a suis ordinibus, vel ab altaris ministerio perpetuo removendi. 1. De adulteriis vero et aliis criminalibus quae sunt minora, potest Episcopus cum clericis post peractam poenitentiam dispensare *ut in ordinibus suis deserviant*." These latter words in italics appear only in the *Compilatio Prima*, and not in the Gregorian Decretals—Jaffe places this letter before the year 1179—JL, n. 14091. Cf. also Kehr, *Italia Pontificia* (7 vols., Romae, 1903), VII, 360, n. 49.

[37] Cf. Glossa ad c. 22, D. L.

[38] Cf. Glossa ad c. 22, D. L.—Cod. MS. in the Vatican Library, n. 2288, fol. 49v, col. 2, cited by Brys, *De Dispensatione*, p. 146.

[39] It should be noted that an exact line of demarcation cannot be placed between the Decretists and the Decretalists. Thus, some Decretists, as Guido De Baysio (+1313), were also Decretalists. Consequently, no strict division

sation somewhat, still used that term as applying to penances imposed for sins, just as the Decretists had,[40] while others objected to that use of the term.[41] Others applied the term to any leniency shown by a judge in inflicting penalties.[42]

The early Decretalists did not clearly distinguish between dispensation from vindicative penalties and absolution from medicinal punishments. This is clear from the fact that they applied to dispensations the decretal of Pope Innocent III (1199),[43] which treated only of absolution from excommunication.[44]

These early Decretalists, especially those who wrote before the promulgation of the Decretals of Gregory IX, did not agree as to the power of bishops. Some favored the teachings of the Decretists that the bishops could dispense from vindicative penalties of the general law only when that power was expressly granted to them.[45]

is here intended. Cf. Kuttner, *Repertorium der Kanonistik (1140-1234)* (Romae, 1937), p. 57.

[40] Cf. Ioannes de Deo (+ after 1253): "Sic est tenendum quod pro quocumque mortali debet septennis imponi poenitentia si major vel minor non invenitur a canone . . . sed tamen dicimus quod potest moderari a sacerdote ex causa . . . potest ergo presbyter dispensare in poenitentiis, ratione duce consideratis considerandis."—*Liber Dispensationum,* cited by Brys, *De Dispensatione,* p. 169, nota 1.

[41] Cf. St. Raymond of Peñafort, *Summa S. Raymundi de Pennafort Barcinonensis, de poenitentia et matrimonio* (Veronae, 1744), L. III, tit. XXIX, *de poenitentia et remissione* (hereafter cited as *Summa*).

[42] Cf. Archdiaconus (Guido De Baysio), *Rosarium domini Guidonis archidiaconi Bononiensis super Decreto,* glossa ad v. *nisi,* c. 5, C. I, q. 7.

[43] C. 29, X, *de sententia excommunicationis,* V, 39: ". . . quia tamen conditor canonis eius absolutionem sibi specialiter non retinuit, eo ipso concessisse videtur facultatem aliis relaxandis."

[44] Cf. for example, glossa ordinaria ad v. *de adulteriis,* c. 4, X, de iudiciis, II, 1; ad v. *Plerisque,* ad v. *miror,* c. 4, D. L; ad v. *permissa,* c. 15, X, *de temporibus ordinationum et qualitate ordinandorum* I, 11.

[45] Cf. Joannes Teutonicus, *glossa ordinaria,* ad dictum Gratiani ante c. 1, D. L: "Secundum quosdam in omnibus criminibus dispensat (episcopus) ubi non prohibetur, Extra, de excomm., Nuper . . . Petrus Hispanus contrarium dicit. Nam cum in quibusdam certis casibus ei permittitur dispensare . . . ergo in aliis prohibetur. Et credo quod Episcopus semper possit dispensare, nisi ei prohibeatur expresse a iure." Cf. Gillman, "Des Petrus Hispanus Glosse zur Compilatio I,"—*AKKR,* CII (1922), 70.

Others, among them those who applied the decretal of Innocent III [46] to dispensations, held that the bishops could dispense except in cases where that power was expressly denied to them.[47] It should be noted that these latter Decretalists spoke of general dispensations, and made no distinction between dispensation from law in the strict sense and dispensation from vindicative penalties. Among these was Alanus (ante a. 1210), who states the common teaching of the time:

> Quia de dispensatione hic tractat Gratianus, ideo videamus, quid sit dispensatio, unde dicatur, et que sint indispensabilia, que dispensabilia, quis possit dispensare, et qua de causa dispensari debeat.
>
> Dispensatio est iuris communis relaxatio, et dicitur a dispensosas, tractum ab officio procuratoris fabri vel domini qui unicuique tribuit secundum merita sua. . . .
>
> Papa potest dispensare contra omnia statuta dispensabilia, Inferiores episcopi dispensare possunt contra canones continentes penas iuris ordine infligendas in minoribus criminibus, ut infra de iudiciis, At si clerici. Sed hoc plenius declaratum est L. DI. in princ. et c. Si quis presbiter. Contra canones Penitentiales omnes potest episcopus dispensare, saltim quantum ad rigorem penitentie, Inferiores prelati canones iudiciales dispensare non possunt, poenitentiales possunt, ut infra de pen. di. i. Mensuram, L. di. De his clericis, Hi qui, et infra de XXVI, q. VII. Tempora. . . .[48]

However, that distinction was made by the later Decretalists, particularly by those who wrote after the promulgation of the Decretals of Gregory IX. These later Decretalists, even though they did not always distinguish the concepts of dispensation and absolution,

[46] C. 29, X, *de sententia excommunicationis,* V, 39.

[47] Cf. *glossa ordinaria* ad c. 4, *At si clerici,* X, *de iudiciis,* II, 1: ". . . nonnullis asserentibus Episcopum dispensare posse ubicumque non invenitur prohibitum in qua sententia fuerunt Tancredus, et Laurentius et est magister B. et notatur per ipsum in isto capitulo (Nuper) aliis in contrarium sentientibus, ut G. Naso." Cf. also Joannes Teutonicus, in *glossa ordinaria* ad dictum Gratiani ante C. 5, C. I, q. 7: "De dispensatione Episcoporum dico quod ubicumque non est prohibita dispensatio, ibi possint dispensare. . . ."

[48] Glossa (set II) ad dictum Gratiani post c. 5, C. I, q. 7, v. *"discipline."* Transcribed for the author from the manuscript (MS. Vat. Ross. 595, fol. 97v) in the Vatican Library by Dr. Stephen Kuttner. Cf. for authenticity of this gloss, Kuttner, *Repertorium der Kanonistik (1140-1234),* p. 57 ff.

recognized that the decretal of Innocent III applied to absolution from the medicinal penalty of excommunication and not to dispensations in general.[49] Thus, though they distinguished the concept of general dispensations from that of absolution, they considered dispensation from vindicative penalties as a form of absolution, "quae est favorabilis, et per quam ius commune non vulneratur,"[50] and applied special rules for such dispensations based upon the general norms of absolution. Thus, Innocent IV (1243-1254) clearly stated the general principle, which later all Decretalists affirmed. Dispensations in the strict sense of relaxation of law could be given by bishops only when the law granted them such power. As to dispensations in the wider sense, he proposed two rules, one more probably tenable than the other. Bishops could dispense from all vindicative penalties inflicted by general law or by the law of superiors except when that power was expressly denied to them. This power was denied to bishops by the decretal of Alexander III in dispensations from penalties incurred by major crimes. However, the more probable rule was that bishops could not dispense from such penalties unless the law either tacitly (by a simple or impersonal grant of

[49] Cf. Archdiaconus, glossa ad c. 14, *de electione*, I, 6, in VI°: ". . . Si obiiciatur de decretali infra, De Sententia excommunicationis, Nuper [c. 29, X, V, 39] dic superstitiosam esse talem obligationem, et inutilem, cum non loquatur de dispensatione quae habet ius vulnerare . . . et quod communiter prohibita est; ut probant iura superius allegata, sed loquitur de absolutione ab excommunicatione, quae est favorabilis, et per quam ius commune non vulneretur." Cf. also Joannes Hispanus, De Petesella, *Summa super titulos Decretalium*, ad tit. *De Filiis presbyterorum*: ". . . expresse confunditur sententia antiquorum . . . Illa decretalis infra, Nuper (c. 29, X, V, 39) que eos induxit in errorem non iuvat eos namque loquitur in sententia excommunicationis, cuius exsecutionem et absolutionem non solum episcopus sed etiam simplex sacerdos in ipsa ordinum receptione recipit. . . . Simplex sacerdos enim habet claves ligandi et solvendi, maxime cum recipit (simul) ordinariam administrationem, excommunicare non est ordinis tantum sed iurisdictionis et sic absolvere excommunicatos potest. Ergo cum episcopus absolvendi excommunicatos potestatem habeat, ut supra probatum est, quemlibet excommunicatum absolvere poterit, nisi expresse a canone vel ab homine prohibeatur et sic loquitur decretalis Nuper."

[50] Cf. Archdiaconus, cited in note immediately preceding.

power) or expressly permitted them to do so.[51] This faculty, expressly granted by law, of dispensing from vindicative penalties in the case of the crime of adultery and of lesser crimes, (c. 4, X, *de iudiciis,* II, 1) therefore, could be exercised unless it was expressly prohibited; and in cases involving major crimes (maiori crimine adulterii) dispensations could be granted by bishops only when this faculty was expressly given to them.[52] Examples of such express

[51] Cf. *Apparatus,* ad c. 15, *Dilectus,* X, *de temporibus ordinationum et qualitate ordinandorum,* I, 11; "Nota non licere dispensare Episcopo nisi ubi invenitur concessum. Argumentum contra infra, *de sententia excommunicationis, Nuper* (V, 39, 29). Sed potest dici Episcopo non licere dispensare in his quae pertinent ad generalem statum Ecclesiae, nisi ubi invenitur expressum ut hic (c. 15, I, 11). Argumentum supra, eodem, c. Sane (c. 2, I, 11). In criminibus autem licet semper Episcopo dispensare, nisi prohibeatur, et sic loquitur contrarium (c. Nuper). Vel dic non licere Episcopo dispensare super faciendo, scilicet ut aliquid fiat contra canones, nisi ubi permittitur a iure, ut hic, supra, *de constitutionibus,* c. 1 (c. Canonum 1, 2), nisi contraria consuetudine et praescripta esset eis derogatum. . . . Super eo autem quod factum est, semper dispensare potest ut toleretur, nisi prohibeatur ut in contrario. Argumentum ad hoc XXII, q. 5, c. *Hoc videtur* (c. 9), et dicit et forte melius, quod ubi ius concedit dispensationem simpliciter, Episcopus dispensare potest, et sic loquitur infra, *de sententia excommunicationis,* c. Nuper, c. 29, X, V, 39, infra, *de clerico excommunicato ministrante, Postulastis,* c. 7, X, V, 27. Si autem dispensatio non conceditur a canone numquam Episcopus potest dispensare, ut hic, etiam si in canone inveniatur quod Papa dispensat . . .," cited by Van Hove, *Commentarium Lovaniense in C. I. C.,* Vol. I, Tom. V, p. 167.

[52] Cf. Joannes Hispanus, De Petesella, *Summa super titulos Decretalium,* ad tit. *De Filiis presbyterorum*: ". . . Et ad decre(talem) illam, infra *De iudiciis, At si clericis* (c. 4, X, II, 1), que dicit episcopos posse dispensare in occultis et minoribus criminibus. R. Verum esse etiam si super hiis non invenitur dispensatum, in minoribus enim adulterio, nisi dispensatum inveniatur, non poterunt, dispensare, aliis, scil, P. Yspano et fere omnibus novis doctoribus in contrarium sentientibus. Ideo hanc materiam hic plenius explicemus. Unde dico cum P. Yspan. viro excellentissimo scientiae . . . episcopum in maiori crimine adulterio licet inveniat dispensatum nisi ei a iure specialiter concedatur dispensare non posse. In minoribus bene. . . ." Cf. also Hostiensis, *Lectura Aurea,* ad c. 4, X, II, 1: "Tu dicas quod Episcopus potest dispensare in adulterio et minoribus criminibus, nisi in iure expressa prohibeatur. Sed et in maioribus, ubi hoc in iure concessum invenitur." Cf. Antonius De Butrio, *Commentarii,* ad c. 15, *Dilectus,* I, 11: ". . . Aut volunt dispensare super facto, et tunc aut volunt dispensare in delictis, ex toto poenam tollendo, et in quibus

powers granted by law to bishops in relation to major crimes are cited by St. Raymond of Penafort (1175-1275):[53] viz., crimes of heresy for which clerics were deposed or deprived of office[54] and crimes of sacrilege. St. Raymond limited this power somewhat: when the crimes were public, bishops were acknowledged by him to have faculties to dispense in crimes of adultery and minor crimes; in major crimes only in cases expressly granted by the law. In all occult crimes bishops could dispense unless they were expressly prohibited to do so by law.[55]

Besides the explicit grant of dispensatory power to bishops, Innocent III had mentioned the simple or tacit grant. The Decretalists commonly claimed for bishops this implicit concession of faculties to dispense from vindicative penalties inflicted by law, even by the general councils. They rested this claim upon certain impersonal concessions established in the IV General Council of the Lateran, celebrated under Pope Innocent III in the year 1215. In that council some penalties were imposed "nisi cum eis fuerit miseri-

possunt dispensare, et in quibus non, servandum est quod habetur, de iudiciis, *At si clerici,* § 1 (c. 4, X, II, 1), quia in gravioribus adulterio et supra non dispensant, nisi ubi appareat permissum; in inferioribus dispensant, nisi appareat prohibitum. Aut volunt dispensare in delictis, infamiam abolendo, id est tollendo, et non possunt, *de re iudicata, Cum te* (c. 23, X, II, 27). . . ." Cf. also Abbas Panormitanus (Nicolaus De Tudeschis), *Commentaria in Quinque Libros Decretalium,* 5 vols. in 7 (Venetiis, 1588), ad c. 15, *Dilectus.*

[53] *Summa,* lib. III, tit. XXIX, § II, *de dispensationibus.*

[54] Cf. Council of Ancyra, canon 1: ". . . cessare autem debent ab omni Sacro ministerio, ita ut nec panem. nec calicem offerant, nec Evangelium pronuntient, nisi forte aliqui Episcopum conscii sint laboris eorum, et humilitatis et mansuetudinis, et voluerunt eis aliquid amplius tribuere, vel adimere. Penes ipsos ergo de his erit potestas . . ."—Mansi, II, 528.

[55] ". . . Episcopus potest dispensare . . . in adulterio, et minoribus criminibus; in maioribus adulterio nequaquam, nisi in casibus a iure expressis . . . dum . . . intelligitur de peccatis manifestis per facti evidentiam, vel per confessionem in iure sponte factam, non metu probationis; et credo quod in adulteriis potest Episcopus dispensare, in maioribus autem adulterio criminibus manifestis dispensare non potest, nisi in casibus supra a iure concessis. Episcopus dispensare in omni crimine . . . nisi expresse prohibeatur sibi a iure . . . credo veram esse de omnibus criminibus occultis, quantumcumque sint, et quantumcumque enormia, si tamen exigant dispensationem."—*Summa,* lib. III, tit. XXIX, II.

corditer dispensatum." [56] Innocent IV was the first to formulate the general rule of this implicit concession, although others before him, especially Joannes Teutonicus (+ 1245),[57] had formulated much the same opinion. Innocent stated that bishops, because of an implicit grant of power, could dispense where the law makes a simple or impersonal grant of dispensation.[58] The reason is obvious: the clause, "nisi fuerit misericorditer dispensatum," contains a faculty of dispensing. But it is clear that the Pope has the power to dispense from these laws. Therefore the faculty of dispensation contained in the law pertains to the bishops and not to the Pope.[59] However, when such a grant of faculty was not at least implicit, the bishop could not dispense.[60] Some Decretalists disagreed with this opinion of Innocent, and denied to bishops this implicit grant of power in the matter of statutes of general councils.[61]

The Decretalists also claimed for bishops the power of dispensing from the common law whenever urgent necessity or the evident utility of the Church demanded such dispensations. They did not claim this power expressly as to dispensations from vindicative penalties, but applied it to dispensations in general. Various reasons were

[56] Cf. cc. 10, 26, 64—Mansi, XXII, 1051; cf. also c. 12, X, *de poenis,* V, 37: ". . . talium in clericorum collegium nullatenus admittantur, neque in domibus regularibus, alicuius praelationis assequantur honorem, nisi cum eis fuerit misericorditer dispensatum." Cf. also c. 2, X, *de torneamentis,* V, 13.

[57] Cf. glossa ad c. 12, X, *de poenis,* V, 37: ". . . cum non determinetur a quo possit dispensari, videtur quod episcopus potest dispensare, ex quo Papa sibi specialiter non retinuit dispensationem."

[58] *Apparatus* ad c. 12, X, *de poenis,* V, 37: ". . . dicit et forte melius, quod ubi ius concedit dispensationem simpliciter, Episcopus dispensare potest, et sic loquitur infra, *de sententia excommunicationis,* c. *Nuper* . . ."

[59] *Loc. cit.*

[60] "Si autem dispensatio non conceditur a canone numquam Episcopus potest dispensare . . . etiam si in canone inveniatur quod Papa dispensat . . . quia cum Episcopi debeant servare canones, non debent contra facere, nisi expresse concedatur."—*Loc. cit.*

[61] Cf. Antonius De Butrio, *Commentarii,* ad c. 15, *Dilectus,* I, *de temporibus ordinationum et qualitate ordinandorum,* 11; Panormitanus, *Commentaria,* ad c. 43, *Quisque,* X, *de electione et electi potestate,* I, 6, n. 8; ad c. 12, *In quibusdam,* X, *de poenis,* V, 37, n. 5.

given for this right: natural equity demanded it,[62] and the contrary norm of action would be irrational and burdensome to the Church.[63] The Decretalists required a very grave cause, one of public good, for the use of this power. The impossibility of having recourse to the proper superior, or the inconvenience of such recourse, was not expressly included, although Sandeus (1444-1503) stated that the dispensation could be granted by the bishop only if the legislator could not be consulted.[64] A cause of a private nature did not seem to suffice for the use of this power. Innocent IV stated "propter scandalum vitandum legitima est dispensatio," but it seems rather clear that he applied this norm only to the power of dispensing from the law of fasting granted to simple priests when recourse to the bishop was impossible.[65]

[62] Cf. Abbas Antiquus (Bernard of Montmirat), *Lectura Aurea* (Argentina, 1510), ad c. 28, *de multa,* X, *de praebendis,* III, 5.

[63] Cf. Hostiensis, *Lectura,* ad c. 28, X, *de praebendis,* III, 5: "Igitur, si evidens utilitas, et maxime urgens necessitas ecclesiae requirit dispensationem fieri in talibus, quae constitutio irrationabilis, et Ecclesiae onerans . . . et ideo ubicumque Ecclesiae necessitas vel evidens utilitas id exposcit dispensare potest. A qualibet constitutionis prohibitione necessitas et utilitas videt ut excepta." Cf. also Joannes Andreae, *Commentaria Novella,* ad c. 28, X, *de praebendis,* III, 5, n. 21; also Boich, *In Quinque Decretalium Libros Commentaria* (Venetiis. 1756), *Commentaria,* ad c. 28, X, *de praebendis,* III, 5, n. 22; Panormitanus, *Commentaria,* ad c. 4, X, II, 1; Sandeus, *Commentaria,* ad c. 4, X, II, 1.

[64] *Commentaria,* ad c. 4, X, II, 1.

[65] *Apparatus,* ad c. 1, *Ex parte,* X, *de observatione ieiunorum,* III, 46, n. 2: ". . . propter scandalum vitandum possit sacerdos dispensare etiam in (ieiunis) indicatis, nam propter scandalum vitandum legitima est dispensatio."

CHAPTER V

FROM THE COUNCIL OF TRENT TO THE CODE OF CANON LAW

ARTICLE I. THE VINDICATIVE PENALTIES

THE vindicative penalties during these centuries remained practically the same. Corporal punishments were inflicted occasionally as vindicative penalties, although many of these penalties ceased shortly after the Council of Trent.[1] Some irregularities were considered as vindicative penalties, or at least as partaking of the nature of such penalties.[2]

ARTICLE II. THE DISPENSATION FROM PENALTIES

The Council of Trent (1545-1563) made few changes in the legislation on dispensations from vindicative penalties. It granted to bishops the faculty of dispensing in all cases of irregularity and suspension resulting from secret crime, except that arising from willful homicide and from crimes that had been denounced before a tribunal.[3] Bishops could dispense from the vindicative penalty of suspension, whether *a iure* or *ab homine*,[4] arising from an occult crime, even if that suspension was reserved to the Holy See.[5] It

[1] Cf. Wernz, *Ius Decretalium*, VI, tit. V, pp. 105 ss.

[2] Cf. Schmalzgrueber, *Ius Ecclesiasticum Universum*, lib. V, tit. XXXVII, n. 69.

[3] Sess. XXIV, *de ref.*, c. 6: "Liceat episcopis in irregularitatibus omnibus et suspensionibus, ex delicto occulto provenientibus, excepta ea, quae oritur ex homicidio voluntario, et exceptis aliis deductis ad forum contentiosum, dispensare, et in quibuscumque casibus occultis, etiam Sedi Apostolicae reservatis, delinquentes quoscumque sibi subditos in dioecesi sua per se ipsos aut vicarium ad id specialiter deputandum in foro conscientiae gratis absolvere, imposita poenitentia salutari. Idem et in haeresis crimine in eodem foro conscientiae eis tantum, non eorum vicariis, sit permissum."

[4] Cf. Schmalzgrueber, *Ius Ecclesiasticum Universum*, lib. V, tit. XXXIX, n. 316.

[5] Cf. Wernz, *Ius Decretalium*, VI, tit. IV, n. 92.

should be noted, however, that the grant of power excepted those cases which had been denounced before a tribunal; and therefore, once the penalty was inflicted as an *ab homine* penalty through the sentence of a judge, it was excluded from the dispensatory power of the bishops.[6] They could exercise this power only over their subjects,[7] but outside the diocese,[8] and could also delegate this power of dispensation.[9] This dispensation was not limited to the forum of conscience, as in the case of absolution, but could be given in the external forum.[10] The power of absolving in all occult cases, granted by the Council, was not to be so extended as to include the power of dispensing from vindicative penalties in such cases, since this latter grant of power referred only to absolution in occult cases from censures.[11] Since this faculty allowed the granting of dispensations only in suspension and irregularities, bishops could not, by virtue of this grant, dispense from other vindicative penalties, even in occult cases, which remained reserved to the Pope.[12]

However, though this grant of power in *all* occult cases was not made by the Council of Trent in the matter of dispensations from all vindicative penalties, commentators commonly held that

[6] Lega, *De Delictis et Poenis*, n. 129.

[7] Commentators applied this limit of the bishops' power, mentioned in the canon as applying to absolution from censures, to dispensations. Cf. Schmalzgrueber, *Ius Ecclesiasticum Universum*, lib. V, tit. XXXVII, n. 117; Wernz, *Ius Decretalium*, VI, tit. IV, n. 94; D'Annibale, *Summula Theologiae Moralis* (5. ed., 3 vols., Romae: Desclée, Lefebvre et Soc., 1908), I, n. 322 (hereafter cited as *Summula*).

[8] Cf. D'Annibale, *loc. cit.*: ". . . haec verba 'in dioecesi sua' . . . ad absolutiones, non ad dispensationes pertinent." Cf. also Sanchez, *De Sancto Matrimonii Sacramento* (Antwerpiae, 1926), lib. II, disp. XI, n. 12.

[9] Cf. Putzer, *Commentarium in Facultates Apostolicas*, n. 25; Thesaurus, *De Poenis Ecclesiasticis Praxis Absoluta et Universalis* (Romae, 1760), pars I, cap. 23, dic. IV (hereafter cited as *De Poenis Ecclesiasticis*); D'Annibale, *Summula*, I, n. 322; Schmalzgrueber, *op. cit.*, lib. V, tit. V, n. 113.

[10] Cf. D'Annibale, *Summula*, I, n. 322; Schmalzgrueber, *Ius Ecclesiasticum Universum*, lib. V, tit. XXXVII, nn. 119, 326.

[11] Cf. Lega, *De Delictis et Poenis*, n. 112; D'Annibale, *Summula*, I, n. 316.

[12] Cf. Thesaurus, *De Poenis Ecclesiasticis*, pars I, cap. 23; Piatus Montensis, *Praelectiones Iuris Regularis* (3. ed., 3 vols., Tornaci, 1905), II, 101; Wernz, *Ius Decretalium*, VI, tit. V, n. 113.

bishops had such power to dispense from any vindicative penalty in occult cases, that is, in occult crimes, in cases of grave necessity, when the Pope could not be approached without serious inconvenience. Such cases of grave necessity included the danger of scandal or serious injury or infamy.[13] D'Annibale (+1892) extended this power of bishops to dispense from all penalties, whether in occult cases or public, "quoties gravis necessitas urget, et R.P. sine gravi incommodo adiri non potest," and as reason for this power he referred to the "natura legum humanorum, quarum nulla est obligatio cum incommodo gravi."[14] Wernz (+1914), in refuting this opinion of D'Annibale as "juridically incongruous" and as lacking any basis in Church law, reluctantly admitted that in cases of occult vindicative penalties the bishop may dispense when grave inconvenience prevents recourse to Rome and when infamy would follow upon the observance of the penalty.[15] Schmalzgrueber (+1735), in speaking of irregularities, proposed the same principle: in cases of voluntary homicide—reserved expressly to the Pope by the Council of Trent—the bishop could dispense in the forum of conscience, in the event of urgent necessity to avoid infamy or scandal or other grave sins, if convenient recourse to the Pope was not possible. However, this dispensation was rather a suspension of the penalty, for a dispensation later had to be sought from the Pope.[16]

[13] Cf. Thesaurus (*De Poenis Ecclesiasticis,* pars I, cap. 23, dic. V): "Concessum est Episcopo dispensare super poenis, latac sententiae ex iure communi, et etiam ex conciliari constitutione, etiam Papae reservatis, in casu gravis necessitatis, idest cum alias scandala, vel damna gravia sequeretur, et non potest haberi recursus opportunus ad Sedem Apostolicam, ut ob inopiam, vel temporis brevitatem." Cf. also Sanchez (*De Sancto Matrimonii Sacramento,* lib. II, dist. XL, nn. 3, 8, 9): ". . . quia ius soli Pontifici reservat dispensationem, cum ergo is consuli nequeat, poterit episcopus tamquam pastor ordinarius dispensare. . . . Episcopus solum potest . . . dispensare, ratione necessitatis urgentis, sed quando adest potens dispensare, ad quem confugi potest, necessitas cessat, ergo non poterit episcopus."

[14] *Summula,* I, n. 315 ss.

[15] *Ius Decretalium* (VI, tit. IV, n. 91, nota 71): ". . . nullo allegato iuris textu suam assertionem probat. . . . Pro poenis *occulte incursis,* quarum executio secum traherit infamiam aut scandalum, minor etiam apparet iuridica incongruentia."

[16] *Ius Ecclesiasticum Universum,* lib. V, tit. XII, n. 250: "Excipitur 1. casus

In public cases, the norms established by Innocent IV were followed, at least in substance, by the commentators who wrote after the Council of Trent. Some propounded the first principle stated by Innocent: that bishops could dispense from all *latae sententiae* vindicative penalties unless they were expressly prohibited to do so in certain reserved cases.[17] Others, and they were by far the greater number, held the second principle of Innocent, which he also preferred: that bishops could not dispense in these penalties unless the power was granted to them, either tacitly or expressly.[18]

Thus Innocent's teaching as to the simple, tacit, or impersonal grant of dispensatory power was admitted by all commentators.[19]

urgentis necessitatis ad vitandam infamiam vel scandalum, aut iliud grave peccatum, et si non sit facilis recursus ad papam; nam tunc dispensare cum irregulari, qui occultum commisit homicidium, pro foro conscientiae potest episcopus, ut in ordinibus etiam sacris ministrare, et celebrare possit, et quamdiu culpa, et defectus occultus manet, et donec dispensatio a papa inpetretur."

[17] Cf. Thesaurus (*De Poenis Ecclesiasticis,* pars I, cap. 23, dic. II): "Circa poenas latae sententiae ex ipso iure iam . . . incursas, varias esse DD. sententias. . . . Prima esserit, inferiorem Praelatum posse dispensare super poenis huiusmodi, ubicumque non reperitur prohibitum, etiamsi sint latae a iure pontificio, quia eo ipso censetur esse de genere permissorum."

[18] Cf. Suarez. *Tractatus de Legibus et Deo Legislatore* (Conimbriae, 1612), I, tit. VI, c. 14, nn. 2, 4, 6; Thesaurus (*op. cit.,* pars I, cap. 23, dic. II): "Secunda sententia probabilior asserit Episcopum, seu Praelatum non posse dispensare super poenis latae sententiae, nisi ubi ius tacite, vel expresse illi dispensare concedit." Cf. also D'Annibale, *Summula,* I, n. 314; Piatus Montensis, *Praelectiones Iuris Regularis,* II, 582, 596 ss. Wernz (*Ius Decretalium,* VI, tit. IV, n. 88) wrote: "Potestos remittendi poenam . . . per dispensationem per se illi competit, qui poenam tulit, vel qui huius sit superior aut successor vel delegatus. . . . Quare licet Ordinarius aliique ab ipso delegati possint dispensare a poenis iure diocesano constitutis, a poenis iuris communis dispensare non valent, nisi in quantum habeant ad hoc facultatem sive specialem a R. Pontifice acceptam sive generalem per ius commune concessum . . . certe facultas dispensandi tacite fit ipso iure. . . ." Cf. Vermeersch, *De Religiosis Institutis et Personis* (4. ed., 2 vols., Brugis, 1907), I, nn. 418, 425 ss.

[19] Cf. Suarez, *Tractatus de Legibus et Deo Legislatore,* I, tit. VI, c. 14, n. 8; Sanchez, *De Sancto Matrimonii Sacramento,* lib. I, disp. V, nn. 2, 5; Thesaurus (*De Poenis Ecclesiasticis,* pars I, cap. 23, dic. III): "Dico III quod dispensandi facultas super poenis latae sententiae censetur concessa Episcopis seu Inferioribus habentibus episcopalem iurisdictionem, quoties canon permittit dispensationem impersonaliter, ut per illa verba 'nisi cum illo fuerit misericorditer dispensatum.' " Cf. also Wernz (*Ius Decretalium,* VI, tit. IV, n. 90): ". . . in . . . poenis latae

Commentators after the Council of Trent also taught the doctrine of the Decretalists in regard to the dispensation from penalties incurred for major and minor crimes, with, however, some new distinctions. All taught that the bishop could not dispense from vindicative penalties incurred through the commission of the major crimes unless that faculty was expressly granted to him.[20] As to the minor crimes, such as adultery or even lesser crimes, there were different opinions. Some held, as the Decretalists had, that the bishop could dispense from any and all vindicative penalties incurred through these minor crimes, unless they were prohibited from doing so in special cases, either explicitly or implicitly.[21] Such implicit prohibitions were said to have existed if the incurred penalty was one which endured for a definite length of time,[22] or if the penalty demanded execution by a third party.[23] Thus, according to this opinion, bishops could dispense from such penalties as infamy, irregularity *(sic)*, ineligibility for office, or verbal deposition; they could not dispense from privation of benefice, or office, or revenue after judicial sentence.[24] The reason given for this wide grant of power

sententiae iure communi sine interventu iudicis incursis, certe facultas dispensandi tacite fit ab ipso iure Episcopis aliisque Praelatis iurisdictionem quasi episcopalem habentibus, quoties ius permittit dispensationem quin determinat personam a qua dari debet; satis enim intelligitur R. Pontificem in iure commune dispensare posse; ergo facultas dispensandi in lege contenta non ad R. Pontificem sed ad inferiores Praelatos est referenda." See also Chelodi, *Ius Poenale,* p. 35; Roberti, *De Delictis et Poenis,* p. 306.

[20] Cf. Thesaurus, *De Poenis Ecclesiasticis,* pars I, cap. 23, dic. IV; D'Annibale, *Summula,* I, n. 315; Lega, *De Delictis et Poenis,* n. 12.

[21] Cf. Thesaurus (*De Poenis Ecclesiasticis,* pars I, cap. 23, dic. IV): "In poenis latae sententiae ex ipso iure incursis ob crimina etiam publica minora seu non maiora adulterio . . . concessum esse a iure Episcopo, seu Praelato habenti episcopalem iurisdictionem pro utroque foro dispensare; dummodo specialiter non reperiatur prohibitum. . . ." Cf. D'Annibale, *Summula,* I, n. 315; Lega, *De Delictis et Poenis,* n. 12.

[22] Cf. Thesaurus (*De Poenis Ecclesiasticis,* pars I, cap. 23, dic. IV): ". . . Et sufficit si poena sit lata ad tempus determinatum quia hoc ipso est reservata dispensatio." Cf. Suarez, *De Censuris,* Dist. XXIX, sec. I, n. 20.

[23] Cf. Thesaurus, *loc. cit.*

[24] Cf. Thesaurus (*loc. cit.*): "Unde poterit dispensare in iis casibus super poena infamiae, vel irregularitatis vel inhabilitatis, vel depositionis verbalis, non autem super privatione beneficii, vel officii, vel bonorum privatione post factam iudicis ministerio."

to the bishops was the fact that these minor crimes were very frequently committed, and it would have been burdensome to appeal to Rome in each case.[25]

The other opinion limited the power of bishops in regard to these minor crimes. Suarez (+1617) and others admitted this power only in the case of suspensions and depositions, for the decretal of Alexander III, on which this grant of power depended, treated only of those penalties.[26] Wernz also rejected the distinction between penalties which demanded execution by a third party and those which did not; he proved that such a principle in itself was uncertain, to say the least.[27] Thus, according to this opinion, bishops could dispense clerics who had been suspended through the commission of an occult minor crime. Likewise, they could dispense clerics who had been deposed for the crime of adultery or for lesser crimes. But since infamy of law followed deposition,[28] and this could be removed only by the Roman Pontiff,[29] the commentators introduced a distinction. Bishops could generally dispense in such cases, and *indirectly* remove the infamy, since the penalty of infamy had not been directly inflicted, but had resulted from another penalty. The Pope alone could *directly* remove the infamy.[30]

[25] Cf. Thesaurus (*De Poenis Ecclesiasticis,* pars I, cap. 23, dic. IV): ". . . quia cum ea minora crimina frequentiora consulendum fuit, ne tam frequenter necessarius esset recursus ad Sedem Apostolicam."

[26] Cf. c. 4, X, *de iudiciis,* II, 1: ". . . dummodo sint talia crimina propter quae suspendi debeant vel deponi"; and in the Friedberg edition of the Corpus is added: ". . . potest episcopus cum suis clericis post peractam poenitentiam dispensare, ut in ordinibus suis deserviant." Cf. Wernz, *Ius Decretalium,* VI, tit. IV, n. 91, also note 71; Suarez, *De Censuris,* Dist. XXIX, sec. I, n. 21.

[27] *Ius Decretalium, ibid.,* nota 71.

[28] C. 17, C. VI, q. 1.

[29] C. 23, X, *de sententia et re iudicata,* II, 27.

[30] Cf. Suarez, *De Censuris,* Dist. XLVIII, sec. II, nn. 6-8; Reiffenstuel, *Ius Canonicum Universum,* lib. V, tit. 37, nn. 28, 29; Gonzalez-Tellez, *Commentaria Perpetua in Singulos Textus Quinque Librorum Decretalium Gregorii IX,* lib. II, tit. I, cap. 4, § 2, n. 2; Schmalzgrueber, *Ius Ecclesiasticum Universum,* lib. V, tit. XXXVII, n. 137; Wernz, *Ius Decretalium,* VI, tit. V, n. 126; *Pontificale Romanum, Summorum Pontificum iussu editum a Benedicto XIV et*

All the commentators, however, agreed that the distinction between major and minor crimes was a difficult criterion to recognize in practice.[81] They agreed that the gravity of the crime was not to be judged according to theological norms regarding the gravity of sin; but rather it was to be considered grave or major, and beyond the dispensatory power of bishops, in line with the gravity of the punishment attached to a particular crime. This principle made the distinction more practical in deciding the actual powers of bishops. Bishops could dispense in penalties incurred through the crimes of adultery, theft, sacrilege, perjury, the false giving of testimony; they could not dispense in the major crimes of heresy, simony, or homicide.[82]

The principles of dispensation from vindicative penalties, therefore, remained practically the same during these centuries. Only in particular instances, when applications of these principles were made, was there any change from the practice of the previous centuries. The power of dispensing from vindicative penalties was reserved to the legislator who inflicted the penalty, or to his successor or superior, or to one delegated by him. Therefore a judge who merely applied the penalty established by a superior had no power whatsoever to dispense from that penalty, unless, of course, he enjoyed delegated power from the superior to do so.[83]

However, as Wernz pointed out,[84] the application of the principles was difficult, since the entire principle of major and minor crimes was an uncertain and unreliable one, and the commentators looked forward to definite regulations from Rome establishing in particular

Leone XIII Pont. Max. recognitum et Castigatum (3 vols., Ratisbonae, Neo Eboraci et Cincinnati, 1908), tit. *degradationis forma.*

[81] Cf. Thesaurus, *De Poenis Ecclesiasticis,* pars I, cap. 23, dic. IV; Schmalzgrueber, *loc. cit.*; Wernz, *op. cit.,* VI, tit. IV, n. 91. Cf. also Chelodi, *Ius Poenale,* p. 36; Roberti, *De Delictis et Poenis,* pp. 305, 306.

[82] Cf. Thesaurus, *De Poenis Ecclesiasticis,* pars I, cap. 23, dic. IV.

[83] Cf. Thesaurus, *De Poenis Ecclesiasticis,* pars I, cap. 23, dic. I; Wernz, *Ius Decretalium,* VI, tit. IV, nn. 88, 89; Schmalzgrueber, *Ius Ecclesiasticum Universum,* lib. V, tit. XII, n. 239.

[84] *Ius Decretalium,* VI, tit. IV, nn. 88, 89.

the vindicative penalties from which the bishops could dispense. These definite rules were established in the Code of Canon Law and the dispensatory power of the bishops was definitely decided. In occult cases the power was extended; in public cases it was limited. Likewise certain powers were granted to confessors in extraordinary cases.[85]

[85] Canon 2290.

HISTORICAL SUMMARY

In the early Church, as in so many matters of ecclesiastical law, the penal legislation did not possess that clarity and completeness which was to develop through the centuries. There was no clear distinction between vindicative and medicinal penalties; most penalties inflicted by the Church combined both elements. The terms used to designate the various penalties were not uniform; moreover, the internal and external forums were not completely separated.

Most of the penalties of the Church were largely vindicative in nature up to the sixth century. But the medicinal element was often prominent. Consequently, the principles of dispensation from penalties likewise lacked clarity and precision, and were often confused with those of absolution from penalties. The bishop dispensed from penalties incurred by his clerics and subjects; and occasionally the Pope granted such dispensations.

In the fourth century the active subject of dispensation was threefold: the bishops, the Pope, and the provincial synods. The Pope and the synods granted dispensations from vindicative penalties more as a matter of vigilance over the bishops' use of their coercive powers. Bishops and synods granted dispensations from vindicative penalties inflicted by the general law, although both often acknowledged the need of applying to the Pope for certain dispensations.

In the ninth century the Popes claimed the right to dispense from penalties inflicted by the general law. Others possessed that right only when it was expressly granted to them. This principle was further developed and clarified in the Gregorian Reform, although not all the bishops acknowledged the claim of the Pope in practice.

The Decretists further developed that principle, in a greater or lesser degree. They allowed bishops to dispense only when the law had given them special faculties. Bishops, by law, could dispense from penalties inflicted for minor crimes, whenever that power was not expressly denied to them; and from penalties inflicted for the so-called major crimes they could dispense only when that power was expressly granted to them. Besides this explicit grant of dispensatory power to bishops, another grant was allowed: the simple or tacit grant of power. Moreover, whenever urgent necessity demanded a dispensation from penalties, the bishops could dispense.

The Council of Trent made few changes, granting special dispensatory powers to bishops in cases of suspensions and irregularities resulting from secret crimes, with a few exceptions. Commentators writing after the Council of Trent also held that bishops had the power to dispense from any vindicative penalty in occult crimes in cases of grave necessity, when the Pope could not be approached without serious inconvenience. The old distinction between major and minor crimes was used by all commentators—with, however, many misgivings. The application of the general principles of dispensation from vindicative penalties was difficult and unreliable; and all looked forward to definite regulations from Rome. These came in the Code of Canon Law when the principles were definitely settled. The powers of the bishops were clearly defined, and certain extraordinary faculties, heretofore unknown, were granted to confessors.

Part II

Canonical Commentary

SECTION I

ORDINARY DISPENSATION FROM VINDICATIVE PENALTIES

CHAPTER VI

GENERAL PRINCIPLES OF DISPENSATION FROM VINDICATIVE PENALTIES

Canon 2289. Poena vindicativa finitur eius . . . dispensatione ab eo concessa qui legitimam habeat dispensandi potestatem ad normam can. 2236.

Canon 2236, § 1. Remissio poenae sive per absolutionem, si agatur dẹ censuris, sive per dispensationem, si de poenis vindicativis, concedi tantum potest ab eo qui poenam tulit, vel ab eius competente Superiore aut successore, vel ab eo cui haec potestas commissa est.

§ 2. Qui potest a lege eximere, potest quoque poenam legi adnexam remittere.

§ 3. Iudex qui ex officio applicat poenam a Superiore constitutam, eam semel applicatam nequit.

Article I. Preliminary Notions

A. *Vindicative Penalties*

Vindicative penalties are those which are intended directly for the expiation of crimes, so that their relaxation does not depend on the mere cessation of contumacy.[1] They are penalties inasmuch

[1] Canon 2286: Poena vindicativae illae sunt, quae directe ad delicti expiationem tendunt ita ut earum remissio e cessatione contumaciae delinquentis non pendeat.

as they are inflicted by lawful ecclesiastical authority for crime by way of some privation, pain or suffering, so that the crime is atoned for and expiated by the privation and suffering of the offender.[2] They have for their primary object the good of the community, the expiation of crime, and the restoration of a violated social order.[3] Unlike censures, they look primarily to the delict committed, that is, to the violation of a law, rather than to the offender or violator of the law.[4] Unlike censures, which intend directly the amendment of the delinquent and which demand absolution as soon as the delinquent's contumacy ceases and he expresses his repentance, vindicative penalties endure *per se* even subsequent to the offender's repentance.[5] Hence the amendment or repentance of the delinquent does not give him the right to be released from them, but they are rather inflicted for a definite time or *in perpetuum*. This temporal element, if it may so be termed, is an exclusive characteristic of vindicative penalties, and is often the only means of determining whether a particular penalty is medicinal or vindicative. Thus the penalties of suspension and interdict may be either censures or vindicative penalties; but if this temporal element is present, the penalty is vindicative and not medicinal.[6]

Vindicative penalties, as has been noted,[7] at one time were tem-

[2] Tarquini, *Institutiones Iuris Publici Ecclesiastici*, n. 25; Hinschius, *Kirchenrecht*, IV, p. 747.

[3] Cf. Lega, *Praelectiones in Textum Iuris Canonici*, lib. II, Vol. III, *De Iudiciis Ecclesiasticis*, pars I, cap. I, n. 56; Ayrinhac-Lydon, *Penal Legislation in the New Code of Canon Law*, n. 156.

[4] Cf. Chelodi, *Ius Poenale*, n. 46; Coronata, *Institutiones Iuris Canonici*, Vol. IV, *De Delictis et Poenis* (Taurini: Marietti, 1935), n. 1819; Wernz-Vidal, *Ius Canonicum*, tom. VIII, n. 332.

[5] Cf. Ayrinhac-Lydon, *Penal Legislation*, n. 156; Wernz-Vidal, *Ius Canonicum*, VII, n. 332; Sipos, *Enchiridion Iuris Canonici* (Pecs: Typographia Haladas, 1926), § 238, I.

[6] *E.g.*, canon 2410: "Superiores religiosi qui, contra praescriptum can. 965-967, subditos suos ad Episcopum alienum ordinandos remittere praesumpserint, ipso facto suspensi sunt per mensem a Missae celebratione." Also canon 2370: "Episcopus aliquem consecrans in Episcopum, Episcopi vel, loco Episcoporum, presbyteri assistentes, et qui consecrationem recipit sine apostolico mandato contra praescriptum can. 953, ipso iure suspensi sunt, donec Sedes Apostolica eos dispensaverit."

[7] Cf. *supra*, p. 22.

poral or corporal punishments, in consequence, it seems, of the influence of the Roman and Germanic laws.[8] But since the Council of Trent, vindicative penalties have been spiritual in nature, involving suspension, either perpetual or temporary, privation of office or of benefice, penal transfer, deposition and degradation.[9]

Vindicative penalties are divided, according to the norms of canon 2217, into fixed and undetermined penalties, penalties *latae sententiae* and *ferendae sententiae,* and penalties *a iure* and *ab homine.* A fixed vindicative penalty is one that is so clearly determined by law or precept, that no doubt may arise as to what is meant. The Code uses the term "taxative statuta" to describe this clarity which must exist. This term involves the following elements: the quality or type of the penalty must be accurately stated, and the length of time must be clearly determined.[10] As often as the law or precept fails expressly to define the type of privation to be suffered or neglects to state the length of time this privation is to endure, the vindicative penalty attached to that law or precept is said to be undetermined or arbitrary. In other words, the penalty is left to the prudent discretion of the judge or superior. This discretion may concern the question whether any penalty is to be inflicted, or what kind of penalty, or in what measure or for what length of time. For the law may clearly determine that a penalty must be inflicted, but leave the kind and measure to the judge. Or it may allow the superior or judge to inflict additional penalties;[11] or it may establish a minimum of penalties, and leave it to the judge to inflict a more severe punishment.[12] The terms by which undetermined vindicative penalties are left for their proper specification to the prudent judgment of the superior or judge are either preceptive or facultative.[13] Preceptive terms implying an

[8] Hinschius, *Kirchenrecht,* IV, 803; V, 36, 51 ss.

[9] It should be noted that a mild form of corporal punishment still exists: "incarceration" or detention in a monastery as a penalty for clerics. Cf. Chelodi, *Ius Poenale,* n. 46.

[10] Cf. Berutti, *Institutiones Iuris Canonici,* Vol. VI (Taurini-Romae: Marietti, 1938), cap. IV, n. 19, III; Wernz-Vidal, *Ius Canonicum,* VI, n. 61.

[11] Cf. canon 2170.

[12] Cf. canons 2321; 2337; 2349; 2361; 2378; 2391, § 2.

[13] Canon 2217, § 1, 1°.

obligatory use of punitive power on the part of superiors or judges, in general are: *debet puniri, privandus, puniendus est, declarandus* or *declaretur infamis;* facultative or arbitrary terms are: *pro gravitate culpae, ad arbitrium superioris.*

Vindicative penalties are likewise divided into *latae sententiae* and *ferendae sententiae.* A fixed or determined vindicative penalty is of a *latae sententiae* character if it is attached either by law or precept to the commission of the crime in such a way that as soon as the crime is committed the penalty is immediately incurred.[14] The penalty is inflicted upon the potential offender, by the legislator or superior who makes the precept, at the very moment that the law or precept is promulgated; and thus the term "latae sententiae" is used, because in reality it may be said that the condemnatory sentence has already been extrajudicially passed upon the offender.[15] The legislator uses such terms as *ipso facto, ipso iure,* etc., to express *latae sententiae* vindicative penalties; the superior, likewise, decrees *(per modum praecepti)* certain vindicative penalties to be incurred *ipso facto.* It is obvious that all *latae sententiae* vindicative penalties are fixed or determined penalties.

Vindicative penalties of a *ferendae sententiae* character are those which are to be inflicted by the judge or superior. They may be determined by law or undetermined, and are expressed by such terms as *deponatur, ab Ordinario puniatur.* They are called "ferendae sententiae" precisely because at the time of the commission of the delict sentence has not yet been passed; and the offender is not obliged to observe the vindicative penalty unless and until that penalty is legitimately applied or inflicted upon him through the intervention of the judge or superior.[16] In order that it may be perfectly clear when an offender incurs a vindicative penalty in the very act of committing a delict, the Code establishes a general norm that the penalty must always be understood to be *ferendae sententiae* unless the law or precept expressly states it to be *latae sententiae,* or unless such terms as *ipso iure,* or *ipso facto,* or similar

[14] Canon 2217, § 1, 2°.

[15] Cf. Berutti, *Institutiones Iuris Canonici,* VI, p. 65.

[16] Cf. Berutti, *Institutiones Iuris Canonici, ibid.,* n. 2; Ayrinhac-Lydon, *Penal Legislation in the New Code of Canon Law,* n. 35.

terms are employed with reference to the manner of incurring the penalty.[17] Such terms are *eo ipso*,[18] *manet*.[19]

Finally, vindicative penalties are divided into penalties which derive *a iure* or *ab homine*. They are said to derive *a iure* when, whether of a *latae sententiae* or a *ferendae sententiae* character, the penalties are determined and established by law, universal or particular, or *ad modum legis*, that is, by a general precept.[20]

They are said to derive *ab homine* when, although established by law, they are inflicted through a special order *per modum praecepti peculiaris*, that is, through a particular precept of the superior, or by a condemnatory judicial sentence. It follows, therefore, that a *ferendae sententiae* vindicative penalty which is attached to a law and is established by it is a penalty *a iure tantum* as long as no condemnatory sentence has been pronounced; but after such a sentence has been issued, it becomes a penalty *a iure et ab homine*, but it is considered as *ab homine*.[21] In other words, vindicative penalties are considered as deriving *a iure* whenever these penalties, whether they be of a *latae* or a *ferendae sententiae* character, are established by law or by a general precept.[22] If the penalty is of a *latae sententiae* nature, it remains a penalty *a iure* even after a declaratory judiciary sentence has been rendered. Vindicative penalties, on the other hand, are considered *ab homine* when they are inflicted through a condemnatory sentence by which a judge applies a *ferendae sententiae* vindicative penalty established by law, or when they are inflicted through a particular precept. It should be noted here that a determined vindicative penalty of *latae sententiae* char-

[17] Cf. canon 2217, § 2.

[18] Canon 2365.

[19] Canon 671, 1°.

[20] Canon 2217, § 1, 3°. Cf. Berutti, *Institutiones Iuris Canonici*, VI, p. 66; Wernz-Vidal, *Ius Canonicum*, VII, n. 146, nota 16.

[21] Cf. canon 2217, § 1, 3°.

[22] A general precept is here included although canon 2217, § 1, 3° mentions merely the establishment of a penalty by *law*. For a general precept is in reality a law, and differs from a law only in the matter of its duration. Cf. Berutti, *Institutiones Iuris Canonici*, VI, p. 66; Beste, *Introductio in Codicem* (Collegeville, Minnesota: St. John's Abbey Press, 1938), p. 889; Lega, *De Delictis et Poenis*, nn. 78, 130; Wernz-Vidal, *Ius Canonicum*, VII, nn. 156, 166 d; Wernz, *Ius Decretalium*, VI, n. 146.

acter which has been confirmed by a declaratory judiciary sentence is not a penalty *ab homine,* but remains a penalty *a iure* after the sentence has been issued; the Code demands a condemnatory sentence passed upon a penalty *ferendae sententiae* in order that a penalty *a iure* may be considered as *ab homine.*[23]

A further problem here presents itself.[24] It concerns the existence of *latae sententiae* vindicative penalties attached to particular precepts, and the further question as to whether such a penalty, attached to a particular precept and incurred *ipso facto* upon the violation of the precept, is an *ab homine* vindicative penalty and as such reserved.

A *latae sententiae* vindicative penalty, as has been seen, is a determined penalty so attached to a law or precept that it is incurred by the very fact that the delict is committed. This principle appears quite clear, with a possibility of difficulty arising only from its application, *i. e.,* whether the terms used in a specific case are equivalent to the *ipso facto* and *ipso iure* of canon 2217, § 1, 2°. In an opinion which he held in 1919, and again repeated in 1925 and 1933, Cappello makes a distinction in the principle established in this canon. He asserts that a *latae sententiae* penalty is one that is attached in such a manner to a law or a general precept that it is incurred *ipso facto* by the violation of the law or general precept.[25]

There seems to be no reason, and Cappello offers none, to limit the coercive power of ecclesiastical authorities or to assert that a

[23] Hollweck, *Die kirchlichen Strafgesetze* (Mainz, 1899), § 23, p. 87, nota 3; Eichmann, *Das Prozessrecht des Codex Iuris Canonici* (Paderborn, 1920), p. 57; Coronata, *Institutiones Iuris Canonici,* IV, n. 1690.

[24] This problem is given particular attention here because of the question, to be treated immediately, whether a dispensation from vindicative penalties is a dispensation in the strict sense of the concept as given in canon 80. The problem will also arise in the treatment of the suspension of vindicative penalties and their dispensation in urgent cases according to canon 2290. It was thought best to solve this question immediately, in the preliminary treatment of *latae sententiae* and *ferendae sententiae, a iure* and *ab homine* vindicative penalties.

[25] *De Censuris* (Augustae Taurinorum: Marietti, 1919), n. 2, 3°; *De Censuris* (2. ed., 1925; 3. ed., 1933), n. 4, 3°: "Vocantur latae sententiae quae ita sunt additae legi vel praecepto generali ut incurrentur ipso facto delicti commissi, quin opus sit sententiae auctoritatis ecclesiasticae."

bishop, for example, in imposing a particular precept, is restricted to *ferendae sententiae* penalties, and that he cannot attach a vindicative penalty to this particular precept in such a way that it is incurred *ipso facto* when the delict is committed, apart from any judiciary procedure. Why, for example, cannot a bishop say to one of his priests: "Do not attend that theater, and if you do, you are *ipso facto* suspended for three months"? No distinction whatsoever is made in canon 2217, § 1, 2°, between a general precept and a particular precept, nor is the distinction made in canon 2220, § 1, which simply states that those who have the power to make laws or impose precepts can attach penalties to the law or precept.[26] Consequently, there seems to be no justification for the assertion that a *latae sententiae* penalty cannot be attached to a particular precept; and consequently it would seem that vindicative penalties of a *latae sententiae* character may be established by particular precepts.

The second problem is whether such a vindicative penalty *latae sententiae* attached to a particular precept is *ab homine* or *a iure*, or neither. According to canon 2217, § 1, 3°, as had been shown, an *ab homine* penalty is one which is inflicted by a particular precept or by a judicial condemnatory sentence, even if the penalty is established in the law; consequently when a *ferendae sententiae* penalty is attached to the law, before the condemnatory sentence it is *a iure*, but after the sentence has been issued it is both *a iure* and *ab homine*, but is considered as *ab homine*.[27] Moriarty, in a discussion of this canon in relation to *ab homine* censures, cites seeming difficulties in the text of this law. In canon 2217, § 1, 3°, he says, there is not an adequate distinction, since there simply is no *ratio distinctionis* for the division in this paragraph of the canon, of penalties into *a iure* and *ab homine*. For the definition of *a iure* penalties is based on the manner in which the penalties are *constituted* or established, while the definition of *ab homine* penalties is based on the manner in which the penalties are *inflicted*. The legislator obviously fore-

[26] Canon 2220, § 1: Qui pollent potestate leges ferendi vel praecepta imponendi, possunt quoque legi vel praecepto poenas adnectere. . . .

[27] Canon 2217. Cf. Moriarty, *The Extraordinary Absolution from Censures*, pp. 95, 96.

saw the possibility of a doubt regarding these two definitions, namely, in the case in which the *ferendae sententiae* penalty is *established* by the law but is *inflicted* by a condemnatory judicial sentence, because it is quite clear that such a penalty would fulfill the definition of a penalty *a iure* (in its establishment in the law) as well as the definition of a penalty *ab homine* (in its infliction by a condemnatory sentence). And so he immediately settled the doubt by explaining that such a penalty, even though after the condemnatory sentence it is both *a iure* and *ab homine*, is for all practical purposes to be considered as *ab homine*. This explanation, Moriarty adds, is not restricted to the definition of *ab homine* penalties in this canon, but pertains to all that precedes it in the first part of canon 2217, § 1, 3°, and therefore the clause "quare poena ferendae sententiae . . ." is not to be considered at all as an indication that an *ab homine* penalty can be only *ferendae sententiae*.[28]

This explanation by Moriarty is excellent. However, it would seem that the legislator in this section of canon 2217 chose his terms carefully in an attempt to avoid confusion. Thus, the term "feratur" seems to have been chosen deliberately, for it is the root term from which both the terms "latae sententiae" and "ferendae sententiae" are derived. Thus, in the case of *latae sententiae* penalties it may well express the *establishment* of these penalties by a particular precept; and in the case of *ferendae sententiae* penalties it equally may express the *infliction* of such penalties by a particular precept or by a condemnatory judicial sentence.[29] A *latae sententiae* penalty may, therefore, be said to be established (in the sense of "feratur") by a particular precept and consequently fall under the definition of a penalty *ab homine*. Similarly, a *ferendae sententae* penalty

[28] Moriarty, *The Extraordinary Absolution from Censures,* p. 96.

[29] Cf. Ayrinhac-Lydon, *Penal Legislation in the New Code of Canon Law,* n. 84; Roberti, in expounding his own opinion—jointly held by Michiels—that *latae sententiae* penalties cannot be *ab homine,* confesses that the term "feratur" as used in canon 2217, § 1, 3° rather expresses the establishment of a penalty than its infliction: "Obstat, fatemur, verbum "feratur," quod magis congruit poenae constitutioni quam irrogationi. . . ."—"An censura latae sententiae per praeceptum constituta sit reservata," *Apollinaris,* VI (1933), 343. This opinion will be treated shortly. Cf. also canon 2236, § 1, where this term is obviously used to express the establishment of a penalty, as well as its infliction.

may be said to be inflicted (in the sense of "feratur") by a particular precept or by a condemnatory sentence, and therefore would be a penalty *ab homine.* Thus, the translation of the term "feratur" in the strict sense of "infliction" does not do justice to that term; and therefore to say that there is no *ratio distinctionis* for the division in this canon of penalties into *a iure* and *ab homine* is not altogether correct. At least as regards penalties *latae sententiae* the *ratio distinctionis* is the establishment of the penalty: in the one case by law (*a iure*), in the other by particular precept (*ab homine*). It is true that the difficulty still remains in regard to penalties *ferendae sententiae,* but this arises rather from the nature of such penalties which are established by law in such a way that their infliction—by particular precept or condemnatory sentence—is to follow. Thus the term "feratur" seems to have been used deliberately to include both penalties *latae sententiae* and penalties *ferendae sententiae.* It has been shown that penalties *latae sententiae* established by particular precepts do exist. They must be either *a iure* or *ab homine.* They are not *a iure* because the legislator has excluded them from his definition of this type of penalty;[30] therefore they must be *ab homine* and the legislator has included them in his definition of that type of penalty.[31]

The majority of canonists[32] admit the existence of the *latae*

[30] Canon 2217, § 1, 3°: ". . . in ipsa lege statuta. . . ."

[31] Canon 2217, § 1, 3°: ". . . si feratur per modum praecepti peculiaris. . . ."

[32] Cf. Coronata, *Institutiones Iuris Canonici,* IV, n. 1690; Sole, *Praelectiones in Liber V Codicis Iuris Canonici, De Delictis et Poenis* (Romae: Pustet, 1920), n. 70 (hereafter cited as *De Delictis et Poenis*); De Meester, *Iuris Canonici et Iuris Canonico-Civilis Compendium,* Vol. IV (Brugis: Desclée de Brouwer, 1928), n. 1708, 5° (hereafter cited as *Compendium*); Ayrinhac-Lydon, *Penal Legislation in the New Code of Canon Law,* n. 35; Berutti, *Institutiones Iuris Canonici,* VI, n. 20, p. 67, nota 1; Ferreres, *Institutiones Iuris Canonici* (2. ed., 2 vols., Barcinone: Subirana, 1920), II, n. 968; Sipos, *Enchiridion Iuris Canonici,* II, § 229, n. 2; Chelodi, *Ius Poenale,* n. 19, c; Cipollini, *De Censuris Latae Sententiae iuxta Codicem Iuris Canonici* (Taurini: Marietti, 1925), p. 7 (hereafter cited as *De Censuris*); Vermeersch-Creusen, *Epitome Iuris Canonici* (3. ed., 3 vols., Mechlinae-Romae: Dessain, 1927-1928), III, n. 406 (hereafter cited as *Epitome*); Salucci, *Il Diritto Penale secondo il Codice di Diritto Canonico,* I (Subiaco: Tipografia dei Monasteri, 1926), p. 198, nota 1 (hereafter cited as *Il Diritto Penale*); Falco, *Corso In Diritto Ecclesiastico* (Padova, 1930), p. 263.

sententiae ab homine vindicative penalty, which is the vindicative penalty *latae sententiae* attached to a particular precept. But Roberti [33] and Michiels [34] and later Vermeersch-Creusen [35] maintain that such a penalty is not *ab homine* but "tamquam a iure." They maintain the complete assimilation of laws and precepts and distinguish two types of precepts: a *praeceptum ad instar legis,* by which a penalty is established in the manner of a penal law, and a *praeceptum ad instar sententiae,* by which a penalty is inflicted in the manner of a condemnatory sentence. The conclusion is drawn that whenever the Code uses the term "praeceptum," it refers to the *praeceptum ad instar legis;* whenever it uses the term "per modum praecepti" it refers to the *praeceptum ad instar sententiae.* Therefore, when a penalty *latae sententiae* is established by a *praeceptum ad instar legis* ("per praeceptum" in the language of the Code) it is not *ab homine,* but *tamquam a iure.* When a penalty is inflicted by a *praeceptum ad instar sententiae* ("per modum praecepti" in the language of the Code, as in canon 2217, § 1, 3°) it is *ferendae sententiae* and *ab homine.* Too, just as a condemnatory sentence pertains to the moment of the infliction of the penalty, so the *praeceptum* mentioned in n. 3 of this canon pertains to the infliction of the penalty and, therefore, the term "feratur" of this canon refers only to a *ferendae sententiae* penalty inflicted by a particular precept *ad instar sententiae* because *latae sententiae* penalties are not "inflicted" but "incurred." The obvious conclusion is drawn: penalties *latae sententiae* attached to particular precepts cannot be *ab homine,* but are *tamquam a iure.*[36]

This opinion of Roberti and Michiels is criticized at length by

[33] "An censura latae sententiae per praeceptum constituta sit reservata," *Apollinaris,* VI (1933), pp. 341, 342.

[34] "De reservatione censurae latae sententiae praecepto peculiari adnexae," *Ephemerides Theologicae Lovanienses* (Brugis, 1924—), IV (1927), pp. 192-204 (hereafter this periodical will be cited as *ETL*).

[35] Cf. *Epitome,* III, n. 406.

[36] Cf. Roberti, "An censura latae sententiae per praeceptum constituta sit reservata," *Apollinaris,* VI (1933), p. 342.

Kinane[37] and by Moriarty.[38] Briefly, the objections raised to the opinion are these: the argument, drawn from canon 2195, § 2, concerning the assimilation of laws and precepts, is not valid, since that canon considers only delicts or the violations of laws and of precepts as similar and not the laws or precepts themselves. Likewise, the assertion that *latae sententiae* penalties are "incurred" but not "inflicted" is unwarranted, since the Code itself uses the term "inflict" in connection with such penalties.[39] Similarly, the assertion that the phrase "per modum praecepti" refers only to the *praeceptum ad instar sententiae* and concerns only penalties *ferendae sententiae* is purely gratuitous inasmuch as the phrase is used by the Code when it speaks of the infliction of penalties by precepts—whether these penalties are *latae* or *ferendae sententiae*.[40] Therefore, when the term "per modum praecepti" is used, it cannot be presumed to apply only to the infliction of a *ferendae sententiae* penalty by a *praeceptum ad instar sententiae,* but it refers likewise to the infliction of a *latae sententiae* penalty by the *praeceptum ad instar legis*—unless, of course, the context clearly indicates that the *ferendae sententiae* penalty alone is included.[41]

These objections against the opinion of Roberti, Michiels and others[42] are justified, but the conclusion which Moriarty draws, namely, "that the *latae sententiae* penalty inflicted by reason of a particular precept, both before and after it is incurred, must be considered as an *ab homine* penalty"[43] is not quite clear. In other words, if Moriarty wishes to state that a penalty *latae sententiae* attached to a law and "inflicted" by the superior upon the delinquent by means of a particular precept after he has incurred it, is

[37] "The Reservation of Censures 'Latae Sententiae' Imposed by a Particular Precept," *Irish Ecclesiastical Record,* XL (1932), pp. 528-534.

[38] *Extraordinary Absolution from Censures,* pp. 101-103.

[39] Cf. canon 2241, § 2; 2220, § 2; 2225.

[40] Cf. canons 1933, § 4; 2217, § 1, 3°; 2225; 2243, § 1.

[41] *E.g.,* canon 1933, 4. Cf. also Moriarty, *Extraordinary Absolution from Censures,* p. 103.

[42] Vermeersch-Creusen, *Epitome,* III, n. 406. Roberti cites Tabera, "Nocion de la pena 'ab homine,'" in *Illustracion del Clero,* 1931, pp. 195-198, 227-230, as holding this same opinion.

[43] *Extraordinary Absolution from Censures,* p. 103.

a penalty *ab homine*, his conclusion is untrue and unwarranted by any arguments on his part. Can such a penalty *latae sententiae* be said to be "inflicted" after it is incurred? The infliction of such a penalty is contained in the very law or precept in the form of a condition; if the law or precept is violated and the condition is thus verified, the infliction of the penalty immediately takes place, and the penalty is incurred. The infliction and incurrence occur at the same moment.[44] Therefore, if such a penalty were "inflicted" by means of a particular precept after it had been incurred, that "infliction" could mean only one thing, a declaration *ad modum praecepti* on the part of the superior. It would be an extrajudicial declaration of the penalty, corresponding to a declaratory judicial sentence, and would in no way change the species of penalty: if it were *a iure* before such a declaration or "infliction" it remains *a iure* after the infliction.[45]

As a result of this discussion, then, several conclusions may be drawn. A vindicative penalty *latae sententiae* may be attached to or established by a particular precept. Such a penalty is *ab homine*. When a *latae sententiae* vindicative penalty established by law or precept is declared or confirmed by a superior by means of a particular precept it is changed in no way whatsoever; if it was *a iure* it remains so after the declaration *ad modum praecepti* has been given.

B. *The Dispensation*

Vindicative penalties are removed by dispensation. Of course, these penalties cease in other ways; for example, the vindicative penalty ceases with the death of the delinquent. They also cease of themselves upon the expiration of the time for which they were inflicted.[46] Prescription, likewise, may cause vindicative penalties to cease.[47] But normally the vindicative penalties indefinite as to

[44] Berutti, *Institutiones Iuris Canonici*, VI, p. 65.

[45] Cf. Coronata, *Institutiones Iuris Canonici*, IV, n. 1690. Also canon 2225.

[46] Canon 2289.

[47] Cf. Wernz-Vidal, *Ius Canonicum*, VII, nn. 205, 206; Lega, *De Delictis et Poenis*, n. 187; Augustine, *A Commentary on the New Code of Canon Law*, VIII (3. ed., St. Louis, Mo.: Herder, 1931), p. 108 (hereafter cited as *A Commentary on the New Code*); Sipos, *Enchiridion Iuris Canonici*, § 232, n. 1;

time are removed by dispensation. And all may be removed this way.

The term "dispensation" in the science of Canon Law possesses a very limited significance. At present, in the Code of Canon Law, it is used only to signify an act of a lawful superior or his delegate, by which, for a reasonable cause, the obligation of a law is removed in a particular case.[48] As has been shown, this precise and clear concept was not always present. On the contrary, for centuries in the early Church the term signified any exception from the law;[49] and it was only in the course of time that the concept became clear and was distinguished from other institutes which resembled dispensation in one aspect or another. But from the very beginning the relaxation of vindicative penalties was considered a dispensation in the strict sense of the concept as it appears in the Code of Canon Law. This relaxation of vindicative penalties was termed a dispensation *ex post* or *in factis,* in counterdistinction to the dispensation *in faciendis.*[50] A dispensation *ex post* or *in factis* was the relaxation of a law, or of the effects of a law, resulting from a past act in a violation of that law; a dispensation *in faciendis* was the relaxation of a law which allowed an act contrary to the law to be placed *in futuro.*[51] When the concept of dispensation had developed and was clearly distinguished from other concepts, the dispensation from vindicative penalties was retained, although it was admittedly governed by special norms exclusive to itself.[52]

Eichmann, *Das Strafrecht des Codex Iuris Canonici* (Paderborn, 1920), § 13 (hereafter cited as *Strafrecht*); Vermeersch-Creusen, *Epitome,* III, nn. 428-432. Cf. also canons 2240, 1703.

[48] Canon 80.

[49] Cf. Brys, *De Dispensatione,* pp. 16, 44.

[50] Cf. Brys, *De Dispensatione,* pp. 16, 26, 106, 107, 121, 132; Van Hove, *Commentarium Lovaniense in C. I. C.,* Vol. I, nn. 329, 331; Innocent IV, *Apparatus,* ad c. 15, *Dilectus,* X, *de temporibus ordinationum et qualitate ordinandorum,* I, II.

[51] Cf. Suarez, *Tractatus de Legibus et Deo Legislatore,* lib. VI, c. 10, n. 9; c. 14, n. 7; Reiffenstuel, *Ius Canonicum Universale,* lib. I, tit. 2, n. 465; Brys, *De Dispensatione,* p. 106.

[52] Pyrrhus, *Praxis Dispensationum Apostolicarum,* lib. I, c. 3; Brys, *De Dispensatione,* p. 249.

It was only in fairly recent times that the relaxation of vindicative penalties was said to be not a dispensation in the strict or proper sense, but rather a dispensation or privilege in a wide, arbitrary sense. Among those who hold this opinion are Hinschius,[53] Eichmann,[54] Mörsdorf,[55] Köstler,[56] and Michiels.[57] The arguments are best given by Michiels. The relaxation or removal of vindicative penalties is not a dispensation because the obligation of the law is in no way relaxed, as is required in a dispensation in the proper sense according to canon 80.[58] The juridical effects of the delinquent's act alone are relaxed or removed, whereas in a dispensation in the proper sense the proper effects of a law are relaxed, the *vinculum legale* proper to a determinate law is broken.[59] Likewise, the removal of vindicative penalties is governed by the special norms of canons 2236, § 1, and 2289, norms which are distinct from those established for dispensations in canons 80-89.

Ojetti, as Van Hove notes,[60] seems to hold this same opinion. At least from the reason which Ojetti gives for excluding the relaxation or absolution of medicinal penalties from the concept of dispensation we may deduce that he would not consider the relaxation of a vindicative penalty as a dispensation. The difference, he says, between dispensations and absolutions (relaxations of censures) consists in the fact that by a dispensation one is exempt from the law itself, while by an absolution the effects of the law alone are relaxed. Therefore, he continues, absolutions concern the past, dispensations the future.[61] Thus he would of necessity seem to include the concept

[53] *Kirchenrecht,* III, pp. 789-792; 825-829.

[54] *Lehrbuch des Kirchenrechts auf Grund des Codex Iuris Canonici* (2. ed., Paderborn: Schoningh, 1926), I, 101 (hereafter cited as *Kirchenrecht*).

[55] *Die Rechtssprache des Codex Iuris Canonici* (Bonn, 1933), p. 388.

[56] *Wörterbuch zum Codex Iuris Canonici* (Munchen, Kosel: Pustet, 1929), p. 125: "Dispensatio."

[57] *Normae Generales Iuris Canonici, Commentarius Libri I Codicis Iuris Canonici* (2 vols., Lublin-Polonia: Universitas Catholica, 1929), II, 453 (hereafter cited as *Normae Generales*).

[58] Canon 80: "Dispensatio, seu legis in casu speciali relaxatio. . . ."

[59] Michiels, *Normae Generales,* II, p. 453, n. 2.

[60] *Commentarium Lovaniense in C. I. C.*, I, n. 331, nota 3.

[61] Ojetti, *Commentarium In Codicem Iuris Canonici* (3 vols., Romae, 1927), I, p. 325.

of relaxation of vindicative penalties in his concept of absolutions and it too would be merely a relaxation of the effect of the law and not of the law itself, and it too would rather concern itself with past acts, violations of the law already placed. In other words, the proponents of this opinion seem to be reviving the old distinction between dispensations *in factis* and *in faciendis,* and seem to admit that the latter alone is a real dispensation.[62]

The majority of canonists do not treat of this question, but simply point out the difference between the absolution from medicinal penalties and dispensation from vindicative penalties, but many of them in making that distinction seem to consider the remission of vindicative penalties as a dispensation in the strict sense.[63] Others [64] correctly and expressly assert that the remission of these penalties is a dispensation in the strict sense of that term. For the law itself is relaxed in a particular case, and to grant such a relaxation the power of dispensing from the law is required.[65] Whenever a dispensation from the penalty of a law is granted, the penal law is relaxed. A penal law, it must be noted, is one which obliges under penalty. It has, in reality, two parts: the stipulation of the law and

[62] Michiels, *Normae Generales,* II, p. 455, n. 4.

[63] *E. g.,* cf. Falco, *Introduzione allo studio del "Codex Iuris Canonici"* (Turin: Fratelli Bocca, 1925), p. 113; Vermeersch-Creusen, *Epitome,* III, n. 429; Coronata, *Institutiones Iuris Canonici,* I, n. 108; Chelodi, *Ius Poenale,* n. 29; Wernz-Vidal, *Ius Canonicum,* VII, n. 210; Beste, *Introductio in Codicem,* tit. VII, p. 898.

[64] Van Hove, *Commentarium Lovaniense in C. I. C.,* I, nn. 329, 331; Berutti, *Institutiones Iuris Canonici,* VI, n. 38, p. 102; Friedberg, *Lehrbuch des katholischen und evangelischen Kirchenrechts* (Leipzig, 1903), p. 274 (hereafter cited as *Lehrbuch*); Del Guidice, *Privilegio, Dispensa ed Epicheia nel Diritto Canonico* (Milano, 1929), pp. 34, 35; Hilling, *Die Allgemeinen Normen des Codex Iuris Canonici* (Friburgi, 1926), p. 83; Chelodi-Bertagnolli, *Ius de Personis iuxta Codicem Iuris Canonici* (Tridenti, 1922), n. 86, p. 154 (hereafter cited as Chelodi, *Ius de Personis*); Haring, *Grundzüge des katholischen Kirchenrechtes. Dritte nach den Codex Iuris Canonici* (Graz, 1924), I, p. 83; Blat, *Commentarium Textus Codicis Iuris Canonici* (Romae, 1921-1927); lib. V, *De Delictis et Poenis* (Romae: Collegio "Angelico," 1924), n. 56 (hereafter cited as *De Delictis et Poenis*).

[65] Cf. canon 2236, § 2: Qui potest a lege eximere, potest quoque poenam legi adnexam remittere. Cf. also Van Hove, *Commentarium Lovaniense in C. I. C.,* I, n. 331.

the penalty attached to that stipulation.[66] The obligation is the same in both parts and since the obligation is the same, only the ecclesiastical authority who has the power to dispense from the law itself can dispense from the vindicative penalty attached thereto.[67] Since the vindicative penalty is definitely a part of the penal law and the obligation of the subject of such a penal law to undergo the prescribed penalty is the same obligation that he has to obey the law itself,[68] it follows that the penal law is relaxed whether he be released from the duties entailed in the law or whether he be released from the penalty prescribed for the violation of those duties. In other words, it may be said that the penal law is relaxed *in part*.[69] The *vinculum poenale* of the law, created when the penalty is incurred or inflicted, is in reality broken. Before the penalty is dispensed, the *vinculum poenale* exists and the offender is bound by the penal law; after the dispensation, the *vinculum* is broken and the offender is loosed and freed from the penal obligation of the law.

It is true that this argument is valid as regards vindicative penalties established by the law itself or by general precepts, penalties *a iure*. But what of the vindicative penalties *ab homine*, those established by particular precepts or inflicted through a condemnatory judicial sentence, or through the extrajudicial particular precept? Unless the complete assimilation of laws and precepts is to be admitted,[70] it would seem that the remission of such penalties cannot possibly be termed the relaxation of law in the sense of canon 80. And yet the above mentioned canonists maintain that it is. The argument is based on the fact that the particular precept bearing the penalty and the condemnatory judicial sentence or precept by which the penalty is inflicted, bind those individuals to whom they are given by the very same obligation which laws as such

[66] Cf. Wernz-Vidal, *Ius Canonicum,* VII, n. 210; Beste, *Introductio in Codicem,* tit. VII, p. 898; Vermeersch-Creusen, *Epitome,* III, n. 430; Woywod, *A Practical Commentary,* II, n. 2076.

[67] Cf. canon 2236, § 2.

[68] Berutti, *Institutiones Iuris Canonici,* VI, n. 38; Woywod, *A Practical Commentary,* II, n. 2076.

[69] Berutti, *loc. cit.*

[70] Cf. arguments of Roberti and Michiels, from canon 2195, § 2: *supra,* p. 63.

impose on all.[71] And therefore a *vinculum legale* is broken when such penalties are dispensed.

The question as to whether the remission of vindicative penalties is a dispensation in the strict sense is, however, merely a theoretical one. For even if all such remissions were dispensations in that restricted sense, the norms established in canons 80-89 for such real dispensations would not be directly applicable to remissions from vindicative penalties, for the Code has established special norms [72] for such dispensations from penalties,[73] norms which are distinct from those in canons 80-89.[74] However, in reality the one power—that of dispensing from the vindicative penalty attached to a law—depends in a large degree on the other—that of dispensing from the law itself. He who has the power to dispense from the law itself can dispense from the penalty attached to the law.[75] Consequently, the general norms of dispensation established in canons 80-89 including extraordinary powers granted by such norms, apply, indirectly perhaps, to the dispensations from vindicative penalties.[76]

The dispensation from vindicative penalties is essentially an act of jurisdiction, an act of that public power, granted by God or bestowed by the Church, of ruling over baptized subjects with a view to securing their eternal salvation.[77] The infliction of coercive measures is an act of jurisdiction pertaining to the external forum, and therefore only those who enjoy jurisdiction in the external forum

[71] Berutti, *Institutiones Iuris Canonici,* VI, n. 38, I.

[72] Canons 2236-2239, 2289, 2290.

[73] Van Hove, *Commentarium Lovaniense in C. I. C.*, I, n. 331; Michiels, *Normae Generales,* II, p. 453.

[74] The similarity of canon 2236, § 1 to canon 80 should be noted, indicating the intention of the legislator to separate these norms.

[75] Canon 2236, § 2.

[76] This relationship between canons 80-89 and the dispensations from vindicative penalties will be discussed at length. Cf. *infra,* p. 112.

[77] Cf. Maroto, *Institutiones Iuris Canonici ad Normam Novi Codicis* (3. ed., Madrid, 1919), I, n. 573 (hereafter cited as *Institutiones*); Vermeersch-Creusen, *Epitome,* I, n. 233; Ayrinhac-Lydon, *Penal Legislation in the New Code of Canon Law,* n. 65; Ojetti, *Commentarium in Codicem Iuris Canonici,* I, p. 327; Wernz-Vidal, *Ius Canonicum,* II, n. 48; Coronata, *Institutiones Iuris Canonici,* IV, n. 1736; Cicognani, *Canon Law* (authorized English version by J. O'Hara and F. Brennan, 2. ed., Philadelphia: The Dolphin Press, 1935), p. 830.

are competent to inflict such measures.[78] Therefore just as a penalty thus inflicted establishes a true juridical tie,[79] the dispensation of these coercive measures is an act of jurisdiction presupposing jurisdiction over the penalty as well as over the matter at issue, proper *per se* to the legislator or reserved to him inasmuch as this power depends on that of inflicting penalties,[80] which latter power in turn depends on the power to legislate or make laws.[81] Only in this wide sense may the dispensation from vindicative penalties be said to be a legislative act.[82]

Although the norms established by the Code in canons 2236-2239 apply equally to the dispensation from vindicative penalties and absolution from censures, these two institutes are essentially different. Absolution is a judicial act performed in accordance with law, interpreted widely, an act of justice,[83] which must be performed in favor of the offender who repents and asks for it, just as the sacramental absolution from sins is due in strict justice under the same circumstances.[84] Once granted, it cannot be revoked.[85] Dispensation from vindicative penalties, however, is entirely an act of favor dependent upon the will of the superior, which may be granted or refused, or

[78] Cf. Cappello, *De Censuris* (3. ed., Taurinorum Augustae: Marietti, 1933), n. 10; Lega, *De Delictis et Poenis*, n. 103.

[79] Wernz-Vidal, *Ius Canonicum*, VII, n. 209; Augustine, *A Commentary on the New Code*, VIII, p. 107.

[80] Canon 2236.

[81] Canon 2220, 2221.

[82] Van Hove, *Commentarium Lovaniense in C. I. C.*, I, n. 323; Friedberg, *Lehrbuch*, pp. 247-277. Cf. also Del Giudice, *Privilegio, Dispensa ed Epicheia nel Diritto Canonico*, pp. 36-47, wherein he maintains contrary to the majority of canonists, that this power is essentially administrative. For the opinions of those who hold that the power is more or less intrinsically legislative in character, cf. Michiels, *Normae Generales*, II, p. 452; Hilling, *Die Allgemeinen Normen des Codex Iuris Canonici*, p. 83.

[83] Vermeersch-Creusen, *Epitome*, III, nn. 429, 491; Chelodi, *Ius Poenale*, n. 29; Wernz-Vidal, *Ius Canonicum*, VII, n. 208; Lega, *De Delictis et Poenis*, nn. 121-123; Woywod, *A Practical Commentary*, II, n. 2076; D'Annibale, *Summula*, I, n. 313, nota 4; Hollweck, *Die kirchlichen Strafgesetze*, § 30, p. 97, nota 1; 69, p. 141, nota 1.

[84] Wernz-Vidal, *Ius Canonicum*, VII, n. 208; Lega, *De Delictis et Poenis*, nn. 103-105.

[85] Sipos, *Enchiridion Iuris Canonici*, § 232, n. 1.

even revoked by the one who has granted the dispensation through ordinary power.[86] There may be times, however, when the superior would be bound by charity or justice, to grant the dispensation, if, for example, grave public or private necessity demanded it.[87] The dispensation, finally, is contrary to law and is liable to strict interpretation.[88]

ARTICLE II. THE PRINCIPLES

A. *Power Exercised in One's Own Right*

> **Canon 2236, § 1. Remissio poenae . . . per dispensationem, si de poenis vindicativis, concedi tantum potest ab eo qui poenam tulit, vel ab ejus competente Superiore aut successore. . . .**

Canon 2236, in paragraphs 1 and 2, establishes an all-inclusive designation of those who are empowered to dispense from vindicative penalties. It includes those who in their own right may grant the dispensation and those who may do so through derived dispensatory power. The designation of those who are empowered to dispense *in their own right* obtains its force not merely from the fact that it is determined by an act which is a dispensation from positive ecclesiastical law. It is, in reality, an expression of an underlying principle, based on the very nature of this dispensation from vindicative penalties. For the granting of the dispensation, as has been shown, implies an act of jurisdiction.[89] And this principle is sufficiently general in character to be applicable to any dispensation from any penalty, whether the penalty be imposed by the general law of the Church or by some particular law, by a general pre-

[86] De Meester, *Compendium*, III, n. 1725; Sipos, *loc. cit.*; Coronata, *Institutiones Iuris Canonici*, IV, n. 1736, nota 5; Beste, *Introductio in Codicem*, tit. VII, p. 897.

[87] Lega, *De Delictis et Poenis*, n. 122; Coronata, *Institutiones Iuris Canonici*, IV, n. 1736.

[88] Sipos, *loc. cit.*; Chelodi, *Ius Poenale*, nn. 29, 30; Lega, *De Delictis et Poenis*, n. 122.

[89] Cf. above, p. 70.

cept or by a particular precept, whether as a penalty *latae sententiae* or *ferendae sententiae.*

In the case of vindicative penalties established in a law, whether general or particular, the principle that he who establishes the penalty has the power to dispense from it is very clear. For it is evident that a legislator has power to relax his own law and the penalty constituted by that law, since the law, and therefore the penalty, derives its binding force only from the will of the legislator.[90] Just as the legislator might, at the time when he attaches the penalty to the law, exempt certain individual persons from the obligation of the penalty, so he has the power, at any other time, to decide that the obligation of the penalty should cease at any given time as far as the designated persons are concerned. This is but an application of the legal maxims which state that "A thing can be dissolved by the same causes which brought it into being," and "He who binds may release."[91] The will of the legislator is the cause which produces the penalty, just as it is his will which produces the law.[92]

It should be noted, however, that this dispensatory prerogative of the legislator is official rather than personal, since ordinary jurisdiction is always attached to an office[93] and the legislator participates in it only because he occupies that office. Any vindicative penalty which he might establish is constituted by him as an ecclesiastical *official,* and not as a man. Similarly, the dispensation from that penalty is an act of his *official* will, and as such an act of jurisdiction. And so, if for any cause he has ceased to occupy the office by reason of which he possessed jurisdictional powers, his right to dispense has simultaneously ceased.

In the case of *latae sententiae* vindicative penalties attached to a particular precept, the principle is the same. The ecclesiastical

[90] Suarez, *Tractatus de Legibus et Deo Legislatore,* VI, c. 14, n. 2; Berutti, *Institutiones Iuris Canonici,* VI, n. 38; Coronata, *Institutiones Iuris Canonici,* IV, n. 1736; Vermeersch-Creusen, *Epitome,* III, n. 411; Van Hove, *Commentarium Lovaniense in C. I. C.,* I, nn. 379-384.

[91] "Omnes res, per quascumque causas nascitur, per easdem dissolvitur"—C. I, X, *de regula iuris,* V, 41; "Ejus enim est solvere, cujus est ligare"—Chelodi, *Ius Poenale,* n. 29; Lega, *De Delictis et Poenis,* n. 129.

[92] Reilly, *The General Norms of Dispensation,* p. 51.

[93] Canon 197, § 1.

superior who establishes such a vindicative penalty by means of a particular precept has the power in his own right to dispense from the penalty. The precept to which the penalty is attached presupposes an act of jurisdiction on the part of the superior who gives the precept. For this precept is, as Noval states,[94] a command given by virtue of jurisdiction. Both canon 2195, § 2, and canon 2220, § 1, wherein the norms for the establishment of these penalties is stated, treat exclusively of precepts which are given by those superiors who have jurisdiction in the Church.[95] Superiors who have jurisdictional powers and who may give such precepts include, beside the Roman Pontiff, the Sacred Congregations, ecumenical councils, local ordinaries, cathedral chapters and vicars capitular, plenary and provincial councils, superiors, even local superiors, of exempt clerical religious communities and their chapters according to the norms of their constitutions.[96] Through a similar act of jurisdiction

[94] *Commentarium Codicis Iuris Canonici* (*De Processibus* [Taurini, 1920], pars III, p. 394): "Iussio Superioris vi jurisdictionis lata."

[95] Cf. Vermeersch-Creusen, *Epitome,* III, n. 383; Berutti, *Institutiones Iuris Canonici,* III, p. 74.

[96] Cf. Vermeersch-Creusen, *Epitome,* III, n. 411; Cavigioli, *De Censuris Latae Sententiae Quae in Codice Iuris Canonici Continentur Commentariolum* (Torino: Libreria Editrice Internazionale, 1918), nn. 6-15 (hereafter cited as *De Censuris*); Eichmann, *Lehrbuch,* n. 60; Ferreres, *Institutiones Iuris Canonici,* II, 974; Coronata, *Institutiones Iuris Canonici,* IV, n. 1693; Cappello, *De Censuris* (3. ed., 1933), nn. 4-7; Augustine, *A Commentary on the New Code,* VIII, pp. 84, 85, 110; Salucci, *Il Diritto Penale,* nn. 99-102; Chelodi, *Ius Poenale,* n. 24, nota 5; Berutti, *Institutiones Iuris Canonici,* IV, nn. 22, 23; Keene, *Religious Ordinaries and Canon 198,* The Catholic University of America Canon Law Studies, n. 135 (Washington, D. C.: The Catholic University of America Press, 1942), pp. 133, 134; Ayrinhac-Lydon, *Penal Legislation in the New Code of Canon Law,* n. 69; Cerato, *Censurae Vigentes Ipso Facto a Codice Iuris Canonici Excerptae* (2. ed., Patavii, 1921), p. 39 (hereafter cited as *Censurae Vigentes*); Cocchi, *Commentarium in Codicem Iuris Canonici ad Usum Scholarum* (2. ed., Taurinorum Augustae: Marietti, 1928), VIII, 86; Fanfani, *De Iure Religiosorum ad Normam Codicis Iuris Canonici* (2. ed., Taurinorum Augustae, 1925), pp. 72, 73 (hereafter cited as *De Iure Religiosorum*); Michiels, *Normae Generales,* II, n. 480; Roberti, *De Delictis et Poenis* (Romae, 1930), I, nn. 305, 306; *Schaefer, Compendium de Religiosis ad Normam Codicis Iuris Canonici* (3. ed., Roma, 1940), pp. 235-237 (hereafter cited as *De Religiosis*); Smith, *The Penal Law for Religious,* The Catholic University of America, Canon Law Studies, n. 98 (Washington: The Catholic University of

the superior may relax or remove the precept, or he may relax or remove the penalty which he has attached to that precept.[97] This vindicative penalty, it should be remembered, is *ab homine*, and is always reserved to the superior who has established the penalty (or his successor or his superior) and may be dispensed by another only if that power is given to him. This principle is a complete reversal of the principle established for similar *ab homine* censures *latae sententiae*, for such censures attached to particular precepts are not reserved unless the reservation is expressly stated in the precept.[98]

A *ferendae sententiae* vindicative penalty likewise may be established by a particular precept,[99] and is likewise a vindicative penalty *ab homine* and reserved to the superior who has given the particular precept to which the penalty is attached. He alone, or his successor and superior, or one whom he has commissioned, may dispense from this penalty. The principle herein stated is the same as that for

America, 1935), p. 130 ss.; Wernz-Vidal, *Ius Canonicum*, I, n. 471; VII, n. 222; Blat, *De Delictis et Poenis*, p. 85; Woywod, *A Practical Commentary*, II, p. 425.

[97] Berutti, *Institutiones Iuris Canonici*, VI, n. 38, II; Ayrinhac-Lydon, *Penal Legislation in the New Code of Canon Law*, n. 65; Lega, *De Delictis et Poenis*, n. 129.

[98] Moriarty, *Extraordinary Absolutions from Censures*, pp. 104, 105, wherein he discusses canon 2245 at length. Cf. also Coronata, *Institutiones Iuris Canonici*, IV, nn. 162, 163; Sole, *De Delictis et Poenis*, n. 173, 2; Salucci, *Il Diritto Penale*, I, nn. 198-200; Reintjes, *De Absolutione Censurae*, (Dissertatio ad obtinendum gradum Doctoratus in Facultate Iuris Canonici in Pontificio Collegio "Angelico" de Urbe Elaborata, 1925), pp. 13, 14; Collison, *Non Omnis Censura Ab Homine Est Reservata* (Dissertatio ad Gradum Doctoris in Facultate Iuris Canonici Consequendum Scripta apud Pontificium Institutum Angelicum, Romae, 1935), pp. 78-79.

[99] Cf. Cappello, "De Absolutione a Censuris 'ab Homine,'" *Nouvelle Revue Théologique* (Tournai, 1869—), XLVII (1920), pp. 525-527; *De Censuris* (1. ed., 1919), nn. 2, 3; *De Censuris* (2. ed., 1925; 3 ed., 1933), nn. 4, 3°, holds the opinion that a superior, in imposing a particular precept, is restricted to *ferendae sententiae* penalties. Cf. *supra*, p. 59; also Moriarty, *Extraordinary Absolutions from Censures*, pp. 94, 95; Coronata, *Institutiones Iuris Canonici*, IV, n. 1690; Vermeersch-Creusen, *Epitome*, III, n. 406; Cipollini, *De Censuris*, p. 7; Sole, *De Delictis et Poenis*, n. 70; Salucci, *Il Diritto Penale*, I, n. 198; DeMeester, *Compendium*, III, nn. 1708, 1735; Ayrinhac-Lydon, *Penal Legislation in the New Code of Canon Law*, n. 35.

similar *ab homine* censures established as *ferendae sententiae* by a particular precept, which censures are always reserved to the superior who attached the censure to the particular precept.[100]

When a *ferendae sententiae* vindicative penalty is inflicted by means of a condemnatory judicial sentence or by means of a particular precept, it becomes a penalty *ab homine.*[101] And in the case of such vindicative penalties an important problem presents itself in regard to the reservation of such penalties. All vindicative penalties are *per se* reserved according to the general norms established in canons 2289 [102] and 2236, § 1. But in reference to *ferendae sententiae* vindicative penalties, the question arises: to whom is the dispensation from such penalties reserved? Is it reserved to the legislator who in the law decrees that for the commission of a certain delict a vindicative penalty must be inflicted, whether through a judicial trial or through an extrajudicial precept, or is it reserved to the jurisdictional superior who, though he is inferior in jurisdiction to the legislator, actually inflicts the penalty by passing the condemnatory sentence upon the offender or by decreeing the particular precept? Or, when such a vindicative penalty is inflicted and becomes thereby a penalty *ab homine,* is it reserved precisely as an *ab homine* penalty to the superior who inflicts it or who passes the judicial sentence, just as similar *ab homine* censures are reserved, in canon 2245, § 2? [103] It is obvious that the matter of reservation of these penalties is of the highest importance in the consideration of the dispensation from vindicative penalties, and in this work the question of the reservation of the *ab homine* vindicative penalty has a very practical bearing in many questions to be treated, first, in regard to the dispensatory competence of ordinaries in regard to these penalties; secondly, in reference to the recourse to be made after the suspension of the penalty by the confessor in the more

[100] Canon 2245, § 2; Moriarty, *Extraordinary Absolution from Censures,* pp. 93, 97, 98, 107.

[101] Canon 2217, § 1, 3°.

[102] Poena vindicativa finitur ejus expiatione vel dispensatione ab eo concessa qui legitimam habeat dispensandi potestatem ad normam can. 2236.

[103] Canon 2245, § 2: Censura ab homine est reservata ei qui censuram inflixit aut sententiam tulit, ejusve Superiori competenti, vel successori aut delegato. . . .

urgent cases in canon 2290. Consequently, it calls for more than a mere cursory treatment.

As in any question of this type, there are proponents and opponents, those who hold that the legislator alone may dispense, and those who are of the opinion that only the superior who actually inflicts the penalty *per se* has the power to dispense from it.[104] The two opinions shall be presented at length, with the arguments proposed. It should be noted, however, that very few canonists treat of this question expressly, and the majority of them use such ambiguous terms that it is often very difficult to discover just what is meant.[105]

1. Whenever *ferendae sententiae* vindicative penalties established in the common law are inflicted by means of a condemnatory judicial sentence or by means of a particular precept, they may not be relaxed by the ecclesiastical superior who passes the sentence or gives the particular precept by which the penalties are imposed, even though that superior has full jurisdiction over the guilty party; but the dispensation is reserved absolutely to the legislator of the common law who has established the penalty, namely, the Roman Pontiff. This right of the legislator thereafter becomes an exclusive right, which no one but the legislator, his successor or one whom he has commissioned may use. This principle, again, is a complete reversal of the principle established for similar *ferendae sententiae* censures. Both the vindicative penalties and the censures thus inflicted are *ab homine* penalties; [106] but *ab homine* censures *ferendae sententiae* are reserved to the one who inflicted them by particular precept or who passed the condemnatory sentence, to his competent superior, his successor or delegate,[107] and not to the legislator of the general

[104] *Per se,* because this power may be exercised by a superior or successor and may be delegated or conceded to others.

[105] *E. g.,* Chelodi, *Ius Poenale,* n. 29; and especially n. 30 as compared with n. 50; Vermeersch-Creusen, *Epitome,* III, n. 430, 3, as compared with n. 491, 2; De Meester, *Compendium,* III, nn. 1726-1727 as compared with n. 1799, 4; Coronata, *Institutiones Iuris Canonici,* IV, n. 1693 as compared with n. 1736; Wernz-Vidal, *Ius Canonicum,* VII, n. 210 as compared with n. 211.

[106] Canon 2217, § 1, 3°.

[107] Canon 2245, § 2.

law which constituted the censure.[108] Lega [109] gives an excellent explanation for this difference between the remission of *ferendae sententiae* censures and the dispensation from *ferendae sententiae* vindicative penalties. In the first place, a vindicative penalty *per se* does not demand its relaxation; it is a penalty in the strict sense, given as a *quid pro quo:* the social order has been violated and the debt to society must be paid. Its relaxation, or dispensation, may not be demanded; it is an act of favor, not of justice.[110] Consequently, the one who is under such a penalty cannot demand a remission or relaxation of the punishment, and therefore does not suffer any inconvenience in being bound to seek such a dispensation of his penalty from the ecclesiastical authority who established it, namely, the Pope.[111] However, one who is under a censure may demand, in strict justice, a remission of his penalty as soon as he is repentant and his contumacy has ceased.[112] Moreover, when an ordinary, or a judge of his court [113] inflicts a *ferendae sententiae* vindicative penalty established in the general law of the Church, he merely *applies* the penalty; he in no way creates the *vinculum poenale.* He acts only as a judge, in deciding whether the accused

[108] Cappello, *De Censuris* (3. ed., 1933), n. 31; Ayrinhac-Lydon, *Penal Legislation in the New Code of Canon Law,* n. 84; Vermeersch-Creusen, *Epitome,* III, n. 441, 442; Sole, *De Delictis et Poenis,* nn. 190-191; Salucci, *Il Diritto Penale,* I, p. 223; Collison, *Non Omnis Censura Ab Homine Est Reservata,* pp. 71, 72; Reintjes, *De Absolutione Censurae,* p. 25; Coronata, *Institutiones Iuris Canonici,* IV, n. 1750; Cavigioli, *De Censuris,* n. 80; Berutti, *Institutiones Iuris Canonici,* VI, n. 48; Blat, *De Delictis et Poenis,* n. 69; De Meester, *Compendium,* III, n. 1736; Farrugia, *De Casuum Conscientiae Reservatione* (2. ed., Augustae Taurinorum, 1922), n. 121; Lega, *De Delictis et Poenis,* n. 130.

[109] *De Delictis et Poenis,* nn. 129, 130.

[110] Chelodi, *Ius Poenale,* n. 29; Lega, *De Delictis et Poenis,* nn. 121-123; Woywod, *A Practical Commentary,* II, n. 2076; D'Annibale, *Summula,* I, n. 313, nota 4; Hollweck, *Die kirchlichen Strafgesetze,* 30, p. 97, nota 1; 69, p. 141, nota 1; Vermeersch-Creusen, *Epitome,* III, nn. 429, 491; Wernz-Vidal, *Ius Canonicum,* VII, n. 208; Sipos, *Enchiridion Iuris Canonici,* § 232, n. 1; Coronata, *Institutiones Iuris Canonici,* IV, n. 1736, nota 5.

[111] Lega, *De Delictis et Poenis,* n. 129.

[112] Lega, *De Delictis et Poenis,* n. 130.

[113] Canons 1572, § 1; 1573, § 2.

is guilty of the delict; and if the accused is found guilty, he applies the vindicative penalty established by law for the commission of the delict. However, when the same judge or ordinary inflicts a censure *ferendae sententiae a iure,* he does more than apply the penalty; he inflicts it. His judgment, or *cognito judicialis,* must begin with the necessary admonitions that the accused recede from his contumacy[114] in the sense of canon 2242, § 3;[115] and only if the accused ignores these admonitions can the judge consider him as persistent in his contumacy.[116] The judge then inflicts the censure. And precisely because the infliction of the censure of necessity presupposes contumacy and contempt for the authority of the judge who condemned the crime, the offender is not considered worthy of absolution unless he obtains it from the judge whom he has offended by his contumacy and whose authority was violated by his contempt. The judge, in this instance, in reality establishes, or rather confirms or reestablishes a *vinculum poenale,* which he alone, or his successor, superior, or delegate may remove. The repentence of the offender and his consequent recession from his former contumacy is satisfaction to the judge to whose authority the offender was contumacious or obstinate or disobedient.[117]

[114] Canon 2233, § 2: Licet id legitime constet, si agatur de infligenda censura, reus reprehendatur ac moneatur ut a contumacia recedat ad normam 2242, § 3, dato, si prudenti ejusdem iudicis vel Superioris arbitrio casus id ferat, congruo ad resipiscentiam tempore; contumacia persistente, censura infligi potest.

[115] Canon 2242, § 3: Contumaciam desiise dicendum est, cum reum vere delicti commissi poenituerit et simul ipse congruam satisfactionem pro damnis et scandalo dederit aut saltem serio promiserit; judicare autem utrum poenitentia vera sit, satisfactio congrua aut eiusdem promissio seria, necne, illius est, a quo censurae absolutio petitur.

[116] Canon 2242, § 2: Si agatur de censuris ferendae sententiae, contumax est qui, non obstantibus monitionibus de quibus in can. 2233, § 2, a delicto non desistit vel patrati delicti poenitentiam cum debita damnorum et scandali reparatione agere detrectat. . . .

[117] Lega (*De Delictis et Poenis,* n. 130, nn. 1-3): "Quamobrem, hac maxima de causa, absolutio petenda est a iudice irrogante censuram quia censurae illatio subaudit necessario contumaciam, seu spretum in auctoritatem iudicis qui illud crimen damnavit; et censuratus non habetur absolutione dignus nisi istam petat ab eo in quem contumacia deliquit eique satisfaciat."

This opinion is held by Lega[118] and Findlay.[119] De Meester[120] seems to hold this same opinion, as also does Cance;[121] but the terms they use are not quite clear and they give no arguments.[122]

2. The second and seemingly the more correct opinion states that whenever *ferendae sententiae* vindicative penalties are inflicted by means of a particular precept or by a condemnatory judicial sentence, they may be relaxed by the ecclesiastical superior who passes the sentence or gives the precept. The vast majority of canonists[123] seem to hold this opinion, although, as has been suggested, some of them are not quite clear or consistent in adhering to the principle established by this opinion. Many of them are content with quoting canon 2236 without treating of *ferendae sententiae* vindicative penalties, and most of them treat canon 2236 as apparently pertaining only to censures and not to vindicative penalties. Those who treat of *ferendae sententiae* vindicative penalties expressly simply state the principle without adducing arguments.[124]

[118] *De Delictis et Poenis,* nn. 129, 130.

[119] *Canonical Norms Governing the Deposition and Degradation of Clerics,* pp. 200, 201.

[120] *Compendium,* III, nn. 1726, 1799.

[121] *Le Code de Droit Canonique* (2. ed., 4 vols., Paris: Libraire Lecoffre, Gabalda, 1929), III, n. 212.

[122] These obscure expressions of De Meester and Cance will be seen shortly, in the critical consideration of this opinion. Cf. *infra,* this Chapter, p. 82.

[123] Cf. Augustine, *A Commentary on the New Code,* VIII, pp. 239, 240; Ayrinhac-Lydon, *Penal Legislation in the New Code of Canon Law,* nn. 65, 70; Woywod, *A Practical Commentary,* II, nn. 2076, 2077; Wernz-Vidal, *Ius Canonicum,* VII, nn. 211, 329, 258, 367; Berutti, *Institutiones Iuris Canonici,* VI, n. 38, II; Coronata, *Institutiones Iuris Canonici,* IV, nn. 1736, 1737; Blat, *De Delictis et Poenis,* nn. 58, 59; Vermeersch-Creusen, *Epitome,* III, nn. 430, 491; Chelodi, *Ius Poenale,* nn. 29, 47; Ferreres, *Institutiones Iuris Canonici,* II, nn. 989, 990; Sipos, *Enchiridion Iuris Canonici,* § 232, n. 2; Salucci, *Il Diritto Penale,* I, p. 164, n. 3; p. 300, n. 2; Sole, *De Delictis et Poenis,* n. 147; Eichmann, *Strafrecht,* pp. 70-73; Haring, *Grundzüge des katholischen Kirchenrechtes. Dritte nach den Codex Iuris Canonici,* p. 932.

[124] *E. g.,* Ayrinhac-Lydon, *Penal Legislation in the New Code of Canon Law,* n. 70; Woywod, *A Practical Commentary,* n. 2077; Salucci, *Il Diritto Penale,* I, pp. 164, 300; Wernz-Vidal, *Ius Canonicum,* VII, nn. 211, 329; Berutti, *Institutiones Iuris Canonici,* VI, n. 38.

The entire problem centers around the interpretation of the single word "tulit" in canon 2236, § 1. This canon states: "Remissio poenae . . . per dispensationem, si de poenis vindicativis, concedi tantum potest ab eo qui poenam tulit, vel ab eius competente Superiore aut successore, vel ab eo cui haec potestas commissa est." The problem is further complicated by the fact that this canon treats of the remission of penalties in general, including both vindicative and medicinal penalties, and since these penalties differ in so many respects and especially in reference to the competence of superiors and others to remit them, the application of the single principle enunciated in canon 2236, § 1 becomes very difficult. Further, special norms are established for the remission or absolution of censures, norms which are exceptions to canon 2236, § 1,[125] whereas the remission, or dispensation of vindicative penalties is ruled solely by the general principle of canon 2236, § 1,[126] which principle is stated, of necessity, in very general terms which permit wide interpretations. The phrase "poenam tulit" is one of these.

The word "tulit" is translated variously as "establish"[127] or "inflict"[128] or as "establish or inflict."[129] As may be noted, as this term is interpreted, so the two opinions are naturally formed. For if the term is to be understood in the sense of "establish," then canon 2236, § 1 restricts the power of dispensation of all vindicative

[125] *E. g.*, canon 2245, § 1 and § 4.

[126] Canon 2289.

[127] De Meester, *Compendium*, III, n. 1726; Findlay, *Canonical Norms Governing the Deposition and Degradation of Clerics*, p. 201; Gange, *Le Code de Droit Canonique*, III, n. 212, 2. Coronata (*Institutiones Iuris Canonici*, IV, n. 1693) establishes the principle that "poenam ferre" as a term of the Code is to be translated "to establish a penalty" ("Poenas . . . ferre . . . significat legem poenalem aut poenale praeceptum ferre. . . .") and in n. 1736 interprets the phrase as the infliction of a penalty (". . . poenam tulit . . . valet . . . modo absoluto . . . pro poenis inflictis sententia condemnatoria. . . .").

[128] Woywod, *A Practical Commentary*, II, n. 2076; Sipos, *Enchiridion Iuris Canonici*, §232, n. 2; Salucci, *Il Diritto Penale*, I, p. 164, 3; 300, 2; Coronata, *Institutiones Iuris Canonici*, IV, n. 1736.

[129] Cf. Chelodi, *Ius Poenale*, n. 24; nota 1; Blat, *De Delictis et Poenis*, n. 58; Berutti, *Institutiones Iuris Canonici*, VI, n. 38, II; Augustine, *A Commentary on the New Code*, VIII, p. 107, § 1.

penalties to the one who established them by law or precept; [180] and therefore if a *ferendae sententiae* vindicative penalty is established by the common law, the legislator, namely the Roman Pontiff, alone has the power to dispense from it and other superiors who may inflict the penalty by means of a condemnatory sentence or particular precept have no power whatsoever over its remission or relaxation.[181] However, if the term is interpreted in the sense of "inflict" or "establish or inflict," then the reservation of vindicative penalties is vastly different:

1. *Latae sententiae* vindicative penalties established and determined by law *(a iure)* are reserved to the legislator who established them in the law, whether general or particular.[182]

2. Likewise, vindicative penalties *latae sententiae* attached to a particular precept *(latae sententiae ab homine)* are reserved to the superior who established the particular precept.

3. *Ferendae sententiae* vindicative penalties established by particular precept or by general or particular law but inflicted by particular precept or condemnatory sentence *(ferendae sententiae ab homine)* are reserved to the jurisdictional superior who inflicted them, namely, the superior who passed the sentence or issued the precept.

This latter interpretation of the word "tulit"—in the sense of "inflict" or "inflict or establish"—is the correct one. This conclusion is based not only on the consideration of the term in itself but even more so on the cumulative arguments which will be adduced. The word "ferre" is used in the Code in the sense of "inflict" [183] but

[180] De Meester (*Compendium,* III, n. 1726): "ab eo qui poenam tulit lege vel praecepto"; Cance (*Le Code de Droit Canonique,* III, n. 212, 2): "La remise des peines peut etre accordee seulement . . . par l'auteur de la loi ou du precepte. . . ."

[181] Findlay, *General Norms Governing the Deposition and Degradation of Clerics,* p. 201.

[182] All canonists admit this principle. It may be helpful to emphasize what should be clear from this treatment in these and the following pages, namely, that the problem considered here is concerned only with the vindicative penalties *ferendae sententiae a iure* inflicted by a condemnatory sentence or particular precept.

[183] Canon 2242, § 1.

more often in the sense of "establish or inflict." [134] This of itself would prove nothing; but the use of the term "tulit" in canon 2236, § 1 proves that it cannot be interpreted in the singular exclusive sense of "establish." For if this were so, the general rule of canon 2236, § 1 would in no way apply to censures. It would not apply to *latae sententiae* censures, whether established in law or precept, because such censures are not *per se* reserved to the legislator who established the law or the superior who gave the precept. On the contrary, they are never reserved unless the reservation is *expressly* stated in the law or precept.[135] Neither would it apply to *ferendae sententiae* censures because such penalties are reserved, not to the legislator or superior who established the censure, but to the superior who inflicts it or passes the condemnatory sentence.[136] Therefore the very principle which is established for the remission of censures: "Remissio poenae . . . per absolutionem, si agatur de censuris . . . concedi tantum potest ab eo qui poenam tulit . . ." is not applicable to censures.

It might be argued that the interpretation of "tulit" in the sense of infliction of the penalty [137] likewise restricts the application of canon 2236, § 1 to *ferendae sententiae* penalties exclusively, since these penalties alone are "inflicted" and *latae sententiae* penalties are not "inflicted" but "incurred" or "established." [138] But *latae sententiae* penalties may be said to be "inflicted"; the Code itself

[134] Canons 13, § 1; 2217, § 1, 3°; 2247, § 1. Cf. Köstler, *Wörterbuch zum Codex Iuris Canonici*, p. 160: "ferre"; Chelodi, *Ius Poenale*, n. 24, nota 1; Blat, *De Delictis et Poenis*, n. 58.

[135] Canon 2245, § 4: Censura latae sententiae non est reservata, nisi in lege vel praecepto id expresse dicatur; et in dubio sive iuris sive facti reservatio non urget." Cf. also Moriarty, *Extraordinary Absolution from Censures*, pp. 104, 105.

[136] Canon 2245, § 2: "Censura *ab homine* est reservata ei qui censuram inflixit aut sententiam tulit, eiusve Superiori competenti, vel successori aut delegato. . . ."

[137] Sipos, *Enchiridion Iuris Canonici*, § 232, n. 2; Woywod, *A Practical Commentary*, II, n. 2076; Salucci, *Il Diritto Penale*, I, p. 164, 3; p. 300, 2; Coronata, *Institutiones Iuris Canonici*, IV, n. 1736.

[138] Michiels, *"De reservatione censurae latae sententiae praecepto peculiari adnexae," ETL*, IV (1927), pp. 190-194; Roberti, "An censura latae sententiae per praeceptum constituta sit reservata," *Apollinaris*, VI (1933), pp. 341, 342.

uses the term "inflict" in connection with *latae sententiae* penalties.[139] *Latae sententiae* penalties are, in reality, inflicted in the very act of the establishment of the penalties.[140] The best translation, however, of the term "ferre" is "to establish or inflict." [141]

From the foregoing consideration, it seems unquestionably evident that the term "tulit" involves not only the notion of the establishment of the vindicative penalty by the legislator or jurisdictional superior, but also the infliction of the penalty through a judicial sentence or a particular precept.

Moreover, the argument of Lega that *ferendae sententiae* censures *a iure* are really inflicted and a *vinculum poenale* is definitely created by the superior who inflicts them whereas vindicative penalties *ferendae sententiae a iure* are merely applied by the jurisdictional superior who in turn in no way creates or establishes a *vinculum poenale* is woefully weak. What he says about the infliction of *ferendae sententiae* censures is true and his arguments to prove his contention are sound. But to state that in inflicting a vindicative penalty *ferendae sententiae a iure* the superior acts only as a judge is not true. He acts not as a mere judge, but as a jurisdictional superior who has full jurisdiction over the accused.[142] It is true that the judge who is chosen by the superior to hear the case merely applies the penalty *ex officio*. But such a judge possesses no power of jurisdiction over the accused in *foro externo*, that is, outside the exercise of his office of judging.[143] The superior, however, who constitutes the judge must have full jurisdictional power over the accused offender who is being tried. Similarly, the superior who inflicts a vindicative penalty *ferendae sententiae* by means of a particular precept must have jurisdiction over the person to be punished.[144]

In the case of *ferendae sententiae a iure* vindicative penalties,

139 Canon 2225: ". . . si poena latae vel ferendae sententiae inflicta sit ad modum praecepti particularis. . . ."

140 Cf. *supra*, p. 57; Moriarty, *Extraordinary Absolution from Censures*, p. 102.

141 Cf. *supra*, p. 61.

142 Berutti, *Institutiones Iuris Canonici*, VI, n. 38, VI.

143 Berutti, *Institutiones, loc. cit.*

144 Canons 2217, § 1, 2°; 2220, § 1.

the law determines the penalty *to be inflicted.* The *vinculum poenale* is not created when the penalty is determined in the law; otherwise one who would violate the law would immediately be liable to that *vinculum.* But in *ferendae sententiae* penalties such is not the case. The *vinculum poenale* is not created until the penalty is actually inflicted,[145] and the offender is not bound by the penalty until it is inflicted by a superior who has jurisdiction over the offender. The superior establishes the bond upon one of his subjects; of him it may be said, "fert poenam." [146]

Finally, the conclusion may be reached that whenever *ferendae sententiae* vindicative penalties are inflicted by means of a condemnatory judicial sentence or by means of a particular precept, they may be dispensed only by the ecclesiastical superior who passes the sentence or gives the precept or his superior, successor, or delegate. The penalties are *ab homine* and are reserved, not precisely because they are *ab homine* but rather because they are vindicative penalties.[147]

Canon 2236, § 1 also states that a successor or superior to one who establishes or inflicts a vindicative penalty may likewise dispense, in his own right, from the penalty. A successor can dispense penalties constituted by his predecessor because officially he is identical with his predecessor. *Ex officio* he has exactly the same jurisdiction, since he occupies the same office and enjoys all the powers of that office. This is merely another application of a Rule of Law: "He who succeeds to the right of another must make use of the same right." [148]

One who is superior in jurisdiction to another who establishes or inflicts a vindicative penalty can relax that penalty at will, because the jurisdiction of the inferior depends upon the jurisdiction of the

[145] Wernz-Vidal, *Ius Canonicum,* VII, nn. 209, 211; Berutti, *Institutiones,* VI, n. 38; Salucci, *Il Diritto Penale,* I, p. 164, n. 3.

[146] Canon 2236, §; Wernz-Vidal, *Ius Canonicum,* VII, nn. 209, 211.

[147] Canon 2236, § 1.

[148] Reg. 46, *R.J.*: in VI°: "Is qui in ius succedit alterius, eo iure, quo ille, uti debebit"; cf. Beste, *Introductio In Codicem,* tit. VII, p. 897; Blat, *De Delictis et Poenis,* n. 58.

superior.[149] To deny this right to a superior would be tantamount to affirming that an inferior has the right to limit and impede the jurisdiction of the superior.[150]

I. The Roman Pontiff

Inasmuch as the jurisdiction of the Sovereign Pontiff is supreme and coextensive with the Church, it reaches every member of the Church immediately and touches every law or jurisdictionary precept of the Church. Consequently, his dispensatory power includes within its scope all vindicative penalties established or inflicted throughout the entire Church, whether these penalties have been attached to laws enacted by himself, by one of his predecessors, by the Apostles, by an ecumenical council, or by a legislator who exercises jurisdiction over some particular territory or particular society, or whether these penalties have been constituted by particular precepts by any jurisdictional superior in the Church, or, finally, whether the vindicative penalties have been inflicted by means of a condemnatory judicial sentence or a particular precept. In other words, all vindicative penalties are subject to his dispensatory power, penalties *a iure* or *ab homine, latae sententiae* or *ferendae sententiae,* established or inflicted by any and all ecclesiastical superiors. In all these cases the Roman Pontiff is either equal or superior, jurisdictionally, to the legislator or superior.[151] As legislator, he may dispense from any vindicative penalty established or inflicted by himself; as successor, he may relax any penalty established or inflicted by his predecessor; as superior, he may remit any penalty constituted or inflicted by all other inferior prelates. Common law and particular law are subject to him.

This universal papal dispensatory power is not created by the

[149] Cf. Suarez, *Tractatus de Legibus et Deo Legislatore,* VI, c. 14, n. 2; Lega, *De Delictis et Poenis,* n. 129.

[150] Cf. Coronata, *Institutiones Iuris Canonici,* IV, n. 1736; Ballerini-Palmieri, *Opus Theologicum Morale* (7 vols., Prati: Giachetti, 1889-1893), VII, n. 134; Wernz-Vidal, *Ius Canonicum,* VII, n. 209; Wernz, *Ius Decretalium,* VI, .n 88, nota 67; 175, nota 150; Lega, *De Delictis et Poenis,* n. 129; Augustine, *A Commentary,* VIII, p. 107.

[151] Cf. Suarez, *Tractatus de Legibus et Deo Legislatore,* VI, c. 14, n. 2.

mere positive law of the Code as expressed in canon 2236, § 1. It is rather a facet of the doctrine of the plenitude of jurisdiction enjoyed by the Pope, who, in the words of the Vatican Council,[152] "has . . . supreme and full power of jurisdiction in the universal Church . . . over those things which pertain to the discipline and government of the Church throughout the entire world." Accordingly, all vindicative penalties are subject to this universal dispensatory power, so that the Pope can dispense from any of them at any time.

The power to relax, in his own right, a *latae sententiae* vindicative penalty established by the common or general law of the Code resides in the Roman Pontiff alone, as an exclusive power. Both reason and the positive deposition of law expressed in canon 2236, § 1 confirm the absolute exclusiveness of this prerogative of the Pope. For the same power is necessary to loose as was required to bind; [153] and this power is entirely lacking in any authority below that of the Roman Pontiff when there is a question of vindicative penalties of the common or general law of the Church. And canon 2236, § 1 makes the positive statement that the Pope alone, as the legislator who established the *latae sententiae* vindicative penalties in the general law, has the power to dispense from them. It follows, therefore, that as far as these penalties are concerned, ordinaries other than the Roman Pontiff enjoy only participated or derived power.

This is not the case in regard to censures, as has been shown. For *latae sententiae* censures of the common law are exceptions to the norm set down in canon 2236, § 1. They are not *per se* reserved to the legislator, the Roman Pontiff, who constituted the censures in the law, but are reserved to him only if it is expressly stated in the law that the censures are reserved *simpliciter, speciali modo*, or *specialissimo modo* to the Apostolic Sea.[154]

[152] Sess. IV, cap. 3, De primatu Romani Pontificis—Denzinger-Bannwart, *Enchiridion Symbolorum, Definitionum et Declarationum de Rebus Fidei et Morum* (16. et 17. ed., Friburgi Brisgoviae: Herder, 1928), n. 1831.

[153] Chelodi, *Ius Poenale*, n. 29; Const. Benedict XIV, Bulla, "Magnae," 29 iunii, 1748.

[154] Canon 2245, § 1, 2. Cf. Coronata, *Institutiones Iuris Canonici*, IV, n.

An ecumenical council enjoys the same right as the Roman Pontiff with reference to vindicative penalties which it may attach to laws enacted by itself [155] or by a former council, but in practice a council never grants a dispensation.[156]

Mention should be made here of other vindicative penalties reserved to the Roman Pontiff through the major causes *per accidens*.[157] Any vindictive penalties that might be inflicted according to the rule of canon 2227, § 1 may be dispensed only by the Roman Pontiff. For he alone, by the positive withdrawal of certain matters from the scope of the bishop's jurisdiction and exemptions of certain persons from the direct control of the ordinary, as established in canons 2227, § 1, and 1557, § 1, has the power to dispense from any vindicative penalties that might be inflicted upon those who hold the highest governmental rank in a nation, their sons and daughters, and those who have the immediate right of succession. Among these would be included the king or queen of a nation and his or her consort, as well as the president of a republic; in short, the person who is considered the ruler in any particular nation.[158]

1736; Wernz-Vidal, *Ius Canonicum,* VII, n. 90; Ayrinhac-Lydon, *Penal Legislation in the New Code of Canon Law,* n. 65.

[155] Canon 2220, § 1; canon 228, § 1; Vermeersch-Creusen, *Epitome,* III, n. 411; Pesch, *Praelectiones Dogmaticae* (Romae, 1909), I, n. 459; Wernz-Vidal, *Ius Canonicum,* II, n. 461; Bouix, *Tractatus de Papa* (Parisiis, 1869-1870), II, pp. 415, 687; Palmieri, *De Romano Pontifice,* p. 691; Eichmann, *Kirchenrecht,* p. 146.

[156] Cf. Reilly, *The General Norms of Dispensation,* p. 54.

[157] Cf. Cavagnis, *Institutiones Iuris Publici Ecclesiastici* (2. ed., 2 vols., Romae, 1888), II, 438, 439; Coronata, *Institutiones Iuris Canonici,* I, n. 309; Eichmann, *Kirchenrecht,* p. 145; Chelodi, *Ius de Personis,* n. 152; Toso, *Ad Codicem Iuris Canonici Commentaria Minora* (5 vols., Romae: Marietti, 1920-1934), lib. II, tom. II, p. 14 (hereafter cited as *Commentaria Minora*); Ryan, *Principles of Episcopal Jurisdiction,* The Catholic University of America, Canon Law Studies, n. 120 (Washington: The Catholic University of America Press, 1939), pp. 66, 91; Billot, *Tractatus de Ecclesia Christi* (5. ed., Romae: Apud Aedes Universitatis Gregorianae, 1927), I, 713.

[158] Coronata, *Institutiones Iuris Canonici,* IV, n. 1713; Ayrinhac-Lydon, *Penal Legislation in the New Code of Canon Law,* n. 46; Cappello, *De Censuris* (3. ed., 1933), n. 18; Vermeersch-Creusen, *Epitome,* III, n. 417.

Another group enjoying this special privilege is that consisting of Cardinals, Legates of the Holy See, and all bishops.[159]

It is interesting to note here that in the event of the death of the Pope, the College of Cardinals, *sede vacante,* in no way enjoys the powers of a successor to the Pope: it has no jurisdiction to grant dispensations which were reserved to the Pontiff.[160]

II. Those Having Inferior Jurisdiction (to the Roman Pontiff)

A further application of this canon is made to others, inferior in jurisdiction to the Roman Pontiff, who may dispense from vindicative penalties with proper power. All who have the power of jurisdiction in the external forum and exercise that power in attaching vindicative penalties, according to the norms of canon 2220, § 1 [161] to laws or jurisdictional precepts which they have made, may in their own right dispense from those penalties.

(a) *Local Ordinaries*

1. Residential Bishops

A residential bishop has proper power to dispense from all vindicative penalties *latae* or *ferendae sententiae, a iure* or *ab homine,* attached to the particular or diocesan law established either by himself or by one of his predecessors, even if such a penalty were enacted in a diocesan synod, for in a synod there is only one legislator, namely, the bishop. The others who attend a synod have merely a consultive vote.[162] The bishop need not seek the consent or counsel

[159] Canon 1557, § 1, 2°, 3°.

[160] "Sedis Apostolicae vacatione durante, S. Collegium Cardinalium in iis, quae ad Pontificem Maximum dum viveret pertinebant, nullam omnino potestatem aut jurisdictionem habeat, neque gratiam neque justitiam faciendi, aut factam per Pontificem mortuum exsecutioni demandandi; sed ea omnia futuro Pontifici reservare teneatur": Pius X, Const. *"Vacante Sede Apostolica,"* 25 Dec., 1904, n. 1.

[161] Canon 2220, § 1: "Qui pollent potestate leges ferendi vel praecepta imponendi, possunt quoque legi vel praecepto poenas adnectere; qui judiciali tantum, possunt solummodo poenas, legitime statutas, ad normam iuris applicare."

[162] Canon 362.

of his cathedral chapter—or diocesan consultors, in places where no cathedral chapter has been constituted—in order to grant this dispensation, even though the chapter or body of consultors had been asked to give consent to the enactment of the law to which the penalty was attached, and had actually consented.[163] This power, since it is proper or ordinary, may be delegated or commissioned by the bishop to others.[164]

When a bishop attaches a vindicative penalty *latae sententiae* to a particular precept, if, for example, he were to say to one of his priests: "You must stay away from that place, and if you go there again, you are *ipso facto* suspended for a year," that penalty is *ab homine,* and as such is reserved to the bishop, so that he alone has the proper power to dispense from the penalty. Similarly, if the bishop establishes a *ferendae sententiae* vindicative penalty and that penalty is inflicted upon the offender by a judge, or by the bishop himself by means of a particular precept, the penalty is *ab homine,* and reserved to the bishop.[165]

According to canon 2236, § 1, bishops also enjoy proper power in relation to vindicative penalties established in the common law. They cannot, as has been seen, dispense from *latae sententiae* penalties of the common law except through participated or derived power. But in relation to *ferendae sententiae* vindicative penalties of the general law of the Church, they do enjoy, in their own right, the power to dispense. For once such a penalty, even though established definitely and completely in the common law, is inflicted by a court or by a particular precept, it becomes a penalty *ab homine,*[166] and as such falls under the jurisdiction of the ordinary who gave the particular precept or whose court issued the condemnatory sentence.[167] For example, if the law states that a cleric should be sus-

[163] Reilly, *The General Norms of Dispensation,* p. 56; Benedict XIV, *De Synodo Dioecesana,* lib. XIII, c. 5, n. 7.

[164] Canons 199, § 1; 2236, § 1. Cf. Coronata, *Institutiones Iuris Canonici,* IV, n. 1736.

[165] Lega, *De Delictis et Poenis,* n. 129.

[166] Canon 2217, § 3.

[167] Ayrinhac-Lydon, *Penal Legislation in the New Code of Canon Law,* n. 70; Coronata, *Institutiones Iuris Canonici,* IV, nn. 1736, 1737; Berutti, *Institu-*

pended for a definite time if guilty of a certain delict, and a court, finding him guilty of the violation, actually imposed this vindicative penalty, the ordinary alone has the proper power to dispense from the *ab homine* penalty. The ordinary is not merely a judge who applies the penalty *a iure*, but a jurisdictional superior who inflicts the penalty and thereby makes it *ab homine.*[168] And if a person who is bound by such a vindicative penalty *ab homine* changes his residence and acquires a domicile in another diocese, he cannot be dispensed by his new ordinary, but only by the ordinary who inflicted the penalty.[169] Again it should be observed that this penalty is reserved not precisely because it is *ab homine,* but because it is a vindicative penalty and all vindicative penalties are reserved to the superior who has established or inflicted the penalty, or his superior or successor. Others enjoy the power only if it is granted to them by the superior. It is important to keep this principle always in mind to avoid confusing the remission of vindicative penalties with the absolution from censures, which is ruled by entirely different principles.

They who rule the diocese temporarily or during the interregnum when the episcopal see is vacant may be considered as successors of the bishop and as such may dispense from vindicative penalties with the same jurisdictional power as the bishop himself. This power belongs innately to the residential bishop and adheres in his office no matter who may be the administrator of the diocese.[170] The cathedral chapter and the board of diocesan consultors both possess this power [171] during the eight days of their rule.[172] And when they elect a vicar capitular or, where the board of diocesan consultors exist, an administrator, the vicar capitular or administrator receives all

tiones Iuris Canonici, VI, n. 38, I, VI; Wernz-Vidal, *Ius Canonicum,* VI, n. 175, nota 150; Sipos, *Enchiridion Iuris Canonici,* § 232, p. 915.

168 Cf. Berutti, *Institutiones Iuris Canonici,* VI, n. 38, VI.

169 Coronata, *Institutiones Iuris Canonici,* IV, n. 1736; Wernz-Vidal, *Ius Canonicum,* VII, n. 215, nota 22; Salucci, *Il Diritto Penale,* I, p. 168; Berutti, *Institutiones Iuris Canonici,* VI, n. 38, III.

170 Cf. Ryan, *Principles of Episcopal Jurisdiction,* pp. 141-144.

171 Canon 435, § 1.

172 Canon 432, § 1.

the power formerly held by the chapter or board of consultors.[173] Obviously, therefore, this vicar capitular or administrator becomes the recipient of ordinary and not merely delegated episcopal jurisdiction. He becomes, in reality, the jurisdictional successor of the bishop and necessarily the *ordinarius loci*.[174] In consequence of this power being handed over to the vicar capitular or administrator he can exercise the jurisdictional functions proper to the episcopal office and can dispense from vindicative penalties just as the bishop.[175] He must, of course, abstain from using this power of dispensation in cases which would prove inopportune, or detrimental to the welfare of the diocese, or prejudicial to his successors.[176]

Others who are successors to the bishop and possess his power of dispensing from vindicative penalties because they hold his office temporarily are: (1) a transferred bishop from the time he receives authentic notification of his transfer until he takes canonical possession of his new see; [177] (2) the vicar capitular who, at the special suggestion of the Holy See, is appointed by the archbishop or bishop; [178] (3) the administrator who is elected by the cathedral chapter or the board of diocesan consultors to administer a quasi-vacant diocese.[179] Mention must be made, too, of the Apostolic Administrator who is commissioned for a stipulated period of time

[173] Canons 435, § 1; 437. Cf. Coronata, *Institutiones Iuris Canonici*, I, n. 461; Hermes, *De Capitulo Sede Vacante vel Impedito et de Vicario Capitulari* (Dissertatio Historico-Canonica, Lovanii: Vilinthout Fratres, 1873), p. 143; Wernz-Vidal, *Ius Canonicum*, II, n. 710; McDonough, *Apostolic Administrators*, The Catholic University of America Canon Law Studies, n. 139 (Washington, D. C.: The Catholic University of America Press, 1941), pp. 91-94.

[174] Maroto, *Institutiones*, I, n. 701; Cocchi, *Commentarium In Codicem Iuris Canonici ad Usum Scholarum*, II, 343.

[175] Berutti, *Institutiones Iuris Canonici*, VI, n. 38, III; Jaeger, *The Administration of Vacant and Quasi-vacant Dioceses in the United States*, The Catholic University of America Canon Law Studies, n. 81 (Washington, D. C.: The Catholic University of America, 1932), p. 170; Ryan, *Principles of Episcopal Jurisdiction*, p. 124; Vermeersch-Creusen, *Epitome*, III, n. 411.

[176] Canons 435, § 3; 436.

[177] Canon 430, § 3, 1°.

[178] Canon 431, § 2.

[179] Canon 429, § 3. Cf. Jaeger, *The Administration of Vacant and Quasi-vacant Dioceses in the United States*, pp. 169, 170.

to rule a diocese either *sede plena* or *sede vacante*.[180] Oftentimes he is assigned to a diocese whose affairs he is to administer until prevalent abuses are eradicated, or until a sick bishop is sufficiently recovered to resume active administration, or until the return of a bishop who has been summoned to Rome.[181] During the time of his administration, the temporary apostolic administrator is vested with the same power as the vicar capitular,[182] and is a jurisdictional successor, although only temporarily, of the bishop, and as such possesses the latter's proper ordinary power of dispensing from vindicative penalties.[183]

The only jurisdictional superior empowered to dispense from vindicative penalties established or inflicted through proper power of a bishop, is the Roman Pontiff or one delegated by him, and not the Metropolitan or Primate.[184] The Metropolitan, at the time of his visitation, possesses no power to dispense from vindicative penalties imposed by any of his suffragan bishops, since he undertakes this visitation, not as one jurisdictionally superior to the suffragan bishop, but rather as one vicariously empowered by the Roman Pontiff.[185] He may, as the court of appeals, remit vindicative penalties judicially inflicted by one of his suffragan bishops, when the sentence of the bishop has been proven unjust.[186] But in that event, because the judicial sentence of the suffragan bishop is put aside as null and void, the penalty as a matter of fact was never

[180] Canon 315, § 2.

[181] McDonough, *Apostolic Administrators*, pp. 96-100.

[182] Canon 315, § 2, 1°.

[183] Canon 2236, § 1.

[184] Canon 274, 5°, 7°. Cf. Coronata, *Institutiones Iuris Canonici*, IV, n. 1736; Wernz-Vidal, *Ius Canonicum*, VII, n. 209, nota 14; Lega, *De Delictis et Poenis*, n. 122; Ballerini-Palmieri, *Opus Theologicum Morale*, VII, n. 134; Ayrinhac-Lydon, *Penal Legislation in the New Code of Canon Law*, n. 65; De Meester, *Compendium*, III, n. 1726.

[185] Cf. canon 274. Also Ryan, *Principles of Episcopal Jurisdiction*, p. 97; Zollinger, *Institutiones Iuris Naturalis et Ecclesiastici Publici* (Romae, 1823), III, n. 359; Toso, *Commentaria Minora*, p. 98; Chelodi, *Ius Poenale*, n. 24, nota 1; Cavigioli, *De Censuris*, n. 12; Eichmann, *Kirchenrecht*, p. 165; Wernz-Vidal, *Ius Canonicum*, II, n. 528.

[186] Canon 1594, § 1. Cf. Berutti, *Institutiones Iuris Canonici*, VI, n. 38, II, 2.

really incurred and consequently needed no dispensation. The Metropolitan, in cases of appeal, in reality merely reverses the sentence of his suffragan and declares, retroactively, that the defendant was never guilty of the delict and therefore never deserved the penalty; he does not dispense from the penalty.[187]

It is true that the Metropolitan, during the time of his visitation, may punish notorious crimes with whatever penalties he deems just and may proceed against those who openly and notoriously commit any crime or delict against the Metropolitan himself or any of his entourage.[188] And he may dispense, according to canon 2236, § 1, from any vindicative penalties which he may thus inflict. But he does so, not as one jurisdictionally superior to the bishop of the place, but as one appointed by the Pope to act in this particular time in place of the bishop.[189] Further powers of dispensation from vindicative penalties may be obtained only through a particular grant of the Supreme Pontiff.[190]

2. Abbots and Prelates Nullius

Abbots and Prelates *nullius,* abbots or prelates with territorial jurisdiction,[191] since they have full ordinary power of jurisdiction, also in the external forum, over all the subjects, whether cleric or lay, of the territory assigned to them, have all the rights and faculties which the Code gives to ordinaries [192] and can truly be said to exercise a quasi-episcopal power over the territory assigned to them,[193]

[187] Wernz-Vidal, *Ius Canonicum,* VII, n. 209, p. 221, nota 14; Lega, *De Iudiciis Ecclesiasticis,* IV, n. 491; Thesaurus, *De Poenis Ecclesiasticis,* P. I, c. 24.

[188] Canon 274, § 5. Cf. Chelodi, *Ius Poenale,* n. 24, nota 1.

[189] Eichmann, *Kirchenrecht,* p. 165.

[190] Eichmann, *Kirchenrecht,* p. 165; Wernz-Vidal, *Ius Canonicum,* II, n. 528.

[191] For the difference between abbots and prelates *nullius,* cf. canon 319, § 1; also Coronata, *Institutiones Iuris Canonici,* I, n. 385. Abbots *nullius* are always regulars; prelates *nullius* may be either regulars or seculars. Cf. canons 324; 326; 327.

[192] Canon 198.

[193] Canons 319, 323. Coronata, *Institutiones Iuris Canonici,* I, nn. 372, 389; Vermeersch-Creusen, *Epitome,* I, nn. 437, 438; Bouix, *De Episcopo,* I, n. 1859; Wernz-Vidal, *Ius Canonicum,* II, nn. 563, 569, 815; Chelodi, *Ius Poenale*; Blat, *Commentarium Textus Codicis Iuris Canonici,* II, nn. 278, 281; Augustine, *A*

may inflict [194] vindicative penalties and dispense from them, just as a residential bishop. The two powers are exactly the same. Therefore these abbots and prelates may dispense from all vindicative penalties *latae* or *ferendae sententiae, a iure* or *ab homine,* attached to the particular law of the territory, even if the penal law was enacted in a synod of that territory.[195] The abbot or prelate does not need the consent or counsel of the chapter—whether that chapter is a secular one [196] or religious [197] or a board of diocesan consultors [198]—in order to grant the dispensation, even though the chapter or board of consultors had been asked to give consent to the enactment of the penal law and had consented. The abbot or prelate may likewise attach vindicative penalties to any of his precepts, and the dispensation from these penalties are reserved to him, whether the penalty is *latae sententiae* attached to a particular precept or *ferendae sententiae* and inflicted by a judge or by the abbot or prelate himself by means of a particular precept or condemnatory sentence.

In the case of vindicative penalties *ferendae sententiae* of the common law, the abbot or prelate *nullius* possesses the same power as the residential bishop. They may, therefore, dispense from any of these penalties which they themselves or through the agency of one of their judges have inflicted either judicially by means of a condemnatory sentence or extrajudicially through a particular precept. These penalties are *ab homine* and are reserved to the abbot or prelate.[199] This power is proper and ordinary, and therefore

Commentary on the New Code, II, pp. 331-336; Ripoll, *Novisimas Instituciones de Derecho Canonico* (Madrid, 1920), I, n. 690; Santamaria, *Comentarios al Codigo Canonico* (Madrid, 1922), I, n. 387; Schaefer, *De Religiosis,* n. 165.

[194] Canon 2220, § 1.

[195] Cf. Schaefer, *De Religiosis,* n. 165, d.

[196] Canons 324, 391.

[197] Canon 324.

[198] Canons 326, 423-428.

[199] Canon 2236, § 1. Cf. Coronata, *Institutiones Iuris Canonici,* IV, nn. 1736, 1737; Ayrinhac-Lydon, *Penal Legislation in the New Code of Canon Law,* n. 70; Berutti, *Institutiones Iuris Canonici,* VI, n. 38, I, VI; Wernz-Vidal, *Ius Canonicum,* VII, nn. 209, 211.

may be delegated or commissioned by the abbot or prelate to others.[200]

The successor of an abbot or prelate *nullius* acquires his power of dispensing from the above mentioned penalties, just as in the case of a bishop. When the abbacy or prelacy is vacant, the religious [201] or secular chapter, or, as the case may be, the board of diocesan consultors, rule the abbacy or prelacy; and consequently may dispense from vindicative penalties with the same power and with the same restrictions as the abbot or prelate.[202] The vicar capitular who is chosen by the chapter or by the consultors enjoys exactly the same dispensatory power.[203]

As in the case of residential bishops, the only jurisdictional superior who can dispense from vindicating penalties established or inflicted by the abbot or prelate is the Roman Pontiff.[204] Vindicative penalties judicially inflicted by an abbot or prelate may be remitted, on appeal, by the neighboring Metropolitan or by another bishop whom the abbot or prelate has chosen as Metropolitan, with the approval of the Holy See, according to the norm of canon 285.[205] But this remission on appeal of vindicative penalties is not strictly a dispensation.[206]

3. Vicars General

As to the power of the vicar general, in his own right, to dispense from vindicative penalties according to the first paragraph of canon

[200] Canons 199, § 1; 2236, § 1. Cf. Coronata, *Institutiones Iuris Canonici,* IV, n. 1736.

[201] In the case of a religious chapter, the particular constitution of the particular order may call for a different procedure: cf. canon 327, § 1: "nisi constitutiones aliud ferant. . . ."

[202] Canon 327, § 1.

[203] Canons 327, § 1; 432; 435, § 1.

[204] Cf. Coronata, *Institutiones Iuris Canonici,* IV, n. 1736; Lega, *De Delictis et Poenis,* n. 122; Ayrinhac-Lydon, *Penal Legislation in the New Code of Canon Law,* n. 65; De Meester, *Compendium,* III, n. 1726; Wernz-Vidal, *Ius Canonicum,* VII, n. 209.

[205] Canons 1594, § 3; 285.

[206] Cf. *supra,* p. 93. Cf. also Lega, *De Iudiciis Ecclesiasticis,* IV, n. 491; Wernz-Vidal, *Ius Canonicum,* VII, n. 209; Thesaurus, *De Poenis Ecclesiasticis,* P. I, c. 24; Berutti, *Institutiones Iuris Canonici,* VI, n. 38, II, 2.

2236, again there is divided opinion. Under the term vicar general is understood both the vicar general of a residential bishop and the vicar general of an abbot or prelate *nullius*.[207] The question here concerns itself as to whether the vicar general may dispense from vindicative penalties *in his own right* or whether he needs, for the exercise of his power, a special mandate from the bishop, abbot or prelate. There is no question here of the power which the vicar general uses, whether it is ordinary or delegated. For the vicar general always acts by reason of his office with ordinary power,[208] whether before [209] or after he had received a special mandate.[210] Neither is there a question here of whether the vicar general may act with *proper* power as the bishop, abbot, or prelate does; for the vicar general always acts with vicarious, though ordinary power.[211]

Canonists who affirm that the vicar general may in his own right, and without a special mandate from his superior, dispense from vindicative penalties according to canon 2236, § 1, base their contention on the general statement of the powers and rights accorded to the vicar general, as given in canon 368, § 1.[212] For this canon states that the vicar general by virtue of the office which he holds possesses the same jurisdiction within the limits of the diocese, over spiritual

[207] Canon 198, § 1.

[208] Canon 197, § 2. Cf. Maroto, *Institutiones*, I, 831-832.

[209] Cf. Cappello, *Summa Iuris Canonici* (Romae, 1928), II, n. 394; Vermeersch-Creusen, *Epitome*, I, n. 355; Campagna, *Il Vicario Generale del Vescovo*, The Catholic University of America Canon Law Studies, n. 66 (Washington, D. C.: The Catholic University of America, 1931), pp. 5-8 (hereafter cited as *Il Vicario Generale*).

[210] Cf. Maroto, *Institutiones*, I, 830; Wernz-Vidal, *Ius Canonicum*, II, nn. 678-679; Vermeersch-Creusen, *Epitome*, I, n. 357. Cf. also a lengthy discussion on this question: Roelker, "The Vicar General and the Special Mandate," *The Jurist*, II (1942), pp. 346-362; cf. also Chelodi, *Ius De Personis*, p. 330; Kearney, *The Principles of Delegation*, The Catholic University of America Canon Law Studies, n. 55 (Washington, D. C.: The Catholic University of America, 1929), pp. 72-74; Campagna, *Il Vicario Generale*, pp. 133-135; Hilling, *Das Personenrecht des Codex Iuris Canonici* (Paderborn, 1924), p. 183.

[211] Canon 197, § 1.

[212] "Vicario Generali, vi officii, ea competit in universa dioecesi iurisdictio in spiritualibus ac temporalibus, quae ad Episcopum iure ordinario pertinet, exceptis iis quae Episcopus sibi reservaverit, vel quae ex iure requirant speciale Episcopi mandatum."

and temporal matters, as the bishop himself enjoys by ordinary law. The only exceptions to this power are those matters which the bishop expressly reserves to himself or which by common law require a special mandate of the bishop. Therefore, unless the bishop reserves the dispensation from some particular vindicative penalty or penalties to himself, or unless the general law demands a special mandate from the bishop before the vicar general may dispense from vindicative penalties, the vicar general may exercise the same jurisdictional power of dispensing from vindicative penalties as the bishop enjoys. And, the argument proceeds, since the general law, as expressed in canon 2236, § 1, makes no mention whatsoever of the necessity of a special mandate, the vicar general may dispense from all penalties established or inflicted through ordinary power by the bishop. Therefore, according to this opinion, the vicar general possesses the same powers as were enumerated above,[213] as pertaining to residential bishops, abbots and prelates *nullius*. Proponents of this opinion are Coronata,[214] Sole,[215] and Hofmann.[216]

Van Hove [217] and others [218] hold that the vicar general always needs a special mandate to dispense from vindicative penalties according to canon 2236, § 1. This opinion seems to be the more correct, from the consideration of both canon 2236, § 1, and canon 368, § 1. Canon 368, § 1 states that the vicar general cannot exercise the same jurisdictional power of his bishop in matters which the bishop reserves to himself or in cases where a special mandate is required by common law. It is true that canon 2236, § 1 does not require a special mandate, but that is because this canon establishes a distinct reservation of the dispensation to the one who established

[213] Cf. this chapter, p. 89.

[214] *Institutiones Iuris Canonici,* IV, n. 1736: "Vicarius generalis probabiliter potest auferre poenas ab Ordinario Loci statutas potestate ordinaria."

[215] *De Delictis et Poenis,* nn. 83, 147.

[216] *Die freiwillige Gerichtsbarkeit in kanonischen Recht* (Paderborn, 1929), p. 40.

[217] *Commentarium Lovaniense in C. I. C.,* I, n. 331, p. 312, nota 1.

[218] Augustine, *A Commentary on the New Code,* VIII, 108; Von Kienitz, *Generalvikar und Offizial auf Grund des Codex Iuris Canonici* (Freiburg, 1931), pp. 106-107; Blat, *De Delictis et Poenis,* n. 38; Pistocchi, "De Superiore Potestatem Coactivam Habente," *Il Monitore Ecclesiastico,* IX (1937), p. 13.

or inflicted the penalty. To determine who is, therefore, the competent superior of dispensation, it must be determined first who in the law may establish or inflict vindicative penalties. In other words, canon 2236, § 1 in determining the competent superior refers directly to canon 2220 wherein these superiors are enumerated.[219] Two persons are expressly excluded, one absolutely, the other conditionally: the judge who, with only judicial power, applies a penalty already established by law, and the vicar general if he acts without a special mandate from the bishop.[220] Both of these are incompetent to act under the circumstances—and therefore cannot establish or inflict vindicative penalties. Consequently, both of them are excluded, under the same circumstances, from acting under canon 2236, § 1, because neither, if the circumstances are verified, fulfills the stipulations of the phrase "qui poenam tulit" in canon 2236, § 1. The judge is excluded absolutely because he simply does not have the power to establish or inflict penalties; he merely applies them. The vicar general is conditionally excluded because, if he acts without the special mandate of his bishop, he too does not have the power to establish or inflict penalties.[221] If the vicar general cannot, without a special mandate from the bishop, establish or inflict vindicative penalties, which act is in complete accordance with the law, *a fortiori* he cannot, without a similar mandate, grant a dispensation

[219] Canon 2220: § 1. Qui pollent potestate leges ferendi vel praecepta imponendi, possunt quoque legi vel praecepto poenas adnectere; qui iudiciali tantum, possunt solummodo poenas, legitime statutas, ad normam iuris applicare.
§ 2. Vicarius Generalis sine mandato speciali non habet potestatem infligendi poenas.

[220] Cf. Blat, *De Delictis et Poenas,* n. 38; Chelodi, *Ius Poenale,* n. 24; Coronata, *Institutiones Iuris Canonici,* IV, n. 1693; Pistocchi, "De Superiore Potestatem Coactivam Habente, *loc. cit.;* Salucci, *Il Diritto Penale,* p. 99; Sole, *De Delictis et Poenis,* n. 83; Wernz-Vidal, *Ius Canonicum,* VII, n. 165; Esswein, *The Extrajudicial Coercive Powers of Ecclesiastical Superiors,* The Catholic University of America, Canon Law Studies, n. 127 (Washington: The Catholic University of America Press, 1941), pp. 70-71.

[221] Cf. Coronata, *Institutiones Iuris Canonici,* IV, n. 1693: ". . . non potest, ne valide quidem, poenas legi aut praecepto a se dato adnectere; nec sententia condemnatoria reum poenae a iure latae subiicere."

from them, an act entirely contrary to the law.[222] In other words, if he has the mandate of the bishop, he may inflict or establish penalties; and he may dispense from vindicative penalties only if he has the mandate of the bishop.

Again it must be emphasized that this problem concerns only the question whether the vicar general, in his own right and authority, may dispense from vindicative penalties according to canon 2236, § 1. For the vicar general may, through the exercise of vicarious or participated power, dispense, according to canon 82, from laws enacted by the principal ordinary or his predecessors. The vicar general is himself a local ordinary[223] and consequently is included under the terms of canon 82.[224] And if these particular diocesan laws are penal laws, the vicar general may certainly dispense from the vindicative penalty, either indirectly by dispensing from the law itself, or directly by dispensing, in virtue of canon 2236, § 2, from the penalty attached to the law.

4. Permanent Apostolic Administrators

The permanent apostolic administrator who is sent by the Sovereign Pontiff to rule or administer a diocese either *sede plena* or *sede vacante*[225] enjoys the same power that is granted to residential bishops.[226] Unlike the temporary apostolic administrator, who rules only for a time of emergency, the perpetual administrator rules indefinitely in the place of a residential bishop. In most instances the permanent apostolic administrators are neighboring residential bishops who assume the rule of smaller neighboring dioceses.[227] Since they are, in reality, non-residential bishops of the diocese over which they rule, and since they have all the powers of a resi-

[222] Cf. Van Hove, *Commentarium Lovaniense in C. I. C.*, I, n. 331; Augustine, *A Commentary on the New Code,* VIII, 108.

[223] Canon 198, § 2.

[224] Cf. Reilly, *The General Norms of Dispensation,* pp. 56-57.

[225] Canon 312.

[226] Canon 315, § 1.

[227] *Acta Apostolicae Sedis, Commentarium Officiale* (Romae, 1909—), XI (1919), 72; cf. also McDonough, *Apostolic Administrators,* pp. 158-166; Eichmann, *Kirchenrecht,* p. 174; Vermeersch-Creusen, *Epitome,* I, n. 431; Wernz-Vidal, *Ius Canonicum,* II, n. 557; Toso, *Commentaria Minora,* p. 138.

dential bishop, they may dispense from vindicative penalties, just as the residential bishop, even if the residential bishop is still in possession of the see to which the administrator has been appointed. For when the administrator is assigned to the diocese *sede plena,* the jurisdiction of the bishop and of his vicar general is suspended.[228] The apostolic administrator alone is the competent superior to dispense from vindicative penalties reserved by canon 2236, § 1 to the residential bishop.

5. Vicars and Prefects Apostolic

According to canon 294, § 1, vicars and prefects apostolic enjoy in their own assigned territories the same jurisdiction as that enjoyed by a residential bishop in his diocese,[229] unless, in the letter of appointment, the Holy See limits that jurisdiction. This jurisdiction which they exercise is ordinary, being annexed to the very office which they hold.[230] As *ordinarii* and *ordinarii locorum* of canon 198, they have all the rights and faculties which the Code gives to ordinaries; thus they can truly be said to exercise a quasi-episcopal power over the territory assigned them.[231] They therefore have the same dispensatory power as a bishop in regard to vindicative penalties. They may inflict vindicative penalties according to the norms of canon 2220, § 1; and they may dispense from such penalties according to the rule of canon 2236, § 1, unless, of course, this particular power is excluded expressly in the letter of appointment from the Holy See.[232]

[228] Canon 316, § 1.

[229] Canon 294, § 1: Vicarii et Praefecti Apostolici iisdem iuribus et facultatibus in suo territorio gaudent, quae in propriis dioecesibus competunt Episcopis residentialibus, nisi quid Apostolica Sedes reservaverit.

[230] Canon 197. Cf. Chelodi, *Ius de Personis,* n. 183; Vermeersch-Creusen, *Epitome,* I, n. 404; Wernz-Vidal, *Ius Canonicum,* II, n. 544.

[231] Cf. Coronata, *Institutiones Iuris Canonici,* I, nn. 372, 389.

[232] Cf. Winslow, *Vicars and Prefects Apostolic,* The Catholic University of America Canon Law Studies, n. 24 (Washington, D. C.: The Catholic University of America, 1924), pp. 15, 61-69; Coronata, *Institutiones Iuris Canonici,* I, n. 373; Eichmann, *Kirchenrecht,* p. 170; Wernz-Vidal, *Ius Canonicum,* II, nn. 545, 569; Toso, *Commentaria Minora,* pp. 147, 155; Chelodi, *Ius de Personis,* n. 183; Pugliese, "De Vicario Delegato in territorio missionum," *Apollinaris,* VI (1933), 196-217.

(b) *Other Ordinaries*

1. Major Superiors of Clerical Exempt Religious

Major superiors of clerical exempt religious,[233] since they have ordinary jurisdictional power,[234] can dispense their subjects [235] from any penal law or any vindicative penalty attached to such a law which they themselves have established or which one of their predecessors or inferiors has enacted.[236] They may likewise dispense from any vindicative penalties attached to any precept, general or particular, which, in virtue of canon 2220, § 1, they or their predecessors or inferiors have established.[237] Moreover, they may dispense from *ferendae sententiae* vindicative penalties which they have inflicted upon their subjects by means of a condemnatory judicial sentence or particular precept. In other words, their power of dispensing is the same as that of the residential bishop in regard to his subjects, with, however, one exception. Common law defines the limits of episcopal power of dispensation from vindicative penalties; not only the general law, but the particular constitutions of the various

[233] Included under the term "major superior" are the following: 1. Abbot primate and abbot general of a monastic Congregation (abbot president, abbot superior, or superior general), 2. abbot of an exempt monastery, 3. supreme moderator of a religion, 4. the provincial superior, 5. vicars of the foregoing, 6. all others who have authority like to that of provincials. Cf. canon 198, § 1; 488, 8°; Larraona, "Commentarium Codicis: Canon 488," *Commentarium pro Religiosis* (later [1935] *Commentarium pro Religiosis et Missionariis*, Romae, 1920—), IV (1923), 39-46 (hereafter cited as *CpR* or *CpRM*); Keene, *Religious Ordinaries and Canon 198*, pp. 2, 3.

[234] Canons 198, § 1; 501, § 1. Cf. Berutti, *Institutiones Iuris Canonici*, III, n. 23; Coronata, *Institutiones Iuris Canonici*, IV, nn. 1693, 1736; Ayrinhac-Lydon, *Penal Legislation in the New Code of Canon Law*, n. 37; Salucci, *Il Diritto Penale*, p. 104; Woywod, *A Practical Commentary*, II, n. 2056; Cavigioli, *De Censuris*, pp. 6-15; Eichmann, *Kirchenrecht*, p. 60; Santamaria, *Comentarios al Codigo Canonico*, VI, n. 90; Ferreres, *Institutiones Iuris Canonici*, II, n. 974; Cappello, *De Censuris* (3. ed., 1933), n. 11; Augustine, *A Commentary on the New Code*, VIII, 84, 85; Chelodi, *Ius Poenale*, n. 24; Cerato, *Censurae Vigentes*, n. 6.

[235] Since the jurisdiction of religious superiors binds only their subjects, their dispensatory power likewise may be exercised only over their subjects.

[236] Canon 2236, § 1. Cf. Reilly, *The General Norms of Dispensation*, p. 57.

[237] Cf. Berutti, *Institutiones Iuris Canonici*, III, n. 23; VI, n. 22.

religious communities may determine the limits of the power of major superiors to dispense from vindicative penalties.[238]

Thus, for example, ordinarily this power of dispensation is reserved, not to the provincial superior, but to the general chapter of the community.[239]

The general chapter of a clerical exempt religion may dispense from vindicative penalties which it may have attached to its laws or precepts, always, however, according to the norms of particular constitutions.[240] Also the provincial chapter, within the limits of particular constitutions, can dispense from all vindicative penalties which the chapter had attached to precepts issued by itself.[241]

The supreme moderator of the clerical exempt religion and the general chapter, or the supreme moderator of a monastic congregation, as the case may be, are the respective jurisdictional superiors who, according to canon 2236, § 1, can dispense from vindicative penalties established or inflicted in the courts of these provincial superiors or local abbots.[242] But, as has been demonstrated, if a remission is granted on appeal it is, in reality, but a declaration of innocence and not a real dispensation from the vindicative penalties.[243]

2. Local Superiors of Clerical Exempt Religious

Minor or local superiors of clerical exempt religions, although not ordinaries, also have jurisdiction over their subjects in the external forum.[244] Therefore, they too may attach vindicative penal-

[238] Berutti, *Institutiones Iuris Canonici,* III, n. 23, II; Coronata, *Institutiones Canonici,* IV, n. 1693.

[239] Cf. Chelodi, *Ius Poenale,* n. 24, nota 2; Schaefer, *De Religiosis,* n. 107, p. 228, nota 72; Berutti, *Institutiones Iuris Canonici,* VI, n. 38, II, 3.

[240] Canon 2236, § 1; Berutti, *Institutiones Iuris Canonici,* VI, n. 22, VI.

[241] Berutti, *Institutiones Iuris Canonici,* VI, n. 22, VII.

[242] Coronata, *Institutiones Iuris Canonici,* IV, n. 1736; Berutti, *Institutiones Iuris Canonici,* VI, n. 38, II, 3; Wernz, *Ius Decretalium,* VI, 88, 175; Lega, *De Delictis et Poenis,* n. 129.

[243] Cf. Wernz-Vidal, *Ius Canonicum,* VIII, n. 209; Lega, *De Iudiciis Ecclesiasticis,* IV, n. 491; Thesaurus, *De Poenis Ecclesiasticis,* P. I, c. 24.

[244] Canon 501, 1. Cf. Coronata, *Institutiones Iuris Canonici,* IV, n. 1693; Berutti, *Institutiones Iuris Canonici,* III, n. 26, VII; Vermeersch-Creusen;

ties to jurisdictional precepts which they give,[245] unless the particular constitutions of the religious community restricts this power.[246] An example of this restricted power is the one cited by Schaefer: [247] among the Capuchin Friars Minor only the major superior may inflict penalties. But according to the general law these local or minor religious superiors may dispense from the penalties which are attached to precepts established by themselves or their predecessors, except in those instances where the coercive power of local superiors is restricted by particular constitutions. For if they have no coactive power under their constitutions to inflict vindicative penalties, they have no power, under canon 2236, § 1, to dispense from vindicative penalties.

Chelodi [248] and others [249] would seem therefore to deny this dispensatory power to minor superiors of clerical exempt religions. For they deny that such religious superiors have power from the common law to attach vindicative penalties to precepts and that they enjoy that power only when it is expressly granted to them by their particular constitutions.[250] The argument is based entirely on

Epitome, III, n. 411; Cavigioli, *De Censuris,* pp. 6-15; Ferreres, *Institutiones Iuris Canonici,* II, n. 974; Perathoner, *Kirchliches Gerichtswesen und Kirchliche Strafrecht* (Brixen, 1919), p. 90 (hereafter cited as *Kirchliches Gerichtswesen*); Augustine, *A Commentary on the New Code,* VIII, p. 84, 85; Chelodi, *Ius Poenale,* n. 24; Eichmann, *Das Strafrecht,* p. 60.

245 Cf. canon 2220, § 1.

246 Cf. O'Brien, *The Exemption of Religious in Church Law* (Milwaukee: Bruce, 1943), pp. 43, 44; Coronata, *Institutiones Iuris Canonici,* IV, n. 1693; Vermeersch-Creusen, *Epitome,* III, n. 411; Cavigioli, *De Censuris,* p. 15; Eichmann, *Strafrecht,* p. 60; Claeys-Bouuaert-Simenon, *Manuale Iuris Canonici ad Usum Seminariorum,* III (4. ed., Grandae et Leodii, 1934), n. 1256 (hereafter cited as *Manuale Iuris Canonici*); Santamaria, *Comentarios al Codigo Canonico,* VI, 90; Perathoner, *Kirchliche Gerichtswesen,* p. 90; Ferreres, *Institutiones Iuris Canonici,* I, 809; II, 974; Schaefer, *De Religiosis,* n. 107, p. 228; Goyeneche, *CpR,* III (1922), 139-144.

247 *De Religiosis,* n. 107, p. 228.

248 *Ius Poenale,* n. 24, nota 3.

249 Cf. Salucci, *Il Diritto Penale,* pp. 102, 103; Cappello, *De Censuris* (3. ed., 1933), p. 13, nota 8; Biederlach-Führich, *De Religiosis* (Oeniponte, 1919), n. 43.

250 Chelodi, *Ius Poenale,* n. 24: "Neque ex iure communi superiores religiosi locales videntur posse dare praeceptum cum adnexa vera poena canonica. . . .

the fact that in pre-Code law this power was not certain.[251] However, there seems to be no reason to deny to local superiors this particular exercise of jurisdiction, since the Code makes no distinction between major and minor superiors in either canon 501, § 1 or in canon 2220, § 1.[252] Consequently, those local superiors can dispense from those vindicative penalties which they or their predecessors *actually* inflicted or established by jurisdictional precept, a principle which may be accepted by proponents of either of the above opinions.

Other superiors, who have only dominative power [253] cannot dispense from vindicative penalties, because they cannot inflict them. They may issue orders or precepts (non-jurisdictional) to which they may attach so-called "paternal penalties," such as prayers or fastings or other such works.[254] But these penalties are not canonical penalties, and are ruled, not by general, but by the particular law of individual constitutions.[255]. Similarly, these superiors may "dispense" from these paternal penalties, within the limits and restrictions, of course, established by the individual constitutions, but again the dispensation is not a true one, but rather a license or permission.[256] A religious superior with mere dominative power cannot dispense from vindicative penalties of the general law or of particular law, therefore, unless that power of jurisdiction is granted to him by a superior who has ordinary jurisdiction.[257]

The person jurisdictionally superior to local religious superiors of clerical exempt religions who, according to canon 2236, § 1 is competent to dispense from vindicative penalties inflicted by local

In iure novo non apparet satis probata, nisi expresse in eorum constitutionibus contineatur."

[251] Chelodi, *loc. cit.*; Wernz, *Ius Decretalium*, III, 692.

[252] Cf. O'Brien, *The Exemption of Religious in Church Law*, pp. 43, 44.

[253] Canon 501, § 1. Chapters and superiors of non-exempt religions and of lay exempt religions are included under this class. Cf. Berutti, *Institutiones Iuris Canonici*, VI, n. 22, Scholion A.

[254] Berutti, *Institutiones Iuris Canonici*, III, n. 25, I; VI, n. 22, Scholion A.

[255] Schaefer, *De Religiosis*, n. 107, p. 228.

[256] Reilly, *The General Norms of Dispensation*, p. 2; Berutti, *Institutiones Iuris Canonici*, III, n. 25, III; Schaefer, *De Religiosis*, n. 113, c.

[257] Berutti, *loc. cit.*

superiors is the respective major superior, namely, either the general chapter or the supreme moderator of the community or the provincial superior or the provincial chapter, subject, as usual, to any particular norms established by the particular religious constitutions. This applies to all vindicative penalties inflicted by the local superior, whether the penalties are those established by the religious constitution and inflicted by the local superior, or penalties attached to the local superior to jurisdictional precepts given by him. Moreover, the supreme moderator or general chapter, as judges of appeal,[258] may remit vindicative penalties judicially inflicted by provincial superiors; and the supreme moderator of a monastic congregation has similar power in regard to penalties judicially inflicted by the local abbot. But this remission is not strictly a dispensation, but rather a declaration or interpretation of the accused's innocence.

3. Plenary and Provincial Councils

Plenary and provincial councils,[259] although certainly not ordinaries, have jurisdiction to establish and pass laws and precepts to which are attached vindicative penalties for their respective territories and subjects.[260] These councils, therefore, have the power, too, of dispensing from these penalties thus established by a former council, but in practice a council never grants a dispensation.[261] Special powers are conceded to local ordinaries in regard to laws of plenary and provincial councils in canon 82 and canon 291, § 2; but since the power they receive is derived or participated power, it shall be treated in its proper place.[262]

B. *Derived Dispensatory Power*

Canon 2236, § 1. Remissio poenae . . . per dispensationem, si de poenis·vindicativis, concedi . . . potest . . . vel ab eo cui haec potestas commissa est.

258 Canon 1594, § 4.

259 Canons 281, 283.

260 Canon 2220, § 1. Cf. Berutti, *Institutiones Iuris Canonici,* VI, n. 22, V; Vermeersch-Creusen, *Epitome,* III, n. 411; Coronata, *Institutiones Iuris Canonici,* IV, nn. 1693, 1736.

261 Cf. Reilly, *The General Norms of Dispensation,* p. 54.

262 Cf. *infra,* p. 112.

§ 2. Qui potest a lege eximere, potest quoque poenam legi adnexam remittere.

"Potest quis per alium, quod potest facere per seipsum," states the rule of law.[263] A person who possesses the right to do something possesses fundamentally the corresponding right to commission someone else to perform that act in his stead.[264] Since this is true, it follows that the superior who is jurisdictionally competent, under canon 2236, § 1, together with his successor or his superior, can empower another person to grant dispensations from vindicative penalties established or inflicted by that superior, just as the legislator or his superior or successor can empower another to grant dispensations from his laws.[265] Such a concession of power can be made, obviously, only to a cleric, because clerics alone are capable of obtaining the power of jurisdiction required by this canon.[266] The vicar general, thus, may be commissioned by the ordinary to dispense from vindicative penalties in a particular case, or the ordinary may be commissioned by the Pope, etc.[267] This concession of power to dispense from vindicative penalties is expressed in the words of canon 2236, § 1: ". . . cui haec potestas commissa est."

This concession of power may be either explicit or implicit. An explicit concession of dispensatory power is made whenever a superior clearly grants such a power either by the express words of a law or special indult, or by means of some other sign which distinctly and clearly expresses it.[268] Such an explicit concession is made by

[263] Regula 68, *R.J.*, in VI°.

[264] Blat, *De Delictis et Poenis*, n. 58; Augustine, *A Commentary on the New Code*, VIII, 108; Wernz-Vidal, *Ius Canonicum*, VII, n. 210; Brys, "De potestate Episcoporum dispensandi in legibus Ecclesiae generalibus," *Collationes Brugenses*, XXXIX (1929), p. 145; Reilly, *The General Norms of Dispensation*, pp. 57, 66; Coronata, *Institutiones Iuris Canonici*, I, n. 107; Michiels, *Normae Generales*, II, 480-481.

[265] Canon 80.

[266] Canon 118.

[267] Augustine, *A Commentary on the New Code*, VIII, 108.

[268] Reilly, *The General Norms of Dispensation*, pp. 66, 67; Coronata, *Institutiones Iuris Canonici*, I, n. 107; Michiels, *Normae Generales*, II, 480; Brys,

the general law itself in canon 2237 to ordinaries. Similar concessions are made to the various dicasteries of the Roman Curia,[269] to each of which the Pope entrusts a share of his jurisdiction. Special concessions of faculties are sometimes made by the Roman Pontiff personally or by the competent Roman Congregations; and still another example of such a concession are the quinquennial faculties granted to bishops by the Holy See. Other superiors, who are jurisdictionally inferior to the Pope, may also make these concessions to others of powers of dispensing which they have in virtue of canon 2236, § 1.

An implicit concession of dispensatory power is one which, even though not specifically stated, is nonetheless contained in an explicitly granted power "as an effect in its cause, . . . as a part in the whole or a species in the genus." [270] An example of this implicit grant is stated in canon 2236, § 2. For, according to the second paragraph of this canon, the power to dispense from a law implicitly contains the power to dispense from the vindicative penalties which may be attached to that law. The vindicative penalty is contained in the penal law "ut pars in toto"; [271] and if the power to dispense from the whole is granted to a person, the power to dispense from the part is also granted implicitly.[272] This is but an application of the rule of law which states that "without doubt the part is contained in the whole." [273]

This power of jurisdiction which is conceded—either explicitly or implicitly—may be either ordinary or delegated power. At times the legislator may explicitly grant delegated dispensatory power to another. Thus the Pope may delegate a bishop to dispense from a particular vindicative penalty reserved to the Roman Pontiff; or a bishop may delegate one of his priests to dispense from a penalty

"De potestate Episcoporum,"—*ibid.*, p. 145; Augustine, *A Commentary on the New Code*, VIII, 108; Wernz-Vidal, *Ius Canonicum*, VII, n. 210.

[269] Cf. Reilly, *The General Norms of Dispensation*, pp. 61, 62.

[270] Michiels, *Normae Generales*, II, 481.

[271] Cf. Michiels, *Normae Generales*, II, 481; Wernz-Vidal, *Ius Canonicum*, VII, n. 210; Beste, *Introductio in Codicem*, p. 898; Berutti, *Institutiones Iuris Canonici*, VI, n. 38.

[272] Cf. Chelodi, *Ius Poenale*, n. 29.

[273] "In toto partem non est dubium contineri": Reg. 80, *R.J.*, in VI°.

reserved to himself.[274] At other times the legislator makes an explicit concession, in the law itself, of dispensatory power which is bestowed directly on a certain office and only indirectly on the incumbent because he is actually occupying that office, as in canon 2237; and at such times the jurisdiction which the commissioned person enjoys is not delegated but ordinary power.[275]

Some canonists [276] maintain that this power which is granted by the law itself is always delegated and never ordinary. For ordinary power consists in more than the mere concession of a faculty to an office; it must be proper, they say, to the office; it must belong to the office *per se*—and not through a commission—"according to the preformed juridical concept in the constitutional law." [277] However, this opinion of ordinary power cannot stand against canon 197,[278] which is a restatement of the old law, under which this commissioned power was considered as ordinary,[279] and according to canon 6, 2° it is thus to be understood in the new law of the Code. Moreover, canon 912 states explicitly that such concession of ordinary power to a jurisdictional inferior by law is not contrary to the juridical concept of ordinary power.[280]

Either ordinary or delegated power may be conceded implicitly. Thus the conceded ordinary power which an ordinary enjoys in virtue of canon 81 to dispense from the common law includes implicitly the ordinary power of dispensing from any vindicative penalties which may be attached to such general laws. The power of dispens-

[274] Canon 199.

[275] Canon 197. Cf. Michiels, *Normae Generales,* II, 469-471; De Meester, *Compendium,* I, nn. 444-448; Vermeersch-Creusen, *Epitome,* I, n. 277; Coronata, *Institutiones Iuris Canonici,* I, n. 278, nota 3; Crisci, "Evolutio historica delegationis a iure," *Apollinaris,* IX (1936), 270-299; Reilly, *The General Norms of Dispensation,* pp. 57-59.

[276] Blat, *De Delictis et Poenis,* pp. 469, 470; Ojetti, *Commentarium in Codicem Iuris Canonici,* I, 328, nota 10.

[277] Ojetti, *Commentarium in Codicem Iuris Canonici,* I, 328.

[278] Canon 197: § 1. Potestas jurisdictionis ordinaria ea est quae ipso iure adnexa est officio; delegata, quae commissa est personae.

[279] Cf. Crisci, "Evolutio historica delegationis a iure," *Apollinaris,* IX (1936), 514; Michiels, *Normae Generales,* II, 469 ss.

[280] Canon 912: ". . . ii tantum possunt potestate ordinaria indulgentias elargiri, quibus id expresse a iure concessum est."

ing from the vindicative penalty, in this instance, is ordinary power conceded implicitly.[281]

Likewise, delegated power to dispense from a law contains within itself the delegated power to dispense from the vindicative penalty which might be part of that law. A priest, thus, who has been delegated by the bishop to dispense from a particular penal law, may dispense from the penalty of the law—and this in virtue of delegated, not ordinary, power. This is an implicit concession of delegated power to dispense from vindicative penalties.

I. Implicit Grant of Power to Dispense from Vindicative Penalties

> **Canon 2236, § 2. Qui potest a lege eximere, potest quoque poenam legi adnexam remittere.**

Canonists [282] are wont to treat of the power of dispensing from vindicative penalties enunciated in this second paragraph of canon 2236 in relation to superiors who have the power to dispense from laws *in their own right.* They state the principle upon which this power is based: the dispensation from the obligation of observing a law is proportionately greater than the dispensation from the vindicative penalty which is attached to the law. For the vindicative penalty is part of the penal law [283] because the vindicative penalty is in reality contained in the penal law. Therefore, it follows that the

[281] Canon 2236, § 2. Sipos seems to deny that conceded ordinary power to dispense from a law includes the power to dispense from the penalty of the law; and asserts that the legislator alone has power to dispense from the penalties of his laws. Cf. Sipos, *Enchiridion Iuris Canonici,* § 232, p. 915.

[282] Cf. Blat, *De Delictis et Poenis,* n. 58; Berutti, *Institutiones Iuris Canonici,* VI, n. 38, V; Sipos, *Enchiridion Iuris Canonici,* § 232, p. 915; De Meester, *Compendium,* III, n. 1726; Coronata, *Institutiones Iuris Canonici,* IV, n. 1726; Roberti, *De Delictis et Poenis,* n. 268, B; Ayrinhac-Lydon, *Penal Legislation in the New Code of Canon Law,* n. 66; Augustine, *A Commentary on the New Code,* VIII, 108; Wernz-Vidal, *Ius Canonicum,* VII, n. 210; Gange, *Le Code de Droit Canonique,* III, n. 212, 2, 5°; Cavigioli, *Manuale Di Diritto Canonico,* p. 725, nota 1; Ferreres, *Institutiones Iuris Canonici,* II, n. 990; Woywod, *A Practical Commentary,* II, n. 2076; Salucci, *Il Diritto Penale,* I, 165, 166.

[283] Cf. Berutti, *Institutiones Iuris Canonici,* VI, n. 38, V; Wernz-Vidal, *Ius Canonicum,* VII, n. 210; Beste, *Introductio in Codicem,* p. 898.

superior, or legislator, who has the power in his own right to dispense from the whole, has the right and power to dispense from the part. Examples of the application of the principle are cited: the Roman Pontiff, since he or his successor alone has the power in his own right to dispense from the general penal law, has the power to dispense from any vindicative penalties attached to the law; and ordinaries who have the power to dispense, in their own right, from diocesan law or laws enacted by provincial or plenary councils [284] have the corresponding power to dispense from the vindicative penalties enacted in such laws.[285]

Now, the principle as stated and explained is correct but the application of the principle to those who *in their own right* may dispense from laws seems to be quite beyond the intention of the legislator when he formulated the principle in this second paragraph of canon 2236. For to state that the legislator, or his successor, who has formulated and promulgated a penal law has the power to dispense from the penalty of that law is but to repeat the principle already established in the first paragraph of canon 2236: Remissio . . . per dispensationem . . . concedi . . . potest ab eo qui poenam tulit, vel ab eius competente Superiore aut successore. . . ." Quite obviously, the legislator who has enacted the penal law, has likewise established or enacted the penalty. Consequently, he acquires the power to dispense from the penalty rather from the fact that he—or his predecessor or inferior—has established the penalty [286] than from the fact that he—or his superior or successor—has the power to dispense from his own law.[287] Both principles, it is true, apply; but the legislator seems to have intended that the first principle, that of the first paragraph of this canon, should be applied to those who *in their own right* have the power to dispense from laws; and that the second principle, that stated in the second paragraph, should be applied to those who enjoy the power of dispensing from laws, not in their own right, but by concession or delegation.[288] Otherwise,

[284] Canons 82, 291, § 2.

[285] Cf. Sipos, *Enchiridion Iuris Canonici,* § 232, p. 915; Blat, *De Delictis et Poenis,* n. 58; Coronata, *Institutiones Iuris Canonici,* IV, n. 1736.

[286] Canon 2236, § 1.

[287] Canon 2236, § 2.

[288] Chelodi, *Ius Poenale,* n. 29.

this second paragraph of canon 2236 seems to be a needless repetition of the first. In other words, legislators may dispense from vindicative penalties because they have established them in their laws; inferiors may dispense from those same vindicative penalties whenever they have been conceded ordinary power, or have been given delegated power to dispense from the laws to which the penalties are attached. In the first instance, the legislator has the power to dispense from vindicative penalties in his own right; and this is but an application of the first paragraph of canon 2236. In the second instance, the inferiors have the power to dispense from vindicative penalties, not in their own right, but because of participated power, because of the implicit concession of that power by superiors who possess the power in their own right; and this is but an application of the second paragraph of canon 2236.

This concession, then, of dispensatory power is an implicit grant of power to others than the legislator by which they may dispense from vindicative penalties otherwise reserved to the legislator or his superior or successor.

(a) *Implicit Ordinary Power to Dispense from Vindicative Penalties*

The implicit ordinary power to dispense from vindicative penalties is contained, as has been stated, in the explicit concession of ordinary power to dispense from the law to which the penalty is attached. Thus anyone who has been granted ordinary power to dispense from a law may dispense from the penalty which may be a part of that law.

It is apparent, therefore, that in order to discover who may enjoy this implicit grant of ordinary power to dispense from vindicative penalties, it must first be decided who precisely enjoys the explicit grant of ordinary power to dispense from laws to which penalties might be attached. In other words, a summary treatment must be made of the general norms of dispensation from laws, as contained in canons 80-83 in relation to derived on conceded power.

Canon 80 states that a dispensation from law may be granted by the one to whom the legislator or his successor or superior has conceded the faculty of dispensing.[289] As is obvious, such a one dis-

[289] Canon 80: "Dispensatio . . . concedi potest . . . nec non ab illo cui

penses from the law, not in his own right, but rather through participated or derived power, power which he has obtained from the legislator or his successor or superior. This power may be either ordinary or delegated. Here only the granting of ordinary derived power is to be considered.

The Roman Pontiff is the supreme legislator in the Church. But since it would be impossible for him personally to attend to all of the numerous affairs of the Church, he often concedes ordinary power to others to dispense from laws which are reserved, as it were, to himself. This power he concedes either to the Roman Curia or to ordinaries.

1. The Roman Curia

Occupying, it may be said, a middle position between the dispensatory power personal to the Roman Pontiff and the dispensatory power possessed by the inferior ordinaries of the Church is the power invested in the various dicasteries of the Roman Curia. The Sacred Congregations, Tribunals, and Offices, each given its respective competence, have been constituted by the Pope; and to each of these the Roman Pontiff grants or entrusts a share of his jurisdiction over the laws of the Church.[290] Each of the various Congregations or Tribunals or Offices are empowered to expedite matters pertinent to its own designated field of activity as often as these matters are brought to the attention of the Holy See. These various dicasteries, as they are called, function entirely in the name of the Roman Pontiff and with only such powers as have been conceded to them by him.[291] Consequently, their authority is quasi-supreme, although naturally it is lower than the absolutely supreme authority possessed personally by the Pope. The power which they enjoy is, of course, ordinary derived power, power which has either been conceded to them by the Pope by means of the general law, or may be given to them at any time directly by the Pope.[292]

iidem [conditor legis, eius successor vel Superior] facultatem dispensandi concesserint."

[290] Canon 243.

[291] Canon 243, § 1.

[292] Cf. canons 246-264. As an example of jurisdiction granted over and above the powers mentioned in the Code, cf. the *Motu proprio* of Pius XI,

Therefore, when one of the dicasteries, acting within its competence as established by law or by the Pope directly, may dispense from a certain law or precept of the Church, it may likewise dispense from any vindicative penalties which may be attached to that particular law or precept. Thus, for example, the Sacred Congregation of the Council may dispense the secular clergy and faithful from precepts given to them by their proper local ordinary.[293] Consequently this Congregation may likewise dispense clergy and laity from any vindicative penalties which may be attached to such precepts.[294] The power which the Congregation here exercises in dispensing from the precept or law is ordinary derived power, because the Pope alone, as superior jurisdictionally to the local ordinary in this instance, has the power to dispense from such precepts or laws; and the Congregation enjoys this same power because that power has been conceded to it by the Pope in the common law. And the power which the Congregation here exercises in dispensing from the vindicative penalty is implicit ordinary power, because it enjoys that power only because it has been given the ordinary power of dispensing from the precept: which is merely an application of canon 2236, § 2. It should be noted, however, that in respect to such dispensations pontifical approval is necessary, unless faculties for granting the dispensation in question have been given to the dicastery which is dealing with the case.[295]

2. Ordinaries

In order to facilitate the government of the Church at large and the better to provide for the greater good and salvation of the faithful, it has always been the custom of the Holy See to grant ample dispensatory powers to ordinaries. This power is expressly conferred in various ways, either directly by the Pope or the Sacred

Sancta Dei Ecclesia, March 25, 1938—*AAS,* XX (1938), 154-159, which extended the jurisdiction of the Sacred Congregation for the Oriental Church.

293 Canon 250, § 1, § 2.

294 Cf. Berutti, *Institutiones Iuris Canonici,* VI, n. 38, II, 1, b, p. 102.

295 Canon 244, § 2: "Gratiae quaevis . . . indigent pontificia approbatione, exceptis iis pro quibus eorundem Officiorum, Tribunalium, Congregationum Moderatoribus speciales facultates tributae sint. . . ."

Congregations of the Roman Curia, or by the law of the Code. These express concessions shall be treated here briefly.[296]

Special concessions of faculties are sometimes made by the Pope personally or by the competent Congregation of the Roman Curia to ordinaries. Thus, the Roman Pontiff may, during trying times, such as those immediately following a world-wide war, grant to ordinaries special powers to dispense from certain general laws of the Church.[297] If any vindicative penalties were attached to such laws, they too could be dispensed by the ordinary. The quinquennial faculties granted to the bishops of the United States are another example of such an explicit concession of dispensatory power.[298]

The law itself occasionally grants to ordinaries ordinary power to dispense from the general law of the Church. This concession of power is made at times to all ordinaries and at other times only to local ordinaries. A commentary of each individual instance of explicit concession of dispensatory power is beyond the scope of this dissertation; some instances, however, warrant at least brief commentaries.

Canon 15 states that in a doubt of fact an ordinary can dispense

[296] Cf. Reilly, *The General Norms of Dispensation,* pp. 64-94 for a more complete treatment. Cf. also Brys, "De potestate Episcoporum dispensandi in legibus Ecclesiae generalibus," *Collationes Brugenses,* XXIX (1929), 144-164; Vermeersch-Creusen, *Epitome,* I, n. 174; Brys, *De Dispensatione,* pp. 125 ss.; Augustine, *A Commentary on the New Code,* I, 178; Van Hove, *Commentarium Lovaniense in C. I. C.,* I, nn. 389-391; 396-414; Coronata, *Institutiones Iuris Canonici,* I, n. 279; Hilling, "Begriff und Umfang der potestas jurisdictionis ordinaria et delegata," *AKKR,* CIV (1924), 195 ss.; Del Guidice, *Privilegio, Dispensa ed Epicheia,* p. 47; Michiels, *Normae Generales,* II, 468; Maroto, *Institutiones,* I, nn. 689-690; Prümmer, *Manuale Iuris Canonici* (4. ed., Friburgi Briscoviae: Herder, 1922), Q. 86; Gasparri, *Tractatus Canonicus de Matrimonio* (Parisiis, 1892), I, n. 405; Crisci, "De Delegatione a iure in iure canonico vigente," *Apollinaris,* X (1937), 522-525; Toso, *Commentaria Minora,* II, 165; Chelodi, *Ius de Personis,* n. 127; Wernz-Vidal, *Ius Canonicum,* II, n. 366; V, n. 411; Von Kienitz, *Generalvikar und Offizial auf Grund des Codex Iuris Canonici,* pp. 74-76.

[297] Cf. Decretum S. Congr. Consist., Oct. 25, 1918—*AAS,* X (1918), 481-486 for such examples.

[298] Cf. Bouscaren, *Canon Law Digest* (2 vols., Milwaukee: Bruce Publishing Co., 1934-1941), II, 5, canon 66 for the latest formula of quinquennial faculties for the United States.

from all laws provided that the law in question is one from which the Roman Pontiff is wont to grant a dispensation.[299] A doubt of fact exists when it is uncertain whether an act or a person has the conditions required for the application of the law.[300] Not every doubt of fact suffices, however; the uncertainty must be positive: weighty reasons must be present both for affirming and denying the fact. Moreover, the doubt must have some objective foundation: there must be something which objectively gives rise to the doubt existing in the mind. A merely negative or subjective doubt certainly does not suffice, for such a doubt is equivalent to ignorance.

The concession of power, too, is made only when there is a question of a law which the Pope is accustomed to relax. Obviously, it would not be reasonable if an ordinary were to be empowered to grant a dispensation which the Roman Pontiff would not ordinarily grant. There are certain laws which the Roman Pontiff does not relax, even though he could do so.

Whenever, consequently, the conditions of this canon are fulfilled, the ordinary is empowered to grant the doubtfully required dispensation. The power is ordinary derived power, explicitly conceded to all ordinaries.[301] It follows, then, that, under these same conditions these ordinaries may dispense from any vindicative penalties that might be attached to such laws. In other words, if the positive objective doubt in regard to a penal law exists, the ordinary has the power, in virtue of the implicit grant of canon 2236, § 2, to dispense from the vindicative penalties which are but a part of the penal law. For example, if there exists a positive doubt with a clear objective foundation that the norms of the law forbidding a plurality of residential benefices[302] are not applicable in a particular case, the ordinary has the power to dispense from that law. And precisely

[299] Canon 15: ". . . in dubio autem facti potest Ordinarius in eis dispensare, dummodo agatur de legibus in quibus Romanus Pontifex dispensare solet."

[300] Cf. Coronata, *Institutiones Iuris Canonici,* I, n. 18; Cicognani, *Canon Law,* p. 585.

[301] Canon 15 speaks of ordinaries without qualification, and therefore, under the circumstances, this power is enjoyed not only by local ordinaries, but also by major superiors of clerical exempt institutes with respect to their own subjects. Cf. canons 198, § 1; 488, 2°, 8°.

[302] Cf. canons 156; 1439.

because he enjoys the power to dispense from the law, he may, if in the case a priest already had willfully taken possession of the benefices, dispense that priest from the vindicative penalty *latae sententiae* established in canon 2396.[303]

Another express concession by law of dispensatory power to ordinaries in regard to general laws is made in canon 81. In her customary solicitude for the welfare of her subjects the Church has wisely considered the possibility that harm rather than good might result if a situation should arise which demands an immediate dispensation but which the ordinary can not grant, because he finds himself without an express faculty to provide for the emergency; and so she has made an express concession of ordinary power whereby ordinaries [304] are empowered to grant any dispensation from the general law which the Holy See itself is wont to grant, under certain conditions: if it would be difficult to have recourse to the Holy See to obtain the required reserved dispensation and at the same time there would be danger of grave harm in delay.[305]

The conditions must be present. Difficulty of recourse involves several elements: recourse should be difficult, not impossible, and the difficulty should be judged in reference to the time which might be allowed to elapse before the reasonably feared harm will arise.[306]

[303] Canon 2396: Clericus, qui assecutus pacificam possessionem officii vel beneficii cum priore incompatibilis, prius quoque retinere praesumpserit contra praescriptum can. 156, 1439, utroque privatus ipso iure exsistat."

[304] Again, canon 81 also treats of ordinaries without qualification and thereby includes all ordinaries, not only local ordinaries. Cf. canon 198, § 1.

[305] Canon 81: "A generalibus Ecclesiae legibus Ordinarii infra Romanum Pontificem dispensare nequeunt, ne in casu quidem peculiari . . . nisi difficilis sit recursus ad Sanctam Sedem et simul in mora sit periculum gravis damni, et de dispensatione agatur quae a Sede Apostolica concedi solet." Cf. also Suarez, *Tractatus de Legibus et Deo Legislatore,* VI, c. 14, n. 10; Ojetti, *Commentarium in Codicem Iuris Canonici,* I, pp. 330-332; Brys, *De Dispensatione,* pars I, sect. 2, cap. 3; Maroto, *Institutiones,* I, n. 302; Chelodi, *Ius de Personis,* n. 86; Van Hove, *Commentarium Lovaniense in C. I. C.,* I, nn. 396-401; 408-413; Biederlach-Führich, *De Religiosis,* n. 39; Vermeersch-Creusen, *Epitome,* I, n. 594; II, nn. 305, 556; Vromant, *Ius Missionariorum, Introductio et Normae Generales,* n. 195 ss.; Michiels, *Normae Generales,* II, 484; Coronata, *Institutiones Iuris Canonici,* I, n. 112.

[306] Cf. Reilly, *The General Norms of Dispensation,* p. 75; Cicognani, *Canon Law,* p. 838.

The recourse is to be understood as the ordinary means of recourse, not extraordinary methods; and this ordinary recourse is that made to the Holy See, prescinding from the possibility or ease of approaching someone close at hand who might have the necessary power.[807] Danger of grave harm, or a reasonable fear of any grave harm, which may result if someone must wait until a dispensation can be obtained from the Holy See, is sufficient. And, finally, for the same reason mentioned above,[808] the concession of power is made only when there is a question of a law which the Pope is accustomed to relax. Under these conditions, any ordinary may dispense from any general law of the Church.

And in these same cases the ordinary may dispense from vindicative penalties which may have been incurred because of the violation of such laws.[809] Citing the same example used above, if, in time of emergency—as during a war—one priest had taken two or even three parishes under his care in violation of canon 1439, the local ordinary, under the conditions set forth in canon 81, would have the power to dispense that priest from the restrictions and stipulations of canon 1439; and he would likewise have the power then to dispense that priest from the vindicative penalty which he had incurred in virtue of canon 2396. The bishop, in this instance, would be using the dispensatory power expressly granted to him by canon 81 to dispense from the general law of canon 1439; and he would be using the dispensing power implicitly granted to him by canon 2236, § 2 in dispensing from the vindicative penalty of canon 2396. This latter power, it should be noted, is far more extensive than the power the ordinary enjoys under canon 2237,[810] which shall be treated shortly.

A further concession of dispensatory power is made in canon 82,[811] and it is obviously a derived power which is enjoyed only by

[807] Cf. Reilly, *The General Norms of Dispensation,* p. 76.

[808] Cf. *supra,* p. 116.

[809] Cf. Coronata, *Institutiones Iuris Canonici,* IV, n. 1736; Chelodi, *Ius Poenale,* n. 29; Ayrinhac-Lydon, *Penal Legislation in the New Code of Canon Law,* n. 66; Augustine, *A Commentary on the New Code,* VIII, 108.

[810] Cf. Coronata, *Institutiones Iuris Canonici,* IV, n. 1736.

[811] Canon 82: "Episcopi aliique locorum Ordinarii dispensare valent . . . in legibus Concilii provincialis ac plenarii ad normam can. 291, § 2, non vero in

local ordinaries. For canon 82 confers on each local ordinary of the territory over which the jurisdiction of the particular council extends, the ordinary power to dispense, in accordance with canon 291, § 2, that is, "in particular cases and for a just cause,[312] the laws enacted by plenary or provincial councils. This is a concession of power to the local ordinary, since he possesses no inherent authority to relax laws enacted by such councils.[313] For to the council as a collegiate group the supreme legislator has bestowed jurisdiction superior to that possessed personally and separately by the members of the council; and the legislator in a council is the *coetus episcoporum*,[314] and not any one individual of the assembled members.[315] In consequence, therefore, the power which the local ordinary possesses in virtue of canon 82 to dispense from laws thus enacted is communicated or expressly conceded ordinary power.

Applying canon 2236, § 2 once again, the local ordinary may dispense from any and all vindicative penalties established by the conciliar law from which he may dispense "in particular cases and for a just cause." And once again the local ordinary receives an implicit grant of power to dispense from vindicative penalties because he enjoys an express grant of power to dispense from a law which in general is beyond his jurisdiction.

(b) *Implicit Delegated Power to Dispense from Vindicative Penalties*

Just as implicit ordinary power to dispense from vindicative penalties is contained in the explicit concession of ordinary power to dispense from the law to which the vindicative penalty is attached, so implicit delegated power to dispense from vindicative penalties

legibus quas speciatim tulerit Romanus Pontifex pro illo peculiari territorio, nisi ad normam can. 81."

[312] Canon 291, § 2: "Decreta Concilii plenarii et provincialis promulgata obligant in suo cujusque territorio universo, nec Ordinarii locorum ab iisdem dispensare possunt, nisi in casibus particularibus et justa de causa."

[313] Cf. Reilly, *The General Norms of Dispensation*, pp. 89, 90.

[314] Cf. Chelodi, *Ius de Personis*, p. 364; Wernz, *Ius Decretalium*, I, 263-264; Suarez, *Tractatus de Legibus et Deo Legislatore*, VI, c. 15, n. 4.

[315] This is denied by Sipos, who seems to hold that the local ordinary here dispenses as legislator. Cf. Sipos, *Enchiridion Iuris Canonici*, § 232, p. 915.

is included in the express delegation to dispense from laws which have penalties attached thereto. Thus anyone who has been delegated to dispense from a law may dispense from the vindicative penalty which may be a part of that law.[316]

Canon 80 establishes the general norm for dispensations from law. The legislator, and his successor and superior, who have ordinary power to dispense in their own right from their own laws may delegate another to dispense from these laws. The Roman Pontiff alone as supreme legislator may delegate another to dispense from the general law of the Church; as supreme superior he may delegate another to dispense from any laws established by any other authority in the Church. All other superiors who have legislative power to make laws or jurisdiction to constitute precepts may delegate others to dispense from their particular laws; and the successors and superiors of the above legislators may likewise grant the same delegation of dispensatory power.[317] Whoever, therefore, has received this express delegation to dispense from a law may dispense from the vindicative penalty added to that law; and he does so with merely delegated power. For example, a Metropolitan may receive from the Roman Pontiff the delegated power to dispense his suffragan bishops under peculiar or unusual circumstances and according to his prudence and considered judgment from the stipulation of canon 955, § 1.[318] He may, in other words, receive delegation to dispense these bishops from the obligation of acquiring dimissorial letters before ordaining priests. And since the Metropolitan has this delegated power to dispense from the general law, he may dispense any of his suffragan bishops, who may have neglected to obtain the necessary dispensation from him, from the vin-

[316] Cf. Blat, *De Delictis et Poenis,* n. 58; Chelodi, *Ius Poenale,* n. 29; Coronata, *Institutiones Iuris Canonici,* IV, n. 1736; Ayrinhac-Lydon, *Penal Legislation in the New Code of Canon Law,* n. 66; Salucci, *Il Diritto Penale,* I, 165, 166; Wernz-Vidal, *Ius Canonicum,* VII, n. 210.

[317] Canon 80: "Dispensatio . . . concedi potest a conditore legis, ab eius successore vel Superiore, nec non ab illo cui iidem facultatem dispensandi concesserint."

[318] Cf. canon 955, § 1: "Unusquisque a proprio Episcopo ordinetur aut cum legitimis eiusdem litteris dimissoriis."

dicative penalty of suspension which they had incurred by virtue of canon 2373.[319]

Sipos [320] and Roberti [321] deny that the second paragraph of canon 2236 applies to those who may dispense from a law through delegated power, although neither gives reasons for the unique [322] opinion that only those who have ordinary power to dispense from a law may dispense from the penalty attached to the law. There seems to be no reason for restricting canon 2236, § 2 in this manner, since the Code makes no such distinction. Reason, too, upholds the other opinion. He who is delegated to dispense from a penal law may dispense his subject from the law and thereby dispense from the penalty before the delict is committed.[323] In other words, he has the power to remove the obligation of the entire law, including, therefore, the penalty which is but part of the law: when he exempts his subject from observing the law he exempts him likewise from observing the penalty which would have been incurred except for the dispensation. If he is empowered to dispense thus "ante patratum delictum," he enjoys the same power "post patratum delictum." [324]

II. Explicit Grant of Power to Dispense from Vindicative Penalties

> **Canon 2236, § 1. Remissio poenae . . . per dispensationem, si de poenis vindicativis, concedi . . . potest . . . ab eo cui haec potestas commissa est.**

[319] Canon 2373: "In suspensionem per annum ab ordinum collatione Sedi Apostolicae reservatam ipso facto incurrunt:

"1. Qui contra praescriptum can. 955, alienum subditum sine Ordinarii proprii litteris dimissoriis ordinaverint."

[320] *Enchiridion Iuris Canonici,* § 232, p. 915, nota 4.

[321] *De Delictis et Poenis,* n. 268, B.

[322] The majority of other canonists, *i. e.,* those who treat of the subject expressly, admit the opposite principle enunciated in this treatise. Cf. Ayrinhac-Lydon, *Penal Legislation in the New Code of Canon Law,* n. 66; Blat, *De Delictis et Poenis,* n. 58; Chelodi, *Ius Poenale,* n. 29; Coronata, *Institutiones Iuris Canonici,* IV, n. 1736; Salucci, *Il Diritto Penale,* I, pp. 165, 166; Wernz-Vidal, *Ius Canonicum,* VII, n. 210.

[323] Cf. Blat, *De Delictis et Poenis,* n. 58, p. 82.

[324] Cf. Blat, *De Delictis et Poenis,* n. 58, p. 82.

Just as in the dispensations from law there are certain express delegations and concessions of power granted by the legitimate superior, so in dispensations from vindicative penalties those who in accordance with canon 2236 have the power in their own right to dispense from these penalties [325] may concede or delegate this power directly to others. This express grant of power, therefore, may be either ordinary or delegated power.

(a) *Explicit Grant of Delegated Power to Dispense from Vindicative Penalties*

The similarity of terminology in canon 80 and canon 2236, § 1 is a clear indication of the similarity of principles. For the principle is exactly the same: "Potest quis per alium, quod potest facere per seipsum." [326] Whoever, therefore, has the power to dispense in his own right [327] from vindicative penalties may delegate that power to another directly. The Roman Pontiff may grant delegation to an inferior to dispense from any vindicative penalty of the common law; and other ordinaries may likewise delegate others to dispense from vindicative penalties of particular law. This is but an application of the norms of canon 199, the commentary of which is beyond the scope of this treatise. It will suffice to state that the power of dispensing from vindicative penalties may be delegated in accordance with the stipulations of canon 199.[328]

(b) *Explicit Grant of Ordinary Power to Dispense from Vindicative Penalties*

The Roman Pontiff, as supreme legislator, may concede ordinary power to dispense from the vindicative penalties of the common or general law of the Church whenever he sees fit to do so. He may do so directly. For example, during trying times of emergency, the Pope may grant this ordinary power to local ordinaries or to other

[325] Cf. *supra*, p. 72.

[326] Regula 68, *R.J.* in VI°.

[327] Cf. *supra*, p. 72.

[328] Canon 199: 1. Qui iurisdictionis potestatem habet ordinariam, potest eam alteri ex toto vel ex parte delegare, nisi aliud expresse iure caveatur.

ordinaries. Or ordinary dispensatory power may be conceded directly by the general law of the Church. The grant of power is express because it is given directly; it is ordinary power because it is conceded directly to a particular office and indirectly to the incumbent who occupies that office.[329] It is derived or participated power because it belongs to the office not by its very nature, but rather by concession of legitimate authority.[330]

There are many examples of this concession of ordinary power by law—to the various dicasteries of the Roman Curia, to ordinaries, and, finally, to confessors.

1. The Roman Curia

Just as the Roman Pontiff has entrusted to the various dicasteries of the Roman Curia a share in his supreme jurisdiction over the laws of the Church,[331] so he has also conceded to them power and jurisdiction to dispense from vindicative penalties within the limits of their respective competencies. In matters of the internal forum, the Sacred Penitentiary may grant dispensations from vindicative penalties *a iure* or *ab homine* established by general or particular law or inflicted by any ecclesiastical superior.[332] The Sacred Congregation of the Council may dispense from vindicative penalties inflicted upon clerics or the faithful *per modum praecepti* by their proper local ordinaries.[333] Exactly the same power is enjoyed by the Sacred Congregation of the Propagation of the Faith in relation to the clerics and faithful under its jurisdiction.[334] The Sacred Congregation for Religious may remit penalties inflicted *per modum praecepti*

[329] Canon 197, § 1.

[330] Canon 197, § 2. Cf. Michiels, *Normae Generales,* II, 469-471; Vermeersch-Creusen, *Epitome,* I, n. 277; Coronata, *Institutiones Iuris Canonici,* I, n. 278, nota 3; De Meester, *Compendium,* I, nn. 444-448; Crisci, "Evolutio historica delegationis a iure," *Apollinaris,* IX (1936), 270-299; idem, "De delegatione a iure in iure canonico vigente," *Apollinaris,* X (1937), 513-535; Reilly, *The General Norms of Dispensation,* pp. 57-59.

[331] Cf. *supra,* p. 113.

[332] Canon 258. Cf. Berutti, *Institutiones Iuris Canonici,* VI, n. 38, II, 1, a, p. 102.

[333] Canons 250, 1601. Cf. Berutti, *Institutiones Iuris Canonici,* VI, n. 38.

[334] Canon 252. Cf. Berutti, *Institutiones Iuris Canonici,* VI, n. 38.

bý a superior in a clerical exempt religious institute, and those penalties inflicted by any religious superior upon members of any religious institute or society of men or women who live together "more religiosorum." [335] Finally, the Sacred Roman Rota, as a court of appeals, may remit any and all vindicative penalties inflicted by means of condemnatory judicial sentence by any ecclesiastical authority inferior jurisdictionally to the Roman Pontiff.[336] This latter remission of a penalty, as has been noted before,[337] is in reality not a dispensation of the vindicative penalty.

2. Ordinaries

The general law of the Church also concedes ordinary power to dispense from vindicative penalties of the general law to ordinaries in canon 2237. This concession of power will be treated in detail in the following chapter.

3. Confessors

Express concession of dispensatory power are granted to confessors in canon 2290, in more urgent cases as defined in that canon, first in regard to suspending the vindicative penalty and secondly in regard to a real dispensation in extraordinary cases. This express concession of power to confessors will be treated in its proper place.[338]

C. *Ex Officio Dispensatory Power of Judges*

Canon 2236, § 3. Judex qui ex officio applicat poenam a Superiore constitutam, eam semel applicatam remittere nequit.

Whenever a vindicative penalty is inflicted by means of a judicial sentence, it is the judge appointed to hear the particular case who

[335] Canon 251. Cf. Berutti, *Institutiones Iuris Canonici,* VI, n. 38.

[336] Canons 259, 1599. Cf. Berutti, *Institutiones Iuris Canonici,* VI, n. 38, II, 1, c, p. 103.

[337] Cf. *supra,* p. 93.

[338] Cf. *infra,* p. 124.

applies the penalty. The penalty itself has been established by the competent and legitimate superior in accordance with canon 2220, § 1, either by law, general or particular, or by precept. If the vindicative penalty is established as a *ferendae sententiae* penalty, the judge applies the penalty by means of a condemnatory judicial sentence; if it is a *latae sententiae* penalty the judge, either at the prudent will of his superior, or at the insistance of an interested party, or finally *ex officio* because of the common good, officially confirms the penalty by means of a declaratory judicial sentence.[339] In either case, the judge acts merely as a judge *ex officio*, who has no jurisdiction over the accused in the external forum outside of his judicial power; [340] he merely applies a penalty which is established or inflicted [341] by his superior. When the judge has decided a case commissioned to him by his superior and has applied the penalty, his power over the case ceases and he has no further authority to act, unless he has received special authorization *ex alio titulo* to act.[342] Thus, for example, the *officialis* of the diocese, as judge, may apply a *ferendae sententiae* vindicative penalty of the general law. Once he has applied the penalty, he may not dispense from it, unless, of course, he has received the faculty to do so either from the competent superior, or the Code,[343] or the competent Sacred Congregation. This principle is but a corollary of the principle established in the first paragraphs of canon 2236 and canon 2220. The judge is not competent to dispense from the penalties precisely because he has neither established nor inflicted them.[344] The vindicative penalties thus applied by means of a condemnatory sentence by the judge *ex officio* may be dispensed only by the superior who has constituted the judge, or his superior, successor, or by one to

[339] Cf. canons 2223, § 4; 2225.

[340] Cf. Berutti, *Institutiones Iuris Canonici*, VI, n. 38, VI.

[341] Cf. canon 2236, § 1.

[342] Cf. Wernz-Vidal, *Ius Canonicum*, VII, n. 210; Ayrinhac-Lydon, *Penal Legislation in the New Code of Canon Law*, nn. 35, 66; Augustine, *A Commentary on the New Code*, VIII, 108; Coronata, *Institutiones Iuris Canonici*, IV, n. 1736; Berutti, *Institutiones Iuris Canonici*, VI, n. 38, VI.

[343] Cf. canon 1640, § 2.

[344] "De se judex ius dicit, non condit."—Wernz-Vidal, *Ius Canonicum*, VII, n. 165.

whom he has commissioned the power.[345] Penalties *latae sententiae* applied by means of a declaratory sentence by the judge *ex officio* may be dispensed only by the ecclesiastical superior who has established the penalty—or his successor, superior, or by one commissioned to do so by the legitimate and competent authority.[346]

Canon 2236, § 3 speaks only of judges who "*ex officio apply* a penalty constituted by a superior." If the judge himself establishes or inflicts a vindicative penalty, in accordance with canon 1640, § 2,[347] upon contumacious parties or those who exhibit a definite lack of reverence and obedience to the ecclesiastical tribunal,[348] he may dispense from that penalty during the course of the trial.[349] This is an application of canon 2236, § 1, for the judge does not apply a penalty, but in reality establishes and inflicts it in accordance with the faculty given him by the Code.

[345] Cf. Berutti, *Institutiones Iuris Canonici,* VI, n. 38, VI; Wernz-Vidal, *Ius Canonicum,* VII, n. 165.

[346] Canon 2236, § 1.

[347] Canon 1640, § 2: "Omnes, judicio assistentes, qui reverentiae et obedientiae tribunali debitae graviter defuerunt, iudex, etiam illico et incontinenti si coram tribunali sedente in id quis peccaverit, potest censuris quoque aliisve congruis poenis ad officium reducere, advocatos praeterea et procuratores etiam iure alias causas apud tribunali ecclesiastica pertractandi privare."

[348] Cf. Ayrinhac-Lydon, *Penal Legis lation in the New Code of Canon Law,* n. 35.

[349] Cf. Coronata, *Institutiones Iuris Canonici,* IV, n. 1736; Berutti, *Institutiones Iuris Canonici,* VI, n. 38, VI; Wernz-Vidal, *Ius Canonicum,* VII, nn. 210, 211.

CHAPTER VII

EXTENDED POWERS OF ORDINARIES TO DISPENSE FROM VINDICATIVE PENALTIES

Canon 2237, § 1. In casibus publicis potest Ordinarius poenas latae sententiae iure communi statutas remittere, exceptis:

1°. Casibus ad forum contentiosum deductis;

3°. Poenis inhabilitatis ad beneficia, officia, dignitates, munera in Ecclesiae, vocem activam et passivam eorumve privationis, suspensionis perpetuae, infamiae iuris, privationis iuris patronatus et privilegii seu gratiae a Sede Apostolica concessae.

2. In casibus vero occultis, firmo praescripto can. 2254 et 2290, potest Ordinarius poenas latae sententiae iure communi statutas per se vel per alium remittere, exceptis censuris specialissimo vel speciali modo Sedi Apostolicae reservatis.

Article I. General Notions

A. *The Dispensation*

By virtue of their office ordinaries may dispense from *latae sententiae* vindicative penalties established by themselves or by their predecessors; but in order that the need of recurring to Rome may not arise too often, more extensive powers have been granted to them by common law. Canon 2237 is a direct and express concession to ordinaries of ordinary power to dispense from vindicative penalties of the common law of the Church. It is an application of canon 2236, § 1, which states that vindicative penalties can be remitted or dispensed from "ab eo cui haec potestas commissa est," for to the ordinary is conceded a power over the general laws of the Church, a power which normally is reserved to the Roman Pontiff. As has been shown,[1] *latae sententiae* vindicative penalties of the

[1] Cf. *supra*, p. 87.

general law may be remitted by ordinaries other than the Roman Pontiff only through participated or derived power. Such derived power, although ordinary, is conceded in canon 2237. Consequently, the dispensation which the ordinary is empowered to grant is a dispensation in the strict sense of that term; it is the total remission of the vindicative penalty, an act of jurisdiction.

There is no prescribed form for the dispensation from vindicative penalties granted by ordinaries in virtue of canon 2237.[2] The ordinary needs but to express the fact that a dispensation from the penalty is granted; he may do so verbally or he may grant the dispensation in writing, for example, in the mandates which he may give to a penitent in response to a recourse to him as the competent superior. However, if the vindicative penalty was inflicted in writing, it is best for the ordinary to grant the dispensation likewise in writing, although there is no obligation to do so.[3]

B. *The Subject of the Dispensatory Power*

The dispensatory power conceded in canon 2237 is granted to ordinaries. Consequently, all ecclesiastical authorities who are comprehended in that term, according to canon 198,[4] enjoy the dispensatory power over vindicative penalties granted in canon 2237. These, then, are the jurisdictional superiors who possess the dispensatory power over vindicative penalties, which power will vary in accordance with the extent of the individual superior's jurisdiction.

The most fundamental principle underlying the designation of those who may grant dispensations from vindicative penalties is set forth in canon 201, §1, which states that "the power of jurisdiction

[2] Cf. canon 2239. Cf. also Chelodi, *Ius Poenale,* n. 29.

[3] Cf. canon 2239, § 2.

[4] Cf. canon 198, § 1: In iure nomine *Ordinarii* intelliguntur, nisi quis expresse excipiatur, praeter Romanum Pontificem, pro suo quisque territorio Episcopus residentialis, Abbas vel Praelatus *nullius* eorumque Vicarius Generalis, Administrator, Vicarius et Praefectus Apostolicus, itemque ii qui praedictis interim ex iuris praescripto aut ex probatis constitutionibus succedunt in regimine, pro suis vero subditis Superiores maiores in religionibus clericalibus exemptis.

2. Nomine autem *Ordinarii loci* seu *locorum* veniunt omnes recensiti, exceptis Superioribus religiosis.

can be exercised directly only over subjects."[5] Accordingly, a superior-subject relationship must be established before any claim to dispensatory power over an individual person can be substantiated. In other words, an ordinary who is granted dispensatory power can exercise that power only over those over whom he has jurisdiction.[6]

In regard to local ordinaries, who are territorial superiors, this superior-subject relationship arises in various ways. It is determined primarily by valid baptism, and in addition[7] by possession of a domicile,[8] or of a quasi-domicile,[9] or, in the case of *vagi,* by actual residence in the territory of the one who has the dispensatory power.[10] In the first two cases it is possession of the domicile or quasi-domicile which establishes the jurisdictional relationship and not the actual presence in the territory. Therefore, a person who is temporarily absent from his domicile or quasi-domicile does not cease to be a subject of the superior of that territory and the latter can exercise his dispensatory power in favor of such a subject even when he is outside the territory.[11] Similarly, this jurisdictional relationship arises, in the case of clerics, from the fact of incardination into a particular territory;[12] and in the case of non-exempt religious, from the location of the religious house to which they are attached.[13]

If the dispensatory power is exercised in the internal sacramental

[5] Cf. canon 201, § 1: Potestas jurisdictionis potest in solos subditos directe exerceri.

[6] Cf. Reilly, *The Principles of Dispensation,* pp. 95-99; Blat, *De Delictis et Poenis,* n. 59.

[7] Cf. canons 12; 87.

[8] Cf. canons 92, § 1, § 3; 94, § 1, § 3.

[9] Cf. canons 92, § 2, § 3; 94, § 1, § 3.

[10] Cf. canons 91; 94, § 2.

[11] Cf. canon 201, § 3: "Nisi aliud ex rerum natura aut ex iure constet, potestatem iurisdictionis voluntariam seu non-iudicialem quis exercere potest . . . extra territorium existens, aut in subditum e territorio absentem." Cf. also Wernz-Vidal, *Ius Canonicum,* VII, n. 215; Reilly, *The General Norms of Dispensation,* p. 98.

[12] Cf. canon 111. Cf. also McBride, *Incardination and Excardination of Seculars,* The Catholic University of America Canon Law Studies, n. 145 (Washington, D. C.: The Catholic University of America Press, 1941), pp. 387, 388; Blat, *De Delictis et Poenis,* n. 59.

[13] Cf. canon 500, § 1. Cf. also Blat, *De Delictis et Poenis,* n. 59.

forum, the jurisdictional relationship is verified by the penitential character of the one who presents himself to the competent superior. Consequently, if a local ordinary is approached in the confessional, his jurisdiction extends over all those over whom he has sacramental jurisdiction according to canon 881, § 1,[14] and is not limited as it is in the external forum.

In regard to major religious superiors, this dispensatory power may be exercised only over their subjects.[15] A person becomes the subject of a religious superior by reason of juridic membership in the community which that superior governs.[16] Consequently, all religious—whether they be local superiors or their subjects—belonging to the various local communities which are united to form a province or similar division are the subjects of the major superior who is placed at the head of the province; and all members of the institute are the subjects of the Supreme Moderator of the institute.[17] The foregoing is true of the customary religious institutes. In some instances the principles will be different, as in the case of the members of monasteries *sui iuris* and monastic congregations. For the subjection of the members in a monastic congregation is not as complete with respect to the *Abbas Primas* and *Abbas Praeses* as is that of religious of other institutes to their respective major superiors. Except for the powers contained in canons 655 and 1594, § 4, the jurisdiction of the *Abbas Primas* and *Abbas Praeses* is determined by the constitutions of the institute and the special decrees of the Holy See.[18]

[14] Cf. canon 881, § 1.

[15] Cf. canon 198, § 1. Cf. also Augustine, *A Commentary on the New Code*, VIII, p. 110; Berutti, *Institutiones Iuris Canonici*, VI, n. 38, IV, p. 106; Blat, *De Delictis et Poenis*, n. 59, 2; Claeys-Bouuaert-Simenon, *Manuale Iuris Canonici*, I, p. 135; Cappello, *Summa Iuris Canonici*, III, n. 410 (hereafter cited as *Summa*); Cocchi, *Commentarium in Codicem Iuris Canonici*, VIII, 86; Fanfani, *De Iure Religiosorum*, pp. 72, 73; Michiels, *Normae Generales*, II, n. 480; Pejška, *Ius Canonicum Religiosorum* (3. ed., Friburgi in Brisg., 1932), p. 237; Pelle, *Le Droit Penal de L'Eglise* (Paris: P. Lethielleux, 1939), p. 70; Roberti, *De Delictis et Poenis*, I, 305, 306; Salucci, *Il Diritto Penale*, I, p. 167; Schaefer, *De Religiosis*, pp. 235, 236; Vermeersch-Creusen, *Epitome*, III, n. 254.

[16] Cf. Michiels, *Normae Generales*, II, n. 494.

[17] Cf. canon 502. Cf. also Blat, *De Delictis et Poenis*, n. 59, p. 85.

[18] Cf. canon 501, § 3.

As to the status of *peregrini*[19] as passive subjects of the dispensatory power of those ordinaries in whose territory the *peregrini* are actually staying, canonists are not agreed. In other words, prescinding from any express concessions of power granted by a competent superior, and presupposing that materially the particular dispensation from a certain vindicative penalty is within the limits of the dispensing ordinary's power, some canonists deny that the ordinary has the authority from the general law to dispense from vindicative penalties those *peregrini,* or transients, who are actually in his territory;[20] while others affirm that ordinaries do have the power to dispense *peregrini* in these cases.[21]

Those who deny this power of the ordinary in regard to *peregrini* state that canon 94 is an all-inclusive, and therefore exclusive, determination of subjects; and consequently they maintain that *peregrini* cannot be considered as true subjects of such a superior. The Code, they state, gives no general principle in regard to the exercise of jurisdiction over *peregrini;* but rather the Code's express inclusion of *peregrini* in some particular cases and instances[22] clearly indicates that they are to be excluded in other cases, and particularly in regard to the dispensation from vindicative penalties.[23]

Those who affirm this dispensatory power in regard to *peregrini* assert that no law is to be found which expressly declares that the temporary sojourn of *peregrini* is not sufficient to constitute a *titulus subjectionis* to the superior of that territory.[24] On the contrary, in at least one instance, the subjection of *peregrini* to a superior of the territory is determined by the very fact that they are present in

[19] Cf. canon 91: "Persona dicitur . . . peregrinus, si versetur extra domicilium et quasi-domicilium quod adhuc retinet."

[20] Cf. Wernz-Vidal, *Ius Canonicum,* VII, n. 215; also p. 225, nota 22; Coronata, *Institutiones Iuris Canonici,* I, n. 113, ad 2°; Chelodi, *Ius de Personis,* p. 145, nota 1; Roberti, *De Delictis et Poenis,* n. 271.

[21] Cf. Cappello, *Summa,* I, n. 130, ad 2°; Michiels, *Normae Generales,* II, n. 495; Maroto, *Institutiones,* I, n. 364; Claeys-Bouuaert-Simenon, *Manuale Iuris Canonici,* I, 233, p. 135; Reilly, *General Norms of Dispensation,* p. 100; Berutti, *Institutiones Iuris Canonici,* VI, n. 38, IV, p. 106.

[22] Cf. *v.g.,* canons 1043; 1045; 1245; 1313; 1320.

[23] Cf. Wernz-Vidal, *Ius Canonicum,* VII, p. 225, nota 22.

[24] Cf. Reilly, *The General Norms of Dispensation,* p. 100.

his territory.[25] They also appeal to the milder discipline introduced by the Code, declaring that it is far more in conformity with the spirit of the Code to amplify than to diminish dispensatory power which is granted in favor of the faithful in general.[26]

Although the former opinion seems more correct, the second opinion must be regarded as at least probable. And consequently, since there is a doubt of fact concerning the point in question, namely, that *peregrini* are to be regarded as subjects with reference to the dispensatory power of an ordinary, the ordinary can exercise his power of dispensing from vindicative penalties in accordance with canon 15.

It should be noted that the dispensatory power granted to ordinaries by canon 2237 allows dispensations from the vindicative penalties of the general law, in other words, dispensations from laws of an authority superior jurisdictionally to the dispensing ordinary. Consequently, it follows that an ordinary must have a just, reasonable cause for dispensing from the penalty; without such a cause the dispensation is illicit and invalid.[27] Only the Roman Pontiff can dispense validly from *latae sententiae* penalties of the common law without the valid reason required for dispensations imparted by prelates inferior to the Sovereign Pontiff.[28]

Such just and reasonable causes required before an ordinary can exercise the dispensatory power conceded to him in canon 2237 may be of various kinds, all of which may be reduced either directly or indirectly to that designated as *ad bonum commune.*[29] Such causes

[25] Cf. canon 14, § 1, 2°: (Peregrini adstringuntur) neque legibus territorii in quo versantur, iis exceptis quae ordini publico consulunt, vel actuum solemnia determinant.

[26] Cf. canon 200, § 1. Cf. also Reilly, *The General Norms of Dispensation,* p. 100; Michiels, *Normae Generales,* II, n. 495; Maroto, *Institutiones,* I, n. 364.

[27] Cf. canon 84, § 1: A lege ecclesiastica ne dispensetur sine justa et rationabili causa, habita ratione gravitatis legis a qua dispensatur; alias dispensatio ab inferiore data illicita et invalida est.

[28] Cf. DeMeester, *Compendium,* III, n. 1727; Coronata, *Institutiones Iuris Canonici,* IV, n. 1736; Augustine, *A Commentary on the New Code,* VIII, p. 107; Berutti, *Institutiones Iuris Canonici,* VI, n. 38, III, p. 108.

[29] Cf. DeMeester, *Compendium,* III, n. 1727; Berutti, *Institutiones Iuris Canonici,* VI, n. 38, III, p. 108.

may be private spiritual or temporal benefit or necessity, as in canon 2290, *v.g.*, the spiritual dignity of the person asking for the dispensation or his merit within the Church, or the amendment or reparation of damage or scandal.[30] Other similar causes may be present, but a just and reasonable cause must be present. If there is a doubt as to whether the cause is sufficient to allow the granting of the dispensation from the vindicative penalty, the ordinary may validly and licitly grant the dispensation.[31]

C. *The Object of the Dispensatory Power*

The object of the dispensation according to canon 2237 consists of "poenae latae sententiae iure communi statutas," in other words, all *latae sententiae* vindicative penalties established by the general law of the Church, excepting those which are expressly excluded in canon 2237, § 1. Therefore, the ordinary may dispense from such *latae sententiae* penalties of the common law, penalties which, according to the norms and principles established in canon 2236, § 1, are *per se* reserved to the Roman Pontiff. At first sight, because of the "reservation" of such penalties to the Pope as supreme legislator, it would seem that canon 2237 is an exception to canon 2236, § 1, and it is thus considered by some authors.[32] However, canon 2237 is in no way an exception to canon 2236, § 1; on the contrary, it is a direct application of that canon. For canon 2236, § 1 establishes the norm that *latae sententiae* vindicative penalties *a iure communi* are reserved, not only to the Roman Pontiff and his successor, but also to anyone to whom the Pope, either personally or through the agency of the general law of the Church, concedes such power.[33] The *latae sententiae* vindicative penalties of the general law are

[30] Cf. Augustine, *A Commentary on the New Code*, VIII, p. 107; Berutti, *Institutiones Iuris Canonici*, VI, n. 38, III, p. 108; DeMeester, *Compendium*, III, n. 1727.

[31] Cf. canon 84, § 2: Dispensatio in dubio de sufficientia causae licite petitur et potest licite et valide concedi.

[32] Cf. *v. g.*, Coronata, *Institutiones Iuris Canonici*, IV, n. 1736, p. 133.

[33] Cf. canon 2236, § 1: Remissio poenae . . . per dispensationem, si de poenis vindicativis, concedi tantum potest . . . vel ab eo cui haec potestas commissa est.

per se beyond the dispensatory powers of the ordinaries, and it is only through a concession of derived ordinary power that the latter enjoy the power to dispense from them.

All other *latae sententiae* vindicative penalties, therefore, are outside the dispensatory power of the ordinary as specified by canon 2237: those established by particular law or general precept, as well as *latae sententiae ab homine* vindicative penalties, namely, those established by particular precept. *Ferendae sententiae* vindicative penalties, too, whether established by general or particular law or precept, are beyond the scope of the dispensatory power conceded to ordinaries by this canon.[84] All such penalties are dispensed according to canon 2236.[85] It is to be noted, however, that *latae sententiae* vindicative penalties established in a particular territory by the Holy See or by an Ecumenical Council are by their very nature to be considered as *latae sententiae* vindicative penalties of the common law, and as such are included in the object of the dispensatory power of canon 2237. Therefore, the ordinary has the power to dispense from such *latae sententiae* penalties established for a particular territory.[86] No distinction is to be made here between *latae sententiae* vindicative penalties established for a particular territory by particular decrees of the Roman congregations and those which the Roman Pontiff has established for a particular territory.[87] Both are enacted by the Holy See, for the power of the Congregations and Offices of the Roman Curia is vicarious power, exercised in the name and by the authority of the Roman Pontiff,[88] and, therefore,

[84] Cf. Blat, *De Delictis et Poenis*, n. 59.

[85] Cf. Coronata, *Institutiones Iuris Canonici*, IV, n. 1737; Woywod, *A Practical Commentary*, II, n. 2077; Ayrinhac-Lydon, *Penal Legislation in the New Code of Canon Law*, nn. 67-70; Blat, *De Delictis et Poenis*, n. 59; Sole, *De Delictis et Poenis*, n. 147; Lega, *De Delictis et Poenis*, n. 131.

[86] Cf. Berutti, *Institutiones Iuris Canonici*, VI, n. 38, IV, 3; p. 105, nota 1.

[87] Cf. Coronata, *Institutiones Iuris Canonici*, I, p. 108, nota 5, wherein he makes such a distinction.

[88] Cf. Reilly, *The General Norms of Dispensation*, p. 91; Augustine, *A Commentary on the New Code*, I, p. 178; Blat, *Commentarium Textus Codicis Iuris Canonici*, I (Romae: in Instituto Pii IX, 1921), n. 153; Cappello, *Summa*, I, n. 318, ad 3; Const. Pii X, *Sapienti Consilio*, 29 Iunii, 1908—*AAS*, I (1909), 7-9.

both are to be considered as *latae sententiae* penalties of the common law, ordinarily entirely beyond the dispensatory powers of the ordinary,[39] but, by virtue of canon 2237, within the scope of his derived dispensatory power.

Article II. The Dispensatory Power of Ordinaries in Public Cases

Canon 2237, § 1. In casibus publicis potest Ordinarius poenas latae sententiae iure communi statutas remittere, exceptis:

1°. Casibus ad forum contentiosum deductis;

3°. Poenis inhabilitatis ad beneficia, officia, dignitates, munera in Ecclesia, vocem activam et passivam, eorumve privationis, suspensionis perpetuae, infamiae iuris, privationis iuris patronatus et privilegii seu gratiae a Sede Apostolica concessae.

A. *The Public Cases*

The first paragraph of this canon determines the dispensatory power of ordinaries in regard to *latae sententiae* vindicative penalties established in the common law when the case presented is public. A public case is distinct from a public delict, for it involves not only the delict but the vindicative penalty incurred as a result of the commission of the delict. If the delict is public, according to the norms of canon 2197, 1°, the *latae sententiae* vindicative penalty incurred is presumed to be likewise public; and the case is a public case. However, in such a case it does not necessarily follow that the *latae sententiae* penalty incurred is always public, for it may occur that the delict is public in the sense that it has been committed publicly and the malice and blame ("dolus et cupla") of the delinquent has been divulged and publicized, but the *latae sententiae* penalty incurred by the commission of that delict is unknown to others. In such a case, the delict is considered as formally occult; [40] and

[39] Cf. canon 82. Cf. also Reilly, *loc. cit.*; Augustine, *loc. cit.*

[40] Cf. Coronata, *Institutiones Iuris Canonici,* IV, n. 1648; Lega, *De Delictis*

since the *latae sententiae* vindicative penalty incurred is occult, the case is an occult case.

A public case, therefore, in the sense of canon 2237, § 1 is one which involves a formally public delict or a public vindicative penalty or both. According to canon 2197, 1°, a public delict is one which has been divulged or publicized or is bound to be divulged or to become widely known because of the circumstances which surround it.[41] A delict may become public, therefore, in three distinct ways:

1. If the delict has been divulged;
2. If the delict has been committed under such circumstances that it is likely or bound to be divulged;
3. If the delict here and now is surrounded by such circumstances that the delinquent can and is likely to be detected.[42]

If the delict committed has been divulged, the delict is considered public. It makes no difference by whom it has been divulged or publicized, by the offender or by others who may have knowledge of it; neither does the fact that the delict has been divulged in good faith or bad, justly or unjustly, change its public nature. To determine just when a delict has been divulged or publicized is difficult. The Code itself is silent on this matter; and authors do not agree on the degree of publicity that must be present to allow one to state that the delict has been divulged. It is safe, however, to say that the delict may be said to be divulged if it is already known to the people of a community, or at least to the greater or major part of the inhabitants of a community,[43] no matter how they acquired the knowledge of the delict. If the delict is known to many persons of a community, but not to the major part, the delict is to be considered as not having been divulged, and, consequently, from the

et Poenis, n. 131; D'Annibale, *Summula,* I, n. 242, nota 52; Blat, *De Delictis et Poenis,* n. 120.

[41] Cf. canon 2197, 1°: [Delictum est] publicum, si iam divulgatum est aut talibus contigit seu versatur in adiunctis ut prudenter iudicari possit et debeat facile divulgatum iri.

[42] Cf. canon 2197, 1°. Cf. also Coronata, *Institutiones Iuris Canonici,* IV, n. 1645; Augustine, *A Commentary on the New Code,* VIII, p. 16.

[43] Cf. Ayrinhac-Lydon, *Penal Legislation in the New Code of Canon Law,* n. 6, b; Coronata, *Institutiones Iuris Canonici,* IV, n. 1645, a; Vermeersch-Creusen, *Epitome,* III, n. 384, 3.

standpoint of divulgence and publicity is not public. It may be public or become so in one of the other two ways, to be explained immediately, namely, by reason of the circumstances surrounding it either at the time of its commission or later, by which the delict is likely or bound to be divulged.

If the delict has been committed under such circumstances that it is likely or bound to be divulged, the delict also is public. In other words, if certain persons witnessed the commission of the delict, and the characters of these persons are such that they will certainly publicize their knowledge, the delict is a public one. The number of the persons possessing such knowledge is not important; the characteristics of such persons are. The original witnesses to the fact may have been few, but if they are talkative, the fact will be known to many.[44] On the other hand, quite a large number of persons may have witnessed the commission of the delict, and still the delict may remain occult, because such persons, who, for example, may be relatives of the guilty party, certainly will not reveal the fact to others. In other words, no definite norm may be established because this entire matter is one of fact, and a prudent judgment is the only possible rule to be followed. However, it should be particularly noted that it is not sufficient that the publicity of the fact *may* be foreseen, but the divulgence or publicity or the delict *must* be foreseen before the delict is to be considered public.[45]

If the delict here and now, after its commission, is surrounded by such circumstances that the delict can and must be detected, the delict is public. It matters not under what circumstances the delict was actually committed, whether or not it was perpetrated in the presence of witnesses. But here and now, by virtue, perhaps, of the carelessness or imprudence of the offender, or because of the diligence of interested parties or of public authority, the delict is bound to become known and publicized. These circumstances may be many

[44] Cf. Ayrinhac-Lydon, *Penal Legislation in the New Code of Canon Law*, n. 6, b; Coronata, *Institutiones Iuris Canonici*, IV, n. 1645; Vermeersch-Creusen, *Epitome*, III, n. 384; Lega, *De Delictis et Poenis*, n. 244, 4; Chelodi, *Ius Poenale*, n. 4, nota 6; Woywod, *A Practical Commentary*, II, n. 2027.

[45] Cf. canon 2197, 1°. Cf. also Coronata, *Institutiones Iuris Canonici*, IV, n. 1645.

and varied, according to the particular case in question, but if because of them the delict can be and is bound to be divulged or publicized, the delict is public.[46]

It may occur, under certain circumstances, that one and the same delict is occult in one place and public in another; or that a delict, at one time occult, may now be public. The peculiar circumstances surrounding the delict at the present time are to be considered in forming a prudent judgment as to whether the delict is public here and now.[47]

The vindicative penalty, likewise, may be public in the same manner. If it has been divulged or publicized or become known to the people of the community, or at least to the major part of the inhabitants of a community, the vindicative penalty may be considered to be public. If the penalty, however, is known to many persons of the community, but not to the greater or major part of them, it is to be considered as not having been divulged and, consequently, is not public, at least from the viewpoint of publicity. It may be public, or become so, by reason of the circumstances which surround it at the time of its incurrence or later, by which the penalty is likely or bound to become known. Thus, if the persons who have witnessed the commission of the delict and are, consequently, aware of the vindicative penalty incurred by the offender, or if persons who know, from some other source, of the vindicative penalty, even if they be very few in number, will publicize the fact, that penalty is public.[48] Again it should be noted that a vindicative penalty may be public in one place and occult in another, or public at some other time and occult here and now.[49] And circumstances which surround the pen-

[46] Cf. Coronata, *Institutiones Iuris Canonici,* IV, n. 1645.

[47] Coronata, *Institutiones Iuris Canonici,* IV, n. 1648; Berutti, *Institutiones Iuris Canonici,* VI, n. 3, III, C, 2, pp. 9, 10; Lega, *De Delictis et Poenis,* n. 313; Hollweck, *Die kirchlichen Strafgesetze,* § 5, nota 7.

[48] Cf. Rossi, "De sacerdotibus qui matrimonium etiam civile tantum contrahere praesumpserint quoad absolutionem a censura de qua in 2388, § 1"—*Perfice Munus,* XI (1936), p. 532, nota 2; p. 534, nota 1.

[49] Cf. Blat, *De Delictis et Poenis,* n. 120; Coronata, *Institutiones Iuris Canonici,* IV, n. 1648; Gasparri, *Tractatus canonicus de matrimonio,* I, n. 160; Hollweck, *Die kirchlichen Strafgesetze,* 5, nota 7; Chelodi, *Ius Poenale,* n. 4; Wernz, *Ius Decretalium,* VI, n. 17, V.

alty at the present time are to be taken into consideration in determining whether the penalty at the present time and in the present place is public.

A public case, therefore, in the sense of canon 2237, § 1 is one which involves a formally public delict or a public vindicative penalty or both. If the delict is public here and now, and the vindicative penalty incurred is public, the case is a public case. If the penalty is public here and now, even though previously or in another place it was occult, the case also is public. Consequently, if a declaratory judicial sentence has been given publicly or has been publicized, the case is a public case, since the vindicative penalty has now become public.[50] On the contrary, if the delict is either materially or formally occult here and now, the case cannot be a public case. Similarly, if the penalty is occult here and now, even though previously or in another place it was public, the case cannot be public in the sense of this canon.

B. *The Dispensatory Power*

The dispensatory power granted to ordinaries in canon 2237, § 1 to dispense in public cases from *latae sententiae* vindicative penalties of the common law of the Church is ordinary derived power.[51] Consequently, it may be delegated to others.[52] Thus, the ordinary may delegate this power to confessors of his diocese or territory.[53]

[50] Cf. Berutti, *Institutiones Iuris Canonici,* VI, n. 38, IV, 4; n. 86, II, p. 216, nota 2.

[51] Cf. canon 197, § 1. Cf. also Ayrinhac-Lydon, *Penal Legislation in the New Code of Canon Law,* n. 69; Chelodi, *Ius Poenale,* n. 30; Coronata, *Institutiones Iuris Canonici,* IV, n. 1737.

[52] Cf. canon 199, § 1. Cf. also Ayrinhac-Lydon, *Penal Legislation in the New Code of Canon Law,* n. 69; Berutti, *Institutiones Iuris Canonici,* VI, p. 106, Scholion; Chelodi, *Ius Poenale,* n. 30; Coronata, *Institutiones, Iuris Canonici,* IV, n. 1737; DeMeester, *Compendium,* III, n. 1727, p. 161, nota 4; Salucci, *Il Diritto Penale,* p. 167; Sole, *De Delictis et Poenis,* nn. 146, 147, 3; Wernz-Vidal, *Ius Canonicum,* VII, nn. 211, 215.

[53] Some canonists deny that this power may be delegated. Cf. Blat, *De Delictis et Poenis,* n. 59, n. 84: ". . . 'per se vel per alium,' quod bene adnotetur fuisse in § 1 omissum." Cf. also Augustine, *A Commentary on the New Code,* VIII, p. 110.

Moreover, this dispensatory power may be exercised in both the internal and the external forums,[54] for canon 202, § 3 states that if the forum for which the power is given is not expressed, the power is to be understood as applying to both the internal and external forums, unless the nature of the case demands one or the other.[55] Since canon 2237, § 1 concerns public cases, there is no demand to limit the exercise of the dispensatory power to one or the other of the forums.

C. The Excluded Cases

Certain *latae sententiae* vindicative penalties of the general law of the Church are excluded, in canon 2237, § 1, from the dispensatory power of ordinaries. As has been noted, the *latae sententiae* vindicative penalties of the common law of the Church are *per se* entirely beyond the jurisdiction of the ordinary. He enjoys dispensatory power over them solely by reason of a concession of derived power from the supreme legislator of the Church. In conceding such power, the Holy See, through the general law as enunciated in the Code, may restrict or limit its exercise. This it does in two instances, as outlined in canon 2237, § 1, 1°, 3°. In these cases—and many *latae sententiae* vindicative penalties fall into these classifications—the penalties remain beyond the scope of the dispensatory power of the ordinary and are reserved, as it were, to the Roman Pontiff as supreme legislator of the common law. He alone may dispense from them when the case is a public case.

1. Cases Brought to the Contentious Forum

As soon as a case is brought to a judicial court, the *latae sententiae* public vindicative penalty involved is removed from the dispensatory jurisdiction of the ordinary. This is but a restatement of a similar restriction of the dispensatory powers of ordinaries as

[54] Cf. Blat, *De Delictis et Poenis,* n. 59, 2; Berutti, *Institutiones Iuris Canonici,* VI, n. 38, IV, 3.

[55] Cf. canon 202, § 3: Si forum, pro quo potestas data est, expressum non fuerit, potestas intelligitur concessa pro utroque foro, nisi ex ipsa rei natura aliud constet.

established by the Council of Trent.[56] And since the phrase "casus ad forum contentiosum deducti" was introduced into the Code directly from the old law, it should be interpreted according to the old law[57] and according to the interpretations of approved authors and commentators of that law.[58] Consequently, whenever a case is brought to a judicial court, either in a criminal trial for the purpose of declaring the incurrence of a *latae sententiae* vindicative penalty of the common law[59] or in a civil trial for the purpose of determining the damages caused by an offense,[60] the case is said to have been brought to the contentious forum, and the dispensatory power of the ordinary ceases in regard to the *latae sententiae* vindicative penalties of the common law involved in the case.[61] This is true whether the case is brought before an ecclesiastical or a lay or civil court, provided, of course, that the civil or lay court is competent to treat of the matter at issue.[62] Some authors[63] maintain that the contentious forum of canon 2237, § 1, 1° is to be understood in the sense of the contentious trial mentioned and defined in canon 1552, 2, 1°;[64] and, therefore, only cases brought before a civil ecclesiastical court in civil actions instituted in order to obtain damages

[56] Cf. *supra*, p. 44. Conc. Trid., sess. XXIV, *de ref.*, c. 6.

[57] Cf. canon 6, 3°.

[58] Cf. canon 6, 2°.

[59] Cf. canon 2210, § 1, 1°.

[60] Cf. canon 2210, § 1, 2°.

[61] Cf. Ayrinhac-Lydon, *Penal Legislation in the New Code of Canon Law*, n. 70; Berutti, *Institutiones Iuris Canonici*, VI, n. 38, IV; Blat, *De Delictis et Poenis*, n. 59, 1°; Cocchi, *Commentarium in Codicem Iuris Canonici*, V, n. 56; Coronata, *Institutiones Iuris Canonici*, IV, n. 1737; Gasparri, *Tractatus Canonicus de Sacra Ordinatione*, I, n. 225; Salucci, *Il Diritto Penale*, pp. 169, 170; Sole, *De Delictis et Poenis*, n. 148; Santamaria, *Comentarios al Codigo Canonico*, VI, n. 109; Vermeersch-Creusen, *Epitome*, III, n. 431; Wernz-Vidal, *Ius Canonicum*, VII, n. 214, 3; Woywod, *A Practical Commentary*, II, n. 2077.

[62] Cf. canon 1553. Cf. Blat, *De Delictis et Poenis*, n. 59, 1°; Coronata, *Institutiones Iuris Canonici*, IV, n. 1737; Sole, *De Delictis et Poenis*, n. 148; Woywod, *A Practical Commentary*, II, n. 2077.

[63] Cf. Augustine, *A Commentary on the New Code*, VIII, 109; Eichmann, *Strafrecht*, p. 73; and his later work, *Kirchenrecht*, p. 689, n. 2.

[64] Cf. canon 1552, § 2, 1°: [Objectum iudicii sunt] personarum physicarum vel moralium iura persequenda aut vindicanda, vel earundem personarum facta iuridica declaranda; et tunc iudicium est *contentiosum*.

for a crime are to be included under canon 2237. This unique opinion, however, is untenable in view of the interpretation of the old law, the interpretation upheld commonly by canonists.[65]

As to the moment when a case may be considered to have been brought to the contentious forum, or—which is the same problem—when the dispensatory power of the ordinary ceases, canonists are not in agreement. Blat [66] maintains that a case is to be considered as brought to the contentious forum as soon as the judge, either in a trial instituted to declare a penalty or in one begun in order to obtain damages for a crime, accepts the libellus of the injured party or the accusation against the accused delinquent. From that moment the dispensatory power of the ordinary ceases in regard to the *latae sententiae* vindicative penalty involved in the case.

Reiffenstuel [67] is of the opinion—and gives arguments for his contention—that the moment of the *contestatio litis,* or the discussion between the parties involved in a particular case to determine the precise matter to be dealt with in the trial, determines whether a case has been brought to the contentious forum or not. D'Annibale,[68] denying that the citation of the accused party brings the case to trial, states that as soon as the judge begins to hear the case, as soon as he actually begins to listen to an account of the case, even though no witnesses have as yet been called, the case is to be considered as having been brought to the contentious forum. The very same opinion seems to be held by Sole,[69] although he rather vaguely states that the case is brought to the contentious forum as soon as the competent judge begins to treat of the case in question.

[65] Cf. Coronata, *Institutiones Iuris Canonici,* IV, p. 136, nota 3; Blat, *De Delictis et Poenis,* n. 59, 1°; Sole, *De Delictis et Poenis,* n. 148.

[66] Cf. *De Delictis et Poenis,* n. 59, 1°.

[67] Cf. *Ius Canonicum Universum,* lib. V, tit. 12, n. 232: "Ad forum contentiosum deductum dicitur omne et solum illud homicidium, vel aliud delictum, super quo ad iudicem iam delato facta est contestatio litis. . . . Ratio est, quia forum contentiosum dicitur ex eo, quod in illo contenditur seu litigetur, atque non contenditur in eo donec partes litigantes detur contradictio et contentio quod fit per litis contestationem."

[68] Cf. *Summula* (I, 252): "*Deductum ad forum contentiosum* accipimus, cum iudex per narrationem negotii causam audire ceperit."

[69] Cf. *De Delictis et Poenis,* n. 148: "Tunc casus dicitur deductus ad forum contentiosum cum iudex competens negotium pertractare ceperit."

The third, and more common, opinion [70] is that a case is considered to have been brought to the contentious forum as soon as the accused offender is legitimately cited by the judge to appear to answer charges, either civil (contentious) or criminal. The decree of citation must be legitimate, that is, issued by a competent judge, either at the insistence of the party suing for damages in contentious matters, or at the insistence of the promoter of justice or of the competent superior to declare a *latae sententiae* vindicative penalty in a criminal trial.[71] If, therefore, the judge before whom the case has been brought is absolutely incompetent,[72] whether he be a judge of an ecclesiastical or a civil court, the case is considered as not having been brought to the contentious forum.[73] Consequently, the case cannot be said to be brought to trial when the preliminary acts and inquisitions undertaken in preparation for a criminal trial [74] are being conducted.[75] Nor is the case brought to the contentious forum when the ordinary conducts an administrative—and not judicial—investigation in preparation for the declaration of a *latae sententiae* vindicative penalty *per modum praecepti*.[76]

Of these three basic opinions, the last is the correct opinion. The three opinions are formed according to the emphasis which their proponents place upon various words of the phrase used in canon 2237, § 1, 1°: "Exceptis casibus ad forum contentiosum deductis." The first opinion, that of Blat, seems to emphasize the word "deductis." In other words, a case is *brought* to the contentious forum as soon as the judge receives the libellus or the complaint of the

[70] Cf. Ayrinhac-Lydon, *Penal Legislation in the New Code of Canon Law*, n. 70; Woywod, *A Practical Commentary*, II, n. 2077; Coronata, *Institutiones Iuris Canonici*, IV, n. 1737; DeMeester, *Compendium*, III, n. 1717, p. 161, nota 5; Berutti, *Institutiones Iuris Canonici*, VI, n. 38, IV, 3°; Wernz-Vidal, *Ius Canonicum*, VII, n. 214; Vermeersch-Creusen, *Epitome*, III, n. 431.

[71] Cf. Berutti, *Institutiones Iuris Canonici*, V, n. 38, IV, 3°; Coronata, *Institutiones Iuris Canonici*, IV, n. 1737.

[72] Cf. canon 1557; 1558.

[73] Cf. Coronata, *Institutiones Iuris Canonici*, IV, n. 1737; Blat, *De Delictis et Poenis*, n. 59; Sole, *De Delictis et Poenis*, n. 148.

[74] Cf. canons 1939-1953.

[75] Cf. Wernz-Vidal, *Ius Canonicum*, VII, n. 214.

[76] Cf. D'Annibale, *Summula*, I, nn. 242, 322; Roberti, *De Delictis et Poenis*, n. 270; Wernz-Vidal, *Ius Canonicum*, VII, n. 214.

injured party in contentious matter or as soon as the judge accepts the accusation of the promoter of justice in criminal proceedings. The second opinion, that of Reiffenstuel and D'Annibale and Sole, seems to emphasize the word "contentiosum." A case, therefore, is brought to the *contentious* forum as soon as the parties involved in the civil or criminal case have taken part in the *contestatio litis* and have asserted their contentions or have responded with rebuttal.[77] The third opinion rather stresses the term "exceptis"; and its proponents base their contention on the purpose or reason of the exclusion of these cases from the dispensatory power of the ordinary.

Those cases brought to the contentious forum are excluded from the dispensatory power of the ordinary so that the use of proper jurisdiction on the part of the judge is not intruded upon by any jurisdictional act of another, in this instance by the dispensatory power of the ordinary.[78] In other words, as soon as the judge who is to hear a particular case on trial acquires jurisdiction over the matter at issue, the jurisdiction of others, in this case that of the ordinary, is forbidden by law to be exercised over the same matter. This is but a further application of the principle established in canon 1725, 5°: "lite pendente, nihil innovetur." And the judge acquires jurisdiction over the matter at issue, and the case becomes proper and exclusive to his court as soon as the accused is legitimately cited by the judge.[79] Moreover, the general principles of prevention, as established in canon 1568,[80] seem to apply in this case, so that

[77] Cf. Reiffenstuel (*Ius Canonicum Universum*, lib. V, tit. 12, n. 232): "Ratio est, quia forum contentiosum dicitur ex eo quod in illo contendatur seu litigetur, atque non contenditur in eo donec partes litigantes detur contradictio et contentio quod fit per litis contestationem."

[78] Cf. Berutti (*Institutiones Iuris Canonici*, VI, n. 38, IV, 3°): ". . . secus enim ordo iudiciorum et usus jurisdictionum perturbarentur." Cf. also Coronata (*Institutiones Iuris Canonici*, IV, n. 1737, p. 136, nota 4): ". . . . cum ratio hujus exceptionis eo tendat ne intercipiatur ordo iurisdictionum. . . ." Cf. also Lega, *De Delictis et Poenis*, nn. 130, 131; Wernz-Vidal, *Ius Canonicum*, VII, n. 215, p. 225, nota 23.

[79] Cf. canon 1725: Cum citatio legitime peracta fuerit . . . causa fit propria illius judicis aut tribunalis, coram quo actio instituta est . . . lis pendere incipit; et ideo statim locum habet principium: "lite pendente, nihil innovetur."

[80] Cf. canon 1568: Ratione preventionis, cum duo vel plures iudices aeque

the dispensatory power of the ordinary ceases, or rather is restricted, as soon as the judge has legitimately cited the accused offender.[81] It is to be noted, however, that this limitation or restriction of dispensatory power over *latae sententiae* vindicative penalties of the general law applies, not to the ordinary to whose tribunal or court the case has been brought, but to other ordinaries. The jurisdiction by which the court operates is the jurisdiction of the local ordinary, who is, in reality, the judge; [82] and other judges who are chosen to hear cases in the tribunal act with power delegated to them by the ordinary.[83] Consequently, if the ordinary to whose tribunal the case has been brought exercises the dispensatory power which he possesses in virtue of canon 2237, § 1 over a vindicative penalty brought to his court, he in no way interferes with the jurisdiction of the court, which interference is the reason and purpose of the limitation of power in canon 2237, § 1, 1°.[84]

If a case involving a *latae sententiae* vindicative penalty of the general law has been brought to trial and the accused offender, though guilty, has been cleared of all guilt by the court or by the injured party who had brought suit against him, or if the court had decided that the case is to be dismissed,[85] even though such decisions were induced through false witnesses or other fraudulent means, the case is considered as not having been brought to the contentious forum,[86] and, therefore, not included in the exceptions mentioned in canon 2237, § 1, 1°. In fact, the crime involved in such a case is considered as an occult delict, for the offender, although conscious of his guilt and of the *latae sententiae* vindicative penalty he has in-

competentes sunt, ei ius est causam cognoscendi qui prius citatione reum legitime convenit.

[81] Cf. Coronata, *Institutiones Iuris Canonici,* IV, n. 1737, p. 136, nota 4; DeMeester, *Compendium,* III, n. 1727, p. 161, nota 5.

[82] Cf. canon 1572.

[83] Cf. canon 1574.

[84] Cf. Coronata, *Institutiones Iuris Canonici,* IV, n. 1737.

[85] Cf. canon 1702; 1902.

[86] Cf. Lega, *De Delictis et Poenis,* n. 131, p. 179, nota 1; Salucci, *Il Diritto Penale,* p. 170; Blat, *De Delictis et Poenis,* n. 59; Coronata, *Institutiones Iuris Canonici,* IV, n. 1737; Sole, *De Delictis et Poenis,* n. 148; *Berutti, Institutiones Canonici,* VI, n. 38, IV, 3, a; Gasparri, *Tractatus Canonicus de Sacra Ordinatione,* I, n. 225.

incurred, has been publicly vindicated.[87] Such an offender, guilty of such an occult delict and conscious of the *latae sententiae* vindicative penalty which he has incurred, may obtain a dispensation from the penalty from his ordinary according to the norms established for occult cases in canon 2237, § 2.[88]

Quite obviously, if the declaratory sentence has already been passed upon the guilty offender, and the *latae sententiae* vindicative penalty of the common law has been juridically declared, the case is entirely beyond the dispensatory power of the ordinary. For the penalty has not only been brought to the contentious forum; it has been declared by judicial sentence. The offender must observe the penalty also in the external forum,[89] and he can obtain a dispensation from the penalty only from the Roman Pontiff.[90] In other words, once a case involving a *latae sententiae* vindicative penalty of the general law has been brought to the contentious forum, the derived dispensatory power of the ordinary is restricted ***in perpetuum***, that is, even after the judge has passed sentence against the offender, not, however, as has been demonstrated, if the offender, though guilty, has been vindicated by the court.[91]

2. Vindicative Penalties Expressly Excluded

Besides the *latae sententiae* vindicative penalties of the general law involved in cases brought to the contentious forum, there are other *latae sententiae* vindicative penalties of the common law which are expressly excluded from the dispensatory powers of ordinaries. These are enumerated in canon 2237, § 1, 3°: penalties involving ineligibility to hold benefices, offices, dignities, functions in the Church, or active and passive vote and the privation of all of these;

[87] This is a splendid example of a delict and penalty which, though public at one time, have through particular circumstances, become occult. Cf. *infra*, p. 164.

[88] Cf. Lega, *De Delictis et Poenis*, n. 131, p. 179, nota 1; Berutti, *Institutiones Iuris Canonici*, VI, n. 38, IV, 3, a.

[89] Cf. canon 2232.

[90] Cf. Berutti, *Institutiones Iuris Canonici*, VI, n. 38, IV, 3, a.

[91] Cf. Coronata, *Institutiones Iuris Canonici*, IV, n. 1737; Berutti, *Institutiones Iuris Canonici*, VI, n. 38, IV, 3, a.

perpetual suspension; infamy by law; privation of advowson, that is, of the right of patronage; and the privation of any privilege or favor granted by the Holy See. If any of these vindicative penalties are involved in a case which is public, a dispensation granted by the ordinary is of no avail; the Holy See alone may act.

Prior to the publication of the Code of Canon Law, these penalties were considered as included among those penalties from which ordinaries could dispense, at least if the penalty had no special clause attached which reserved that power to the Roman Pontiff.[92] The Code, however, in clarifying and defining the dispensatory powers of ordinaries, limited that power considerably, particularly in reference to the vindicative penalties enumerated here.

There are several reasons for this restriction of the dispensatory power of the ordinaries. All the penalties enumerated in canon 2237, § 1, 3° concern the public welfare of the Church and not merely that of the offender.[93] Consequently, the treatment of such penalties is a matter of public policy rather than private expediency. Moreover, these penalties are all such that change a state, so that they cannot properly be said to be remissable. For example, if an offender is deprived of a benefice or office, it cannot be said that he may be "dispensed" from such a penalty. Rather, the Holy See permits him either to acquire the benefice or office of which he was deprived or to obtain another.[94] Some of these penalties—for example, inability to hold office or benefice—may be inflicted only by the Holy See, for only the supreme authority in the Church can take away from a person the rights he possesses by common law; [95] and it is but logical that the Holy See should reserve to itself the removal of such a punishment.

Then, too, many of these penalties are very grave penalties, inflicted only for more serious crimes.[96] It should be noted, however, that the two very grave penalties, deposition and degradation, are

[92] Cf. *supra*, p. 39. Cf. also Thesaurus, *De Poenis Ecclesiasticis*, I, 23.

[93] Cf. Coronata, *Institutiones Iuris Canonici*, IV, n. 1737; Augustine, *A Commentary on the New Code*, VIII, p. 110.

[94] Cf. Wernz-Vidal, *Ius Canonicum*, VII, n. 214, 2°.

[95] Cf. canon 2296, § 1.

[96] Cf. Coronata, *Institutiones Iuris Canonici*, IV, n. 1737.

not included among the excluded penalties. They are not *latae sententiae* but always *ferendae sententiae* penalties, and as such are governed by the principles established in canon 2236. Moreover, these two penalties include disqualification for office, which is explicitly mentioned among the penalties reserved to the Roman Pontiff.[97]

These vindicating penalties which are expressly excluded from the dispensatory power of ordinaries will be here considered summarily.

(a) *The Ineligibility to Hold Benefices, Offices, Dignities, Functions, and the Incapability of Sharing in an Active or Passive Vote*

Ineligibility or disability is a punishment by which an offender is made or declared unfit for, and incapable of being appointed validly to an office, benefice, dignity, or particular function in the Church or incapable of exercising an active or passive vote. In itself it may be either *latae sententiae* or *ferendae sententiae*,[98] but in the present discussion only those which are *latae sententiae* are considered. These vindicative penalties are enumerated in the list in canon 2291,[99] of the principle vindicative penalties common to clergy and laity, which affect any member of the Church according to his guilt; and also in the list of the vindicative penalties which are imposed only on clerics, as given in canon 2298.[100]

Since the laity cannot acquire benefices, offices or dignities in the Church, the only penalty of disability which would affect the laity would be that of ineligibility to perform some ecclesiastical

[97] Cf. canons 2303; 2305. Cf. also Findlay, *Canonical Norms Governing the Deposition and Degradation of Clerics*, pp. 200, 201; Ayrinhac-Lydon, *Penal Legislation in the New Code of Canon Law*, n. 175; Coronata, *Institutiones Iuris Canonici*, IV, n. 1737.

[98] Cf. canons 2294, § 1; 2390, § 2; 2394, § 1; 2395; 2345; 2346; 2368, § 1; 2413.

[99] Cf. canon 2291, 9°: Inhabilitas ad gratias ecclesiasticas aut munia in Ecclesia quae statum clericalem non requirant, vel ad gradus academicos auctoritate ecclesiastica consequendos.

[100] Cf. canon 2298, 5°: Inhabilitas ad omnes vel ad aliquot dignitates, officia, beneficia aliave munera propria clericorum.

functions or duties which do not require the clerical state. Such functions would be all those which may be exercised or performed in matters ecclesiastical without involving or including any participation in ecclesiastical power, either of jurisdiction or orders. Such functions, for example, would be those of an advocate in an ecclesiastical court [101] or of an administrator of church goods or of a member of a council of administration.[102]

Clerics, however, may, through the incurrence of a *latae sententiae* vindicative penalty, become ineligible to receive benefices,[103] offices,[104] dignities and functions,[105] all of which include participation in ecclesiastical power of jurisdiction or of orders. However, there are other functions, which, although they do not partake of ecclesiastical power, nevertheless are reserved exclusively to clerics, such as that of chancellor,[106] or of defender of the bond or promoter of justice.[107]

If the penalty of disability or ineligibility is *latae sententiae,* it is incurred as soon as the delict to which it is attached has been committed; and, strictly speaking, one thus canonically infamous, who is conscious of the penalty which he has incurred, even by a secret crime, should refuse any appointment for which he is ineligible, although such an appointment were offered to him before there has been any declaratory sentence passed upon him. It is admitted, however, that this obligation of refusing, or of stating the reason for the refusal really exists only in cases of notorious crimes, for the Church does not expect or demand culprits to publicize their occult guilt.[108]

The capacity or ability to obtain validly any or many or all of

[101] Cf. canon 1657.

[102] Cf. canon 1520. Cf. also Berutti, *Institutiones Iuris Canonici,* VI, n. 87, II, 9°.

[103] Cf. canons 118; 1409; 1412.

[104] Cf. canons 118; 145-147.

[105] Cf. canons 394-396.

[106] Cf. canon 372, § 1.

[107] Cf. canon 1589, § 1. Cf. also Berutti, *Institutiones Iuris Canonici,* VI, n. 89, II, 5°.

[108] Cf. Ayrinhac-Lydon, *Penal Legislation in the New Code of Canon Law,* n. 162, c.

these offices, benefices, dignities or functions, or to exercise active or passive vote, may be removed or taken away by the vindicative penalty of disability, either for a determined time or perpetually.[109] However, it should be noted that, since the penalty of disability or disqualification concerns only the future and not the past, rights which have already been acquired are not taken away by the supervening penalty of disability.[110] If, however, the penalty of privation is added to that of disability, it is evident that such acquired rights may also be taken away, not, however, in virtue of the penalty of disability but solely by reason of the added penalty of privation; for it lies in the nature of privation that a man cannot be deprived of what he possesses by a disability looking to future possession.[111]

The *latae sententiae* vindicative penalties of disability in the common law are the following:

> **Canon 2294, § 1. Qui infamia iuris laborat, non solum est irregularis ad normam can. 984, n. 5, sed insuper est inhabilis ad obtinenda beneficia, pensiones, officia et dignitates ecclesiasticas, ad actus legitimos ecclesiasticos perficiendos, ad exercitium iuris aut muneris ecclesiastici, et tandem arceri debet a ministerio in sacris functionibus exercendo.**
>
> **Canon 2390, § 2. Quod si electioni a collegio clericorum vel religiosorum paragendae, laici vel saecularis potestas sese illegitime, contra libertatem canonicam, immiscere praesumpserint, electores qui hanc immixtionem sollicitaverint vel sponte admiserint, ipso facto privati sunt pro ea vice iure eligendi; qui vero suae electioni taliter factae scienter consenserit, fit ad officium vel beneficium, do quo agitur, ipso facto inhabilis.**

[109] Cf. Berutti, *Institutiones Iuris Canonici*, VI, n. 89, II, 5°.

[110] Cf. canon 2296, § 2: Iura iam quaesita non amittuntur ob supervenientem inhabilitatem, nisi huic addatur poena privationis.

[111] Cf. canon 2296, § 2. Cf. also Augustine, *A Commentary on the New Code*, VIII, 250; Berutti, *Institutiones Iuris Canonici*, VI, n. 87, II, 9°; n. 89, II, 5°; Blat, *De Delictis et Poenis*, n. 128; Ayrinhac-Lydon, *Penal Legislation in the New Code of Canon Law*, n. 162.

Canon 2394. Qui beneficium, officium vel dignitatem ecclesiasticam propria auctoritate occupaverit vel, ad ea electus, praesentatus, nominatus in eorundem possessionem vel regimen seu administrationem sese ingesserit, antequam necessarias litteras confirmationis vel institutionis acceperit easque illis ostenderit, quibus de iure debet:

1°. Sit ipso iure ad eadem inhabilis et praeterea ob Ordinario pro gravitate culpae puniatur.

Canon 2395. Qui scienter acceptat collationem officii, beneficii vel dignitatis de iure non vacantis et patiatur se in eius possessionem immitti, sit ipso facto inhabilis ad illa postea assequenda aliisque poenis pro modo culpae puniatur.

All the above *latae sententiae* vindicative penalties of the common law, if involved in public cases, are excepted from the dispensatory power of ordinaries; only in occult cases can ordinaries dispense from them.[112]

(b) *The Deprivation of Office, Benefice, Dignity, Functions, or Active and Passive Vote*

Deprivation is a punishment by which an offender is deprived of an office, benefice, dignity, functions, or active or passive vote, which he has in his possession. Unlike the penalty of disability, privation concerns the past directly, and not the future; it deprives the offender of something which he had possessed until the commission of the delict to which the *latae sententiae* penalty is attached. This vindicative penalty is by its very nature perpetual,[113] although

[112] Cf. Ayrinhac-Lydon, *Penal Legislation in the New Code of Canon Law,* n. 162, d; Augustine, *A Commentary on the New Code,* VIII, n. 250; Berutti, *Institutiones Iuris Canonici,* VI, n. 38, IV, 3, c. Coronata (*Institutiones Iuris Canonici,* IV, n. 1829, p. 258, nota 2) holds the unique opinion—but offers no argument for it—that the penalty of disability, even in occult cases, is excluded from the dispensatory power of ordinaries.

[113] Cf. Berutti, *Institutiones Iuris Canonici,* VI, n. 89, II, 6°.

some authors[114] maintain that the penalty of deprivation may be complete and perpetual, or it may be only partial and temporary—for example, a cleric holding an office or benefice or a particular dignity may simply be forbidden, for a time, to exercise some of its functions, such as preaching, hearing confessions, etc.[115] However, as Berutti notes,[116] this latter penalty is not strictly a partial or temporary deprivation of office or benefice but rather a partial and temporary suspension from office or benefice.[117]

The vindicative penalty of deprivation may also be either *latae sententiae* or *ferendae sententiae*,[118] but in the present discussion only those *latae sententiae* are considered. These vindicative penalties are enumerated in the list, in canon 2291,[119] of the principle vindicative penalties common to both clergy and laity, which affect any member of the Church; and also in the list of vindicative penalties which are imposed exclusively upon clerics, as given in canon 2298.[120]

Since the laity cannot acquire offices, benefices, or dignities in the Church, the deprivation of these does not concern the laity, but only the clergy, who alone may acquire them.[121] However, the laity may be deprived of performing some ecclesiastical function or duty which does not require the clerical state, which may be exercised in matters ecclesiastical without involving any participation in ecclesiastical power, either of jurisdiction or of orders. Similarly, they

[114] Cf. *e.g.*, Ayrinhac-Lydon, *Penal Legislation in the New Code of Canon Law*, n. 165.

[115] Cf. canon 2299, § 2.

[116] Cf. *Institutiones Iuris Canonici, loc. cit.*

[117] Cf. also Coronata, *Institutiones Iuris Canonici*, IV, n. 1831.

[118] Cf. canon 2396; 2397; 2398; 2266; 2385; 2314, § 1; 2331, § 2; 2340, § 2; 2343, § 2; 2345; 2346; 2350, § 2; 2354, §2; 2359, § 1, § 3; 2368, § 1; 2381, § 2; 2406, § 1.

[119] Cf. canon 2291, 10°: Privatio vel suspensio ad tempus muneris, facultatis vel gratiae iam obtentae;

11°: Privatio iuris praecedentiae vel vocis activae et passivae vel iuris ferendi titulos honoris, vestem, insignia, quae Ecclesia concesserit.

[120] Cf. canon 2298, 4°: Privatio alicuius iuris cum beneficio vel officio coniuncti;

6°: Privatio poenalis beneficii vel officii cum vel sine pensione.

[121] Cf. canon 118.

may be deprived of the exercise of active or passive vote which they may have, for example, in a religious institute or confraternity.[122]

The *latae sententiae* vindicative penalties of deprivation in the general law of the Church are the following:

Canon 2266. Post sententiam condemnatoriam vel declaratoriam excommunicationis manet privatus fructibus dignitatis, officii, beneficii, pensionis, muneris, si quod habeat in Ecclesia; et vitandus ipsamet dignitate officio, beneficio, pensione, munere.

Canon 2385. Firmo praescripto can. 646, religiosus apostata a religione, ipso iure incurrit in excommunicationem, proprio Superiori majori vel, si religio sit laicalis aut non exempta, Ordinario loci in quo commoratur, reservatam, ab actibus legitimis ecclesiasticis est exclusus, privilegiis omnibus suae religionis privatus; et si redierit, perpetuo caret voce activa et passiva, ac praeterea aliis poenis pro gravitate culpae a Superioribus puniri debet ad normam constitutionum.

Canon 2386. Religiosus fugitivus ipso facto incurrit in privationem officii, si quod in religione habeat, et in suspensionem proprio Superiori maiori reservatam, si sit in sacris; cum autem redierit, puniatur secundum constitutiones, et si constitutiones nihil de hoc caveant, Superior maior pro gravitate culpae poenas infligat.

Canon 2396. Clericus, qui assecutus pacificam possessionem officii vel beneficii cum priore incompatibilis, prius quoque retinere praesumpserit contra praescriptum can. 156, 1439, utroque privatus ipso iure exsistat.

Canon 2397. Si quis ad dignitatem cardinalitiam promotus, iusiurandum, de quo in can. 234, emittere recusaverit, ipso facto cardinalitia dignitate privatus perpetuo maneat.

Canon 2398. Si quis ad episcopatum promotus, contra praescriptum can. 333 intra tres menses consecrationem suscipere neglexerit, fructus non facit suos,

[122] Cf. Wernz-Vidal, *Ius Canonicum*, VII, n. 343.

fabricae ecclesiae cathedralis applicandos; et si postea in eadem negligentia per totidem menses perstiterit, episcopatu privatus ipso iure manet.

In public cases, all the above *latae sententiae* vindicative penalties of deprivation of the common law are beyond the dispensatory powers of ordinaries which they possess in virtue of canon 2237. Theoretically in occult cases, ordinaries may dispense from these penalties by virtue of canon 2237, § 2. However, just as canonists prior to the publication of the Code taught that the *latae sententiae* privation of office incurred through the commission of an occult delict did not bind the offender,[123] so the Code, as a matter of fact, attaches the *latae sententiae* vindicative penalty of deprivation only to notorious delicts.[124]

(c) *Perpetual Suspension*

Suspension as a vindicative penalty differs from the censure of suspension in that it is imposed either in perpetuity, for a determined time, or at the will of the superior,[125] whereas the censure of suspension includes no element of time, but is imposed until the offender recedes from contumacy.[126] In its nature the vindicative penalty of suspension is the same as the censure, and its definition must be derived from the definition of the censure of suspension as given in canon 2278, § 1, since the Code nowhere defines the vindicative penalty of suspension. It is, therefore, a penalty by which an ecclesiastic is forbidden the use of the powers or rights belonging to him by reason of his office or benefice or both.[127] Since the penalty of suspension forbids the use of rights which are special to clerics as such,

[123] Cf. Hollweck, *Die kirchlichen Strafgesetze*, 90, p. 158, nota 11; Wernz, *Ius Decretalium*, VI, n. 116; Chelodi, *Ius Poenale*, n. 51.

[124] Cf. canons 2266; 2396-2398. Cf. also Coronata, *Institutiones Iuris Canonici*, IV, n. 1830.

[125] Cf. canons 2278, § 1; 2298, 2°. Cf. also Coronata, *Institutiones Iuris Canonici*, IV, n. 1799; Berutti, *Institutiones Iuris Canonici*, VI, n. 89, II, 2°.

[126] Cf. canon 2241, § 1.

[127] Cf. canon 2278, § 1: Suspensio est censura qua clericus officio vel beneficio vel utroque prohibetur. Cf. also Ayrinhac-Lydon, *Penal Legislation in the New Code of Canon Law*, n. 146.

this penalty is listed among the vindicative penalties which are imposed exclusively on clerics.[128] The powers affected by suspension include the power of orders as well as that of jurisdiction, with, however, one difference, namely, that the power of orders cannot be taken away entirely, even temporarily, inasmuch as it is of divine institution [129] and has been conferred through the sacrament. The power of orders can only be bound in such a way that its use becomes unlawful; while the power of jurisdiction, whether ordinary or delegated, can be withdrawn entirely. It should be noted that the vindicative penalty of suspension does not take away the office itself or the benefice but only the use or exercise of the power or rights connected with it. In this respect the penalty of suspension differs from the penalties of deposition and degradation.

The vindicative penalty of suspension may be either *latae* or *ferendae sententiae,* but in the present discussion only those penalties *latae sententiae* are considered; it may be either *a iure* or *ab homine,* but canon 2237 is restricted to a consideration only of those vindicative penalties of suspension which are established in the common law. Since the effects of suspension are divisible,[130] this vindicative penalty may be either partial or total; it may also be particular or general, that is, inflicted on individual persons or on moral bodies, such as religious communities or colleges of clerics. For chapters and colleges may have rights and possessions which belong to the body, not to the individual members of that body; and consequently the moral body may be deprived of them by law or suspended from the use of them.

The main division of the vindicative penalty of suspension, like that of the medicinal penalty, is into

(a) suspension from office only, by which a cleric is forbidden to exercise the functions of his office or the power of orders and jurisdiction;[131]

[128] Cf. canon 2298, 2°: Suspensio in perpetuum vel ad tempus praefinitum vel ad beneplacitum Superioris.

[129] Cf. canons 107; 108, § 3.

[130] Cf. canon 2278, § 2.

[131] Cf. canon 2279, § 1.

(b) suspension from benefice by which he is deprived of the income and administration of his benefice; [182]

(c) suspension from both office and benefice.[183]

Suspension from benefice is subdivided into privation of the income of the benefice and loss of its administration.[184] Suspension from office, however, can be subdivided as many times as there are powers of which the cleric possessing the office may be deprived or which he may be forbidden to use.[185]

Suspension decreed absolutely, without restriction,[186] implies suspension from both office and benefice.[187] Suspension from office does not include suspension from benefice, and, vice versa, suspension from benefice does not entail suspension from office, unless the contrary is expressly or implicitly stated.[188]

Suspension from office or from benefice, without restriction, is to include suspension from all offices or benefices possessed within the jurisdiction of the superior who inflicted the penalty; but—and this should be noted—if the penalty is established as a *latae sententiae* vindicative penalty by the general law of the Church, it applies to all offices or benefices in any province of the Church.[189]

All the above mentioned vindicative penalties of suspension, established as *latae sententiae* penalties in the common law, may be either perpetual or definitely or indefinitely temporary. If the suspension is perpetual and involved in a public case, it cannot be dispensed by ordinaries by virtue of the power granted to them in canon 2237, § 1. However, there are no perpetual suspensions established as *latae sententiae* vindicative penalties in the Code of Canon Law, and, consequently, strictly speaking, this exception to the dispensatory powers of ordinaries at the present time has little practical

[182] Cf. canon 2280, § 1.

[183] Cf. canon 2278, § 2.

[184] Cf. canon 2280, § 1.

[185] It is beyond the scope of this work to treat of these divisions in detail. Cf. canons 2279-2285.

[186] Cf. *e.g.*, canon 2370.

[187] Cf. canon 2278, § 2.

[188] Cf. canon 2278, § 2. Cf. also Ayrinhac-Lydon, *Penal Legislation in the New Code of Canon Law*, n. 152.

[189] Cf. canon 2282.

bearing. And yet there are certain *latae sententiae* vindicative penalties of suspension established in the Code which, although not expressly established as perpetual, are nevertheless excluded from the dispensatory powers of ordinaries in public cases. These penalties are the following. The first four penalties are established as suspensions "ad beneplacitum Superioris," the last as a strictly temporary suspension.

Canon 671. Si vero dimittatur ob delicta minora iis de quibus in can. 670:

1°. Ipso facto suspensus manet, donec a Sancta Sede absolutionem obtinuerit.

Canon 2370: Episcopus aliquem consecrans in Episcopum, Episcopi vel, loco Episcoporum, presbyteri assistentes, et qui consecrationem recipit sine apostolico mandato contra praescriptum can. 953, ipso iure suspensus sunt, donec Sedes Apostolica eos dispensaverit.

Canon 2387. Religiosus clericus cuius professio ob admissum ab ipso dolum nulla fuerit declarata, si sit in minoribus ordinibus constitutus, e statu clericali abiiciatur; si in maioribus, ipso facto suspensus manet, donec Sedi Apostolicae aliter visum fuerit.

Canon 2394. Qui beneficium, officium vel dignitatem ecclesiasticam propria auctoritate occupaverit vel, ad ea electus, praesentatus, nominatus in eorundem possessionem vel regimen seu administrationem sese ingesserit, antequam necessarias litteras confirmationis vel institutionis acceperit, easque illis ostenderit, quibus de iure debet:

3°. Capitula vero, conventus aliique omnes ad quos spectat, huiusmodi electos, praesentatos vel nominatos ante litterarum exhibitionem admittentes, ipso facto a iure eligendi, nominandi vel praesentandi suspensi manet ad beneplacitum Sedis Apostolicae.

Canon 2373. In suspensionem per annum ab ordinum

collatione Sedi Apostolicae reservatam ipso facto incurrunt:

1°. Qui contra praescriptum can. 955, alienum subditum sine Ordinarii proprii litteris dimissoriis ordinaverint;

2°. Qui subditum proprium, qui alibi tanto tempore moratus sit ut canonicum impedimentum contrahere ibi potuerit, ordinaverint contra praescriptum can. 993, n. 4, 994;

3°. Qui aliquem ad ordines maiores sine titulo canonico promoverint, contra praescriptum can. 974, § 1, n. 7;

4°. Qui, salvo legitimo privilegio, religiosum, ad familiam pertinentem quae sit extra territorium ipsius ordinantis, promoverint, etiam cum litteris dimissorialibus proprii Superioris, nisi legitime probatum fuerit aliquem e casibus occurrere, de quibus in can. 966.

(d) *Infamy by Law*

Infamy is a penalty by which a person suffers the total loss of good name or reputation as a result of a fault that is serious and in many cases attended with public contempt.[140] A person may become canonically infamous in two ways. His own evil deeds may cause him to lose his reputation among others; this is infamy of fact and the penalty is suffered when the ordinary decides that the fact of infamy is present and makes known his judgment.[141] Or a person may become infamous by a disposition of general ecclesiastical law which pronounces him such because of some delict or crime he has committed; this is infamy of law.[142] Infamy of law is a common vindicative penalty which may be imposed upon clergy and laity.[143] It may be either *latae sententiae* or *ferendae senten-*

[140] Cf. Ayrinhac-Lydon, *Penal Legislation in the New Code of Canon Law*, n. 161.

[141] Cf. canon 2293, § 3.

[142] Cf. canon 2293, § 2.

[143] Cf. canon 2291, 4°.

tiae; but in the present discussion only penalties of infamy established as *latae sententiae* by the common law are considered.

In public cases infamy by law established as a *latae sententiae* vindicative penalty in the general law of the Church is excluded from the dispensatory powers of ordinaries. This is by virtue of the express exclusion of this penalty in canon 2237, § 1, 3° and also by reason of canon 2295, which states that infamy of law can be removed only by a dispensation from the Holy See.[144]

The following are *latae sententiae* vindicative penalties of infamy by law of the general law:

> Canon 2314, § 1. Omnes a christiana fide apostatae et omnes et singuli haeretici aut schismatici:
>
> 3°. Si sectae acotholicae nomen dederint vel publice adhaeserint, ipso facto infames sunt et, firmo praescripto can. 188, n. 4, clerici, monitione incassum praemissa, degradentur.
>
> Canon 2320. Qui species consecratas abiecerit vel ad malum finem abduxerit aut retinuerit, est suspectus de haeresi; incurrit in excommunicationem latae sententiae specialissimo modo Sedi Apostolicae reservatam; est ipso facto infamis, et clericus praeterea est deponendus.
>
> Canon 2328. Qui cadavera vel sepulcra mortuorum ad furtum vel alium malum finem violaverit, interdicto personali puniatur, sit ipso facto infamis, et clericus praeterea deponatur.
>
> Canon 2343, § 1. Qui violentas manus in personam Romani Pontificis iniecerit:
>
> 2°. Est ipso iure infamis.
>
> Canon 2351, § 2. Ipsi vero duellantes et qui eorum patrini vocantur, sunt ipso facto infames.

[144] Cf. canon 2295: Infamia iuris desinit sola dispensatione a Sede Apostolica concessa. . . . Canonists commonly consider this reservation as applying only in public cases. In occult cases, ordinaries can dispense from the penalty of infamy of law. Cf. Ayrinhac-Lydon, *Penal Legislation in the New Code of Canon Law,* n. 161.

Canon 2356. Bigami, idest qui, obstante coniugali vinculo, aliud matrimonium, etsi tantum civile, ut aiunt, attentaverint, sunt ipso facto infames. . . .

Canon 2357, §1. Laici legitime damnati ob delicta contra sextum cum minoribus infra aetatem sexdecim annorum commissa, vel ob stuprum, sodomiam, incestum, lenocinium, ipso facto infames sunt, praeter alias poenas quas Ordinarius infligendas iudicaverit.

(e) *The Deprivation of Advowson, and of Privileges or Favors Granted by the Holy See.*

The deprivation of privileges and favors granted by the Holy See and of the unique privilege or right of patronage granted by the Church in particular instances is a vindicative penalty which may be imposed upon any member of the Church, cleric or lay, who may possess the privilege or favor.[145] The deprivation of these rights and privileges, like the privation of office or benefice, dignities or special functions, concerns the past; it deprives the offender of the rights, favors, or privileges which he has in his possession. This penalty also may be either *latae sententiae* or *ferendae sententiae.* However, in the present consideration only those which are *latae sententiae* of the common law are to be discussed.

The right of patronage comprehends the sum total of the privileges which, together with certain duties, are conceded by the Church to Catholic founders of a church, chapel, or benefice, or also to those who have acquired the right of patronage from the founders.[146] At the present time the Code has abolished henceforth the right of patronage, although it respects such a right wherever acquired before the promulgation of the Code.[147] The right of patronage has not and does not exist in the United States: the Second Plenary Council of Baltimore, confirming former decrees of the Provincial Councils of Baltimore, did not admit the existence of the right of patronage

[145] Cf. canon 2291, 7°, 10°.

[146] Cf. canon 1448.

[147] Cf. canon 1450.

in this country.[148] However, where the right of advowson exists, the one who possesses the right may be deprived of it by incurring the *latae sententiae* vindicative penalty of deprivation as established in canon 1470, § 1, 6°: "Si patronus ius patronatus simoniace in alium transferre attentaverit; si lapsus fuerit in apostasiam, haeresim aut schisma; si bona ac iura ecclesiae vel beneficii iniuste usurpaverit aut detineat; si rectorem vel alium clericum ecclesiae servitio addictum aut beneficiarium per se vel per alios occiderit vel mutilaverit." The vindicative penalty for such delicts is *latae sententiae* but in order that the patron should lose his right of patronage as a result of the commission of any of these delicts, it is required that a declaratory judicial sentence be passed upon him.[149]

Other privileges and favors acquired from the Holy See are likewise liable to *latae sententiae* vindicative penalties of the general law,[150] although such privileges are usually lost by reason of *ferendae sententiae* penalties.[151]

In public cases, therefore, the *latae sententiae* vindicative penalty of deprivation of any of these rights, privileges or favors is excluded from the dispensatory power of ordinaries.

Article III. The Dispensatory Power of Ordinaries in Occult Cases

Canon 2237, § 2. In casibus vero occultis, firmo praescripto can. 2254 et 2290, potest Ordinarius poenas latae sententiae iure communi statutas per se vel per alium remittere, exceptis censuris specialissimo vel speciali modo Sedi Apostolicae reservatis.

A. *The Occult Cases*

The second paragraph of this canon determines the dispensatory power of ordinaries in regard to *latae sententiae* vindicative penalties established in the general law when the case presented is occult.

[148] Cf. *Acta et Decreta Concilii Plenarii Baltimorensis II* (Baltimorae: Joannes Murphy, 1894), n. 184.

[149] Cf. canon 1470, § 3.

[150] Cf. *e. g.*, canon 2393.

[151] Cf. canon 78.

An occult case is distinct from an occult delict, for it involves not only the delict but the vindicative penalty incurred as a result of the commission of the delict. Thus, if the delict is at least formally occult, the *latae sententiae* vindicative penalty incurred also is occult; and an occult case exists. If the delict is public, however, the *latae sententiae* vindicative penalty incurred is presumed to be likewise public; and the case is a public case. It may so happen that a delict has been committed publicly and the guilt of the offender has been widely publicized, and yet the *latae sententiae* penalty incurred is absolutely unknown to others. In such a case, infrequent, it is true, but possible, the delict seems to be public and yet the penalty is occult. But such a delict is considered as formally occult.[152] Consequently, an occult case involves a delict which is at least formally occult.

According to canon 2197, 4°, an occult delict is one which is not public; that is, a delict which has not been divulged or has little likelihood or ever being divulged or publicized.[153] Therefore, even if several persons know of a particular delict committed by another, that delict remains occult as long as these persons do not reveal it to others, do not intend to do so, and are not likely to be obliged to do so, *v. g.*, in a trial before a court.[154]

The concept of an occult delict is not opposed to that of a notorious delict, but rather to the concept of a public delict.[155] Consequently, a notorious delict may be occult, either materially or formally so.[156] Moreover, the type and characteristics of persons

[152] Cf. Lega, *De Delictis et Poenis*, n. 131; Blat, *De Delictis et Poenis*, n. 121; D'Annibale, *Summula*, I, n. 242, nota, 52; Coronata, *Institutiones Iuris Canonici*, IV, n. 1648; Gasparri, *Tractatus Canonicus de Matrimonio*, I, n. 260.

[153] Cf. Wernz-Vidal, *Ius Canonicum*, VII, n. 35, V; Michiels, *De Delictis et Poenis* (Lublin-Polonia, 1934), I, 117; Berutti, *Institutiones Iuris Canonici*, VI, n. 3, III, C; Coronata, *Institutiones Iuris Canonici*, IV, nn. 1648, 1739; Lega, *De Delictis et Poenis*, n. 244, 4; Chelodi, *Ius Poenale*, n. 4; Woywod, *A Practical Commentary*, II, n. 2027; Ballerini-Palmieri, *Opus Theologicum Morale*, VII, n. 149.

[154] Cf. Berutti, *Institutiones Iuris Canonici*, VI, n. 3, III; Coronata, *Institutiones Iuris Canonici*, IV, n. 1648.

[155] Cf. canon 2197, 4°.

[156] Cf. Coronata, *Institutiones Iuris Canonici*, IV, n. 1648.

who have knowledge of the delict are to be considered rather than the number of persons who know of the fact.[157] Obviously, if no one but the offender knows about the commission of the delict, that delict is absolutely occult.[158]

The delict may be either materially or formally occult. It is materially occult if the delict itself is not divulged or is not likely to be divulged.[159] This may occur in one of two ways:

1. If the delict has been committed but it is not known publicly that a delict has taken place. Thus, if John were to kill James as they were climbing mountains, but others were under the impression that James accidentally fell into a mountain pass, the delict would be materially occult.

2. If the perpetrator of the delict were unknown as such, though the fact that the delict was committed was well known by others. Thus, if it was evident that James was killed by someone but the person who had killed him was not known, the delict also would be materially occult.

A delict is formally occult if the imputability of the delict is unknown or unpublicized.[160] The fact that a delict has been committed may be well known; but if it is not known that the perpetrator of the delict acted out of malice or fault, that delict is said to be formally occult. For example, John kills James in a public place before witnesses, who, however, arrive only at the moment of the killing and consequently have no way of knowing whether John acted in self-defense and was therefore innocent, or whether he was the unjust aggressor; and as a result it is commonly believed by all that John is entirely innocent. Materially the delict stands in the external forum, imputable to the killer until he proves his inno-

[157] Cf. Lega, *De Delictis et Poenis*, n. 244, 4; Coronata, *Institutiones Iuris Canonici*, IV, n. 1648; Chelodi, *Ius Poenale*, n. 4, nota 6; Woywod, *A Practical Commentary*, II, n. 2027.

[158] Cf. D'Annibale, *Summula*, n. 242, nota 50; Wernz, *Ius Decretalium*, VI, n. 17, V; Coronata, *Institutiones Iuris Canonici*, IV, n. 1648; Berutti, *Institutiones Iuris Canonici*, VI, n. 3, III; Kerin, *The Privation of Christian Burial*, The Catholic University of America Canon Law Studies, n. 136 (Washington, D. C.: The Catholic University of America Press, 1941), pp. 134-137.

[159] Cf. canon 2197, 4°.

[160] Cf. canon 2197, 4°.

cence;[161] but formally the delict is occult. Similarly, the delict remains formally occult in the same case where John, having been brought to trial, has been proven free of all grave imputability in the killing of James.[162]

It may occur, under certain circumstances, that one and the same delict is public in one place and occult in another; or that in one particular place the delict, once public, may now be occult.[163] The circumstances which surround the delict at the present time are to be taken into consideration in determining whether the delict is occult here and now.[164]

An occult case, as has been noted, involves not only an occult delict but also an occult penalty. Consequently, it should be noted that, according to the practice of the Sacred Penitentiary, vindicative penalties, like delicts, may be occult by reason of the persons who know them, by reason of place, and by virtue of time.[165] Therefore, a vindicative penalty that is known to a few persons, though public if such persons will publicize it, will be occult if they are of such character that they will not divulge their knowledge of the penalty to others. A vindicative penalty may be public in one place, and occult in another; it may have been public in a certain place at one time, but has become occult in the same place with the passing of time.

An occult case, therefore, in the sense of canon 2237, § 2, is one which involves a delict at least formally occult or an occult vindicative penalty or both. If the delict is either materially or formally occult here and now, the case is an occult case. If the vin-

[161] Cf. canon 2200, § 2.

[162] Cf. Berutti, *Institutiones Iuris Canonici,* VI, n. 3, II.

[163] For an excellent example, cf. *supra,* p. 146, wherein is cited the case of an offender who, though guilty and conscious of his guilt, has been vindicated in court.

[164] Cf. Coronata, *Institutiones Iuris Canonici,* IV, n. 1648; Berutti, *Institutiones Iuris Canonici,* VI, n. 3, III; Lega, *De Delictis et Poenis,* n. 313; Gasparri, *Tractatus Canonicus de Matrimonio,* I, n. 160; Hollweck, *Die kirchlichen Strafgesetze,* § 5, nota 7; Chelodi, *Ius Poenale,* n. 4; Wernz, *Ius Decretalium,* VI, n. 17, V.

[165] Cf. Rossi, "De sacerdotibus qui matrimonium etiam civile tantum contrahere praesumpserint quoad absolutionem a censura de qua in 2388, 1"—*Perfice Munus,* XI (1936), p. 532, nota 2; p. 534, nota 1.

dictative penalty is occult here and now, even though previously or in another place it was public, the case is occult. If the delict is public but the penalty here and now is occult, the case is occult, because the delict, in this instance, is in reality formally occult.[166]

On the contrary, if the delict is public and the penalty incurred is public or if the penalty here and now is public, even though the delict previously was occult, the case cannot be occult in the sense of this canon.[167]

B. *The Dispensatory Power*

The dispensatory power granted to ordinaries in canon 2237, § 2 to dispense in occult cases from all *latae sententiae* vindicative penalties of the common law of the Church is ordinary derived power.[168] Consequently, this power may be delegated to others.[169] Thus, the ordinary may delegate the dispensatory power to priests or confessors of his diocese, either for each separate case or habitually.[170]

Ordinaries may exercise this dispensatory power, however, only in the internal forum.[171] For canon 202, § 3 states that if the forum for which a particular power is granted is not expressly determined in the law, it is to be understood as applying to both the internal and the external forums unless from the nature of the particular case it is clear that the power is to be exercised in one or the other of the forums. Since the dispensatory power granted in canon 2237, § 2 is to be exercised only in occult cases, which, by reason of

[166] Cf. Blat, *De Delictis et Poenis,* n. 120.

[167] Cf. Berutti, *Institutiones Iuris Canonici,* VI, n. 38, IV, 4; n. 86, II, p. 216, nota 2.

[168] Cf. Canon 197, § 1. Cf. also Wernz-Vidal, *Ius Canonicum,* VII, n. 215; Ayrinhac-Lydon, *Penal Legislation in the New Code of Canon Law,* n. 69; Coronata, *Institutiones Iuris Canonici,* IV, n. 1738; De Meester, *Compendium,* III, n. 1727; Salucci, *Il Diritto Penale,* p. 167; Sole, *De Delictis et Poenis,* nn. 146, 147, 3.

[169] Cf. canon 2237, § 2: "per se vel per alium." Cf. also Wernz-Vidal, *Ius Canonicum,* VII, n. 215.

[170] Cf. Canon 199, § 2. Cf. also Augustine, *A Commentary on the New Code,* VIII, p. 110.

[171] Cf. Wernz-Vidal, *Ius Canonicum,* VII, n. 215, maintains that this power may be exercised in both the internal and external forums, but gives no arguments for his opinion.

the occult delicts involved in such cases, pertain only to the internal forum, from the nature of such cases it is clear that the power is to be exercised in the internal forum alone.[172]

The object of this dispensatory power, as has been noted, includes all *latae sententiae* vindicative penalties of the general law of the Church without exception, as long as the cases in which these penalties are involved are occult. Consequently, confessors who suspend the obligation of observing *latae sententiae* vindicative penalties in the more urgent occult cases according to canon 2290, § 1, may always inform the penitent that recourse may be made to the ordinary, who has the power to dispense from the penalties. Similarly, if the confessor undertakes the obligation of recourse for the penitent, he is to apply to his ordinary for the dispensation.

Certain *latae sententiae* vindicative penalties established in the common law are expressly reserved to the Holy See,[173] and the question arises whether such penalties may be dispensed by ordinaries in virtue of canon 2237, § 2. It seems that such penalties certainly come within the scope of canon 2237, § 2, for that canon states that ordinaries can dispense, in occult cases, from all *latae sententiae* vindicative penalties of the common law. Certain exceptions are expressly made in the case of censures which are reserved to the Holy See *specialissimo* vel *speciali modo,* while those reserved *simpliciter* to the Holy See are included.[174] Consequently, if the legislator wishes to exclude certain reserved vindicative penalties, it would seem that such exceptions would be expressly established in the law. Moreover, since *latae sententiae* censures which are reserved simply to the Holy See are liable to this dispensatory power of ordinaries, it seems but logical to include reserved *latae sententiae* vindicative penalties. Therefore, if the case is occult, the ordinary can dispense from any of the *latae sententiae* vindicative penalties of the common law which are reserved expressly to the Holy See.[175]

[172] Cf. Blat, *De Delictis et Poenis,* n. 59; Berutti, *Institutiones Iuris Canonici,* VI, n. 38, IV, 4, p. 106.

[173] Cf. canons 671, 1°; 2295; 2370; 2373; 2387; 2394, 3°.

[174] Cf. canon 2237, § 2: . . . exceptis censuris specialissimo vel speciali modo Sedi Apostolicae reservatis.

[175] Cf. Ayrinhac-Lydon, *Penal Legislation in the New Code of Canon Law,*

Another problem presents itself. If a case involving a *latae sententiae* vindicative penalty of the general law has been brought to the judicial forum and is pending there, but has not been declared, can the vindicative penalty be dispensed in the internal forum? It is presumed that the penalty is occult, for the fact that it has been brought to the judicial forum does not necessarily mean that the penalty has become public.[176] The question has been proposed by D'Annibale,[177] who answers it in the affirmative, and by Wernz-Vidal,[178] who answer in the negative. For several reasons, it would seem that such a dispensation could not be given, for it does not seem that the Church would allow a faculty to be exercised if such an exercise would definitely embarrass or harm the judge of the external forum. Moreover, there is a certain juridical incongruity in permitting the very *vinculum poenale,* which is being judged in the court, to be dissolved by another outside the court. Such an exercise of dispensatory power certainly at least exposes the power of the judge and his exercise of that power to contempt.[179]

n. 161; Berutti, *Institutiones Iuris Canonici,* VI, n. 88, IV; Blat, *De Delictis et Poenis,* n. 230.

[176] Cf. Coronata, *Institutiones Iuris Canonici,* IV, n. 1648.

[177] Cf. *Summula,* n. 346.

[178] Cf. *Ius Canonicum,* VII, n. 215, p. 225, nota 23.

[179] Cf. Wernz-Vidal, *Ius Canonicum,* VII, n. 215, p. 225, nota 23. Cf. also *infra,* p. 197, wherein the same problem is considered in relation to canon 2290.

SECTION II

DISPENSATION FROM VINDICATIVE PENALTIES IN THE MORE URGENT CASES

CHAPTER VIII

THE USUAL METHOD—CANON 2290, § 1

Canon 2290, § 1. In casibus occultis urgentioribus, si ex observatione poenae vindicativae latae sententiae, reus seipsum proderet cum infamia et scandalo, quilibet confessarius potest in foro sacramentali obligationem servandae poenae suspendere, iniuncto onere recurrendi saltem intra mensem per epistolam et per confessarium, si id fieri possit sine gravi incommodo, reticito nomine, ad S. Poenitentiariam vel ad Episcopum facultate praeditum et standi eius mandatis.

§ 2. Et si in aliquo casu extraordinario hic recursus sit impossibilis, tunc ipsemet confessarius potest dispensationem concedere ad normam can. 2254, § 3.

Article I. The More Urgent Cases

A. *General Notions*

It has been seen in the historical section of this work that, although the Church has always prescribed particular norms for the dispensation from vindicative penalties, it was not until the Code of Canon Law was promulgated that definite deviations from these norms were permitted. For it was the Code of Canon Law which granted definite faculties to ordinaries to dispense from these penalties under certain defined conditions,[1] and at the same time granted faculties to confessors to suspend or dispense from vindicative penalties in certain more urgent or extraordinary cases.

[1] Cf. *supra*, p. 127.

These latter faculties, in the *"casus urgentiores,"* were established and embodied in canon 2290 of the Code.

The number of the more urgent cases is variously regarded as one [2] or two,[3] depending on whether the danger of scandal or infamy is considered as constituting one or two distinct urgent cases. The Code itself uses the phrase *"si . . . reus seipsum proderet cum infamia et scandalo . . ."*, thus seeming to combine both elements, of infamy to the guilty one and of scandal to others, in one case. But does the legislator mean to state that both infamy and scandal or the danger of both must be present before the case may be considered more urgent? Some canonists [4] seem to think that both elements must be present. However, it would seem that either element suffices to provide the more urgent case demanded by the canon. In the first place, the Code often uses the term "et" in the disjunctive sense of *"vel."* In fact, in this same canon 2290, that term is used precisely in that sense: ". . . *per epistolam et per confessarium.*" [5] Also the clear analogy between this canon and canon 2254, § 1 demands that interpretation,[6] for in canon 2254, § 1, the phrase used is *"scandali vel infamiae."* This certainly seems to be the correct interpretation of the phrase, so that either infamy or scandal may produce the more urgent case demanded in this canon.[7] But the two

[2] Cf. Coronata, *Institutiones Iuris Canonici,* IV, n. 1823; Vermeersch-Creusen, *Epitome,* III, n. 491; Berutti, *Institutiones Iuris Canonici,* VI, n. 86, II.

[3] Cf. Kelly, *Jurisdiction of the Confessor According to the Code of Canon Law* (New York, Cincinnati, Chicago: Benziger Brothers, 1929), 235 (hereafter cited as *Jurisdiction of the Confessor*); Ayrinhac-Lydon, *Penal Legislation in the New Code of Canon Law,* n. 157.

[4] Cf. Coronata, *Institutiones Iuris Canonici,* IV, n. 1823; Vermeersch-Creusen, *Epitome,* III, n. 491; Berutti, *Institutiones Iuris Canonici,* VI, n. 86, II.

[5] Cf. Coronata, *Institutiones Iuris Canonici,* IV, n. 1823, p. 252, nota 2; Chelodi, *Ius Poenale,* n. 47, p. 52, nota 4; Moriarty, *Extraordinary Absolution from Censures,* pp. 196, 197.

[6] Cf. Wernz-Vidal, *Ius Canonicum,* VII, n. 34°, 2°; Woywod, *A Practical Commentary,* II, n. 2131; De Meester, *Compendium,* III, n. 1787, 3°; Chelodi, *Ius Poenale,* n. 47; Santamaria, *Comentarios al Codigo Canonico,* VI, p. 169; Ayrinhac-Lydon, *Penal Legislation in the New Code of Canon Law,* n. 157; Eichmann, *Das Strafrecht,* p. 111.

[7] Kelly, *Jurisdiction of the Confessor,* p. 235; Ayrinhac-Lydon, *Penal Legislation in the New Code of Canon Law,* n. 157.

cases, in fact, are usually concomitant. For the scandal undoubtedly is bred by the infamy, just as the personal infamy of the guilty person is produced, more or less, by the scandal on the part of others. It is important to note that the more urgent cases are only those mentioned in canon 2290, § 1.[8]

Just as in canon 2254,[9] for the use of the faculties of canon 2290 at least one of the more urgent cases must be verified, and this for the validity of the dispensation.[10] For it is evident that the general delegation of faculties in canon 2290 is given for the particular circumstances of the more urgent cases, that outside of these more urgent cases the norms of canon 2236 for ordinary cases must be used, that if the condition of the more urgent case is not present the confessor does not possess the faculties granted for such urgent cases.

In passing, it is of practical value to call attention to the difference between canon 2254 and canon 2290 in regard to the kind of cases regarded as more urgent as demanded therein. In addition to the causes for dispensation given in canon 2290, canon 2254, in treating of extraordinary absolutions from censures, establishes as a further reason for absolution the hardship of remaining in grave sin until a competent superior can be approached. Thus in canon 2254 there are three urgent cases,[11] while in canon 2290 there are only two. Likewise, as a result, the faculties granted in canon 2254 are not restricted to occult cases of urgency,[12] for a penitent who is laboring under a public censure and finds it hard to remain in sin may take advantage of the special faculties of confessors in canon 2254. But since the only urgent cases established in canon 2290

[8] Cf. Coronata, *Institutiones,* IV, n. 1823.

[9] Cf. Moriarty, *Extraordinary Absolution from Censures,* p. 144.

[10] Cf. Kelly, *Jurisdiction of the Confessor,* p. 236; De Meester, *Compendium,* III, n. 1748, a; Cappello, *De Censuris* (3. ed., 1933), n. 124.

[11] Cf. Cappello, *De Censuris* (3. ed., 1933), n. 124, 2; Cerato, *Censurae Vigentes,* pp. 43, 44; Salucci, *Il Diritto Penale,* I, 225; Cocchi, *Commentarium in Codicem Iuris Canonici,* V, 124.

[12] Cf. Coronata, *Institutiones Iuris Canonici,* IV, n. 252; De Meester, *Compendium,* III, n. 185, nota 5; Sole, *De Delictis et Poenis,* n. 185; Chelodi, *Ius Poenale,* n. 40; Salucci, *Il Diritto Penale,* I, 216; Cappello, *De Censuris* (3. ed., 1933), nn. 97-100; Cipollini, *De Censuris,* pp. 35, 36; Berutti, *Institutiones Iuris Canonici,* VI, nn. 57, 58.

involve infamy or scandal, it follows that use of canon 2290 is restricted to occult cases of urgency. This matter will be treated in detail in the discussion of the dispensation of vindicative penalties in these occult cases.[13]

B. *The Occult Cases*

The more urgent cases of canon 2290 are only those which are occult, that is, cases which involve a delict at least formally occult. The matter of occult cases has been treated at length previously.[14] It is enough to note here that the case, although public elsewhere or at some other time, must *de facto* be occult now in the place in which the delinquent is morally forced to place the act prohibited by the penalty.

It is of great importance to note that the mere presence of an occult case does not permit the confessor to use the dispensatory faculties granted in canon 2290. The case must be an occult *more urgent* case. The essentially intimate relation between an occult and the conditions for establishing the more urgent case, namely, the infamy or scandal which would necessarily follow from the observance of a vindicative penalty incurred by the occult delict, has been mentioned in passing.[15] The occult case is established by the fact that the delict is at least formally occult or the penalty is occult; and the more urgent case is established by the fact that as a result of the observance of the penalty incurred the delinquent would make known his secret sin, which would entail loss of reputation and scandal.[16] The existence of the one, the occult case, depends necessarily on the existence of the other, the urgent case. For if there is danger of scandal or infamy from the observance of the penalty, the delict and the incurrence of the *latae sententiae* penalty must be occult. If the delict, and consequently the incurrence of the penalty, is public, the person who is commonly known to be under a vindicative penalty will not occasion scandal or suffer infamy by failing

[13] Cf. *infra*, p. 224.

[14] Cf. *supra*, p. 161.

[15] Cf. *supra*, p. 169.

[16] Cf. Ayrinhac-Lydon, *Penal Legislation in the New Code of Canon Law*, n. 157; Berutti, *Institutiones Iuris Canonici*, VI, n. 86, II; Coronata, *Institutiones Iuris Canonici*, IV, n. 1738.

to perform an act prohibited by the penalty; in fact, the very opposite may be true, namely, that the person would rather cause scandal by performing such an action.[17] In other words, there simply is no danger of personal infamy or scandal to others arising from the observance of the vindicative penalty. However, again it must be remembered that vindicative penalties, like delicts, may be occult by reason of time and place, and if such penalties are *de facto* occult, the delict is formally occult, and the entire case is an occult case.[18] Consequently, if it should happen that there is actually danger of scandal or infamy if a person fails to perform an act prohibited by a vindicative penalty because the penalty, although public elsewhere or at some other time, is now *de facto* occult in the place in which the person is morally forced to place the act, he can be dispensed or can have the penalty suspended, according to the norms of canon 2290. The phrase used is "*de facto* occult in the place in which the penitent is morally obliged to place the act" and not "*de facto* occult in the place in which the confession is made"; and the reason for this is clear. If the penitent goes to confession in his own parish, wishing to act against the penalty in that place, the vindicative penalty must be occult in that place, the place of confession, otherwise the confessor cannot suspend or dispense from the penalty, for there will be no scandal or infamy; but if the penitent makes his confession either in his own parish or in some other parish, but must act contrary to the penalty in some other place in which the penalty is *de facto* occult, then the confessor can use the faculties of canon 2290, by reason of the resulting scandal or infamy, regardless of the fact that the penalty is occult or public in the place of the confession. In other words, the public or occult nature of the penalty does not necessarily affect the place of confession, but it certainly does affect the place in which the penitent intends to act, because it is at the latter place that the urgency of the case appears and the infamy or scandal would arise. And if the place of confession and the place of action are the same, as is usually the case, then the vindicative penalty must be occult in the place of

[17] Cf. Cipollini, *De Censuris*, pp. 43, 44.

[18] Cf. Blat, *De Delictis et Poenis*, n. 120; Vermeersch-Creusen, *Epitome*, III, n. 491.

confession, otherwise the danger of scandal or infamy will not be verified.[19]

It is true that scandal may arise from the knowledge of the commission of the delict. Thus the people of a particular parish may be scandalized by the fact that the pastor has committed some delict; but such scandal arising from the public delict is due to the sinful action itself of the particular pastor and not to the observance of any vindicative penalty which he might undergo; and therefore is entirely outside the pale of canon 2290. On the contrary, the observance of the penalty in this instance is rather a public vindication of the publicly known delict and tends rather to remove any scandal that may have been caused. Similarly, a certain amount of infamy may be suffered by such a pastor because of his sin, but such infamy is the result of his own free action and not of the coercive sanction of the Church. Here again the observance of an incurred vindicative penalty tends rather to remove the personal infamy.

Though it follows that whenever there is danger of scandal or infamy arising from the observance of the penalty, the delict and incurrence of the penalty must be occult, it does not follow that every occult delict and its consequent occult incurrence of penalty involves a more urgent case. For if the delict and the penalty incurred are occult, but the vindicative penalty may be observed without scandal or infamy, the more urgent case does not exist and the faculties of canon 2290 may not be used. In these circumstances, the person who has incurred the vindicative penalty has a grave obligation in conscience to observe the penalty unless he has been dispensed by the legitimate and competent superior as established in canon 2236.

In the occult cases mentioned previously, namely, when the delict and imputability are public and the penalty attached to the delict as a matter of fact is occult,[20] the urgency of the case once again depends upon whether infamy or scandal will result from the observance of the penalty. If infamy or scandal will not arise, the case remains merely an occult non-urgent case, and canon 2290 does not apply. If, on the other hand, there is danger of infamy or

[19] Cf. Vermeersch-Creusen, *Epitome,* III, n. 491.

[20] Cf. *supra,* p. 162.

scandal, the occult case becomes a more urgent occult case and thereby becomes subject to the faculties conceded by canon 2290.

C. *The Probability of Infamy or Scandal*

As has been noted, the *casus urgentior* mentioned in canon 2290 is as follows: "si ex observatione poenae vindicativae latae sententiae, reus seipsum proderet cum infamia et scandalo." Consequently, the faculties conceded in canon 2290 may be used if, in an occult case, a *latae sententiae* vindicative penalty cannot be observed without scandal or infamy. The infamy or scandal need not be certain or even very probable; but it is sufficient if the observance of the vindicative penalty and the consequent revelation of a secret delict would at least probably cause the loss of reputation or good name to the delinquent and scandal to the people.[21] It is important to notice that, despite the analogy between canon 2290 and canon 2254, probability on the mere danger of grave scandal or infamy suffices to induce the more urgent case in canon 2254.[22] Likewise, canon 2254 qualifies both the scandal and infamy by the word "gravis," while this term is omitted entirely in canon 2290.

In general, scandal is both that which may offer to another an occasion of sin and the sin which is thus induced.[23] It is divided into active scandal and passive scandal. Active scandal is "dictum vel factum minus rectum, praebens alteri occasionem ruinae spiri-

[21] Cf. Augustine, *A Commentary on the New Code,* VIII, 240; Berutti, *Institutiones Iuris Canonici,* VI, n. 86, II; Ayrinhac-Lydon, *Penal Legislation in the New Code of Canon Law,* n. 157; Woywod, *A Practical Commentary,* II, n. 2130; Wernz-Vidal, *Ius Canonicum,* VII, nn. 263, 340; Kelly, *Jurisdiction of the Confessor,* p. 236. Blat (*De Delictis et Poenis,* n. 210) demands that there be moral certitude that scandal will result.

[22] Cf. canon 2254, § 1: . . . si censurae latae sententiae exterius servari nequeant sine periculo gravis scandali vel infamiae. . . . Cf. Moriarty, *The Extraordinary Absolution from Censures,* p. 145; Cappello, *De Censuris* (3. ed., 1933), n. 124, 3.

[23] Cf. Arregui, *Summarium Theologiae Moralis* (13. ed., Romae, 1937), n. 149; Noldin-Schmidt, *Summa Theologiae Moralis Iuxta Codicem Iuris Canonici* (22. ed., Oeniponte: Rauch, 1934), II, *De Praeceptis Dei et Ecclesiae,* n. 102 (hereafter cited as *Summa Theologiae Moralis*).

tualis." [24] Passive scandal is "ruina ipsa spiritualis proximi orta ex activo," [25] or "ipsum peccatum, ad quod committendum proximo praebetur occasio." [26] In canon 2290, the term "scandal" includes both active and passive scandal, for this canon looks both to those who occasion the spiritual harm [27] and to those who suffer the spiritual harm as a result of another's actions.[28] In this canon the active scandal, or the "factum minus rectum," may be an action which is in itself good or at least indifferent, but which, in the opinion or convictions of others appears to be evil, as, for example, the omission of Mass on Sunday for a just cause unknown to others.[29] Thus, if a priest were to omit the celebration of Mass because of a *latae sententiae* vindicative penalty of suspension, his action, although indifferent in itself, is capable of and likely to give an occasion to the spiritual harm of others inasmuch as it may lead them to the presumption or conviction, spiritually detrimental to such persons, that the ultimate cause for the omission is a serious and grave crime. Unlike canon 2254, which seems to look primarily to those who suffer the spiritual harm and consequently is concerned more with the passive scandal than with the active,[30] canon 2290 seems rather to stress the active scandal and seems to look definitely to the one who, through his action, occasions the scandal.[31] However, canon 2290 does seem to consider the passive scandal as a

[24] St. Thomas Aquinas, *Summa,* II, II, q. 43, a. 1. Cf. Arregui, *Summarium Theologiae Moralis,* n. 149; Noldin-Schmidt, *Summa Theologiae Moralis,* II, n. 103.

[25] Arregui, *Summa Theologiae Moralis,* n. 151.

[26] Noldin-Schmidt, *Summa Theologiae Moralis,* II, n. 103.

[27] Cf. Coronata, *Institutiones Iuris Canonici,* IV, n. 1823; Vermeersch-Creusen, *Epitome,* III, n. 491.

[28] Cf. Berutti, *Institutiones Iuris Canonici,* VI, n. 86, II; Blat, *De Delictis et Poenis,* n. 120; Kelly, *Jurisdiction of the Confessor,* p. 235; Ayrinhac-Lydon, *Penal Legislation in the New Code of Canon Law,* n. 157.

[29] Cf. Noldin-Schmidt, *Summa Theologiae Moralis,* II, nn. 103, 104.

[30] Cf. canon 2254: . . . si censurae latae sententiae exterius servari nequeant sine periculo gravis scandali vel infamiae. . . . Cf. Moriarty, *Extraordinary Absolution from Censures,* p. 146.

[31] Cf. canon 2290: . . . si ex observatione poenae vindicativae latae sententiae, reus seipsum proderet cum infamia et scandalo. . . ." Cf. Coronata, *Institutiones Iuris Canonici,* IV, n. 1823; Vermeersch-Creusen, *Epitome,* III, n. 491.

natural result of the active.[32] This passive scandal may be either *scandalum datum,* as when it results from an action which is evil or has the appearance of evil, and which from its very nature may furnish an occasion of sin; or it may be *scandalum acceptum,* as when it arises from a good action of another, an action which, not by its nature but because of the evil disposition of others, furnishes an occasion for sin. And this latter scandal may be either *scandalum pusillorum,* if it springs from mere weakness or ignorance, or *scandalum pharisaicum,* if it springs from malice.[33] This passive scandal may be occasioned in one person, or several or many persons.[34]

Whenever, therefore, it is foreseen that, when a person who has incurred a *latae sententiae* vindicative penalty must omit an action, the omission of such an action will become an occasion for others, even through mere weakness or ignorance on their part, to commit a sin of any kind, such as detraction or rash judgment, then the vindicative penalty can be suspended by a confessor by reason of canon 2290. This would also seem to apply if there were a probable occasion of a grave diminution of virtue in others, or a grave decrease of esteem for religion or for the priests of that religion. Moreover, it seems that those things which are commonly considered as types of scandal would also be included under this term "scandalum." Consequently, serious indignation on the part of others or harmful rumors would be included in this broad sense of scandal.[35] However, it would seem that *scandalum pharisaicum,* arising solely from the evil dispositions and malice of others, would not be sufficient in itself to allow the use of canon 2290; but such scandal may readily become a source of infamy to the person who omits an action be-

[32] Cf. Blat, *De Delictis et Poenis,* n. 120; Berutti, *Institutiones Iuris Canonici,* VI, n. 86, II; Kelly, *Jurisdiction of the Confessor,* p. 235; Ayrinhac-Lydon, *Penal Legislation in the New Code of Canon Law,* n. 157.

[33] Cf. Noldin-Schmidt, *Summa Theologiae Moralis,* II, n. 103. Authors do not all make these same divisions. Cf. Arregui, *Summa Theologiae Moralis,* n. 151.

[34] Cf. Blat, *De Delictis et Poenis,* n. 120.

[35] Cf. Noldin-Schmidt, *Summa Theologiae Moralis,* II, n. 105; Vermeersch, *Theologiae Moralis Principia, Responsa, Consilio* (2. ed., Brugis: Beyaert, 1927), I, nn. 120-128 (hereafter cited as *Theologia Moralis*); Wouters, *Manuale Theologiae Moralis* (Brugis: Beyaert, 1927), I, nn. 546-553.

cause of a vindicative penalty, and as such would allow the application of canon 2290.

Besides the probability of scandal arising from the observance of a *latae sententiae* vindicative penalty, there is the other cause of the more urgent case: infamy. The more urgent case is established by the fact that there is a probability of infamy arising from the revelation of an occult delict when the perpetrator of the crime observes the *latae sententiae* vindicative penalty which he has incurred. In general, infamy, as understood in canon 2290, may be defined as "amissio bonae existimationis apud fideles probos et graves," [36] arising from the revelation, as it were, of an occult delict. Consequently, if it is foreseen that one's reputation or good name among upright and seriously minded people will be lost or diminished by the observance of an occult *latae sententiae* vindicative penalty by the revelation to them of one's occult crime, either directly inasmuch as their suspicion of the crime would be converted into moral certitude,[37] or indirectly because a strong suspicion would be aroused that the reason for the omission of the prohibited action is a crime imposing the omission as a penalty, then the faculties of canon 2290 may be employed.[38]

Because of the extremely close analogy between canon 2290 and canon 2254, it would seem that in order to establish the more urgent case arising from scandal or infamy, there must be at least the probability that the scandal or infamy will materialize before the confessor can apply for and obtain the proper dispensatory faculties from a competent superior, just as the similar *casus urgentior* of canon 2254 is understood in this sense.[39] In other words, the entire nature of the urgency of this case consists in this: that the dispensation or suspension of the vindicative penalty cannot be deferred without scandal or infamy. Therefore, the probability of infamy or scandal must be imminent in a certain sense, that is, it must be probable that it will be verified before the confessor can obtain the

[36] Cf. canon 2293, § 3. This is, in other words, the definition of *infamia facti*.

[37] Cf. Blat, *De Delictis et Poenis*, nn. 78, 120.

[38] Cf. Vermeersch-Creusen, *Epitome*, III, n. 491.

[39] Cf. Moriarty, *Extraordinary Absolution from Censures*, p. 148.

proper faculties or before the penitent can apply for a dispensation from the competent superior according to canon 2236. If this is not the case, and the penitent will not be exposed to any infamy or will not be the occasion of scandal before the confessor or the penitent can apply to the proper competent superior for a dispensation from the penalty, it simply would not be a more urgent case and could not be used in the application of canon 2290. In other words, if the infamy or scandal is comparatively remote, so that the penitent himself could apply directly to the competent superior for a dispensation before the scandal or infamy will actually arise, it is not understood how this could possibly be a more urgent case or why there would be any need for the confessor to suspend the vindicative penalty in accordance with canon 2290, § 1. However, in practice, this will seldom cause difficulty, because, generally, when this more urgent case is used as a reason for release from the observance of a penalty, it will be a case in which the penitent immediately or shortly after his confession, must perform the act prohibited by the vindicative penalty.[40]

In regard to personal infamy suffered as the result of the observance of a vindicative penalty, the relation between canon 2290 and canon 2232 must be considered. Canon 2232, § 1 states that a *latae sententiae* vindicative penalty is incurred immediately on the transgression of the law, and obliges the culprit to observe the penalty in both the internal and external forum; but if the offender has incurred the penalty by a violation of the law that was not notorious, and he cannot observe the penalty without suffering personal infamy or loss of good name, he is excused from the observance of the vindicative penalty in the external forum until a declaratory judicial sentence has been issued against him, or his offense has become notorious.[41] Since the offender himself is excused, by virtue of and under the conditions of this canon, from observing the penalty in case of infamy, the question may be raised: why, then, are special

[40] Cf. Blat, *De Delictis et Poenis*, n. 120.

[41] Cf. canon 2232, § 1: Poena latae sententiae, sive medicinalis sive vindicativa, delinquentem, qui delicti sibi sit conscius, ipso facto in utroque foro tenet; ante sententiam tamen declaratoriam a poena observanda delinquens excusatur quoties servare sine infamia nequit, et in foro externo ab eo eiusdem poenae observantiam exigre nemo potest, nisi delictum sit notorium, . . .

faculties given the confessor in canon 2290 to suspend the penalty under the same conditions? It is true that the benefit of canon 2232, § 1 can be enjoyed without approaching a confessor, but the submission of the case to the confessor gives the penitent additional benefits not enjoyed under canon 2232, § 1. For the confessor suspends the vindicative penalty entirely while the recourse is pending and consequently the penalty remains suspended even when the danger or probability of loss of reputation has ceased. Moreover, the penitent is freed from the penalty to such an extent that he is excused from observing the penalty not only in the external forum but also in the internal forum; and he can exercise all acts which would otherwise be forbidden to him by the vindicative penalty, not only in cases where the omission of these acts would betray his secret offense to others with the resulting infamy, but also in other cases where there is no danger or probability of betraying himself, or when the danger of scandal or loss of reputation has ceased.[42] In other words, canon 2232, § 1 excuses in the external forum only[43] in such acts as occasion infamy; while canon 2290, § 1 allows a complete suspension of the vindicative penalty. When a confessor cannot be approached, a person under an occult *latae sententiae* vindicative penalty may make use of canon 2232, § 1; and thus this canon seems to be an alternative to canon 2290, § 1, and not a substitute.[44]

Sole[45] has a unique explanation of the relation between canon 2232 and canon 2290. He holds that canon 2290 is but a particular

[42] Cf. Ayrinhac-Lydon, *Penal Legislation in the New Code of Canon Law*, n. 157; Woywod, *A Practical Commentary*, II, n. 2131.

[43] Cf. Ayrinhac-Lydon, *Penal Legislation in the New Code of Canon Law*, n. 57; Augustine, *A Commentary on the New Code*, VIII, 103; Cocchi, *Commentarium in Codicem Iuris Canonici*, VIII, n. 46; Berutti, *Institutiones Iuris Canonici*, VI, n. 36. Coronata, *Institutiones Iuris Canonici*, IV, n. 1723, and Blat, *De Delictis et Poenis*, n. 52 hold that canon 2232, § 1 affects both the internal and external forums.

[44] Cf. Coronata, *Institutiones Iuris Canonici*, IV, n. 1823; Vermeersch-Creusen, *Epitome*, III, n. 491; DeMeester, *Compendium*, III, n. 1787, 3°; Ayrinhac-Lydon, *Penal Legislation in the New Code of Canon Law*, n. 157; Woywod, *A Practical Commentary*, II, n. 2131; Blat, *De Delictis et Poenis*, n. 120; Salucci, *Il Diritto Penale*, pp. 301, 302; Wernz-Vidal, *Ius Canonicum*, VII, n. 340.

[45] *De Delictis et Poenis*, n. 268.

application of the general principle established in canon 2232. Canon 2232 is but a restatement of the principle: *Nemo tenetur prodere semetipsum.* But the individual delinquent may not judge whether there is danger of infamy in his case; he must submit the case to a confessor, who, acting in accordance with canon 2290, makes the judgment. The delinquent may not, through his own authority, excuse himself from the observance of the vindicative penalty, but he must receive the suspension or dispensation of the penalty from his confessor.[46]

If the delinquent, in the case of canon 2290, is unable to find a confessor, and there is danger of scandal or infamy arising from the observance of the vindicative penalty, he may safely use canon 2232 as a quasi-substitute for canon 2290, and may excuse himself from observing the penalty under those conditions. He should, however, make an act of perfect contrition, so that he acts not only validly but licitly.[47]

In general, then, it may be said that a more urgent case involving either personal infamy or scandal to others, when verified, can be invoked for the suspension or dispensation, according to canon 2290, of any *latae sententiae* vindicative penalty which is occult; but the penalty, and consequently the delict, must be occult, at least in the place in which the penitent wishes to perform an act which otherwise is prohibited by the vindicative penalty and in which the revelation of his secret delict and punishment would give rise to infamy to himself or scandal to others from his failure to exercise the act.

[46] Sole (*loc. cit.*): "Ita sane! imo et ipsum ius naturae excusat in casu a poena observandi, quia nemo tenetur prodere semetipsum. Sed animadvertendum, quod nemini licet in causa propria sibi ius dicere; et hallucinationis periculum sedulo vitari debet. Hinc reus, qui delicti sibi sit conscius, non potest suo iudicio suaque auctoritate se eximere a poena incursa observanda; sed expectare debet iudicium confessarii, qui omnibus rite perpensis, et sub conditionibus a iure statutis, obligationem servandae poenae suspendit, imo ex § 2 huius can. et dispensationem concedere potest. . . ."

[47] Cf. Salucci (*Il Diritto Penale*, p. 302): "E ovvio, che quando il delinquente, nel caso di cui al can. 2290, non potesse avere un confessore e intanto non potesse osservare la pena per l'infamia e lo scandalo, può valersi tuta conscientia dal can. 2232, procurando di emettere l'atto di dolore perfetto, affinchè agisca non solo valide ma anche licite." Cf. also DeMeester, *Compendium*, III, n. 1787, 3°, p. 220.

It is the office and duty, ultimately, of the confessor in his prudence to judge whether or not a particular case fulfills the definition of the more urgent case. The confessor, therefore, decides whether the observance of the vindicative penalty will cause loss of reputation or infamy or scandal to others in a particular instance. However, of the actual existence of this condition the penitent may judge and his testimony must be believed. Often the penitent alone may be competent to judge and estimate the probability of infamy or scandal in a peculiar case or particular penalty—for example, suspension from office for a particular time, or refusal to accept a particular dignity offered—of which the confessor might know nothing.[48] The confessor accepts the testimony of the penitent, and forms his prudent judgment as to the existence of the more urgent case. The penitent's testimony also should be accepted as to the existence of the *casus occultus*. Ordinarily he alone may know whether a particular delict or a certain vindicative penalty is occult or public; and the confessor uses his testimony in forming his judgment on the secrecy of the case. If the confessor has at least a positive and probable reason for judging that one of the more urgent cases is present, even though he has some doubt in this regard, he can validly and licitly suspend the penalty in accordance with canon 2290, § 1,[49] or dispense in accordance with canon 2290, § 2, by virtue of canon 209 [50] in conjunction with canon 2290.[51] Even if it subsequently becomes

[48] Cf. Augustine, *A Commentary on the New Code*, VIII, p. 240.

[49] Cf. *infra*, p. 183 as to whether the suspension of the vindicative penalty according to canon 2290, § 1, is an act of jurisdiction. Even if power of suspension is not jurisdiction, however, canon 209 still applies. Cf. Miaskiewicz (*Supplied Jurisdiction According to Canon 209*, The Catholic University of America, Canon Law Studies, n. 122, [Washington: The Catholic University of America Press, 1940], pp. 280-283): Canon 209 supplies not only jurisdiction properly so called but whatever is necessary for the full administration of one's office; that is, the Church supplies all those things whose proper integration is joined with the valid exercise of all the powers inherent in an ecclesiastical office. Cf. also Toso, "Jurisdictio quando ab Ecclesia suppleatur"—*Jus Pontificium*, XVII (1937), p. 100.

[50] Canon 209: In errore communi aut in dubio positivo et probabili sive iuris sive facti, iurisdictionem supplet Ecclesia pro foro tum externo tum interno.

[51] Canon 209 can only be employed under the conditions and stipulations of canon 2290 as to the obligation of recourse, the suitable penance to be im-

evident that the more urgent case was actually and objectively not present at the time of the confession, although the doubt concerning its presence had arisen from a prudent judgment, the suspension of the penalty or the dispensation is certainly valid.[52] Moreover, if the confessor makes a weighed and prudent judgment that a *casus urgentior* and a *casus occultus* is verified in a particular case, the suspension or dispensation from the vindicative penalty is valid, even if subsequent events prove that that judgment was erroneous, as long as the penitent did not, with malice or in bad faith, falsely represent the case as a more urgent case, for example, by asserting the probability of scandal, while knowing that there certainly was no such probability, or by affirming the secrecy of a case while knowing that the case was public.[53]

Article II. The Suspension of the Vindicative Penalty

A. *The Nature and the Form of the Suspension*

Under the faculties of canon 2290, § 1, the confessor does not grant a strict dispensation from the vindicative penalty. Instead he suspends the obligation of the observance of that penalty. In a strict dispensation from vindicative penalties the obligation of the observance is relaxed *in perpetuum,* while in a suspension, the obligation of observing the penalty is relaxed only *ad tempus.*[54] Therefore, the confessor does not remit the penalty, but he suspends the observance of the penalty until recourse is had to the legitimate superior who is competent, according to canon 2236, to remit the pen-

posed, and the satisfaction to be demanded, etc.; otherwise, there would arise the absurd situation that a penitent who is only doubtfully involved in an occult more urgent case would escape the obligation of recourse or penance or satisfaction, while another penitent in whose case true secrecy and urgency are certainly verified, would be bound by such obligations.

[52] Cf. Cappello, *De Censuris* (3. ed., 1933), n. 118, 12; Vermeersch-Creusen, *Epitome,* III, n. 452; Coronata, *Institutiones Iuris Canonici,* IV, n. 1760: this argument is drawn from the analogy between censures and vindicating penalties in canons 2290 and 2254.

[53] Cf. Cappello, *De Censuris* (3. ed., 1933), n. 118; Coronata, *Institutiones,* IV, n. 1760.

[54] Cf. Berutti, *Institutiones Iuris Canonici,* VI, n. 86, II, p. 215, 216.

alty.[55] If the superior refuses to grant the dispensation—and he may in justice do so—and simply gives his mandates,[56] the suspension of the observance of the penalty granted by the confessor ceases, and the vindicative penalty continues to bind the penitent.[57] If the superior grants the dispensation, his act of dispensing is a new act of jurisdiction, essentially distinct from the act of the confessor in suspending the obligation of the observance of the penalty.

The question naturally arises here: for how long a time does the confessor suspend the obligation of the observance of the penalty? Most canonists do not treat of this question at all, being content with merely stating that the obligation of the penalty is suspended. However, it would seem that the penalty is suspended until the reply of the superior is received.[58] In the mandates which the superior sends will be included a statement as to whether the penalty is dispensed by him or whether the penalty is to be observed in the future by the penitent. In the latter case, the superior will give instructions for removing the danger of scandal or infamy in the future,[59] and the suspension of the obligation of the observance of the penalty will cease. If the superior grants the dispensation, the suspension granted by the confessor ceases and the dispensation, the new jurisdictional act of the superior, frees the penitent entirely from the observance of the vindicative penalty.

This power of the confessor to suspend the obligation of observing the vindicative penalty, it seems, is one of jurisdiction. For it is in reality a relaxation of the penalty attached to a penal law, even though it is only a temporary relaxation.[60] Moreover, the obliga-

[55] Cf. Coronata, *Institutiones Iuris Canonici,* IV, n. 1823; Berutti, *Institutiones Iuris Canonici,* VI, n. 86, II; Blat, *De Delictis et Poenis,* n. 120; De-Meester, *Compendium,* III, n. 1787, 3°; Augustine, *A Commentary on the New Code,* VIII, pp. 240-241.

[56] Cf. Ayrinhac-Lydon, *Penal Legislation in the New Code of Canon Law,* n. 157, d.

[57] Cf. Ayrinhac-Lydon, *loc. cit.*

[58] Cf. Vermeersch-Creusen, *Epitome,* III, n. 491.

[59] Cf. *infra,* p. 219 on the nature of the mandates.

[60] Cf. Berutti, *Institutiones Iuris Canonici,* VI, n. 86, II; Coronata, (*Iuris Canonici,* IV, n. 1740, p. 141): "cum omnes effectus poenae suspenduntur ad certum tempus . . . haec remissio, sive dispensatio . . . semper aequivalet partialis legis dispensationi." Cf. also DeMeester, *Compendium,* III, n. 1742, 2, b.

tion of observing the penalty is as thoroughly relaxed during the time allowed for recourse, as that same obligation is relaxed in the complete remission or dispensation granted in accordance with canon 2236. In other words, the power of the confessor touches and relaxes the very obligation of the penal law [61]—clearly an act of jurisdiction. At any rate, the confessor can use this power for the benefit of those, and only those, for whom he possesses sacramental jurisdiction. Canon 2290 does not confer jurisdiction, but it presupposes that the confessor possesses jurisdiction from some other source, and it extends the scope of this jurisdiction to include the suspension of vindicative penalties, which suspension, however, is not an act of sacramental jurisdiction, but rather a "kind of supplement to the jurisdiction the confessor already has." [62]

Unlike the absolution given from a reserved censure by reason of canon 2254, § 1, which absolution is *ad reincidentiam*,[63] the suspension from the obligation of observing the vindicative penalty given by reason of canon 2290, § 1, is not granted with such a resolutive condition.[64] The obligation of recourse is the same as in canon 2254, § 1, but in canon 2290, §1, the obligation of recourse is not demanded *sub poena reincidentiae.* This is so from the very nature of the suspension of the penalty, for such a suspension is not a true and proper remission of the penalty. The vindicative penalty is not removed entirely, but is left suspended, as it were, dependent upon the will of the competent superior who can grant the total removal of the penalty. Consequently, if the recourse is not made within the specified time, the penitent does not incur a new vindicative penalty of the same species, but the same vindicative penalty reacquires its force upon the penitent. In other words, the suspension, after the time for which it is given has elapsed, merely dis-

[61] Cf. *supra*, p. 69. Cf. also Augustine, *A Commentary on the New Code*, VIII, p. 107; Ojetti, *Commentarium in Codicem Iuris Canonici*, I, pp. 327, 328.

[62] Cf. Kelly, *Jurisdiction of the Confessor*, p. 83.

[63] Canon 2254, § 1: ". . . quilibet confessarius . . . absolvere potest . . . sub poena reincidentiae. . . ."

[64] Cf. Coronata, *Institutiones Iuris Canonici*, IV, n. 1740, p. 140; Lega, *De Delictis et Poenis*, n. 135; Hollweck, *Die kirchlichen Strafgesetze*, 31, nota 6; D'Annibale, *Summula*, I, n. 354.

appears and by law loses its force; and the same vindicative penalty continues to bind the offender.[65]

If there is some doubt whether or not a particular case is a *casus urgentior,* but the confessor has a positive and probable reason for believing it to be such, he may suspend the observance of the vindicative penalty absolutely,[66] for canon 209 will supply the necessary jurisdiction if the urgency of the case is not actually or objectively true. When there is a doubt whether or not the penitent has *de facto* incurred a *latae sententiae* vindicative penalty, if it is a doubt of law, then no suspension of the penalty is necessary, for, since a doubtful law does not bind, no penalty can be contracted for the violation of that doubtful law in those of its elements which are doubtful.[67] If the doubt is a doubt of fact, the suspension of the observance of the vindicative penalty is given *ad cautelam,* which is a form of conditional dispensation [68] by which the penitent is given a temporary remission form a doubtful *latae sententiae* vindicative penalty in case it might have actually been incurred and a suspension of the penalty should be needed.[69] The recourse is made as usual to the ordinary.[70]

Just as no particular form is demanded for the dispensation from a vindicative penalty,[71] so there is no need for any special form for the suspension of the obligation of the observance of the

[65] Cf. DeMeester, *Compendium,* III, n. 1787, 3°, p. 220; Berutti, *Institutiones Iuris Canonici,* VI, n. 86, II, p. 217; Ayrinhac-Lydon, *Penal Legislation in the New Code of Canon Law,* n. 157.

[66] Cf. canon 2239, § 1. Cf. Coronata, *Institutiones Iuris Canonici,* IV, n. 1740, p. 140.

[67] Cf. canon 15; canon 2219, § 1. Cf. Lega, *De Delictis et Poenis,* n. 151; Coronata, *Institutiones Iuris Canonici,* IV, n. 1740; Wernz *Ius Decretalium,* VI, n. 177.

[68] Cf. Coronata, *Institutiones Iuris Canonici,* IV, n. 1740, p. 141; Ballerini Palmieri, *Opus Theologicum Morale,* VII, n. 185.

[69] Cf. canon 15. Cf. Coronata, *Institutiones Iuris Canonici,* IV. n. 1740; Cappello, *De Censuris* (3. ed., 1933), n. 94; Ballerini-Palmieri, *Opus Theologicum Morale,* VII, n. 185.

[70] Cf. canons 15, 2237, § 2.

[71] Cf. canon 2239. Cf. Chelodi, *Ius Poenale,* n. 29; Coronata, *Institutiones Iuris Canonici,* IV, n. 1740, p. 143; Wernz, *Ius Decretalium,* VI, n 178; Berutti, *Institutiones Iuris Canonici,* VI, n. 39.

vindicative penalty given by the confessor according to canon 2290, § 1. It is sufficient that the confessor tells the penitent that he is granting the suspension.[72]

B. *The Confessor*

Canon 2290 states that "quilibet confessarius" is given the power to suspend the obligation of observing a vindicative penalty in the more urgent cases or to dispense from the penalty in the extraordinary cases. Consequently any approved confessor can use the faculties of this canon in favor of those over whom he possesses sacramental jurisdiction.[73] All clerics, therefore, who possess sacramental jurisdiction are included under this term "confessor": cardinals; [74] ordinaries and pastors,[75] each to the extent of his particular jurisdiction; secular and religious priests who are approved by the local ordinary for the hearing of confessions of the faithful; [76] priests who are given the special jurisdiction to hear confessions of women religious, according to the stipulations of law; [77] for exempt clerical religious, not only those who have ordinary or delegated jurisdiction in the diocese, but also competent superiors according to the norms of the constitutions, and also any member of the religious or secular clergy who has received delegated jurisdiction from these superiors.[78] Also included is any priest who acts with supplied jurisdiction, in the particular circumstances established by canon 209 in reference to positive doubt of law or fact or common error.

It is important to note that, although the confessor acts, according to canon 2290, in the sacramental forum, it is not necessary for him to have actually absolved the penitent of his sins.[79]

[72] Cf. Berutti, *Institutiones Iuris Canonici,* VI, n. 86, II, p. 216; Blat, *De Delictis et Poenis,* n. 120.

[73] Cf. Augustine, *A Commentary on the New Code,* VIII, p. 107; Blat, *De Delictis et Poenis,* n. 120, p. 172; Ojetti, *Commentarium in Codicem Iuris Canonici,* I, pp. 327, 328.

[74] Cf. canon 239, § 1, nn. 1, 2.

[75] Cf. canons 873, 881.

[76] Cf. canons 874, 881, § 1.

[77] Cf. canons 520-523, 876.

[78] Cf. canons 518, 519, 874, 875, § 1.

[79] Cf. Blat, *De Delictis et Poenis,* n. 120, p. 172; Coronata, *Institutiones*

Before the confessor suspends the vindicative penalty or dispenses from it, he must mention to the penitent his obligation to have recourse; and, unless it is a case in which the recourse will be morally impossible, he must, under pain of grave sin for himself,[80] impose this obligation of recourse upon the penitent. If the confessor were to fail deliberately to impose this obligation of recourse in a case in which the obligation should be given, he would commit a grave sin; but the suspension of the obligation of the observance of the penalty could be valid, for the Code does not require this imposition of recourse under pain of invalidity.[81]

If the penitent unreasonably refuses to undergo the obligation of recourse when it is morally possible, or states that he does not intend to fulfill the mandates which the competent superior may demand, the confessor cannot dispense with the recourse and apply canon 2290, § 2; but he must refuse to grant the suspension of the observance of the vindicative penalty.[82]

The confessor does not impose a penance for the vindicative penalty which he has suspended. Since canon 2290, § 1 requires that recourse be made to the proper competent superior, the mandates which will come from that superior will establish any penance for the penalty which the superior deems fitting. And since the phrase "iniunctis de iure iniungendis" of canon 2254, § 3 applies to canon 2290, § 2, and not to canon 2290, § 1, the mandates from the superior and not the confessor, will indicate whatever is to be enjoined by divine or ecclesiastical law.[83] The confessor, however, must, as he is obliged in every confession, impose a suitable penance for the

Iuris Canonici, IV, n. 1823, p. 252; Woywod, *A Practical Commentary,* II, n. 2131; Kelly, *Jurisdiction of the Confessor,* p. 236.

[80] Cf. Vermeersch-Creusen, *Epitome,* III, n. 454, 4, 1°; DeMeester, *Compendium,* III, n. 1748; Cappello, *De Censuris* (3. ed., 1933), n. 127; Salucci, *Il Diritto Penale,* I, p. 226; Berutti, *Institutiones Iuris Canonici,* VI, n. 57, IV.

[81] Cf. Coronata, *Institutiones Iuris Canonici,* IV, n. 1762; Salucci, *Il Diritto Penale,* I, p. 226; Vermeersch-Creusen, *Epitome,* III, n. 454, 4, 1°; Moriarty, *Extraordinary Absolution from Censures,* p. 155.

[82] Cf. Berutti, *Institutiones Iuris Canonici,* VI, n. 57, IV; Moriarty, *Extraordinary Absolution from Censures,* p. 155; Salucci, *Il Diritto Penale,* I, p. 227.

[83] Cf. Cocchi, *Commentarium in Codicem Iuris Canonici,* V, p. 125.

delict or sin and enjoin those things commanded by the divine positive and natural law, such as the reparation of scandal, restitution of stolen goods, or the dismissal of an accomplice in sin.

Since vindicative penalties are pure penalties, and, unlike censures, do not prevent the reception of the sacraments, it would seem that canon 2290 does not *"ex ipsa rei natura"* affect Orientals, and therefore cannot be used by confessors other than those of the Latin rite.[84]

C. *The Penitent*

Under the term "reus" in canon 2290 is included any penitent, that is, anyone of the faithful who has incurred an occult *latae sententiae* vindicative penalty but cannot observe that penalty in the external forum because of the probable danger of infamy to himself or consequent scandal to others. He is always obliged in conscience to observe the penalty in the internal forum since he can do so without occasioning infamy or scandal; and he is obliged likewise to observe the penalty in the external forum unless there is danger of infamy or scandal, in which latter case he may make use of either canon 2232 *per modum actus,* or of canon 2290 for a complete suspension or dispensation from the vindicative penalty.[85] If he makes use of canon 2232, he is excused from observing the penalty only in the external forum and only in the individual cases in which there will arise infamy or scandal; if as a penitent he uses canon 2290, the observance of the penalty is suspended, not only in the external, but also in the internal forum, and in all cases, whether there is danger of infamy or scandal or not.

Since canon 2290 seems to be restricted to members of the Latin rite,[86] the penitent must be of the Latin rite. Orientals, it seems, are to be excluded from the benefits of this canon. Apparently, therefore, an Oriental penitent cannot be validly and licitly granted a suspension of or a dispensation from a vindicative penalty by a Latin confessor; nor can a Latin penitent obtain the benefits of canon 2290 through the offices of an Oriental confessor. Any benefits which an Oriental penitent might obtain in similar circumstances

[84] Cf. canon 1. Cf. Cicognani, *Canon Law,* pp. 453, 454.
[85] Cf. Berutti, *Institutiones Iuris Canonici,* VI, n. 86, II, p. 216.
[86] Cf. *supra,* p. 186.

or any faculties which a confessor of the Oriental rite might enjoy under similar conditions would be decided by the proper discipline and laws of the Oriental Church.[87]

Just as in the absolution of his sins, the penitent must have the proper dispositions, so in obtaining a suspension of or a dispensation from his vindicative penalty according to canon 2290, he must also have certain requisite dispositions. Thus, for example, he must express his readiness to accept and fulfill the obligation of recourse imposed upon him by the confessor; he must also be ready to fulfill the recommendations enjoined by the confessor, and obey all the instructions or penances which will be contained in the mandates of the superior. And so if the penitent unreasonably refuses to comply with any of these requisites established in canon 2290, he cannot enjoy the supension of the obligation of the observance of the vindicative penalty, for he is not properly disposed. If the recourse to the superior is morally impossible, the confessor should apply the norm of canon 2290, § 2.[88] If the penitent intends to obviate the necessity of recourse by going to a specially authorized or qualified confessor, who has the power to dispense from the vindicative penalty, this is perfectly licit.[89]

The obligation of recourse binds the penitent *sub gravi;* and therefore, when the penitent is aware of the obligation of recourse, he is bound by it even if the confessor, either with or without deliberate fault, did not explicitly impose that obligation upon him;[90] likewise, the penitent is bound by the obligation of recourse when he becomes aware of it, even though the confessor failed to inform him of it.[91]

When the penitent is one who had previously been granted a suspension from the observance of the vindicative penalty in a more urgent case, but has culpably failed to make the prescribed recourse during the time allotted, it is not required that the confessor should

[87] Cf. Cicognani, *Canon Law,* p. 447.

[88] Cf. Berutti, *Institutiones Iuris Canonici,* VI, n. 86, II.

[89] Cf. *infra,* p. 239 for a treatment of this alternative method of canon 2254, § 2 as applied to vindicating penalties.

[90] Cf. *supra,* p. 187.

[91] This obligation of the penitent and the varying opinions on the matter will be treated at length in the article on recourse, *infra,* p. 204.

urge him to make the omitted recourse, for the suspension of the penalty has ceased and the penitent is again bound by the same vindicative penalty.[92] The penitent must be absolved from the grave sin which he has committed by not having made the prescribed recourse; [93] and if the conditions of the occult more urgent case still exist, another suspension from the observance of the vindicative penalty may be again granted by the confessor, and the obligation of recourse, if it is morally possible, must be again imposed upon the penitent under pain of grave sin.

D. *The Forum of the Suspension*

The suspension of the observance of the vindicative penalty, according to canon 2290, § 1, can be granted by the confessor only "in foro sacramentali," that is, only in connection with the act of sacramental confession, when the penitent confesses his sins in the tribunal of Penance for the purpose of obtaining absolution.[94] It is not necessary, however, that the confessor actually absolve the penitent from his sins; if, for some reason, absolution is to be refused, the confessor may use the faculties of canon 2290 in regard to the vindicative penalty.[95] Any use of canon 2290, however, outside the sacramental forum, even in the internal non-sacramental forum, is invalid.[96]

Therefore, although the faculties granted by canon 2290, § 1, are to be used only in the internal sacramental forum, the suspension of the penalty is complete, that is, it removes the effects of the

[92] Cf. *supra*, p. 184.

[93] Cf. *supra*, p. 189.

[94] Cf. Coronata, *Institutiones Iuris Canonici*, IV, n. 1823, p. 252; De-Meester, *Compendium*, III, n. 1748, 1°, c, p. 185; Chelodi, *Ius Poenale*, n. 35, c, p. 42, nota 6; Blat, *De Delictis et Poenis*, n. 78, p. 116, n. 120, p. 172; Cappello, *De Censuris* (3. ed., 1933), n. 126, 7; Berutti, *Institutiones Iuris Canonici*, Vi, n. 86; Kelly, *Jurisdiction of the Confessor*, p. 236; Augustine, *A Commentary on the New Code*, VIII, p. 241; Ayrinhac-Lydon, *Penal Legislation in the New Code of Canon Law*, n. 157.

[95] Cf. Blat, *De Delictis et Poenis*, n. 120, p. 172.

[96] Cf. Coronata, *Institutiones Iuris Canonici*, IV, n. 1823, p. 252; n. 1762, p. 180; Woywod, *A Practical Commentary*, VIII, p. 241; Kelly, *Jurisdiction of the Confessor*, p. 236; Chelodi, *Ius Poenale*, n. 47.

vindicative penalty in the external forum, so that the penitent is freed from the obligation of the observance of the penalty in the external as well as in the internal forum, even in regard to such actions in the external forum as will not cause scandal or infamy.[97]

Article III. The Object of the Suspension

A. *Latae Sententiae Vindicative Penalties*

The object of the suspension granted in virtue of canon 2290, § 1 consists in "poenae vindicativae latae sententiae," and when the conditions required for a more urgent case are verified, that is, when there is danger of scandal or infamy, any confessor "potest . . . obligationem servandae poenae suspendere." Since *latae sententiae* vindicative penalties may be of various kinds, and since few authors have even considered the scope of canon 2290 in this regard, detailed consideration is here given to the various types of *latae sententiae* vindicative penalties.

1. *Latae Sententiae* Vindicative Penalties a Iure

In general, it may be said that all *latae sententiae* vindicative penalties which arise from either general or particular law are properly the object of the suspension which may be granted by reason of canon 2290, § 1. Whether or not this statement is to be restricted or extended will be seen in the course of the discussion in this article.

All *latae sententiae* vindicative penalties which are established by the general law of the Church, and which, therefore, are reserved as regards their dispensation to the Roman Pontiff or his successor

[97] Cf. Coronata, *Institutiones Iuris Canonici*, IV, n. 1823; Woywod, *A Practical Commentary*, II, n. 2131; Ayrinhac-Lydon, *Penal Legislation in the New Code of Canon Law*, n. 157; Vermeersch-Creusen, *Epitome*, III, n. 491; DeMeester, *Compendium*, III, n. 1787, 3°; Blat, *De Delictis et Poenis*, n. 120; Salucci, *Il Diritto Penale*, pp. 301, 302; Wernz-Vidal, *Ius Canonicum*, VII, n. 340. Chelodi (*Ius Poenale*, n. 47) expounds a unique opinion, similar to that of Sole (*De Delictis et Poenis*, n. 268) wherein he states that the suspension and the dispensation of canon 2290 remove the effects of the penalty only in the internal forum. In order to be freed from the observance of the penalty in the external forum, the penitent must resort to canon 2232. Cf. *supra*, p. 178.

or to another if the Pope has conceded such power to him,[98] can be suspended by reason of canon 2290, § 1, provided that they are occult. If they have been brought before the judicial forum, certain considerations must be kept in mind, and they call for special treatment later.[99]

Also all *latae sententiae* vindicative penalties established by general law which are expressly reserved to the Holy See [100] can be suspended by reason of canon 2290, § 1, if they are occult and the conditions of the more urgent case are verified.[101]

All *latae sententiae* vindicative penalties which have been established by particular law or general precept, and which, in consequence, are reserved to the ecclesiastical superior or authority who established them, his successor, his jurisdictional superior, or another to whom he has granted the faculty, can be suspended also by virtue of canon 2290, § 1, if they are occult. Again, such penalties may be brought before a judicial court, in which case special norms are to be applied.

The object of the suspension considered here concerns *latae sententiae* penalties established by common or particular law. It may happen that a particular penalty established in such laws or attached to them may not be clearly established as a vindicative penalty. Thus, although a suggestive list of the more common vindicative penalties is set forth in the Code,[102] there may arise certain doubts about particular penalties. Thus, penal suspension and interdict may be either censures or vindicative penalties.[103] In a doubt of law or in a doubt of fact which cannot be settled, these two penalties are presumed to be censures.[104] They are not included under canon 2290, not only when they are clearly inflicted as censures, but also when there is doubt whether in a particular case they are censures

[98] Cf. canon 2236, § 1.

[99] Cf. *infra*, p. 197.

[100] Cf. canons 671, 1°; 2295; 2370; 2373; 2387; 2394.

[101] Cf. Augustine, *A Commentary on the New Code*, VIII, 248; Berutti, *Institutiones Iuris Canonici*, VI, n. 88, IV; Ayrinhac-Lydon, *Penal Legislation in the New Code of Canon Law*, n. 161.

[102] Cf. canons 2291, 2298.

[103] Cf. canon 2255, § 2.

[104] Cf. canon 2255, § 2.

or vindicative penalties. As to whether a particular vindicative penalty is to be incurred *ipso facto* on the commission of the delict or not, if there is a doubt whether a vindicative penalty established by law or general precept is *latae* or *ferendae sententiae*, it is presumed to be *ferendae sententiae*.[105] In such a case, therefore, since the doubt presumes that the penalty has not been actually inflicted, as *ferendae sententiae*, by way of a judicial sentence or an extrajudicial precept (otherwise the penitent could hardly have such a doubt), then the penalty is to be regarded as a *ferendae sententiae* vindicative penalty which has not yet been contracted, and would in no way come under the faculties of canon 2290.

2. *Latae Sententiae* Vindicative Penalties *ab Homine*

Latae sententiae ab homine vindicative penalties, that is, *latae sententiae* vindicative penalties which are established in particular precepts, may also be suspended by virtue of canon 2290, § 1.[106] In spite of the contrary opinion as held by Cappello, Roberti and Michiels, the existence of such *latae sententiae ab homine* penalties has already been established.[107] Very few authors even treat of such penalties in relation to canon 2290. All authors who treat of canon 2290, § 1 refer to their treatment of canon 2254, § 1, as applicable *servatis servandis* to canon 2290, § 1. Berutti and Vermeersch-Creusen alone even mention such vindicative penalties and seem to admit that such penalties can be suspended under canon 2290, § 1. Most authors are content to state in general that all *latae sententiae* vindicative penalties may be suspended in virtue of this canon.[108] Others[109] admit that *ab homine latae sententiae* censures can be

[105] Cf. canon 2217, § 2.

[106] Cf. Berutti, *Institutiones Iuris Canonici,* VI, n. 86, II, p. 216; Vermeersch-Creusen, *Epitome,* III, n. 454, 1, 1°.

[107] Cf. *supra,* p. 63.

[108] Cf. Chelodi, *Ius Poenale,* n. 47; Salucci, *Il Diritto Penale,* p. 300; Augustine, *A Commentary on the New Code,* VIII, p. 240; Ayrinhac-Lydon, *Penal Legislation in the New Code of Canon Law,* n. 157; Blat, *De Delictis et Poenis,* n. 120; Wernz-Vidal, *Ius Canonicum,* VII, n. 340; Sipos, *Enchiridion Iuris Canonici,* § 238, 5; Ferreres, *Institutiones Iuris Canonici,* II, n. 1055.

[109] Cf. Coronata, *Institutiones Iuris Canonici,* IV, n. 1823; n. 179; Cipol-

absolved by reason of canon 2254, and, therefore, of necessity would seem to hold this same opinion in regard to *latae sententiae ab homine* vindicative penalties and canon 2290, for the two canons are exactly parallel in this respect.[110] For the same reason, others[111] would seem to hold that such *latae sententiae ab homine* vindicative penalties cannot be suspended by a confessor according to canon 2290, § 1, because they expressly exclude *latae sententiae ab homine* censures from the scope of canon 2254.

Now, canon 2290 simply states that all *latae sententiae* vindicative penalties may be suspended by the confessor in the more urgent cases, and since this canon in no way distinguishes between *a iure* vindicative penalties and those *ab homine,* it seems that the distinction should not be made unless clearly demanded by the nature of the canon. DeMeester, speaking of canon 2254, attempts to establish such a demand in canon 2254 by pointing out an implicit exclusion of *ab homine* censures "cum can. 2254, § 1 dicatur recurrendum esse ad S. Poenitentiariam vel ad Episcopum aliumve Superiorem praeditum facultate, non autem 'ad illum qui censuram tulit' uti habet can. 2252."[112] Since the terms used in canon 2290, § 1 are exactly the same,[113] the very same argument may be proposed in asserting that *ab homine* vindicative penalties are excluded from canon 2290, § 1. It must be admitted that the phrase "ad S. Poenitentiariam vel ad Episcopum facultate praeditum" seems to refer only to the recourse for *a iure* vindicative penalties, for it seems absurd for the Code to speak of recourse to a bishop "facultate

lini, *De Censuris,* p. 44; Cerato, *Censurae Vigentes,* p. 28; Kelly, *Jurisdiction of the Confessor,* pp. 169, 170.

110 Cf. canon 2254: "ab iisdem [latae sententiae censuris] . . . absolvere potest"; canon 2290, § 1: "potest obligationem servandae poenae [latae sententiae poenae vindicativae] suspendere."

111 Cf. DeMeester, *Compendium,* III, n. 1787, 3°, b; n. 1748, 1°, b; Cappello, *De Censuris* (3. ed., 1933), n. 4, 3; Woywod, *A Practical Commentary,* II, n. 2097; Wouters, *Manuale Theologiae Moralis,* II, n. 865, 2, b; Blat, *De Delictis et Poenis,* n. 78; Cocchi, *Commentarium in Codicem Iuris Canonici,* V, p. 124.

112 Cf. DeMeester, *Compendium,* III, n. 1787, 3°; also Cappello, *De Censuris* (3. ed., 1933), n. 132.

113 Cf. canon 2290, § 1: "recurrendi . . . ad S. Poenitentiariam vel ad Episcopum facultate praeditum."

praeditum" in the case of a *latae sententiae* vindicative penalty which that bishop had established by a particular precept and the reservation of which, therefore, is reserved to him in virtue of canon 2236, § 1. In other words, the wording "facultate praeditum" at first sight creates the definite impression that the recourse in question is prescribed after the confessor has granted the suspension of the obligation of the observance of some *latae sententiae* vindicative penalty established *a iure communi* and therefore reserved, as to its remission, to the Holy See, but for which a bishop may have a *delegated* faculty to dispense and likewise to receive recourse. But this interpretation of the phrase "facultate praeditum" as meaning "having delegated power or faculty" seems to be incorrect. For if that were the meaning of the phrase, there would appear to be no provision for recourse to an ordinary in the case of an occult *latae sententiae* vindicative penalty established by common law, because in such a case the ordinary would have ordinary power to dispense from the occult *latae sententiae a iure* vindicative penalty,[114] and would not be a bishop "endowed with a faculty" if "faculty" is taken in the sense of a delegated faculty. Consequently, although the phrase "facultate praeditum" may mean merely a delegated faculty in some instances, nevertheless the phrase must be given a broader scope as referring to a bishop, who has the power to dispense, whether that power be ordinary or delegated. And if it is interpreted in this sense, and recourse may be made to the Sacred Penitentiary or to any bishop who has the power to dispense, then there seems to be no reason to exclude the *latae sententiae ab homine* vindicative penalty from canon 2290, § 1 solely from the argument that there is no specific provision for recourse to the person who inflicted or established the penalty. In other words, recourse in canon 2290, § 1 is required after the suspension of the observance of any *latae sententiae* occult vindicative penalty, and the prescription for recourse in this canon is sufficiently broad to include *latae sententiae ab homine* vindicative penalties without any absolute need of the spe-

[114] Cf. Canon 2237, § 2. The power herein treated is ordinary jurisdiction, not jurisdiction delegated by law. Cf. Cappello, *De Censuris* (3. ed., 1933), n. 122, e; n. 126, 6; Chelodi, *Ius Poenale,* n. 30; Blat, *De Delictis et Poenis,* n. 59; Coronata, *Institutiones Iuris Canonici,* IV, n. 1739; Berutti, *Institutiones Iuris Canonici,* VI, n. 38, IV, 4.

cific wording "ad illum qui poenam tulit vel statuit" as demanded by DeMeester.[115]

Another seeming restriction in canon 2290, § 1 is to be noted. In canon 2254, the phrase "ad S. Poenitentiariam vel ad Episcopum aliumve Superiorem praeditum facultate" is used; while in canon 2290, the wording is "ad S. Poenitentiariam vel ad Episcopum facultate praeditum." Must the conclusion be drawn, therefore, that the prescription for recourse in canon 2290 is to be limited only to the Sacred Penitentiary and to bishops who possess the power to dispense? At first glance, this would seem to be the case. And yet the same argument given above would seem to indicate that the interpretation of this phrase in canon 2290, § 1 should be the same as the wording in canon 2254, § 1 and, therefore, should include "alium Superiorem facultate praeditum." For occult *latae sententiae* vindicative penalties established by common law can be dispensed by ordinaries,[116] which term includes not only bishops but other superiors, according to canon 198. Consequently, if the recourse prescribed in canon 2290, § 1 is to be limited only to the Sacred Penitentiary and to bishops, there simply would be no provision for recourse, in the case of an occult *latae sententiae* vindicative penalty *a iure,* to a religious ordinary, since he is not a bishop; and yet by common law he possesses ordinary power to dispense in such instances.[117] Therefore, the recourse of canon 2290, § 1 can be made to the Sacred Penitentiary or to a bishop or superior who has the power to dispense, whether that power be ordinary or delegated; [118] and it follows that occult *latae sententiae ab homine* vindicative penalties established by such superiors are included in the faculties of canon 2290, § 1." [119]

Although, as Moriarty notes,[120] there is so much obscurity in the Code in its provisions for *latae sententiae ab homine* penalties and

[115] Cf. *Compendium,* III, n. 1787, 3°, b; n. 1748, 1°, b, p. 185, nota 4.

[116] Cf. canon 2237, § 2.

[117] Cf. canon 2237, § 2. Cf. Augustine, *A Commentary on the New Code,* VIII, 110; Ayrinhac-Lydon, *Penal Legislation in the New Code of Canon Law,* n. 70.

[118] Cf. Berutti, *Institutiones Iuris Canonici,* VI, n. 86, II, p. 216.

[119] Cf. Berutti, *loc. cit.*

[120] *Extraordinary Absolution from Censures,* p. 167.

for that reason authors like Roberti, Michiels, and Cappello have developed their version of the penalty *tamquam a iure* as a substitute for the *ab homine latae sententiae* penalty,[121] the opinion that *latae sententiae ab homine* penalties are included under the faculties of canons 2290, § 1 and 2254, § 1 has received very great support.[122] Therefore, from such external authority and from the internal authority that the *latae sententiae ab homine* vindicative penalty is not certainly excluded by the wording of canon 2290, § 1, it seems that the very least that can be admitted is that there is a doubt of law, and since in a doubt of law the Church supplies jurisdiction,[123] and also because "favores ampliandi sunt," [124] it can safely be held that the occult *latae sententiae ab homine* vindicative penalty can be suspended by a confessor according to canon 2290, § 1, unless the Holy See decides otherwise.

3. Vindicative Penalties Brought to the Judicial Forum

The question may arise whether, if a delict or a *latae sententiae* vindicative penalty brought to the sacramental tribunal of confession

[121] Cf. *supra*, p. 63.

[122] Among those who directly include such penalties under canon 2290 are Berutti, *Institutiones Iuris Canonici*, VI, n. 86, II, p. 216; Vermeersch-Creusen, *Epitome*, III, n. 454, 1, 1°. Others who indirectly include such penalties under canon 2290 by including them under canon 2254 are: Coronata, *Institutiones Iuris Canonici*, IV, n. 179; Cipollini, *De Censuris*, p. 44; Kelly, *Jurisdiction of the Confessor*, pp. 169, 170; Moriarty, *Extraordinary Absolution from Censures*, p. 168; Cerato, *Censurae Vigentes*, p. 28; Raus, *Institutiones Canonicae*, p. 698; *idem*, "Absolution von Zensuren l. s. ab homine," *TPQ*, LXXXIII (1930), pp. 586, 587; Collison, *Non Omnis Censura Ab Homine Est Reservata*, pp. 58-61; Genicot-Salsmans, *Institutiones Theologiae Moralis*, II, n. 574, 2; Reintjes, *De Absolutione Censurae*, p. 32; Berutti, *Institutiones Iuris Canonici*, VI, n. 57, II; VI, p. 149. To these may be added those who state in general that all occult *latae sententiae* vindicative penalties, without exception, may be suspended under canon 2290, *e. g.*, Augustine, *A Commentary on the New Code*, VIII, 240; Chelodi, *Ius Poenale*, n. 47; Salucci, *Il Diritto Penale*, I, p. 300; Ayrinhac-Lydon, *Penal Legislation in the New Code of Canon Law*, n. 157; Wernz-Vidal, *Ius Canonicum*, VII, n. 340; Sipos, *Enchiridion Iuris Canonici*, 238, 5; Ferreres, *Institutiones Iuris Canonici*, II, n. 1055; Kelly, *Jurisdiction of the Confessor*, p. 236.

[123] Cf. canon 209.

[124] Reg. 15, *R. J.* in VI°.

by a penitent has already been brought to the judicial forum, either to the contentious forum for the declaration of some juridical fact, or to the criminal forum for the declaration of the *latae sententiae* penalty by means of a declaratory judicial sentence,[125] such a *latae sententiae* vindicative penalty may be suspended according to canon 2290, § 1.[126] In other words, if the *latae sententiae* vindicative penalty is brought to the judicial forum, but not yet declared, can a confessor suspend the observance of the penalty under the powers granted to him in canon 2290? Of course, the penalty must be occult to come under the conditions of this canon. However, the fact that the penalty has been brought to the judicial forum does not in any way exclude the possibility that the case may be occult,[127] for if the vindicative penalty has not, and presumably will not easily be divulged, it is occult.[128]

It is the common opinion that if the case has been brought to the judicial forum the penalty cannot be remitted in the internal forum.[129] However, this opinion concerns only the ordinary remission or dispensation of vindicative penalties according to canons 2236 and 2237. Does it apply also to the extraordinary suspension of the penalty, in the more urgent cases, as in canon 2290?

This question is not treated by canonists, who are all too brief and superficial in their treatment of vindicative penalties, and are content with making the very general statement that all *latae sententiae* vindicative penalties are subject to the faculties of the confessor in virtue of canon 2290, § 1. It must be admitted, however, that Cappello [130] and Moriarty [131] treat of this question in relation to canon 2254; and both admit that *latae sententiae* censures brought

[125] Cf. canon 1552, § 2.

[126] A case is commonly considered to have been brought to the judicial forum when the party has been legitimately cited. Cf. *supra*, p. 143.

[127] Cf. Coronata, *Institutiones Iuris Canonici*, IV, n. 1648.

[128] Cf. canon 2197, 1°, 4°.

[129] Cf. *supra*, p. 165. Cf. Wernz-Vidal, *Ius Canonicum*, VII, n. 216, p. 225, nota 23; Coronata, *Institutiones Iuris Canonici*, IV, n. 1737; DeMeester, *Compendium*, III, n. 1746; Cappello, *De Censuris*, n. 119. D'Annibale (*Summula*, n. 346, n. 10), however, holds the opposite opinion.

[130] *De Censuris* (3. ed., 1933), n. 133, 3.

[131] *Extraordinary Absolution from Censures*, p. 74.

to the judicial forum fall under canon 2254, whether they are public or occult censures. The question here concerns only *latae sententiae* penalties which have been brought to the judicial forum and which, nevertheless, are occult.

If such *latae sententiae* vindicative penalties are to be excluded from the scope of canon 2290, it would certainly seem that the legislator would have mentioned the fact expressly, as had been done in canon 2237, § 1. But no such exclusion is made in canon 2290; and the argument used for excluding these penalties from the ordinary dispensation of vindicative penalties, namely, that contempt for the ecclesiastical authority of the judge of the external judicial forum is involved when such penalties are dispensed in the internal forum,[132] is eliminated by the moral necessity implied in the more urgent cases of canon 2290. Besides, the entire matter will ordinarily be submitted to the judgment of the proper ecclesiastical authority by means of the recourse demanded by this canon. Consequently, there appears to be no reason why canon 2290, § 1 cannot be applied, as long as the conditions of this canon are verified, that is, if the case is occult and there is danger of scandal or infamy in the observance of the *latae sententiae* vindicative penalty. Obviously, if the penalty, as a result of its having been brought to the judicial forum becomes public or is likely to become public, the case is beyond the scope of canon 2290 entirely.

4. *Latae Sententiae* Vindicative Penalties Subjected to a Declaratory Sentence

The question to be considered here is whether *latae sententiae* vindicative penalties, after they have been declared or confirmed by means of a declaratory judicial sentence, may be suspended by means of canon 2290, § 1. Berutti [133] expressly excludes all *latae sententiae* vindicative penalties from the scope of canon 2290, § 1 if such penalties are notorious or if they have been confirmed by a declaratory judicial sentence. In holding such an opinion, he seems to believe that in neither case can the penalty be considered as occult, and for

[132] Cf. *supra*, p. 167. Cf. Wernz-Vidal, *Ius Canonicum*, VII, n. 216, p. 225, nota 23.

[133] *Institutiones Iuris Canonici*, VI, n. 86, II, p. 216, nota 2.

that reason can not be included in those governed by the faculties of canon 2290. Several important points must be discussed in the treatment of this question.

First of all, a declaratory sentence is essentially different from a condemnatory sentence. The declaratory sentence does not change the penalty; it remains *latae sententiae a iure* after the sentence has been passed.[184] Secondly, the declaration of a vindicative penalty does not necessarily make that penalty public. For the declaratory judicial sentence is merely a juridical pronouncement by a competent authority that a *latae sententiae* vindicative penalty has been contracted; it is merely a confirmation, as it were, of that fact. It does not *per se* make the penalty public; this is accomplished, rather, by the denunciation of the penalty, which is the act of making public the fact that a vindicative penalty, already incurred and declared, has been contracted, so that the incurrence of the penalty becomes a matter of common knowledge.[185] This denunciation or publication may be done in various ways, for instance, by the insertion of the declaratory sentence in an official periodical.[186] Therefore, when the declaratory sentence is made known generally and the vindicative penalty thereby becomes public, the denunciation is involved. But a declaratory sentence may be given and still not be made public, but rather placed in the secret archives.[187] In this instance, although the vindicative penalty of the delict may be notorious *notorietate iuris*,[188] it may at the same time be occult, inasmuch as it has not been and will not easily be divulged.[189]

Consequently, since a *latae sententiae* vindicative penalty remains such after a declaratory judicial sentence, and since such a *latae sententiae* penalty may be occult, it follows that suspension of the obligation of the observance of such a *latae sententiae* occult vindicative penalty can be granted by a confessor under canon 2290,

[184] Cf. canon 2217, § 1, 3°.

[185] Cf. Moriarty, *Extraordinary Absolution from Censures*, p. 176.

[186] Cf. Coronata, *Institutiones Iuris Canonici*, IV, n. 1723; DeMeester, *Compendium*, III, n. 1596.

[187] Cf. Coronata, *Institutiones Iuris Canonici*, IV, n. 1648.

[188] Cf. canon 2197, 2°.

[189] Cf. canon 2197, 1°, 4°; Coronata, *Institutiones Iuris Canonici*, IV, n. 1648.

§1 as long as conditions required by the *casus urgentior* are verified, that is, if there is danger of personal infamy or scandal to others if the vindicative penalty is observed. If the denunciation of the penalty is made, so that the declaratory sentence is publicized and the case thereby ceases to be occult, canon 2290 cannot be used.

B. *The Question of* Ferendae Sententiae *Vindicative Penalties*

Canon 2290, § 1 expressly limits the faculties therein granted to *latae sententiae* vindicative penalties, just as canon 2254 is expressly limited to *latae sententiae* censures. And, therefore, it would seem that *ferendae sententiae* penalties, whether they be vindicative or medicinal, are absolutely excluded from all consideration in relation to either of these two canons. And yet Coronata [140] and Moriarty,[141] although rejecting arguments offered by Cappello [142] for a similar opinion, offer the assertion that canon 2254 concerns *ferendae sententiae* censures not *per se,* but *per accidens.* And it would seem that the arguments presented would be equally applicable to canon 2290.[143]

Per se, then, canon 2290 concerns only *latae sententiae* vindicative penalties; and correctly, for when a superior or judge inflicts a *ferendae sententiae* vindicative penalty, he will certainly provide that all danger of scandal or infamy will be excluded, and if such is not the case, he will refrain from imposing the penalty or he will defer the infliction according to canon 2223, § 3. Moreover, canon 2232, § 1 does not excuse the delinquent from observing a *ferendae sententiae* vindicative penalty because of the danger of infamy,[144] for this canon presupposes that no such danger will ever arise from the observance of a *ferendae sententiae* penalty. And ordinarily this supposition is true, for the case will seldom, if ever, arise in which the conditions required for the more urgent case will be verified in the observance of *ferendae sententiae* vindicative penalties. Such a

[140] *Institutiones Iuris Canonici,* IV, n. 1762, p. 179, nota 7.

[141] *Extraordinary Absolution from Censures,* pp. 185-188.

[142] *De Censuris* (3. ed., 1933), n. 133, 5.

[143] The arguments here presented are substantially the same as those offered by Moriarty, with the necessary applications to vindicative penalties.

[144] Canon 2232, § 1 concerns only *latae sententiae* vindicative penalties.

case, however, is not impossible. If, for example, the superior or judge has ignored the danger or the probability of scandal or infamy arising from the observance of a *ferendae sententiae* vindicative penalty or has not properly guarded against such an occurrence, the question naturally arises as to whether there is any norm for the extraordinary suspension or dispensation of such a penalty in a more urgent case. As Moriarty notes,[145] law contemplates ordinary contingencies; at times it may make provisions for the extraordinary or even for the exceptional—of which canon 2290 is a good example—but it properly ignores the accidental. Consequently, there is an absence of provision, seemingly as unnecessary, for the extraordinary suspension from the observance of such *ferendae sententiae* vindicative penalties in more urgent cases. But, supposing that such a suspension of the obligation of the penalty should become necessary because of urgency as understood in canon 2290, § 1, there seems to be no reason why, from analogy and in virtue of the norms of canon 20 for just such an absence of provision,[146] canon 2290, § 1 cannot be applied to *ferendae sententiae* vindicative penalties. In employing the analogy, all arbitrary restrictions and extensions of canon 2290 must be studiously avoided.[147] The case, therefore, must be occult. And, just as the issuance of a declaratory sentence does not necessarily mean that the case is publicized,[148] so a condemnatory sentence which is not made known generally may allow the delict and the vindicative penalty to remain occult.[149] Consequently, if *per accidens* there is probability of infamy or scandal from the observance of any *ferendae sententiae* vindicative penalty which is occult in the sense that the penalty or the condemnatory sentence is either generally unknown or unknown in the place in which the penitent is staying, canon 2290, § 1, *per accidens* and by analogy, can be applied, with the corresponding obligations, of recourse to the competent superior, and of obedience to his mandates. Obviously, if the case, as a result of the condemnatory judicial sentence, becomes public, the case is beyond the scope of canon 2290 entirely.

145 *Extraordinary Absolution from Censures*, p. 188.

146 Cf. canon 20.

147 Cf. Vermeersch-Creusen, *Epitome*, III, n. 127.

148 Cf. *supra*, p. 171.

149 Cf. Coronata, *Institutiones Iuris Canonici*, IV, n. 1648.

Article IV. The Recourse

A. *Its Nature*

When a confessor suspends the observance of a *latae sententiae* vindicative penalty according to canon 2290, § 1, he is bound under pain of grave sin to impose upon the penitent the obligation of recourse, when such recourse is morally possible.[150] The term *recursus* is used in various ways by the legislator in the Code[151] signifying at one time the petition addressed to a competent superior for the grant of faculties to absolve or dispense; at another time an appeal to a superior from a precept or penalty of an inferior; at another the approach to a specially authorized confessor for absolution as in canon 2254, § 2; again the communication with a competent authority, by personal approach or by letter, to obtain his mandates after an absolution has been granted as in canon 2254, § 1; and finally the petition addressed to a competent superior for his mandates after a suspension of the obligation of the observance of the penalty has been granted according to canon 2290, § 1 or for a dispensation from a vindicative penalty which has been suspended as in canon 2290, § 1. The recourse, therefore, prescribed in canon 2290, § 1 is not a petition for faculties to dispense a vindicative penalty in a particular case, but a communication to the competent superior to obtain his mandates and, perhaps, to petition for a dispensation from a particular penalty to be granted by the competent superior, for the confessor does not ask the superior for faculties to dispense, but the penitent asks the superior for his mandates or for a dispensation from a vindicative penalty which he has incurred. The recourse, therefore, of canon 2290, § 1 is different from that prescribed in canon 2254, § 1, since the latter is not a petition at all, but a communication with the proper authority for his mandates after the confessor has absolved the penitent of his censure.[152] The recourse of canon 2254 is made after a complete absolution from

[150] Cf. *supra*, p. 187. Cf. DeMeester, *Compendium*, III, n. 1748; Vermeersch-Creusen, *Epitome*, III, n. 454, 1, 1°; Berutti, *Institutiones Iuris Canonici*, VI, n. 57, IV; Salucci, *Il Diritto Penale*, I, p. 226; Cappello, *De Censuris* (3. ed., 1933), n. 127.

[151] Cf. *e.g.* canons 2252; 2254, § 1, 2; 2287; 2290, § 1.

[152] Cf. Moriarty, *Extraordinary Absolution from Censures*, p. 90.

censure has been granted, whereas the recourse of canon 2290, § 1 is made after a suspension of the obligation of a vindicative penalty has been given, in which case the superior may simply give his mandates or he may grant a dispensation from the penalty. In other words, the suspension of the obligation of the observance of the vindicative penalty is a temporary measure conditioned by the moral necessity implied in the *casus urgentiores* and contingent as to a dispensation upon the will of the superior manifested in his reply to the recourse of the penitent in which he includes his mandates. These mandates may or may not contain a dispensation from the vindicative penalty.

B. *Recourse—By Whom*

The obligation of recourse directly and immediately affects the penitent on whom it is imposed by the confessor; and it is clearly a grave obligation,[153] although not imposed *sub poena reincidentiae;* and if it is deliberately and culpably neglected or ignored, it entails a revival, as it were, of the same vindicative penalty.[154]

The penitent may fulfill this obligation of recourse in various ways. He may write or go personally to the competent superior to apply for the necessary dispensation from the vindicative penalty, but in many cases this will be morally or physically impossible. Consequently, if he cannot make it in either of these ways, he must make the recourse *"saltem . . . per epistolam et confessarium."* [155]

The minimum required, therefore, is that the penitent make the recourse through the confessor by means of a letter. If this is impossible, the penitent himself must write or go personally to the

[153] Cf. *supra,* p. 189. Cf. DeMeester, *Compendium,* III, n. 1748, 1°, e, p. 186; Cappello (3. ed., 1933), *De Censuris,* n. 127.

[154] Cf. *supra,* p. 183.

[155] Cf. Coronata, *Institutiones Iuris Canonici,* IV, n. 1762; Cocchi, *Commentarium in Codicem Iuris Canonici,* V, p. 124; Cappello, *De Censuris,* n. 129; Moriarty, *Extraordinary Absolution from Censures,* p. 195. Coronata (*Institutiones Iuris Canonici,* IV, n. 1823, p. 252, nota 2) explains the disjunctive use of the term "et" in canons 2254 and 2290; cf. Chelodi, *Ius Poenale,* n. 47, p. 52, nota 4.

competent superior for the mandates and dispensation.[156] As Coronata notes,[157] the confessor may make the recourse personally, by applying directly and in person to the proper superior, provided, of course, that the name of the penitent is withheld, and that the seal of confession is not violated in any way.[158]

If the confessor cannot write for the penitent, because, for instance, he will not see the penitent again, it is sufficient for the confessor to demand that the penitent himself write to the proper superior, either personally or through some other confessor, asking for the dispensation.[159] However, as Moriarty notes,[160] although a penitent *may* go to another confessor and ask him to undertake the recourse, it is by no means clear that he *must* do so.[161] As for the ability of the penitent to write or go personally to the competent superior directly for the dispensation, it seems certain that, at least in this country, it will be rare that the penitent, unless he be a priest, will be able to write or go personally to the proper superior without grave inconvenience.[162] Consequently, when the penitent is personally incapable of making the recourse directly—which will generally be the case in this country—and if the confessor is prevented by some serious cause from writing for the penitent, or if the penitent will not be able to return to the confessor without serious inconvenience, canon 2290, § 2 may be applied and the confessor himself may grant the dispensation.[163]

If, however, the confessor can write for the penitent, and the

[156] Cf. Coronata, *Institutiones Iuris Canonici,* IV, n. 1762; DeMeester, *Compendium,* III, n. 1748; Cipollini, *De Censuris,* p. 46.

[157] *Institutiones Iuris Canonici, loc. cit.*

[158] Cf. Salucci (*Il Diritto Penale,* I, 227) maintains that the confessor can make recourse only by letter, thus seeming to reject the disjunctive sense of the term "et" in both canon 2254 and canon 2290.

[159] Cf. DeMeester, *Compendium,* III, n. 1748; Blat, *De Delictis et Poenis,* n. 78.

[160] *Extraordinary Absolution from Censures,* p. 196.

[161] Cf. Cerato, *Censurae Vigentes,* p. 41.

[162] Cf. Kelly, *Jurisdiction of the Confessor,* pp. 172, 173; Arregui, *Summarium Theologiae Moralis,* n. 617, 5; Moriarty, *Extraordinary Absolution from Censures,* p. 197.

[163] Cf. Moriarty, *Extraordinary Absolution from Censures,* p. 197; Kelly, *Jurisdiction of the Confessor,* pp. 172, 173.

penitent can return to the confessor to receive the verdict of the superior as to whether a dispensation is granted or not, the confessor is obliged to undertake the recourse.[164] The gravity of this obligation on the part of the confessor depends on various conditions. If the penitent can make the recourse in some other manner, but would prefer to be spared embarrassment, hardship, or difficulty (not serious inconvenience, however, for such would provide an excuse from the recourse itself), then the confessor should, *ex caritate,*[165] undertake the recourse, but it is not evident that he would be bound *sub gravi* to do so.[166] However, if the recourse can be made in no other way than by a letter written by the confessor, and he is not excused from doing so by any just cause, it would seem that in such a case he would be bound *sub gravi* to undertake the recourse, not so much *ex caritate* as *ex munere confessarii.* For the confessor cannot dispense with the obligation of recourse to fit his own convenience, but there must be a serious cause of moral impossibility at least before he is allowed to do so. The penitent definitely has a grave obligation to make the recourse, and if he cannot make it in some other way, he must make it *saltem per epistolam et per confessarium.*[167] Therefore, the two obligations seem correlative: if the recourse can be made in no other way than through the confessor, he has a grave obligation to undertake the recourse, and not merely from charity, but from his office as confessor.

The penitent, when he is aware of his obligation of recourse, is bound by that obligation whether the confessor has or has not, either with or without deliberate fault, expressly imposed it upon him.[168] Moreover, he is bound by the obligation of recourse whenever he does become aware of it, even though the confessor failed to inform him of his grave obligation in this matter at the time of his confession. If the penitent cannot write or personally approach

[164] Cf. Vermeersch-Creusen, *Epitome,* III, n. 454, 3, 1°; Cappello, *De Censuris* (3. ed., 1933), n. 128, 129; DeMeester, *Compendium,* III, n. 1748.

[165] Cf. Vermeersch-Creusen, *Epitome,* III, n. 454, 3, 1°.

[166] Cf. Moriarty, *Extraordinary Absolution from Censures,* p. 197.

[167] Cf. *supra,* p. 204.

[168] Cf. DeMeester, *Compendium,* III, n. 1748; Cappello, *De Censuris* (3. ed., 1933), n. 127; Moriarty, *Extraordinary Absolution from Censures,* p. 198; Berutti, *Institutiones Iuris Canonici,* VI, n. 57, IV.

the competent superior, but can return to the confessor to whom he has confessed, he would be bound to do so, so that the recourse could be made through that confessor.[169] If, however. the confessor refuses to make the recourse when asked to do so, and if the penitent himself cannot write or personally apply to the proper superior, then, although the penitent can make recourse through another more congenial confessor, it is not clear that he is bound to seek the offices of this other confessor. In such a case, the penitent certainly is affected by a serious inconvenience, which will excuse him from recourse.

If the confessor has assumed the burden of recourse at the request of the penitent but has actually neglected to perform it, whatever may be the reason, the grave obligation of recourse still binds the penitent, for the penitent *per se* is bound by that obligation until it is fulfilled. He must make the recourse, in such a case, within a month from the time at which he discovers that the confessor has abandoned the recourse. Of course, if, when he discovers this fact, he cannot without serious inconvenience personally write or go to the superior, and another confessor cannot make the necessary recourse for him, he may receive the dispensation from that confessor in virtue of canon 2290, § 2.

C. *Recourse—To Whom*

The recourse prescribed by canon 2290, § 1 is to be made *"ad S. Poenitentiariam vel ad Episcopum facultate praeditum"* to which should be added *"aliumve Superiorem facultate praeditum."*[170] Whether the recourse is to be made to one or other of these will depend on the nature of the vindicative penalty which is to be suspended. For, since the recourse prescribed in this canon is usually recourse for a dispensation from a vindicative penalty, it follows that the recourse must be made to the superior who is competent, according to the norms of canon 2236, to dispense from the particular vindicative penalty. Since vindicative penalties, unlike censures, are always "reserved," the principles of recourse in canon 2290, § 1, are entirely different from those in canon 2254, § 1.

[169] Cf. canon 2290: "saltem per confessarium."

[170] Cf. *supra*, p. 196.

If the vindicative penalty suspended by reason of canon 2290, § 1 was a *latae sententiae* vindicative penalty *a iure communi*, that is, established by or attached to a general law of the Church, recourse *per se* may be made to the Sacred Penitentiary, for the dispensation of such a vindicative penalty is reserved, according to canon 2236, § 1, to the Holy Father as supreme legislator of the common law. However, since only those vindicative penalties which are occult may be suspended by canon 2290, § 1, and since according to canon 2237, § 2, all ordinaries have the power in occult cases to dispense from all *latae sententiae* vindicative penalties established by the common law, recourse from such penalties can always be made to the local ordinary; and if the penitent is a member of an exempt clerical religious institute, recourse can be made also to the competent major superior by the penitent, and this major superior will usually be the penitent's provincial or general.[171]

If the suspended vindicative penalty was one established by particular law or general precept or attached to either law or precept by a jurisdictional superior who, according to canon 2220, § 1, has the power to do so, the recourse is to be made to the jurisdictional superior who has constituted the penalty or his successor in office, or his jurisdictional superior, or also to another to whom the competent superior has conceded the dispensatory power, provided that the one delegated is a canonical superior,[172] whether the concession is one of ordinary [173] or delegated power, or whether the concession is an explicit [174] or implicit [175] grant of power. Thus, in penalties established in diocesan laws, the competent superior of recourse is

[171] Cf. canons 198, 488, 8°. Cf. Berutti, *Institutiones Iuris Canonici*, VI, n. 86, II.

[172] Cf. canon 2290, § 1; *supra*, p. 196: "ad S. Poenitentiariam vel ad Episcopum aliumve Superiorem facultate praeditum." Thus, although a confessor may have delegated power to dispense from a particular vindicative penalty, recourse may not be made to him, because he is not a canonical superior. Kelly (*Jurisdiction of the Confessor*, p. 237), seems to hold the opposite opinion.

[173] The Roman Pontiff may establish a particular penal law or a general precept for a particular territory and may, therefore, concede ordinary power to dispense from such penalties to others.

[174] Cf. canon 2236, § 1; cf. *supra*, p. 121.

[175] Cf. canon 2236, § 2; cf. *supra*, p. 110.

the local ordinary, or his superior, the Roman Pontiff,[176] or his successor or anyone to whom the local ordinary has conceded this power, either of dispensing directly from the penalty [177] or of dispensing directly from the penal law and indirectly from the penalty attached thereto.[178] Similarly, if the particular law was established by a religious ordinary, that ordinary, his successor, his superior—the respective major religious superior [179] — or one to whom he has delegated this power, is the competent superior of recourse.[180]

If the vindicative penalty suspended under canon 2290, § 1 was a *latae sententiae ab homine* vindicative penalty, the recourse is made to that superior who has given the the particular precept to which the penalty has been attached, or to his own competent superior, successor, or delegate, provided that the last named is a canonical superior. If the particular penal precept was established by a local ordinary, the competent superior of the ordinary is the Roman Pontiff, who may grant the dispensation petitioned by the penitent.[181] However, the Sacred Penitentiary is competent to dispense in the internal forum from such *ab homine latae sententiae* penalties.[182] If the particular penal precept was established by a religious superior, the competent jurisdictional superior of that religious superior is the respective major superior of the religious institute. However, recourse can always be made directly to the Sacred Penitentiary.

If, in some extraordinary case, a *ferendae sententiae* vindicative penalty has been suspended by the confessor according to canon

[176] The Roman Pontiff, and not the Metropolitan, is the superior of the bishop. Cf. *supra*, p. 93. The recourse can be made directly to the Holy Father, but it can also be made to the Sacred Penitentiary, and the Cardinal Major Penitentiary will take care of the case, either granting the dispensation and mandates himself, or referring the matter to the Supreme Pontiff. Cf. Cappello, *De Censuris*, n. 128, 16.

[177] Cf. canon 2236, § 1.

[178] Cf. canon 2236, § 2.

[179] *Supra*, p. 103.

[180] Cf. *supra*, p. 102 for all superiors who are included.

[181] Cf. *supra*, p. 93. Cf. also Berutti, *Institutiones Iuris Canonici*, VI, n. 38, II, 1.

[182] Cf. canon 258, § 1. Cf. Berutti, *Institutiones Iuris Canonici*, VI, n. 38, II, 1.

2290, § 1, by analogy,[183] recourse is made to that superior who has inflicted the penalty, or to his own competent superior, successor, or delegate, provided that the latter is a canonical superior.[184] But in this case it is important to note that, if the vindicative penalty was inflicted by a judge who is not a canonical superior, he has no power to receive the recourse because he has not the power to dispense from the penalty.[185]

As regards the case in which the vindicative penalty has revived because of culpable failure to make the required recourse after the obligation of observing the penalty has been suspended according to canon 2290, § 1, the recourse is exactly the same when that penalty is once again submitted in the tribunal of Penance, for the vindicative penalty is the same vindicative penalty, which merely continues to bind the penitent after the suspension of the penalty has ceased.

It is important to note here that in no case can recourse, in the sense of canon 2290, § 1, be made to a confessor who may enjoy the faculty to dispense from the respective vindicative penalty in the sacramental forum. For the recourse must be made to the Sacred Penitentiary or to a bishop or other *superior* enjoying the faculty. The ordinary confessor who possesses a special faculty is not a superior; and he can only grant a dispensation when the delinquent personally comes to him in the tribunal of Penance, not as to a superior of recourse, but as to a confessor who may dispense the penalty whether the penalty has or has not been already suspended according to canon 2290, § 1. This latter case is but an application of canon 2254, § 2 to vindicative penalties, by which a penitent may, in order to relieve himself of the burden of recourse that would otherwise have to be made to a competent superior, submit his penalty to the privileged confessor as an alternative method to canon 2290, § 1.[186]

183 Cf. *supra,* p. 201.

184 Cf. canon 2236, § 1.

185 Cf. canon 2236, § 3. The competent superior in such a case would be the superior in whose authority the judge acted, or also the Sacred Penitentiary since the matter here treated concerns the internal forum.

186 Cf. *infra,* p. 239, where the application of canon 2254, § 2 is made to vindicative penalties.

D. *Recourse—For What Kind of Vindicative Penalties*

It is obvious that recourse is prescribed whenever any vindicative penalty has been suspended by reason of canon 2290, § 1. Since all vindicative penalties are reserved, it follows that the confessor will use canon 2290, § 1 whenever he possesses no special faculty to dispense from the particular vindicative penalty submitted to him in the tribunal of Penance. If he has the power to dispense from the penalty through some other source than canon 2290, then there is no need, quite obviously, to use this canon; but the confessor will follow the norms of canon 2236 for the ordinary dispensation from vindicative penalties; as is the case, for example, when a confessor who enjoys special faculties, as certain regulars do, dispenses from a vindicative penalty ordinarily reserved to the bishops,[187] or when a confessor, by reason of delegated power, dispenses from a vindicative penalty established by the bishop who has granted the confessor the delegated power, or from an occult vindicative penalty of the common law.[188]

E. *Recourse—When*

In canon 2290, § 1, the confessor must impose upon the penitent the obligation of having recourse "saltem intra mensem. . . ." In other words, the penitent is given a month in which he can comply with this obligation of recourse. Many and varied are the opinions of canonists as to the manner in which this month is to be computed.[189] It is not within the scope of this treatise to treat in detail

[187] *E. g.*, powers granted to confessors of the Passionist Congregation to dispense, in *foro interno*, from all vindicative penalties imposed by the bishop enable them to dispense in virtue of canon 2237, § 2. Cf. Congreg. S. Justinae, Eugenius IV, Bulla, *"Etsi quoslibet,"* 31 maii, 1436.

[188] Cf. canon 2237, § 2, for the ordinary can delegate the dispensatory power given to him in this canon. Cf. *supra*, p. 139.

[189] Cf. Cappello, *De Censuris* (3. ed., 1933), n. 127; Coronata, *Institutiones Iuris Canonici*, IV, n. 1762; Cocchi, *Commentarium in Codicem Iuris Canonici*, V, p. 124; Vermeersch-Creusen, *Epitome*, III, n. 454, 3, 3°; Blat, *De Delictis et Poenis*, n. 78; Roberti, *De Delictis et Poenis*, n. 318; Cipollini, *De Censuris*, p. 45; Moriarty, *Extraordinary Absolution from Censures*, pp. 205-209; Kelly, *Jurisdiction of the Confessor*, p. 173; Rainer, *Suspension of Clerics*, pp. 216, 217; DeMeester, *Compendium*, III, n. 1748; Ferreres, *Institutiones Iuris Canonici*, II, n. 1009.

these varying, often times inconsistent, opinions; but a practical manner of computing this month which is allowed to the penitent for recourse is here presented.

The case in which the penitent knows of his obligation of recourse at the time when he receives the suspension of his penalty, whether he has been informed of it by the confessor or whether he is aware of the obligation from some other source, is to be treated first. Since the *terminus a quo* is expressly assigned as the time when the confessor grants the suspension of the observance of the penalty, the month would not be computed from moment to moment according to canon 34, § 2, but rather would be computed entirely according to the norms of canon 34, § 3. Consequently, the month is to be taken as it is in the calendar, and therefore, is not of necessity made up of thirty days.[190] And since the suspension of the penalty, the *terminus a quo,* does not necessarily coincide with the beginning of the day, the first day, or the day on which the confessor grants the suspension is not computed, and the month will be completed at the end of that day of the following month which has the same date as the day on which the suspension was granted.[191] Thus, if the penitent had received a suspension of the obligation of the observance of a vindicative penalty on November 15, the month in which he must fulfill his obligation of recourse will end at midnight of December 15. According to canon 34, § 3, 4°, if the following month has no day with numerically the same date as the day on which the suspension of the penalty was granted, the month will be completed at the end of the last day of this following month.[192] Thus, if the confessor had suspended the observance of the vindicative penalty on January 30, the month for recourse will end at midnight of February 28, or, in leap year, February 29.

In practice, the computation is not as difficult as it seems at first sight, for the confessor, noting the date on which he is granting the

[190] Cf. canon 34, § 3, n. 1: Menses et anni sumantur prout sunt in calendario. Cf. also canon 32, § 2: In iure nomine mensis venit spatium 30, anni vero spatium 365 dierum, nisi mensis et annus dicantur sumendi prout sunt in calendario.

[191] Cf. canon 34, § 3, 3°.

[192] Cf. canon 34, § 3, 4°.

suspension of the penalty, merely imposes upon the penitent the grave obligation of having recourse before the end of the day in the next month which bears the same number or date. Moreover, the confessor in most cases will assume the burden of recourse for the penitent; and consequently the confessor, knowing the law, will undertake the recourse at the first possible moment.

The month allowed for recourse is *tempus utile*,[193] and, therefore, the time during which the penitent is unable to comply with his obligation of recourse or is completely unaware of such an obligation is not computed.[194] When serious inconvenience prevents complying with the obligation of recourse during part of the time, the obligation of recourse does not cease after a month of continuous time, but it continues during a month of days which offer opportunity for the recourse. In other words, the obligation continues throughout a month of *tempus utile,* which is not computed according to the calendar.[195]

Another conclusion may be drawn from the fact that this month is *tempus utile*. When the penitent has been impeded from making his recourse during the month, he need not make it immediately upon the cessation of the impediment.[196] For the time during which he was prevented from making recourse was not *tempus utile* and simply, therefore, is not to be computed in the month which is *tempus utile*. Only those daye are to be included on which there is opportunity for the fulfillment of the obligation, and for every day on which the penitent is entirely prevented from making recourse, the original month is to be prolonged or extended by an additional day. If the penitent was prevented from making recourse

[193] Cf. Coronata, *Institutiones Iuris Canonici,* IV, n. 1762; DeMeester, *Compendium,* III, n. 1748; Blat, *De Delictis et Poenis,* n. 78; Moriarty, *Extraordinary Absolution from Censures,* p. 207; Cocchi, *Commentarium in Codicem Iuris Canonici,* V, p. 124; Kelly, *Jurisdiction of the Confessor,* p. 173; Rainer, *Suspension of Clerics,* pp. 216, 217; Ferreres, *Institutiones Iuris Canonici,* II, n. 1009.

[194] Cf. canon 35.

[195] Cf. Vermeersch-Creusen, *Epitome,* III, n. 454, 3, 3°; DeMeester, *Compendium,* III, n. 1748.

[196] Cf. Berutti, *Institutiones Iuris Canonici,* VI, n. 57, V; Ferreres, *Institutiones Iuris Canonici,* II, n. 1009; Moriarty, *Extraordinary Absolution from Censures,* p. 208.

during the entire time of the original month, obviously none of the *tempus utile* has been passed, and he has an entire month of *tempus utile* after the cessation of the impediment in which to comply with his obligation of recourse.

The second case to be considered, namely, when the penitent was not aware of his obligation of recourse, therefore, has already been solved. Since the month allowed for recourse is *tempus utile,* the obligation of recourse does not begin until the penitent becomes aware of this obligation.[197] When he learns of his obligation, the *tempus utile* of one month begins immediately. The *terminus a quo* is the time when the penitent learned of his obligation, and the month is computed exactly in the same manner as above.

It is sufficient that the recourse be *begun* within this month.[198] Therefore, it is not necessary that the letter of recourse reach the competent superior within this time or that his dispensation or mandates be received by the penitent within this month allowed for recourse.

When the month of *tempus utile* has passed, and the penitent has failed at least to begin the recourse during a period which offered opportunity for recourse, the suspension of the obligation of observing the vindicative penalty immediately ceases its force, and thereupon the penitent is once again under the same vindicative penalty.

F. *Recourse—In What Manner*

Recourse, as has been noted,[199] may be made in person or by letter, either by the penitent or by the confessor when the penitent is unable to do so. Regarding personal approach to the competent superior for the dispensation and mandates, there is no difficulty. However, certain points must be discussed in reference to recourse by letter.

The letter of recourse should be complete, stating all circumstances exactly and thoroughly. A fictitious name should be used

[197] Cf. *supra,* p. 213.

[198] Cf. Coronata, *Institutiones Iuris Canonici,* IV, n. 1760; Roberti, *De Delictis et Poenis,* I, n. 318; Moriarty, *Extraordinary Absolution from Censures,* p. 209; Ferreres, *Institutiones Iuris Canonici,* II, n. 1009.

[199] Cf. *supra,* p. 204.

to designate the penitent; [200] and the letter should contain the following elements: the title of the superior; the fictitious name of the penitent; the nature of the vindicative penalty or penalties which have been suspended, and the delict or delicts by which the penalty was incurred, with all and any necessary circumstances establishing the fact that the case was an occult one; mention of the fact that the penitent, properly disposed, was granted a suspension of the observance according to canon 2290, § 1, and that he is petitioning now for a dispensation and is prepared to accept the will of the superior in regard to such a dispensation and to accept and fulfill the mandates of the superior; indication of any unusual circumstances which might hinder the penitent from performing in their entirety the mandates ordinarily prescribed in the case in question; the date; the real name and address of the confessor to whom the mandates are to be sent. For composing such a letter of recourse reference may be made to the formulae found in the Appendix of this work, with necessary changes and adaptations to the particular circumstances of an individual case.

It should be noted that the recourse is primarily a recourse for the mandates of the superior, and only secondarily a recourse for the dispensation from the penalty itself,[201] and if the superior wishes to dispense from the vindicative penalty, he will state that fact in the mandates. However, if circumstances are such that they seem to form a definite cause for the dispensation from the penalty, these circumstances should be mentioned to the superior and a petition for the dispensation should be included in the letter. The superior may grant the dispensation or may simply give his mandates for the suspension of the penalty.

A letter of recourse to a local or religious ordinary, or to any competent superior below the Holy See, may be written in the vernacular or in Latin; that to the Sacred Penitentiary may be written in any language, but Latin is preferable.[202]

[200] Cf. canon 2290, § 1: ". . . reticito nomine." Cf. Cappello, *De Censuris*, n. 128.

[201] Cf. *supra*, p. 203.

[202] Cf. Coronata, *Institutiones Iuris Canonici*, IV, n. 1762; Moriarty, *Extraordinary Absolution from Censures*, p. 212; Cappello, *De Censuris* (3. ed., 1933), n. 128, 16.

Since all concessions granted by the Sacred Penitentiary are gratuitous,[203] no offering or fee should be sent with the letter of recourse to the Sacred Penitentiary. However, as Moriarty notes,[204] the sending of a small sum to cover the cost of return postage is not prohibited.

The letter should be sealed and sent directly to the Sacred Penitentiary or to the proper superior. But if the recourse is to be made to the Sacred Penitentiary, the confessor should never send the details of the case to a procurator or agent, so that he may prepare the case better for presentation to the Sacred Penitentiary, even though the name of the penitent is fictitious. If an agent is to be used, the letter of recourse sent to him to be presented to the proper superior or the Sacred Penitentiary must be enclosed in another envelope, which he is strictly forbidden to open, not so much because there is danger of revealing the identity of the penitent, but rather because matters of conscience or anything pertaining to sacramental confession are not to be revealed.[205]

G. *Recourse—The Excusing Cause*

The penitent is obliged to make recourse to the proper superior "si id fieri possit sine gravi incommodo." This serious inconvenience herein mentioned is distinct from the moral impossibility mentioned in canon 2290, § 2, and the latter is not merely an explanation of the serious inconvenience of canon 2290, § 1, although Coronata [206] considers it such. For the serious inconvenience mentioned in canon 2290, § 1 excuses from the recourse after the obligation of recourse has been imposed, whereas the moral impossibility of canon 2290, § 2 allows the confessor to dispense from the vindicative penalty without imposing the obligation of recourse. In the first in-

[203] Cf. Pius XI, const. "Quae divinitus Nobis," 25 martii, 1935, n. 10—*AAS*, XXVII (1935), 111, 112. Cf. Berutti, *Institutiones Iuris Canonici*, VI, n. 57, VII.

[204] Cf. *Extraordinary Absolution from Censures*, p. 213.

[205] Cf. S. Poenit. monitum—*AAS*. XXVII (1935), 62. Cf. Schaaf, "The Seal of Confession: New Precautions"—*Ecclesiastical Review*, XCII (1935), 540, 541; Berutti, *Institutiones Iuris Canonici*, VI, n. 57, VII. Cf. also S.C.S. Off., instr. 9 junii, 1915—Bouscaren, *Canon Law Digest*, I, pp. 413, 414.

[206] *Institutiones Iuris Canonici*, IV, n. 1762.

stance the confessor foresees no difficulty of recourse and imposes the obligation of recourse when he suspends from the penalty; the serious inconvenience subsequently appears and excuses from recourse. In the second instance the confessor foresees at the time of the confession that recourse will be morally impossible and therefore dispenses from the penalty without imposing the obligation of the recourse. The serious inconvenience of § 1 excuses from recourse; the moral impossibility of § 2 allows the confessor to dispense.

The grave or serious inconvenience which excuses from the recourse may be either moral or physical, spiritual or temporal, affecting the penitent himself or involving another. It need not be certain, but if the inconvenience is truly probable, it is sufficient to fulfill the conditions of this canon.[207] Usually this inconvenience will consist in a danger of scandal or infamy arising from the fact that the penitent's crime is liable to become known to others through a revelation of the contents of the letter of recourse or of the letter containing the mandates of the superior. Thus, if there should be actual danger in a particular case that the letters might be opened by someone other than the proper authority—for example, by the civil authorities in time of war—and that the identity of the penitent would become known, with the consequent danger of scandal or infamy or of violation of the seal of confession, such a probability or danger would certainly be sufficient to establish the serious inconvenience to allow at least a deferment of the recourse.[208]

The grave inconvenience might arise in many ways. A prudent judgment is all that is necessary in deciding whether or not, in a particular case, the circumstances give rise to a serious inconvenience sufficient to prevent recourse. This inconvenience amounts to moral impossibility of making recourse arising only after the obligation of recourse had been imposed, and therefore it will always at least suspend that obligation. When the inconvenience ceases, the obligation of recourse remains, and the recourse must be undertaken

[207] Cf. Cappello, *De Censuris* (3. ed., 1933), n. 128, 11; Moriarty, *Extraordinary Absolution from Censures*, p. 213.

[208] Cf. Moriarty, *Extraordinary Absolution from Censures*, p. 214; Coronata, *Institutiones Iuris Canonici*, IV, n. 1764; Cappello, *De Censuris*, n. 128, 11; DeMeester, *Compendium*, III, n. 1750; Cocchi, *Commentarium in Codicem Iuris Canonici*, V. 126.

within the specified time according to what has already been said in regard to the computation of time for the recourse.[209] *Per se* the obligation of recourse remains until it is fulfilled, and the obligation is merely suspended until the excusing cause of serious inconvenience disappears. In other words, the excusing cause of grave inconvenience mentioned in canon 2290, § 1 establishes the time which is not to be computed in the *tempus utile.*

Grave inconvenience, therefore, in excusing from the obligation of recourse as long as the inconvenience continues, suspends that obligation. But the question arises whether the obligation of recourse may cease entirely because of the persistence of the grave inconvenience. And since ignorance of the obligation of recourse likewise suspends that obligation until the penitent becomes aware of his obligation,[210] another corresponding question presents itself, namely, can persistence of ignorance of the obligation of recourse bring about its cessation entirely? The two questions will be treated as one.

Cappello [211] and others,[212] in treating of this question in relation to canon 2254, § 1 establish the principle that if a serious inconvenience which prevents recourse, or if the penitent's ignorance of his obligation of making recourse, persists for a *very long time,* or if the grave inconvenience is foreseen as persisting for a very long time, the obligation can be considered as no longer binding. The very long time thus established as a norm can be regarded as that which extends over at least five years, over an indefinite period of time (beyond five years), or during an entire lifetime.

The same conclusion may be used for canon 2290, § 1 at least theoretically. For, in practice, such a difficulty would rarely, if ever, present itself. For recourse is to be made, in the case of *latae sententiae* vindicative penalties of particular law or precepts to the particular superior who established the law, his successor or delegate. Moreover, recourse to the Holy See from *latae sententiae* vin-

[209] Cf. *supra,* p. 211.

[210] Cf. *supra,* p. 214.

[211] Cf. *De Censuris* (3. ed., 1933), n. 128, 11.

[212] Cf. Coronata, *Institutiones Iuris Canonici,* IV, n. 1760; Cerato, *Censurae Vigentes,* pp. 41, 42; Moriarty, *Extraordinary Absolution from Censures,* p. 215.

dicative penalties of the common law, which alone might possibly offer this difficulty, is not necessary; for ordinaries, under canon 2237, § 2, have the power to dispense from such penalties in occult cases, and consequently recourse can always be made to them.[213]

Article V. The Mandates

A. *The Nature of the Mandates*

The reply of the superior to the recourse of the penitent is called the "mandata" or "mandates." Primarily, the mandates are the orders and instructions which the superior requires the penitent to observe. They usually contain the things enjoined by the superior: the satisfaction to an injured party, the reparation of scandal; together with the penance and satisfaction proportionate to the gravity of the crime. In this sense are the mandates mentioned in canons 2252 and 2254 to be understood.[214] However, the mandates given according to the norms of canon 2290, § 1, although they include the above mentioned elements, contain more, for they are essentially different from those given in either canon 2254, § 1, or canon 2252. This difference arises from the nature and purpose of the recourse demanded in canon 2290, § 1, as compared with the nature and purpose of the recourse to be made in canon 2252 or canon 2254. In canons 2252 and 2254, the absolution from the censure has already been given by the confessor, and the recourse is made by the penitent to receive a rescript containing the order, instructions and penance which the superior requires the penitent to observe. However, in canon 2290, § 1, the vindicative penalty is not dispensed by the confessor, but merely suspended until the mandates of the superior are received. The recourse is made, not only for the instructions and penance of the superior, but also for a dispensation from the penalty, if the superior so wills. This latter element of the recourse is, in reality, the important element.

[213] Cf. *supra*, p. 127.

[214] Cf. DeMeester, *Compendium*, III, n. 1748; Coronata, *Institutiones Iuris Canonici*, IV, n. 1762; Ayrinhac-Lydon, *Penal Legislation in the New Code of Canon Law*, n. 104; Ferreres, *Institutiones Iuris Canonici*, II, n. 1009; Moriarty, *Extraordinary Absolution from Censures*, pp. 128, 217; Berutti, *Institutiones Iuris Canonici*, VI, n. 57.

The mandates of the superior, therefore, will be more or less a total deposition of the case. He will reply to the recourse, and his instructions will state whether the penalty is dispensed or not. If the dispensation is granted, which is a pure act of favor, the superior will add his instructions and orders, and a suitable penance and satisfaction. If a dispensation is not granted—and since the dispensation is a favor, the superior may in strict justice refuse it—his mandates will state that fact, and will include the orders and instructions which the superior deems necessary.

If recourse has been made to the Sacred Penitentiary, the rescript containing the mandates is sent either *in forma gratiosa* or *in forma commissoria necessaria.*[215] The former is sent when the penitent himself makes the recourse and asks for the rescript in this form so that it will not need an executor. The latter is sent when the recourse has been undertaken by the confessor; and ordinarily the rescript will be sent in this form.

When the rescript containing the mandates of the Sacred Penitentiary is thus sent to the confessor, it is sent in a double envelope; and the confessor opens the outside one addressed to him but not the inner envelope which is addressed to the penitent and which contains the rescript. This sealed envelope is delivered sealed to the penitent. On this inner envelope, by way of address, directions are given as to the confessor to be chosen as executor of the rescript. Thus the address may read "Discreto viro confessario ex approbatis ab Ordinario loci" or "Doctori in Theologia vel Iure Canonico.' In the former case, the confessor who undertook the recourse or any other approved confessor may execute the rescript at the time when the penitent goes to confession. In the latter case, the confessor will notify the penitent of a priest who, because he is a Doctor of Sacred Theology or of Canon Law, will be capable of executing the rescript. After the rescript has been executed in the tribunal of penance, it must be burned or destroyed in some other way by the executor as soon as possible, that is, within three days, under pain of *latae sententiae* excommunication.[216]

[215] Cf. canons 36-62 for the concept of rescripts and their execution.

[216] Cf. Ayrinhac-Lydon, *Penal Legislation in the New Code of Canon Law,* n. 104; Ferreres, *Institutiones Iuris Canonici,* II, n. 1009; Arregui, *Summarium Theologiae Moralis,* n. 617, 5.

B. *The Obligation of Obeying the Mandates*

The obligation of obeying the mandates of the superior bind the penitent under pain of mortal sin.[217] The mandates, obviously, will vary according to the varying circumstances of different cases, but this variance in the mandates in no way affects the gravity of the obligation of obeying them. Though they be more or less severe they will always be serious matter, bound to be accepted and obeyed by the penitent under pain of grave sin. The substance of the mandates must be fully performed by the penitent himself, and not by another, unless this is expressly permitted in the mandates; and if the manner of fulfilling the mandates is stipulated, this also must be complied with.

This obligation of obeying the mandates ceases when they are properly carried out.

[217] Cf. Cerato, *Censurae Vigentes*, p. 41; Moriarty, *Extraordinary Absolution from Censures*, pp. 130-132; Berutti, *Institutiones Iuris Canonici*, VI, n. 57.

CHAPTER IX

THE EXCEPTIONAL METHOD—CANON 2290, § 2

Canon 2290, § 2. Et si in aliquo casu extraordinario hic recursus sit impossibilis, tunc ipsemet confessarius potest dispensationem concedere ad normam can. 2254, § 3.

Article I. The Circumstances

When the recourse prescribed in canon 2290, § 1 is morally impossible, or foreseen as such by the confessor, he can dispense from the vindicative penalty without an obligation of recourse. In place of the recourse and its consequent mandate from the superior, the confessor enjoins the things required by law by imposing a suitable penance and satisfaction which must be fulfilled under pain of reincurrence of the vindicative penalty.

In the consideration of the moral impossibility of recourse several important questions must be treated. The first of these concerns the relation between the serious inconvenience mentioned in canon 2290, § 1 and the moral impossibility of canon 2290, § 2. This relationship has been treated earlier in this work,[1] but from a different aspect. It has been established, in relation to the recourse *intra mensem* of canon 2290, § 1, that the month is to be considered as *tempus utile*,[2] and when the obligation of recourse has been actually imposed upon the penitent, he is still obliged to fulfill it even if he has been, because of some serious inconvenience, unable to and consequently excused from performing the recourse within a month of actual time from the suspension of the penalty. However, when the confessor, before granting a suspension of the penalty, foresees that the recourse cannot be made within a month, it seems that he must form his judgment on the calculation of the month, not as

[1] Cf. *supra*, p. 216.

[2] Cf. *supra*, p. 213.

tempus utile, but as *tempus continuum.*[3] Otherwise the provision of canon 2290, § 2 would be practically useless, for in computing the *tempus utile* the time is not considered to begin until the person is able to act, and there would be a consequent and evident contradiction in a norm for moral impossibility which presupposes a calculation that presumes that the person is able to act. Therefore, the confessor, when he foresees that the recourse will be morally impossible within one calendar month from the date on which the case is presented to him in confession, may dispense from the vindicative penalty according to canon 2290, § 2.[4]

The moral impossibility of recourse may arise in many ways. If neither the confessor nor the penitent can make the recourse by letter to the Sacred Penitentiary or to the competent superior, and it is hard for the penitent to go to another confessor and repeat his confession in order that this new confessor may undertake the recourse, the recourse is to be considered as morally impossible.[5] It may be safely stated that almost every penitent will find it hard to go to another confessor to repeat his confession; [6] and moreover, there is no definite obligation for the penitent to make the recourse through any other confessor than the one to whom he originally confessed.[7]

If the confessor is able to write the letter of recourse, but the penitent cannot return to him for the mandates and is, moreover, unable to make the recourse himself, and finds it hard to go to another confessor, the recourse again is considered as morally impossible. Usually at such times as missions or retreats it will happen

[3] Cf. canon 35. Cf. also Coronata, *Institutiones Iuris Canonici,* IV, n. 1762; Moriarty, *Extraordinary Absolution from Censures,* p. 237.

[4] Cf. Moriarty, *Extraordinary Absolution from Censures,* pp. 236-237 for a similar argument in relation to canon 2254. Cf. also Coronata, *Institutiones Iuris Canonici,* IV, n. 1762; Chelodi, *Ius Poenale,* n. 35, c.

[5] Cf. Cocchi, *Commentarium in Codicem Iuris Canonici,* V, 126, nota 1; Salucci, *Il Diritto Penale,* I, p. 227; Kelly, *Jurisdiction of the Confessor,* p. 173; Vermeersch-Creusen, *Epitome,* III, n. 454, 4, 2°; Moriarty, *Extraordinary Absolution from Censures,* p. 237.

[6] Cf. Kelly, *Jurisdiction of the Confessor,* p. 173.

[7] Cf. Moriarty, *Extraordinary Absolution from Censures,* pp. 238, 239 for arguments based on pre-Code legislation.

that the penitent will not be able, at least for an indefinite time, to return to the confessor; and other similar cases may and will arise in which the return to the confessor when the mandates are received will not be possible. Ordinarily, too, as Kelly notes,[8] the penitent will be unable, without serious inconvenience, to go personally to the superior for the mandates, and almost always will be incapable, unless he is a priest, of writing a complete and thorough letter of recourse. Consequently, if the confessor foresees that the penitent is not able to make the recourse and is, moreover, unable to return to the confessor in the event he undertakes the burden of recourse, he may dispense from the vindicative penalty according to canon 2290, § 2.

When the confessor foresees that the serious inconvenience mentioned in canon 2290, § 1 will endure and prevent recourse for at least a month, he may dispense from the penalty because of moral impossibility of recourse.[9] Again it should be noted that the serious inconvenience which produces the moral impossibility of canon 2290, § 2 is the same as that which excuses from or suspends the obligation of recourse of canon 2290, § 1 [10] with this difference: in canon 2290, § 1 the serious inconvenience is not foreseen by the confessor, but appears subsequently; in canon 2290, § 2 the serious inconvenience is foreseen by the confessor before he acts.

Article II. The Dispensation

According to the norms of canon 2290, § 2, the confessor grants a dispensation from the vindicative penalty, a true remission of the penalty. He does this entirely according to the stipulations of canon 2236, § 1, wherein are stated the general norms of dispensation or remission of vindicative penalties. For, as has been shown, the confessor here enjoys an express grant of dispensatory power by law,[11] because the law, as the manifestation of the will of the universal legislator, explicitly concedes that power to him.

[8] *Jurisdiction of the Confessor,* p. 173.

[9] Cf. Chelodi, *Ius Poenale,* n. 35, c; Coronata, *Institutiones Iuris Canonici,* IV, n. 1762.

[10] Cf. *supra,* p. 216.

[11] Cf. *supra,* p. 124.

Of the nature of the dispensation granted according to canon 2290, § 2 very little need be said. It is the same act of jurisdiction and favor as the ordinary dispensation from vindicative penalties.[12] It differs only in the extraordinary circumstances under which it is given.

Likewise, much of the matter discussed under canon 2290, § 1 will apply, by its very nature, to canon 2290, § 2. Thus, the minister of dispensation is the same as the minister of the suspension, namely, the confessor; and the discussion treated before [13] applies here. The forum of the dispensation, too, is exactly the same, that is, the sacramental forum.[14]

Just as no particular form is prescribed for the ordinary dispensation from vindicative penalties [15] or for the suspension of the obligation of the observance of the penalty,[16] so there is no need for any special form to be used by the confessor in dispensing in extraordinary cases according to canon 2290, § 2. It is sufficient for the confessor to notify the penitent that he is dispensed from the penalty.

As has been shown, the suspension of the obligation of the observance of the vindicative penalty granted according to canon 2290, § 1 is not given *ad reincidentiam,* because no penalty or reincidence is incurred as a result of non-fulfillment of the obligation of recourse.[17] However, the dispensation of canon 2290, § 2 is granted with such a resolutive condition based on the fulfillment or non-fulfillment of the penance and satisfaction imposed by the confessor. This question will be treated in detail in Article III of the present chapter.

The object of the dispensation herein granted includes the various penalties discussed in relation to the suspension of the obligation of the observance of such penalties.[18] In other words, all the *latae sententiae* vindicative penalties therein mentioned may be dispensed

[12] Cf. *supra,* p. 65.
[13] Cf. *supra,* p. 186.
[14] Cf. *supra,* p. 190.
[15] Cf. *supra,* p. 65.
[16] Cf. *supra,* p. 182.
[17] Cf. *supra,* p. 184.
[18] Cf. *supra,* p. 191.

by the confessor by reason of the power conceded to him in canon 2290, § 2 and under the circumstances therein specified. These include *latae sententiae* vindicative penalties *a iure; latae sentensententiae ab homine* vindicative penalties; vindicative penalties brought to the judicial forum; *latae sententiae* vindicative penalties subjected to a declaratory sentence; and finally, *ferendae sententiae* vindicative penalties under the peculiar circumstances previously noted.

Article III. The Things to Be Enjoined

A. *Preliminary Remarks*

As regards the conditions and circumstances under which the dispensation of canon 2290, § 2, is granted, the legislator makes express reference to canon 2254, § 3, and thus determines that the dispensation is to be ruled by the norms of the latter canon. Consequently, the present article and the one to follow are based directly on the terminology of canon 2254, § 3. To achieve clarity in this discussion it may be well to paraphrase canon 2254, § 3, combining it with canon 2290, § 2, thus:

"Et si in aliquo casu extraordinario hic recursus sit impossibilis, tunc ipsemet confessarius potest dispensationem concedere, injunctis tamen de iure iniungendis, et imposita congrua poenitentia et satisfactione pro poena vindicativa, ita ut poenitens, nisi intra congruum tempus a confessario praefiniendum poenitentiam egerit ac satisfactionem dederit, recidat in poenam vindicativam."

Before the confessor dispenses from the vindicative penalty, therefore, he must enjoin upon the penitent the things required by law: the "iniunctis de iure iniungendis." There is a great deal of difficulty involved in the interpretation of the phrase "iniunctis de iure iniungendis." The common opinion interprets the phrase as involving three things, namely: satisfaction to an injured party for any harm or damage inflicted by the delict of the penitent; reparation of scandal that may have resulted from his act; and a salutary penance.[19] Moriarty, in a lengthy discussion, declares that such an

[19] Cf. Berutti, *Institutiones Iuris Canonici,* VI, n. 57, IX, D, p. 154; Cappello, *De Censuris,* n. 101; n. 131, 4; DeMeester, *Compendium,* III, n. 1743, 1°; Coronata, *Institutiones Iuris Canonici,* IV, n. 1764; Cipollini, *De Censuris,*

interpretation is at fault and incorrect when applied to canon 2254, § 3.[20] His entire opinion, it seems, is based on a gratuitous assumption, which he does not attempt to prove, namely, that three distinct things are to be done by the confessor: 1. he must enjoin the things required by law; 2. he must impose a penance for the censure; 3. he must impose a satisfaction for the censure. The penitent's observance of the things enjoined is not *sub poena reincidentiae,* whereas the observance of the penance and satisfaction is imposed under such a penalty.[21] His entire argument is built upon that assumption. He states that "it is absolutely clear that the penance to be imposed by the confessor for the censure, according to canon 2254, § 3, is distinct from the *iniunctis de iure iniungendis* and must be performed *sub poena reincidentiae.*" [22] But is that absolutely clear? He immediately draws his conclusion: "Therefore, the common opinion, although it may be true in other instances, is unquestionably incorrect when in reference to canon 2254, § 3, it includes the 'salutary penance' for the censure under the *iniunctis de iure iniungendis.*" Again, he says,[23] "If the 'satisfaction to an injured party' is intended as the *satisfactio pro censura,* then it should not be included in the phrase '*iniunctis de iure iniungendis*' in the treatment of canon 2254, § 3; for the things to be enjoined and the satisfaction are distinguished in this place and have a different binding force, the first to be observed *sub gravi* or *sub levi* according to the particular character of the various things enjoined, and the second to be observed *sub poena reincidentiae.*" Again, his conclusion is drawn: "From the wording of the canon, it seems evident that the *satisfactio pro censura* is distinct not only from the *iniunctis de iure iniungendis* but also from the *poenitentia pro censura.*"

In the first place, it is not absolutely clear that the penance im-

n. 49; Salucci, *Il Diritto Penale,* I, pp. 229, 234; Sole, *De Delictis et Poenis,* n. 198; Blat, *De Delictis et Poenis,* n. 78, p. 120; Kelly, *Jurisdiction of the Confessor,* p. 176; Cerato, *Censurae Vigentes,* pp. 36, 263-265; Ayrinhac-Lydon, *Penal Legislation in the New Code of Canon Law,* n. 106, b; Sipos, *Enchiridion Iuris Canonici,* § 233, n. 10, p. 923, nota 36.

[20] *Extraordinary Absolution from Censures,* pp. 241-246.

[21] Cf. Moriarty, *Extraordinary Absolution from Censures,* pp. 241, 242.

[22] *Ibid,* p. 242.

[23] *Loc. cit.*

posed by the confessor for the censure is distinct from the *iniunctis de iure iniungendis;* nor is it evident that the *satisfactio pro censura* is distinct from the *iniunctis;* and there appears to be no reason for insisting upon such distinctions. The wording of the canon certainly does not force one to that conclusion. The canon merely states that the confessor must enjoin or impose upon the penitent those things required by law, imposing both a suitable penance for the censure and a satisfaction for the censure. It is true that the position of the term "et" might lead to Moriarty's conclusion at first sight; but the two terms "et . . . et" are correlative terms, and the position of the entire ablative absolute phrase "et imposita congrua poenitentia et satisfactione pro censura" indicates that both the penance and satisfaction are to be included in the *iniunctis de iure iniungendis.* Besides the argument derived from the wording of the canon, however, there seems to be no reason whatsoever for demanding a distinction between the *iniunctis* and the penance and satisfaction. Certainly the penance to be imposed for the censure is included among the things required by law.[24] Similarly, the satisfaction for the censure, in other words, the reparation of harm and scandal,[25] is required by law, both natural and positive.[26] Consequently, both the penance and satisfaction, may be included among the *iniunctis de iure iniungendis.* It is true that the *iniunctis* may contain more than the penance and satisfaction, whatever, in fact, may be required by law in the particular case treated; but certainly there is no reason for excluding the penance and satisfaction.

As for the argument that the observance of the things enjoined binds *sub gravi* or *sub levi* while the observance of the penance and satisfaction binds *sub poena reincidentiae,* it appears that the assertion is gratuitously made and *per se* is incorrect. In other words, assuming that there is a distinction between the *iniunctis* and the penance and satisfaction, the statement is true. However, the statement of itself cannot be and is not proved, for if the assumption that

[24] Cf. Cappello, *De Censuris* (3. ed., 1933), n. 101; Berutti, *Institutiones Iuris Canonici,* VI, n. 57, IX, D, p. 154.

[25] Cf. Berutti, *loc. cit.;* Moriarty, *Extraordinary Absolution from Censures,* pp. 244, 248.

[26] Cf. canon 2242, § 3.

there is a distinction between the *iniunctis* and the penance and satisfaction is denied, the statement is not true. Nowhere is it stated in the canon that the *iniunctis* does not bind *sub poena reincidentiae;* the canon merely states that observance of the penance and satisfaction binds *sub poena reincidentiae.* In other words, the *iniunctis de iure iniungendis* includes the penance and satisfaction. It may include other things required by law; but inasmuch as it contains the penance and satisfaction it may be said to bind *sub poena reincidentiae* as regards these two elements. Or, to state it another way, the *iniunctis* may contain many things required by law; the Code mentions two, penance and satisfaction; and these two bind *sub poena reincidentiae.*

Therefore, the common interpretation of the phrase "*iniunctis de iure iniungendis,*" held by all authors consulted in the preparation of this work, may be held as the correct interpretation. The phrase, consequently, embraces the satisfaction to an injured party: the reparation of harm and scandal, and a salutary penance for the penalty,[27] to which may be added whatever is required by law in a particular case.[28] All these things must be enjoined upon the penitent, but the obligation of observing the satisfaction and penance for the censure are to be imposed under penalty of reincidence.

Applying the phrase to canon 2290, § 1, therefore, it may be said that the confessor, before he dispenses from the vindicative penalty, must enjoin upon the penitent the things required by law: he must impose upon the penitent the obligation of repairing the harm and scandal caused by his crime and of observing the salutary penance

[27] Cf. Berutti, *Institutiones Iuris Canonici,* VI, n. 57, IX, D, p. 154; Cappello, *De Censuris,* n. 101, n. 131, 4; De Meester, *Compendium,* III, n. 1743, 1°; Coronata, *Institutiones Iuris Canonici,* IV, n. 1764; Salucci, *Il Diritto Penale,* I, p. 229; Sole, *De Delictis et Poenis,* n. 198; Blat, *De Delictis et Poenis,* n. 78, p. 120; Kelly, *Jurisdiction of the Confessor,* p. 176; Ayrinhac-Lydon, *Penal Legislation in the New Code of Canon Law,* n. 106, b; Sipos, *Enchiridion Iuris Canonici,* § 233, n. 10, p. 923, nota 36.

[28] Cf. canon 2336, § 1: when a penitent is absolved from this censure, he should be required to abjure the sect, etc. Cf. also canon 2319, § 1, 1°: if a penitent has incurred this censure, he must be required to have the marriage convalidated.

which the confessor judges suitable,[29] together with any other things to be enjoined in the particular case at issue.

B. *The Nature of the Penance and the Satisfaction*

The confessor must impose a penance for the vindicative penalty, distinct from the sacramental penance for the crime.[30] For the crime the confessor imposes the same kind of grave penance as he would enjoin if there were no penalty attached to the crime, although it may be mitigated more or less for the reason that another penance has been added because of the vindicative penalty. The penance for the vindicative penalty is to be considered here. And it should be noted that the question of a penance for the vindicative penalty is not treated by any of the canonists directly. Just as in the foregoing discussion, arguments must be based upon norms and opinions advanced in the case of the penance and the satisfaction imposed for censures. In consequence, all authorities quoted will be cited precisely because the opinions they advance for the treatment of censures may be applied to a discussion of vindicative penalties. From this it should not be concluded that the arguments are purely analogical. The arguments advanced are self-supporting; but are bolstered by authorities who advance similar arguments and opinions in regard to censures.

The penance imposed for the vindicative penalty must be grave, because of the grave penalty prescribed for its culpable omission, namely, the reincurrence of the vindicating penalty.[31] There is, however, little consistency of opinion among authors concerning this grave penance, precisely because there are so many elements and

[29] Cf. Chelodi, *Ius Poenale*, n. 47; Vermeersch-Creusen, *Epitome*, III, n. 491, 3; Berutti, *Institutiones Iuris Canonici*, VI, n. 86, II, p. 217; Blat, *De Delictis et Poenis*, n. 120.

[30] Cf. Coronata, *Institutiones Iuris Canonici*, IV, n. 1764; De Meester, *Compendium*, III, n. 1743; Kelly, *Jurisdiction of the Confessor*, p. 176; Cappello, *De Censuris*, n. 101; Berutti, *Institutiones Iuris Canonici*, VI, n. 57, IX, D, p. 154.

[31] Cf. Blat, *De Delictis et Poenis*, n. 78, p. 121; Coronata, *Institutiones Iuris Canonici*, IV, n. 1764; Moriarty, *Extraordinary Absolution from Censures*, p. 246.

factors to be considered, and so many aspects from which the gravity of a penance may be viewed. First of all, the penance should be proportionate to the quantity and quality of the delict committed.[32] Moreover, the character and ability of the penitent must be considered,[33] as well as the seriousness or gravity of the work prescribed as a penance, and the length of time over which it is extended. Consequently, no definite norm can possibly be given which will apply in all cases; and although authors have attempted to give purely objective norms, these will always depend on the circumstances of a particular case from which the confessor who imposes the penance must form a prudent judgment.

The types of principal penances are enumerated in canon 2313; and these are determined prayers, pilgrimages and other like works of piety, particular fasts and alms, and spiritual exercises for a definite time in a religious house. However, in imposing such penances the confessor must keep in mind the gravity of the delict, the character and ability of the penitent; and he must decide upon the gravity of the work to be enjoined and the length of time over which it is to extend according to such considerations.

In moral theology it is generally taught that a grave penance is one which corresponds to a good work prescribed *sub gravi* by the Church, or one which, because of its quantity or quality, would be binding *sub gravi* if it were prescribed by the Church.[34] However, canonists commonly consider such grave penances from the viewpoint of the length of time for which they are given. Thus, for example, Cappello demands that the penance be one that is to be performed each week for a month, each day for a week, or many times a day. For particularly grave penances, he demands that the work be performed each month for half a year, each week for two months, or every day for two or three weeks.[35]

Coronata [36] demands that the penance be performed each day

[32] Cf. canon 2196. Cf. also Berutti, *Institutiones Iuris Canonici,* VI, n. 57, IX, D, p. 154; Cappello, *De Censuris,* n. 101.

[33] Cf. Berutti, *loc. cit.*; Cappello, *loc. cit.*

[34] Cf. Coronata, *Institutiones Iuris Canonici,* IV, n. 1764; Moriarty, *Extraordinary Absolution from Censures,* p. 247; Cappello, *De Censuris,* n. 101.

[35] Cf. Cappello, *De Censuris* (3. ed., 1933), n. 101.

[36] *Institutiones Iuris Canonici,* IV, n. 1764.

for a month, or once a week for three months. As a particularly grave penance he regards one which is to be performed each day for three months, each week for six months, or every month for one or two years.

Other authors [37] give similar opinions as to norms to be used in determining the gravity of the penance to be imposed. But the opinions vary so greatly that it is impossible to determine any definite and sure norm of action. The most that can be said is that the entire matter must be left to the judgment of the confessor and his prudence in forming such a judgment. He must consider the various factors mentioned above: the gravity of the delict and the vindicative penalty, the character and the ability of the penitent, the seriousness and the difficulty of the good work to be enjoined and the length of time during which it is to extend. To the confessor may be applied the admirable admonition given by the Church in canon 2214, § 3, that divine mercy is part of divine justice, that exhortation is more effective than threats, and charity more effective than severity. He should act with mercy and benevolence without harshness or undue rigor, so that those who are corrected be converted from their ways.[38]

A very practical norm of procedure would be to impose the penance which the confessor, by previous experience, knows is demanded by the competent superior which he dispenses from a similar vindicating penance. In most dioceses a uniform penance is imposed by the ordinary for certain censures and vindicative penalties. Any confessor, therefore, who has had fairly wide experience in applying for absolutions from reserved censures or dispensations from vindicative penalties, knows the usual penance imposed. Consequently, when he dispenses, according to canon 2290, § 2, he may impose that same penance.

As has been shown in the preceding article, the satisfaction for the penalty consists in the reparation of any harm and scandal that may have resulted. Obviously, it will be necessary to require the satisfaction only when scandal has actually been given and has not

[37] Cf. Vermeersch-Creusen, *Epitome*, III, n. 491; *idem*, *Theologia Moralis*, III; Ayrinhac-Lydon, *Penal Legislation in the New Code of Canon Law*, n. 106, b; Cerato, *Censurae Vigentes*, pp. 260-263.

[38] Cf. canon 2214, § 2.

been repaired, and when harm has been caused to another and its reparation has not been made or condoned or rejected.[39] When harm has been suffered by another and has not been repaired, the confessor must require that the penitent make restoration for it as best he can. This harm may arise in many ways as a result of the delict of the penitent, even though the delict as such and the resulting penalty were occult.

Likewise, when scandal has been given, the confessor must require that the penitent make reparation in the way which the confessor judges is best. This is to be done, not only because it is prescribed by positive law in this canon, but also because divine law demands that scandal be repaired.[40] Obviously, since in occult cases treated in canon 2290 actual scandal to others will seldom arise, the reparation of scandal rarely will be demanded. However, it may happen that scandal may arise, not from the observance of the vindicative penalty, but from the delict committed; and is such cases the obligation of repairing of the scandal must be imposed by the confessor upon the penitent.

The confessor is to determine specifically and clearly the time within which the penance is to be performed or the satisfaction is to be made,[41] for the penalty of reincidence depends upon that factor. As regards the satisfaction to be given, the time allowed for the reparation of harm and scandal ordinarily should not exceed six months.[42]

C. *The Sanction*

The confessor must clearly specify the time within which the penance and satisfaction which he imposes upon the penitent are

[39] Cf. Coronata, *Institutiones Iuris Canonici,* IV, n. 1764; Cerato, *Censurae Vigentes,* pp. 36, 37; Moriarty, *Extraordinary Absolution from Censures,* p. 249; Berutti, *Institutiones Iuris Canonici,* VI, n. 57.

[40] Cf. S. Poenit. 10 dec., 1860, ad 27: "Reparationem scandali esse necessariam de iure divino, eamque faciendam esse meliori modo quo potest prudenti iudicio Ordinarii seu Confessarii"—*ASS,* I (1865-1866), 566.

[41] Cf. canon 2290, § 2 together with canon 2254, § 3.

[42] Cf. Moriarty, *Extraordinary Absolution from Censures,* pp. 244, nota 23; p. 250, who quotes the norm given for the use of jubilee faculties by Pius XI const. "*Servatori Iesu Christi,*" 25 dec., 1925, pars de facultatibus, III—*AAS,* XVII (1925), 616.

to be performed, and he must, moreover, inform the penitent that if they are not fulfilled within the stated time the same kind of vindicative penalty will be reincurred.[43] If the time has in no way been determined by the confessor, there can be no possible question of reincidence. This is clear from the wording of canon 2254, § 3, from which the norm of canon 2290, § 2, is to be taken. Moreover, if the time has not been determined, it would never be certain when the vindicative penalty would be reincurred, because there is no terminus within which the obligation must be fulfilled. In such a case, Coronata insists that another confessor could specify the time in which the obligation is to be performed.[44] But, as Moriarty notes,[45] that opinion seems very dubious. The determination of the time depends, according to the canon, entirely upon the confessor who dispenses from the penalty. It seems, rather, that in such a case the penitent would be bound *sub gravi* to fulfill his obligation imposed by the original confessor, but not *sub poena reincidentiae.* But if the confessor has specified the time, but has neglected to inform the penitent of the penalty of reincidence in the event of non-fulfillment with the prescribed time, it seems that this could be told the penitent by a subsequent confessor, for this penalty arises directly from the law.

It is important to note that the penance and satisfaction are distinct and the obligations of each are distinct. Therefore, since the fulfillment of each will depend on peculiar and distinct circumstances, a definite time must be specified for each, whether the same time is determined for both or different times are specified, for the penitent reincurs the same kind of vindicative penalty unless he has performed both the determinate penance and the satisfaction within the prescribed time set for each. Consequently, if either the penance or the satisfaction is culpably omitted for the whole of the specified

[43] Cf. Coronata, *Institutiones Iuris Canonici,* IV, n. 1764; Salucci, *Il Diritto Penale,* I, pp. 233, 234; Wernz, *Ius Decretalium,* VI, n. 176; Moriarty, *Extraordinary Absolution from Censures,* p. 250; Berutti, *Institutiones Iuris Canonici,* VI, n. 57, IX, E, p. 155; Ayrinhac-Lydon, *Penal Legislation in the New Code of Canon Law,* n. 106, b.

[44] Cf. Coronata, *Institutiones Iuris Canonici,* IV, n. 1764.

[45] *Extraordinary Absolution from Censures,* p. 250.

time, it is sufficient to involve the reincurrence of the vindicative penalty.[46]

Because of the serious penalty of reincidence which depends upon this factor, it is important that the confessor impose the penance and satisfaction in such away as to leave the least possible, if any, chance for doubt. In other words, a carefully specified penance should be prescribed for a carefully specified time. However, there is likely to be more difficulty in prescribing the satisfaction. Generalities and vague admonitions should not be given, or uncertainty will constantly arise about the reincurrence of the penalty. Thus, it is not sufficient for the confessor to state, "Repair the scandal; mend your life." To attach a penalty of reincidence to such an obligation is absurd. The satisfaction should be as specific as the case allows. The confessor should take all the particulars and the circumstances of the case, the ability of the penitent, and the reason for the scandal or harm into consideration, and then formulate definite prescriptions to be followed, which in his prudent judgment will definitely repair the damage or harm inflicted or the scandal caused.[47]

If the penitent culpably neglects to fulfill the penance and satisfaction within the required time, he reincurs the same kind of vindicative penalty. Therefore, whatever may have been the nature of the original penalty dispensed by reason of canon 2290, § 2, whether it was *a iure* or *ab homine,* whether reserved to the ordinary or to the Roman Pontiff as supreme legislator, the reincurred vindicative penalty is specifically the same, although numerically distinct from the former penalty. In other words, the dispensed vindicative penalty revives and is reincurred.[48]

[46] Cf. Berutti, *Institutiones Iuris Canonici,* VI, n. 57, IX, E, p. 155; Coronata, *Institutiones Iuris Canonici,* IV, n. 1764; Blat, *De Delictis et Poenis,* nn. 78, 120; Moriarty, *Extraordinary Absolution from Censures,* p. 252; Salucci, *Il Diritto Penale,* I, p. 229.

[47] Cf. S. Poenit., 10 dec., 1860, ad 27—*ASS,* I (1865-1866), 566.

[48] The term "revives" used by authors is misleading. The penalty is specifically the same, but not numerically. Cf. D'Annibale, *Summula,* I, n. 354; Cappello, *De Censuris* (3. ed., 1933), n. 95; Coronata, *Institutiones Iuris*

It must be understood that reincidence, or reincurrence of the same kind of vindicative penalty, takes place only if there is grave culpability on the part of the penitent in failing to fulfill the penance or to give proper satisfaction in the specified time. For there is a new vindicative penalty of the same species involved, and consequently for the reincurrence of a vindicative penalty the same factors are necessary as for the incurrence of such a penalty; and therefore before it can be contracted there must be a new delict.[49] And since the salutary penance for the vindicative penalty and the satisfaction are distinct, there are, in canon 2254, § 3 and canon 2290, § 2, apparently two distinct delicts possible, namely, the culpable omission of the penance and the culpable omission of the satisfaction, either of which is sufficient to involve the reincurrence of the vindicative penalty.[50] Moreover, any cause which would excuse from the incurrence of a vindicative penalty, such as ignorance, inadvertance, fear, or forgetfulness, would likewise excuse from the penalty of reincidence attached to the obligation of fulfilling the penance or of giving the satisfaction within the required time.[51] Consequently,

Canonici, IV, n. 1740, 1764; Cipollini, *De Censuris,* pp. 33, 34; Blat, *De Delictis et Poenis,* n. 78; Cocchi, *Commentarium in Codicem Iuris Canonici,* V, pp. 115, 116; Salucci, *Il Diritto Penale,* I, p. 229; Ayrinhac-Lydon, *Penal Legislation in the New Code of Canon Law,* n. 89; Cerato, *Censurae Vigentes,* p. 38; Moriarty, *Extraordinary Absolution from Censures,* pp. 216, 252; Sole, *De Delictis et Poenis,* n. 152, 3; Kelly, *Jurisdiction of the Confessor,* p. 173; Rainer, *Suspension of Clerics,* p. 217; Noldin-Schönegger, *De Censuris* (20. ed., Oeniponte: Rauch, 1928), n. 28; Berutti, *Institutiones Iuris Canonici,* VI, n. 57, IX, E, p. 155.

[49] Cf. canons 2228; 2233, § 1. Cf. also Coronata, *Institutiones Iuris Canonici,* IV, n. 1740; Cappello, *De Censuris* (3. ed., 1933), n. 95, 3, 6, 8; n. 131, 6; Cocchi, *Commentarium in Codicem Iuris Canonici,* V, 115, 116, 126; Blat, *De Delictis et Poenis,* n. 78; Berutti, *Institutiones Iuris Canonici,* VI, n. 57, IX; Chelodi, *Ius Poenale,* n. 35; Cerato, *Censurae Vigentes,* p. 38; Sole, *De Delictis et Poenis,* n. 152, 3; Moriarty, *The Extraordinary Absolution from Censures,* pp. 124, 216, 252.

[50] Cf. Coronata, *Institutiones Iuris Canonici,* IV, n. 1764; Berutti, *Institutiones Iuris Canonici,* VI, n. 57, IX; Salucci, *Il Diritto Penale,* I, 229; *Moriarty, The Extraordinary Absolution from Censures,* p. 252; Blat, *De Delictis et Poenis,* nn. 78, 120.

[51] Cf. canons 2199-2206; 2229. Cf. also Chelodi, *Ius Poenale,* n. 35; Cap-

the penitent must know of the penalty and must not be affected by any of the causes that would preclude blame or that would excuse him from contracting the vindicative penalty.

If either or both the penance for the penalty and the satisfaction were completely omitted culpably, that is, without an excusing cause, for the whole of the time specified by the confessor, it is clear and evident that the delict or delicts are perfect and consummated,[52] and the same kind of vindicative penalty is reincurred. However, the question may arise whether the penitent reincurs the penalty if he has fulfilled the penance or satisfaction, not completely, but only partially. If at least half of the penance and satisfaction are performed, it certainly seems that there is no reincidence or reincurrence of the vindicative penalty, even though the penitent's obligation of completing and continuing the penance and satisfaction would remain until the whole is completed.[53] For the penance is imposed as a single unit; it is given as a penance, not as penances; and the penalty of reincidence is attached to the omission of the penance, and not to the omission of parts of that penance. This is true even if the penance may be made up of various elements, for example, the reception of communion each week for six months. Thus, if such a penance were imposed, it would certainly seem unjustifiably rigorous to insist that a penitent, in culpably omitting the reception of communion once, would be guilty of culpably omitting the penance and would thereby reincur the vindicative penalty. This very same principle applies to the satisfaction. And so it appears safe and justifiable to assert that, if the penitent has fulfilled at

pello, *De Censuris*, n. 127; Blat, *De Delictis et Poenis*, n. 78; Moriarty, *The Extraordinary Absolution from Censures*, pp. 128, 216, 252; Ayrinhac-Lydon, *Penal Legislation in the New Code of Canon Law*, n. 89, c; Sole, *De Delictis et Poenis*, n. 152, 3; Kelly, *Jurisdiction of the Confessor*, p. 173; Cerato, *Censurae Vigentes*, p. 38; Cipollini, *De Censuris*, p. 47; Berutti, *Institutiones Iuris Canonici*, VI, n. 57.

[52] Cf. canon 2228.

[53] Cf. Coronata, *Institutiones Iuris Canonici*, IV, n. 1764; Moriarty, *Extraordinary Absolution from Censures*, p. 252. Coronata seems to be the only author other than Moriarty who has given any attention to this problem. Both, however, treat it in relation to censures according to canon 2254.

least the greater part of both the penance and the satisfaction, it would at least be uncertain whether or not the double delict is perfect or consummated, and, consequently, the vindicative penalty would not be reincurred, though, as has been mentioned, the obligation of completing the penance and the satisfaction would continue to bind the penitent, not now *sub poena reincidentiae,* but *sub gravi.*[54]

[54] Cf. Coronata, *Institutiones Iuris Canonici,* IV, n. 1764; Blat, *De Delictis et Poenis,* n. 78; Moriarty, *Extraordinary Absolution from Censures,* p. 252.

CHAPTER X

THE ALTERNATIVE METHOD—CANON 2254, § 2

Canon 2254, § 2. Nihil impedit quominus poenitens, etiam post acceptam, ut supra, absolutionem, facto quoque recursu ad Superiorem, alium adeat confessarium facultate praeditum, ab eoque, repetita confessione saltem delicti cum censura, consequatur absolutionem; qua obtenta, mandata ab eodem accipiat, quin teneatur postea stare aliis mandatis ex parte Superioris supervenientibus.

ARTICLE I. THE STATUS OF THE QUESTION

Although most authors do not consider the matter to be treated here, the question has been proposed as to whether in similar and analogous circumstances the concession of an alternative method made in canon 2254, § 2, may also be used in reference to canon 2290, that is, by one who is laboring under a vindicative penalty. Kelly [1] responds that, because of the completely analogous circumstances, it would seem that a penitent who had incurred a vindicative penalty, the observance of which was suspended by a confessor by virtue of faculties granted to him by canon 2290, § 1, could still approach a privileged confessor who had faculties to dispense from the particular vindicative penalty, receive a dispensation after confessing again at least the crime and mentioning the vindicative penalty, and thus free himself from the obligation of recourse, or, if recourse has already been made, from the obligation of obeying the mandates that will subsequently come from the superior. It is true that Kelly, in proposing the question, does not respond clearly in the above sense, but seems to confuse the purpose of canon 2254, § 2, as supplying a substitute or alternative method of obtaining the

[1] Kelly, *Jurisdiction of the Confessor*, p. 237. He seems to be the only author who has considered this matter.

mandates.[2] The purpose of canon 2254, § 2 is not to furnish an alternative method of obtaining the mandates, for the privileged confessor, if and because he is not a superior, may not be approached solely for the mandates; [3] but rather to supply an alternative method of obtaining a dispensation, thus obliterating the obligation of recourse to the competent superior, or, if recourse had already been made, from the obligation of obeying the mandates which will subsequently come from that superior.[4] However, although Kelly is not quite clear in his interpretation of canon 2254, § 2, he does apply canon 2254, § 2 to vindicative penalties, which is the important matter at issue here.

There appears to be good reason for this opinion, for certainly a privileged confessor is permitted to use his special faculties whenever a case over which he has jurisdiction is presented to him. If the penitent goes to him without having previously obtained a suspension of the obligation of the observance of the penalty according to canon 2290, § 1 certainly the confessor may use his special faculty without imposing an obligation of recourse,[5] for he is simply using powers granted to him in accordance with canon 2236, § 1, and he is acting strictly according to the norms of that canon. There seems to be no reason why, if the penitent goes to such an authorized or privileged confessor after having previously received a suspension of the penalty from another confessor in virtue of canon 2290, § 1, the faculty of the specially authorized confessor is no longer of any avail. On the contrary, because of the analogous circumstances, it seems very necessary that, just as the notion that the faculties of such a confessor are of no avail is definitely precluded in canon 2254,

[2] Cf. Kelly, *Jurisdiction of the Confessor*, pp. 175, 237, wherein he states that the new and privileged confessor is to be approached for the purpose of obtaining the mandates as a substitute for having recourse to the prescribed superior or awaiting his mandate.

[3] Cf. *supra*, p. 207.

[4] Cf. Moriarty, *Extraordinary Absolution from Censures*, pp. 219-227; Sole, *De Delictis et Poenis*, n. 195; Ayrinhac-Lydon, *Penal Legislation in the New Code of Canon Law*, n. 105; Vermeersch-Creusen, *Theologia Moralis*, III, n. 473, 3; n. 474.

[5] Cf. Coronata, *Institutiones Iuris Canonici*, IV, n. 1763; Cappello, *De Censuris* (3. ed., 1933), n. 130, 1, for similar assertion in regard to absolving from censures.

§ 2, a similar provision is to be allowed in regard to vindicative penalties in canon 2290. Moreover, the argument gains force by comparing the two canons, for in canon 2254, § 1 the censure is definitely absolved, and when the penitent presents himself before a specially authorized confessor, he receives another absolution, this time without the obligation of recourse. In canon 2290, § 2, however, the penitent does not receive a dispensation from the penalty, but merely a suspension of the obligation of observing the penalty; and in approaching a privileged confessor he petitions, not for another suspension, but for a dispensation from the penalty, a favor which the privileged confessor has power to grant in virtue of canon 2236, § 1. In other words, the act of the specially authorized confessor is a new, distinct act, wider in scope and jurisdiction than the act of the original simple confessor; it is an act performed in virtue of canon 2236, § 1, and not of canon 2290, § 1.

Article II. The Circumstances

To transfer the wording, therefore, of canon 2254, § 2, and adapt it to the formulation of canon 2290, it seems that it could be paraphrased as follows:

> Nihil impedit quominus poenitens, etiam post acceptam, ut supra, suspensionem poenae observantiae, facto quoque recursu ad Superiorem, alium adeat confessarium facultate praeditum, ab eoque, repetita confessione saltem delicti cum poena, consequatur dispensationem; qua obtenta, mandata ab eodem accipiat, quin teneatur postea stare aliis mandata ex parte Superioris supervenientibus.

From the wording of this canon: "Nihil impedit quominus . . .", it is clear that a privilege and a distinct benefit is here given to the penitent, so that although the penitent may, at any time, make use of it if he wishes, he is never obliged to accept it.[6]

The terminology "etiam post acceptam suspensionem" as set forth in the paraphrasing adaptation of canon 2254, § 2 should not be accepted or interpreted in the sense that a specially authorized

[6] Cf. Coronata, *Institutiones Iuris Canonici,* IV, n. 1763; Moriarty, *The Extraordinary Absolution from Censures,* p. 219; Vermeersch-Creusen, *Epitome,* III, n. 454, 4, 2°.

confessor—one to whom dispensatory power has been conceded, in virtue of canon 2236, § 1, by the competent superior—cannot use his faculty until the penitent has received a suspension from the observance of the vindicative penalty from another confessor in an urgent case according to the norms of canon 2290, § 1. He can use his special faculty whether the penitent has or has not already approached another confessor and received a suspension of the penalty.[7] If this confessor employs his special faculty in a case in which suspension of the penalty already has been granted, he acts in accordance with the norms of this adaptation of canon 2254, § 2; if he uses his special faculty in a case in which a suspension of the penalty has not previously been granted according to canon 2290, § 1, he is following the norm, not of this canon, but of canon 2236, § 1.

Ordinarily the privileged confessor will be different from the confessor who suspended the obligation of the observance of the vindicative penalty according to canon 2290, § 1. However, it should be noted that the distinction between confessors as established by the canon [8] is not based upon the specification of separate individuals, but rather on the clear differentiation between a confessor who is specially authorized ("facultate praeditum") and a confessor who enjoys no such special faculty. If a confessor has no special faculty, he uses canon 2290, § 1; if a confessor enjoys a special faculty, he employs this particular adaptation of canon 2254, § 2. Consequently, if it should happen that the same confessor, who has granted a suspension of the penalty in virtue of canon 2290, § 1 with the consequent obligation of recourse, should subsequently obtain a special faculty to dispense from the previously suspended vindicative penalty, and if the penitent should return to him before the recourse is begun or before the mandates of the superior are received, there seems to be no reason why the confessor cannot use this, his special faculty, according to the norm of this adaptation of canon 2254, § 2, even though in identity he is not strictly "alius confessarius."

[7] Cf. Coronata, *Institutiones Iuris Canonici*, IV, n. 1763; Cappello, *De Censuris*, n. 130; Moriarty, *The Extraordinary Absolution from Censures*, p. 220.

[8] Cf. "alium adeat confessarium facultate praeditum."

Article III. The Dispensation

A. *Its Nature and Form*

The dispensation which is granted in this, the alternative method, is a dispensation in the strict sense of the term. It is a complete remission of the penalty, according to canon 2236, § 1, granted in strict accordance with the norms of that canon. The penalty is merely suspended in canon 2290, § 1; but in this canon the penalty is dispensed. The penitent may approach the specially authorized confessor and may submit the case for the first time and receive the dispensation from the vindicative penalty. Or the penitent may have gone to a confessor who enjoys no special faculty, and may have received a suspension of the observance of the penalty by reason of canon 2290, § 1, with the obligation of recourse and of obedience to the mandates of the superior. Suppose, however, that before he makes the recourse or before he receives the mandates, he discovers that he could have gone to another confessor who is privileged with special faculties for the particular vindicative penalty, and who in ordinary circumstances, outside of the *casus urgentior*, could have dispensed him without the obligation of recourse, but only with the obligation of obeying the mandates. This penitent, who has shown his good will and good intentions by submitting the case to a confessor and having the penalty suspended according to canon 2290, § 1, should certainly not be in a less favorable position than another penitent who has not done this, but has submitted the case for the first time to a privileged confessor. Consequently, it would seem that the positive declaration which the Church had made in canon 2254, § 2, is applicable in this case. Therefore, even though the vindicative penalty has already been suspended, the penitent may once again go to confession and submit the case, this time to a specially authorized confessor; and this confessor can employ his special faculty in the same way as if no previous approach was made to another confessor, and with the same canonical effect as would be produced if this privileged confessor used his faculties in ordinary circumstances, namely, that there is no subsequent obligation of recourse, and that it is enough to obey the mandates imposed by this confessor. In brief, the privileged confessor merely uses his conceded faculties in strict accordance with canon 2236, § 1; and the penitent is not to be deprived of the advantage of the faculties of the specially authorized confessor, even if he has already had the penalty suspended according to the norm of canon 2290, § 1.

The dispensation which the specially authorized confessor grants is distinct from the suspension granted previously. Consequently, the repeated confession and submission of the delict and vindicative penalty seems to be prescribed not only that the privileged confessor, from his knowledge of the case thus obtained, may give proportionate mandates, but especially that he may be able to use his special faculties to dispense, which, if granted to him as a confessor, can only be used in the sacramental internal forum.

The dispensation granted by the privileged confessor, like the suspension in canon 2290, § 1 and the dispensation in canon 2290, § 2, can be given only in the sacramental forum, for the canon states "quominus poenitens . . . alium adeat confessarium."[9] If the confessor has jurisdiction in the external forum so that he may dispense the penitent from a particular vindicative penalty in the external forum, obviously he may exercise that power; but such a dispensation would not be an application of this adaptation of canon 2254, § 2, but rather of canon 2236, regarding the dispensation granted in the external forum. The dispensation, however, granted under the alternative method is given only within the sacramental internal forum.

There is no special form prescribed for the dispensation which the specially authorized confessor grants. He merely informs the penitent that he is dispensed from the vindicative penalty.

B. *The Confessor*

To employ the faculties in the alternative method of dispensing from a vindicative penalty, the confessor must be one who is "facultate praeditus," that is, one to whom the power to dispense from the particular penalty in question has been conceded in accordance with canon 2236, § 1. His power to dispense, consequently, must proceed from some other source than from the faculties of canon

[9] Cf. Blat, *De Delictis et Poenis*, n. 78, p. 119.

2290, § 2 for more urgent cases. The stipulations of the alternative method, as expressed in canon 2254, § 2 and as applied to vindicative penalties, presupposes that the minister of the dispensation is a specially authorized confessor inasmuch as he possesses a special conceded faculty to dispense in the particular case.

Confessors may possess such powers in various ways. An ordinary is a specially authorized confessor for his subjects as regards those *latae sententiae* vindicative penalties from which he is competent to dispense by law in occult cases; [10] and also for all other vindicative penalties from which he has the power to dispense by reason of quinquennial faculties or particular indults.

Moreover, a confessor may possess delegated powers, granted by the competent superior of dispensation or subdelegated power granted by the ordinary; or the power, or special faculties, may be granted him directly by the Holy See. Thus, certain religious confessors who enjoy the privileges of regulars possess special faculties to dispense from certain vindicative penalties.[11] An apostolic delegate, as a confessor, also may dispense from vindicative penalties in the alternative method, according to the extent of the faculties delegated to him.[12]

All such confessors, therefore, because they have faculties to dispense from vindicative penalties exclusive of more urgent extraordinary cases, can, as far as their jurisdictional faculties extend, grant a dispensation in the sacramental forum from vindicative penalties to a penitent who has already been granted a suspension of the obligation of the observance of the penalty with its concomitant obligation of recourse according to canon 2290, § 1.

Article IV. The Mandates

The privileged confessor who grants a dispensation in the alternative method must give mandates which the penitent is to observe.[13]

[10] Cf. canons 198; 488, n. 8; 2237, § 2. Cf. also Coronata, *Institutiones Iuris Canonici,* IV, n. 1737.

[11] Cf. *e.g.,* the faculties which the confessors of the Congregation of the Passion enjoy by reason of the Congreg. S. Justinae, Eugenius IV, Bulla, "Etsi quoslibet," 31 maii, 1436.

[12] Cf. canon 267.

[13] Cf. canon 2254, § 2: ". . . mandata ab eodem accipiat. . . ."

Just as in canon 2290, § 2, the confessor who grants the dispensation must impose a suitable penance and satisfaction, so the mandates of the specially authorized confessor will consist of an apt penance and fitting satisfaction. It is to be noted that there is no mention, as there is in canon 2290, § 2, of the confessor's obligation to impose the *iniunctis de iure iniungendis,* which, as has been shown,[14] consist primarily of the penance and satisfaction. But those matters which are to be enjoined according to the law, namely, the penance and satisfaction and whatever also is demanded by divine natural or divine positive law, are all included in the mandates which the privileged confessor is to impose upon the penitent, just as the mandates of the superior contain the same elements in canon 2290, § 1.[15] In other words, the mandates of the superior are replaced by those of the privileged confessor in the alternative method, and the mandates of the latter are to consist of the same elements.

Another important point should be noted here. Although the penance and satisfaction imposed by the confessor who dispenses from a vindicative penalty in virtue of canon 2290, § 2 bind the penitent *sub poena reincidentiae,* the mandates given to the penitent by the privileged confessor in the alternative method do not bind under such a penalty. No mention is made of the penalty of reincidence in canon 2254, § 2, for the specially authorized confessor in reality shares in the dispensatory power of the superior, and consequently substitutes, as it were, for the superior in dispensing from the penalty and in imposing the mandates. In other words, his mandates replace those of the superior; and since the superior is not bound by the law to give the mandates in such a way that they oblige under penalty of reincurrence of the vindicative penalty, the same is true of the privileged confessor. Of course, the superior may give the mandates under pain of reincidence, and he may likewise delegate or subdelegate the dispensatory power to the privileged confessor under the condition that he impose mandates *sub poena reincidentiae.* But unless such a condition has been attached to the faculties of the specially authorized confessor, he cannot

[14] Cf. *supra,* p. 228.

[15] Cf. *supra,* p. 219.

impose the mandates under the pain of reincurrence of the vindicative penalty.[16]

However, the mandates which the privileged confessor gives must be grave. and binding upon the penitent *sub gravi,* just as the mandates of the superior bind under pain of mortal sin.[17]

It seems that the penitent who is dispensed from his penalty by the privileged confessor and has received the mandates of that confessor, although he is freed from the obligation of observing the subsequent mandates of the superior which are sent in response to the recourse of canon 2290, § 1, may await these mandates of the superior and fulfill them instead of the mandates of the specially authorized confessor. In other words, the terminology of canon 2254, § 2: "quin teneatur postea stare aliis mandatis ex parte Superioris supervenientibus" seems to allow the penitent a choice, of fulfilling either the mandates of the superior or those of the privileged confessor.[18]

[16] Cf. Cappello, *De Censuris* (3. ed., 1933), n. 94, 1; n. 95, 7, in his treatment of canon 2254, § 2.

[17] Cf. *supra,* p. 221.

[18] Cf. Coronata, *Institutiones Iuris Canonici,* IV, n. 1763; De Meester, *Compendium,* III, n. 1749, p. 118; Cappello, *De Censuris* (3. ed., 1933), nn. 118; 130, 5; Salucci, *Il Diritto Penale,* I, p. 228, nota 1. Chelodi (*Ius Poenale,* n. 35, c. p. 43), however, maintains the opposite is true: that the penitent is bound to observe the mandates of the privileged confessor and cannot fulfill the mandates that come from the superior in response to the recourse. Woywod (*A Practical Commentary,* II, n. 2096) also seems to hold this opinion.

CONCLUSIONS

SINCE there is no evidence of a previous treatise dealing exclusively with the principles of dispensations from vindicative penalties, it may be stated as a general conclusion that authors in general have neglected this particular institute of the Code of Canon Law. It was surprising to find that most canonists were content to treat of this entire matter in perhaps a paragraph or two, and that the adaptation of canon 2254, § 3, to canon 2290, § 2, was neglected entirely. Consequently, many of the more important conclusions arrived at in this study represent an attempt to adapt the opinions of the various authors in regard to canon 2254 to the principles enunciated in canon 2290. The other conclusions, likewise, are mere attempts to establish a clear and thorough groundwork on which others may build. Some of the conclusions drawn represent what, in the mind of the writer, appear to be the better and the more tenable of the varying and contrary opinions offered on certain points.

The conclusions are as follows:

1. While not using the terminology in use at the present time, and lacking that clarity which was to develop through the centuries, the early councils enacted laws involving the principles of the *latae sententiae* vindicative penalty, although the distinction between such vindicative penalties and others which were medicinal in character was not clear.

2. Although most of the penalties of the Church were largely vindicative in nature up to the sixth century, the principles of dispensation from such penalties also lacked clarity and precision, and were often confused with those applying to the absolution from censures.

3. Until the time of the Code of Canon Law, the active subject of dispensation from vindicative penalties was threefold: the Pope, the bishops, and provincial synods, although the extent of the various powers was not at all clear. The application of the general principles was difficult and unreliable, especially in the case of bishops, who by law could dispense from penalties inflicted for minor crimes when-

ever that power was not expressly denied to them, and from major crimes only when that power was granted to them. The Code of Canon Law for the first time clearly and definitely defined the dispensatory powers of bishops and granted certain extraordinary faculties to confessors.

4. The existence of the *latae sententiae ab homine* vindicative penalty has been proved.

5. The remission of vindicative penalties is a dispensation in the strict sense of that term, an act of jurisdiction.

6. According to canon 2236, § 1, the dispensation from *ferendae sententiae* vindicative penalties is reserved to the jurisdictional superior who, though he is inferior in jurisdiction to the legislator who established the penalty in the law, actually inflicts the penalty either by passing the condemnatory sentence upon the offender, or by decreeing the particular precept. His superior, his successor, or one to whom he has granted the faculty, may likewise exercise the same dispensatory power.

7. The competence of various superiors to dispense from vindicative penalties has for the first time been treated in detail in this work.

8. A clear analysis of canons 2236 and 2237 has been attempted, and the division of the dispensatory powers as established in those canons into proper dispensatory power and derived power, which is granted either explicitly or implicitly, has been made for the first time.

9. The prescriptions of canons 15, 81 and 82 apply to the implicit derived ordinary dispensatory power which ordinaries enjoy in virtue of canon 2236, § 2.

10. A case is considered as having been brought to the contentious forum, in the sense of canon 2237, § 1, n. 1, as soon as the accused offender is legitimately cited to appear to answer charges, either civil (contentious) or criminal, either before an ecclesiastical or a civil court.

11. In occult cases, all *latae sententiae* vindicative penalties of the common law, including those which are expressly reserved to the Holy See (*e.g.*, the penalties mentioned in canons 671, 1°; 2295; 2370), may be dispensed by ordinaries in virtue of canon 2237, § 2.

12. If an occult case involving a *latae sententiae* vindicative penalty of the general law has been brought to the judicial forum and is pending there, the vindicative penalty cannot be dispensed in the internal forum.

13. In cases of positive and probable doubt, canon 209 may be employed under the conditions and stipulations of canon 2290.

14. All *latae sententiae* vindicative penalties may be suspended or dispensed according to canon 2290. Consequently, *latae sententiae ab homine* vindicative penalties are included in the object of the powers enjoyed by confessors in virtue of canon 2290.

15. The phrase, "ad S. Poenitentiariam vel ad Episcopum aliumve Superiorem praeditum facultate," used in canon 2254, § 1, is applicable to canon 2290.

16. *Latae sententiae* vindicative penalties which have been subjected to a declaratory sentence, provided that they are occult, are also subject to the suspensory and dispensatory powers of confessors in canon 2290.

17. *Ferendae sententiae* vindicative penalties *per accidens* are included in the object of the powers enjoyed by confessors in canon 2290, that is, if the conditions of an urgent case are verified.

18. In similar and analogous circumstances, the alternative method mentioned in canon 2254, § 2 is applicable to canon 2290.

APPENDIX

Formulae for Recourse

A. General form for recourse after the observance of a vindicative penalty has been suspended by a confessor in an occult and more urgent case.

Recourse through a confessor who will see the penitent again.

Beatissime Pater (Pope):

Eminentissime Princeps (Cardinal):

Reverendissime Domine (Archbishop or Bishop):

Titius (Titia) incurrit poenam vindicativam latae sententiae . . . (mention the penalty, *e. g.*, suspensionis a divinis pro anno) propter . . . (indicate the crime).

Cum sine infamia (vel scandalo) Titius (Titia) poenam istam observare non posset, cumque casus occultus et urgentior esset, infrascriptus confessarius ad normam canonis 2290, § 1, obligationem servandae poenae suspendit.

Nunc vero ad hoc Tribunal recurrit, ut mandata recipiat, ea fideliter exsecuturus (exsecutura). Faveat { Eminentia Vestra / Reverendissimus Dominus, } propter peculiaria adiuncta, dispensationem huius poenae concedere.

Et Deus, etc.

(Date)

N. N.

(true name and address of confessor.)

(N. B. In these various formulae, the wording "Et Deus, etc.," is set down without any further addition.)

B. Forms for recourse to the Sacred Penitentiary.

Address:

All' Eminentissimo Cardinale Penitenziere Maggiore,
Palazzo del S. Officio,
Roma, Italia.

(Recourse to the Sacred Penitentiary may be made through the local ordinary or the apostolic delegate.)

1. *Recourse through a confessor who will see the penitent again.*

(Formula same as above, addressed "Eminentissime Princeps:")

2. *Recourse through a confessor who will not see the penitent again, but knows his name and address and intends to send the rescript to him.*

Eminentissime Princeps:

Titius (Titia) incurrit poenam vindicativam latae sententiae . . . (mention the penalty) propter . . . (mention the crime).

Cum sine infamia (vel scandalo) Titius (Titia) poenam istam observare non posset, cumque casus occultus et urgentior esset, infrascriptus confessarius ad normam canonis 2290, § 1, obligationem servandae poenae suspendit.

Nunc vero ad S. Poenitentiariam per has litteras recurrit, promittens omnia quaecumque mandata se accepturum (accepturam) ac fideliter exsecuturum (exsecuturam). Itaque, propter peculiaria adiuncta humiliter dispensationem petit. Cum Titius (Titia) ad me reverti nequeat, rogo ut mihi tribuatur facultas transmittendi per publicos tabelliones aliove modo rescriptam huius S. Tribunalis.

Et Deus, etc.

(Date)

N. N.

(true name and address of confessor.)

3. *Recourse when the penitent writes the letter, asking that the rescript be sent to some confessor.*

Eminentissime Princeps:

Ego, Titius (Titia) poenam vindicativam latae sententiae . . . (mention the penalty) incurri propter . . . (mention the crime).

Cum sine infamia (vel scandalo) poenam istam observare non possem, cumque casus occultus et urgentior adesset, confessarius ad normam canonis 2290, § 1, obligationem servandae poenae suspendit.

Humillime nunc per has litteras recurrens, promitto quibusvis mandatis me fideliter oboediturum. Faveat Eminentissima Vestra, propter peculiaria adiuncta, dispensationem concedere et rescriptum remittere ad infrascriptum confessarium, quem ad id accipiendum ac implendum adibo.

Et Deus, etc.

(Date)

Dignetur E. V. rescriptum dirigere ad:

N. N.

(name and address of confessor.)

4. *Recourse when the penitent writes the letter, asking that the rescript be sent directly to him.*

Eminentissime Princeps:

Ego poenam vindicativam latae sententiae . . . (mention the penalty) incurri propter . . . (mention the crime).

Cum sine infamia (vel scandalo) poenam istam observare non possem, cumque casus occultus et urgentior esset, confessarius ad normam canonis 2290, § 1, obligationem servandae poenae suspendit.

Humillime per has litteras recurrens, promitto quibusvis mandatis me fideliter oboediturum (oboedituram). Faveat Eminentia Vestra, propter peculiaria adiuncta, dispensationem concedere et rescriptum in forma gratiosa remittere ad me infrascriptum.

Et Deus, etc.

(Date)

N. N.

(true name and address of penitent.)

C. English form of recourse to the local ordinary.

Your excellency,

Titius (Titia) has incurred the latae sententiae vindicative penalty of . . . (mention the penalty) for the crime of . . . (mention the crime).

Since he (she) could not observe the penalty without causing scandal or suffering infamy, I suspended the observance of the penalty in the present occult and urgent case according to the norm of canon 2290, § 1. He (she) now fulfills the obligation of recourse, promising to fulfill the mandates which Your Excellency will impose.

Moreover, under the circumstances, he (she) humbly petitions for a dispensation from the penalty, if it pleases Your Excellency to grant it according to the norm of canon 2237, § 2.

Respectfully,

(Date.) (Confessor—name and address.)

BIBLIOGRAPHY

Sources

Acta Apostolicae Sedis, Commentarium Officiale, Romae, 1909—

Acta et Decreta Concilii Plenarii Baltimorensis II, Baltimorae: Joannes Murphy, 1894.

Ante-Nicene Fathers, Roberts and Donaldson, Editors, American reprint, 10 vols., New York, 1890.

Bouscaren, T. Lincoln, *The Canon Law Digest,* 2 vols. and *Supplement*—1941, Milwaukee: Bruce, 1934-1941.

Canones et Decreta Sacrosancti Oecumenici Concilii Tridentini, Romae: ex typographia polyglotta S. C. de Propaganda Fide, 1882.

Codex Iuris Canonici Pii X Pontificis Maximi iussu digestus Benedicti Papae XV auctoritate promulgatus, Romae: Typis Polyglottis Vaticanis, 1917.

Corpus Iuris Canonici, ed. Lipsiensis 2. post Aemilii Ludovici Richteri curas—instruxit Aemilius Friedberg, Lipsiae: Ex Officina Bernhardi Tauchnitz, 1879-1881. Editio anastatice repetita, Lipsiae, 1928.

Corpus Scriptorum Ecclesiasticorum Latinorum, Editum consilio et impensis Academiae Litterarum Caesareae Vindobonensis, Vindobonae, 1866—

Coustant, *Epistolae Romanorum Pontificum a S. Clementi usque ad Innocentium III,* 3 vols., Parisiis, 1721.

Decretales D. Gregorii Papae IX, una cum Glossis Restitutae, Romae, 1582.

Decretum Francisci Gratiani cum Glossa Bartholomaei Brixiensis, Venetiis, Andreas Calabrensis, 1491.

Denzinger, Henr., et Bannwart, Clem., *Enchiridion Symbolorum, Definitionum et Declarationum de Rebus Fidei et Morum,* 16. et 17. ed., Friburgi Brisgoviae: Herder, 1928.

Friedberg, Aemilius, *Quinque Compilationes Antiquae,* Lipsiae, 1881.

Funk, Francis X., *Patres Apostolici,* Tübingen, 1901.

Hardouin, Jean, *Acta Conciliorum et Epistolae Decretales ac Constitutiones Summorum Pontificum,* 12 vols., Parisiis, 1715.

Jaffé, Philippus, *Regesta Pontificum Romanorum ab condita Ecclesia ad annum post Christum natum MCXCVIII,* Editionem secundam correctam et auctam, auspiciis Gulielmi Wattenbach, curaverunt S. Loewenfeld, F. Kaltenbrunner, P. Ewald; 2 vols. in 1, Lipsiae, 1885-1888.

Liber Sextus Decretalium, una cum Clementinis et Extravagentibus Earumque Glossis Restitutis, Romae, 1582.

Mansi, Joannes D., *Sacrorum Conciliorum Nova et Amplissima Collectio,* 53 vols. in 60, Paris, Arnhem, Leipzig, 1901-1927.

Migne, Jacques Paul, *Patrologiae Cursus Completus, Series Graeca,* 161 vols., Parisiis, 1856-1866.

———, *Patrologiae Cursus Completus, Series Latina,* 221 vols., Parisiis, 1844-1864.

Monumenta Germaniae Historica, 188 vols. incomplete, Hannoverae, 1826—
Leges, 5 vols., I-IV edited by G. H. Pertz; V edited by Pertz-Waitz-Brunner, Hannoverae, 1835-1889.
Libelli de Lite, T. II, edited by Fredericus Thaner, Hannoverae, 1892.
Epistolae, 7 vols., 1887-1928. T. IV, edited by Ernestus Perels, Berolini, 1925.

Pontificale Romanum, Summorum Pontificum iussu editum, a Benedicto XIV et Leone XIII Pont. Max. recognitum et castigatum, 3 vols., Ratisbonae, Romae, Neo Eboraci et Cincinnati, 1908.

Schroeder, H. J., *Canons and Decrees of the Council of Trent,* original text with English translation, St. Louis: B. Herder Book Co., 1941.

———, *Disciplinary Decrees of the Council of Trent,* St. Louis: Herder, 1939.

Thaner, F., *Anselmi Lucensis Collectio Canonum,* 2 vols., Innsbruck, 1906-1915.

Thiel, A., *Epistolae Romanorum Pontificum genuinae a S. Hilario usque ad Hormisdam,* Brunsbergae, 1868.

AUTHORS

Abbas Antiquus (Bernard of Montmirat), *Lectura Aurea,* Argentinae, 1510.

Alterius, Marc., *De Censuris ecclesiasticis nempe de Excommunicatione, Suspensione et Interdicto cum Explicatione Bullae Coenae Dni.,* Romae, 1618.

Arregui, Antonius, *Summarium Theologiae Moralis,* 13. ed., Romae, 1937.

Ayrinhac, H. A., and Lydon, P. J., *Penal Legislation in the New Code of Canon Law,* revised edition, New York, Cincinnati, Chicago, San Francisco: Benziger Brothers, 1936.

[Bachofen], Charles Augustine, *A Commentary on the New Code of Canon Law,* 8 vols.; Vol. VIII: *Penal Code,* 3. ed., St. Louis: Herder, 1931.

Ballerini, A.,-Palmieri, P., *Opus Theologicum Morale,* 7 vols., Prati: Giachetti, 1889-1893.

Barbosa, Augustinus, *Collectanea Doctorum tam Veterum quam Recentiorum in Ius Pontificum Universum,* 6 vols. in 3, Lugduni, 1716.

Baronius, Caesar, *Annales Ecclesiastici,* 36 vols., edited by A. Theiner. Vols. I-XXVIII, Bari Ducis, 1864-1875; Vols. XXIX-XXXVII, Parisiis, 1876-1883.

Batiffol, Pierre, *Etudes d'Histoire et de Théologie Positive,* 1re serie, 4. ed., 2 vols., Paris, 1906; Vol. I, *Les Origines de la Penitence.*

Berardi, Carlo S., *Commentaria in Ius Ecclesiasticum Universum,* 2 vols., Mediolani, 1846.

Bernardus Papiensis, *Summa Decretalium,* ed. Ernestus Laspeyres, Ratisbonae, 1860.

Berutti, Christophorus, *Institutiones Iuris Canonici,* 6 vols., Vol. III, *De Religiosis,* Taurini-Romae: Marietti, 1936; Vol. IV, *De Delictis et Poenis,* Taurini-Romae: Marietti, 1938.

Beste, Udalricus, *Introductio in Codicem,* Collegeville: St. John's Abbey Press, 1938.

Beveridge, William, *Synodicon sive Pandectae Canonum et Conciliorum,* 2 vols., Oxonii, 1672.

Biederlach, J.-Fuhrich, Max., *De Religiosis,* Oeniponte, 1919.

Billot, L., *Tractatus de Ecclesia Christi,* 5. ed., Romae: Apud Aedes Universitatis Gregorianae, 1927.

Blat, Albertus, *Commentarium Textus Codicis Iuris Canonici,* 6 vols., Romae, 1921-1927; Liber V, *De Delictis et Poenis,* Romae: Collegio "Angelico," 1924.

Boehmer, Justus H., *Ius Ecclesiasticum Protestanticum,* 5. ed., 5 vols., Magdeburgi, 1756.

Boich, Henricus, *In Quinque Decretalium Libros Commentaria,* Venetiis, 1756.

Bouix, J., *Tractatus de Papa,* Parisiis, 1869.

Brys, J., *De Dispensatione in Iure Canonico praesertim apud Decretistas et Decretalistas usque ad Medium Saeculum Decimum Quartum,* Brugis: Car. Beyaert, 1925.

Campagna, Angelo, *Il Vicario Generale del Vescovo,* The Catholic University of America Canon Law Studies, n. 66, Washington, D. C.: The Catholic University of America, 1931.

Cance, A., *Le Code de Droit Canonique,* 2. ed., 5 vols., Paris: Libraire Lecoffre, Gabalda, 1929.

Cappello, Felix M., *Tractatus Canonico-Moralis de Censuris iuxta Codicem Iuris Canonici,* Augustae Taurinorum: Marietti, 1919.

———, *Tractatus Canonico-Moralis de Censuris iuxta Codicem Iuris Canonici,* 2. ed., Taurinorum Augustae: Marietti, 1925; 3. ed., Taurinorum Augustae: Marietti, 1933.

Cavagnis, Felix, *Institutiones Iuris Publici Ecclesiastici,* 2. ed., 2 vols., Romae, 1888.

Cavigioli, Ioannes, *De Censuris Latae Sententiae Quae in Codice Iuris Canonici Continentur Commentariolum,* Torino: Liberaria Editrice Internazionale, 1918.

Cerato, Prosdocimus, *Censurae Vigentes Ipso Facto a Codice Iuris Canonici Excerptae,* 2. ed., Potavii: Typis Seminarii, 1921.

Chelodi, Ioannes, *Ius Poenale et Ordo Procedendi in Iudiciis Criminalibus iuxta Codicem Iuris Canonici,* 4. ed., Tridenti: Libreria Moderna Editrice A. Ardesi, 1935.

———, Bertagnolli, Ernesto, *Ius de Personis iuxta Codicem Iuris Canonici,* Tridenti, 1927.

Cicognani, Amleto, *Canon Law,* authorized English Version, by J. O'Hara and F. Brennan, Philadelphia: Dolphin Press, 1935.

Cipollini, Albertus, *De Censuris Latae Sententiae iuxta Codicem Iuris Canonici,* Taurini: Marietti, 1925.

Claeys Bouuaert, F. et Simenon, G., *Manuale Iuris Canonici ad Usum Seminariorum,* 3 vols., Gandae et Loedii, Vols. I and III, 4. ed., 1934; Vol. II, 2. ed., 1935.

Cocchi, Guidus, *Commentarium in Codicem Iuris Canonici ad Usum Scholarum,* 5 vols. in 8, Taurinorum Augustae, 1922-1930; Liber V, *De Delictis et Poenis,* 2. ed., Taurinorum Augustae: Marietti, 1928.

Collison, Paulus J., *Non Omnis Censura Ab Homine Est Reservata,* Dissertatio ad Gradum Doctoris in Facultate Iuris Canonici Consequendum Scripta apud Pontificium Institutum Angelicum, Romae, 1935; typis impressa Lovanii: Bibliotheca S. Alphonsi, 1936.

Conran, E. J., *The Interdict,* The Catholic University of America Canon Law Studies, n. 56, Washington, D. C.: The Catholic University of America, 1930.

Coronata, Matthaeus Conte a, *Institutiones Iuris Canonici,* 5 vols., Taurini (Italia): Marietti, 1928-1936; Vol. IV, *De Delictis et Poenis,* 1935.

D'Annibale, Josephus, *Summula Theologiae Moralis,* 5. ed., 3 vols., Romae: Desclée, Lefebvre et Soc., 1908.

De Baysio, Guido (Archidiaconus), *Rosarium domini Guidonis archidiaconi Buonensis super Decreto,* Editio incunabilis, sine loco et anno.

Del Giudice, V., *Privilegio, Dispensa ed Epicheia nel Diritto Canonico,* Milano, 1929.

De Marca, Petrus, *De Concordantia Sacerdotii et Imperii, seu de Libertatibus Ecclesiae Gallicanae,* 3 vols., Parisiis, 1641.

De Meester, Alphonsus, *Iuris Canonici et Iuris Canonico-Civilis Compendium,* nova ed., 3 vols. in 4, Brugis: Desclée, De Brouwer et Sii, 1921-1928; Vol. III, Pars Secunda, *Liber IV et V Codicis Iuris Canonici,* 1928.

Devoti, Ioannes, *Institutiones Canonicae,* Namurci, 1835.

Durandus (Duranti), Guilelmus, *Speculum Iuris,* Venetiis, 1577.

Eichmann, Eduard, *Lehrbuch des Kirchenrechts auf Grund des Codex Iuris Canonici,* 2. ed., Paderborn, Schöningh, 1926.

Esmein, A., *Le marriage in droit canonique,* 2. ed., 2 vols.; Vol. I edited by R. Genestal, Paris, 1929; Vol. II edited by J. Dauvillier, Paris, 1935.

Esswein, A., *The Extrajudicial Coercive Powers of Ecclesiastical Superiors,* The Catholic University of America Canon Law Studies, n. 127, Washington, D. C.: The Catholic University of America Press, 1941.

Falco, M., *Corso di Diritto Ecclesiastico,* Padova, 1930.

———, *Introduzione allo studio del "Codex Iuris Canonici,"* Turino, Fratelli Bocca, 1925.

Fanfani, L., *De Iure Religiosorum ad Normam Codicis Iuris Canonici,* 2. ed., Taurinorum Augustae, 1925.

Farrugia, Nicolaus, *De Casuum Conscientiae Reservatione,* 2. ed., Augustae Taurinorum: Marietti, 1922.

Ferreres, Joannes, *Institutiones Iuris Canonici,* 2. ed., 2 vols., Barcinone: Subirana, 1920.

Findlay, S. W., *Canonical Norms Governing the Deposition and Degradation of Clerics,* The Catholic University of America Canon Law Studies, n. 130, Washington, D. C.: The Catholic University of America Press, 1941.

Freisen, J., *Geschichte des canonischen Eherechts bis zum Verfall der Glossenlitteratur,* Tübingen, 1888.

Friedberg, J., *Lehrbuch des katholischen und evangelischen Kirchenrechts,* Leipzig, 1903.

Fulton, J., *Index Canonum,* New York, 1892.

Gasparri, Petrus, *Tractatus canonicus de matrimonio,* Parisiis, 1892.

———, *Tractatus Canonicus de Matrimonio,* editio nova ad mentem Codicis Iuris Canonici, Citta Vaticana, 1932.

Genicot, Eduardus, et Salsman, I., *Institutiones Theologiae Moralis,* 11. ed., 2 vols., Bruxellis: Dewitt, 1927.

Gonzalez-Tellez, Emmanuel, *Commentaria Perpetua in Singulos Textus Quinque Librorum Decretalium Gregorii IX,* 5 vols. in 4, Lugduni, 1715.

Haring, J., *Grundzuge des katholischen Kirchenrechtes, Dritte nach dem Codex Iuris Canonici umgearbeitete Auflage,* 2 vols., Graz, Moser, 1924.

Hefele, Charles J., *A History of the Councils of the Church* (translated by W. Clarke), 2. ed., 5 vols., Edinburgh, 1883.

Hefele, Carolus, et Leclercq, Henricus, *Histoire des Conciles,* 10 vols. in 19, Raus, 1907-1938.

Hergenrother, P., Hollweck, J., *Katholisches Kirchenrecht,* Freiburg im Breisgau, 1905.

Hermes, J., *De Capitulo Sede Vacante vel Impedito et de Vicario Capitulari,* Dissertatio Historico-Canonica, Lovanii: Vilinthout Fratres, 1873.

Hilling, N., *Die allgemeinen Normen des Codex Iuris Canonici,* Freiburg im Breisgau: Jas. Waibel, 1926.

Hinschius, Paul, *Das Kirchenrecht der Katholiken und Protestanten in Deutchland,* 6 vols., Berlin, 1869-1897; Vols. I-IV, *System des katholischen Kirchenrechts, Berlin,* 1869-1888.

Hofmann, V., *Die freiwillige Gerichtsbarkeit in kanonischen Recht,* Paderborn, 1929.

Hollweck, Joseph, *Die kirchlichen Strafgesetze,* Mainz, 1899.

Hostiensis, Cardinalis (Henricus de Segusio), *Commentaria in Quinque Decretalium Libros,* 5 vols. in 3, Venetiis, 1581.

———, *Summa Aurea,* Venetiis, 1570.

Hyland, F., *Excommunication, Its Nature, Historical Development, and Effects,* The Catholic University of America Canon Law Studies, n. 49, Washington, D. C.: The Catholic University of America, 1928.

Jaeger, Leo, *The Administration of Vacant and Quasi-vacant Dioceses in the United States,* The Catholic University of America Canon Law Studies, n. 81, Washington, D. C.: The Catholic University of America, 1932.

Joannes Andreae, *In Sex Decretalium Libros Novella Commentaria,* 6 vols. in 5, Venetiis, 1581.

Kahn, L., *Étude dur le délit et la peine in droit canonique,* Paris, 1898.

Kearney, R., *The Principles of Delegation,* The Catholic University of America Canon Law Studies, n. 55, Washington, D. C.: The Catholic University of America, 1929.

Keene, M., *Religious Ordinaries and Canon 198*, The Catholic University of America Canon Law Studies, n. 135, Washington, D. C.: The Catholic University of America Press, 1942.

Kehr, P., *Regesta Pontificum Romanorum, Italia Pontificia*, 7 vols., Berolini, 1906-1923.

Kelly, J., *The Jurisdiction of the Confessor According to the Code of Canon Law*, New York, Cincinnati, Chicago: Benziger Brothers, 1929.

Kerin, C., *The Privation of Christian Burial*, The Catholic University of America Canon Law Studies, n. 136, Washington, D. C.: The Catholic University of America Press, 1941.

Kober, F., *Der Kirchenbann nach den Grundsaetzen des canonischen Rachts*, Tübingen, 1863.

———, *Die Suspension des Kirchendiener*, Tübingen, 1862.

———, *Deposition und Degradation nach den Grundsaetzen des kirchlichen Rechts*, Tübingen, 1867.

Köstler, M., *Wörterbuch zum Codex Iuris Canonici*, München, Kosel, Pustet, 1927.

Krehbiel, E. B., *The Interdict*, American Historical Association, Washington, 1930.

Kuttner, Stephan, *Repertorium des Kanonistik (1140-1234)*, Romae, 1937.

Laspeyres, *Bernardi Papiensis Summa Decretalium*, Ratisbonae, 1860.

Lega, Michael, *Praelectiones in Textum Iuris Canonici*, 4 vols., Romae, 1896-1910, Lib. II, Vols. III, IV, *De Delictis et Poenis*, 2. ed., Romae, 1910.

Maroto, P., *Institutiones Iuris Canonici ad Normam Novi Codicis*, 3. ed., Madrid, 1919.

McBride, J., *Incardination and Excardination of Seculars*, The Catholic University of America Canon Law Studies, n. 145, Washington, D. C.: The Catholic University of America Press, 1941.

McDonough, T., *Apostolic Administrators*, The Catholic University of America Canon Law Studies, n. 139, Washington, D. C.: The Catholic University of America Press, 1941.

Miaskiewicz, F., *Supplied Jurisdiction According to Canon 209*, The Catholic University of America Canon Law Studies, n. 122, Washington, D. C.: The Catholic University of America Press, 1940.

Michiels, G., *Normae Generales Iuris Canonici, Commentarius Libri I Codicis Iuris Canonici*, 2 vols., Lublin, 1929.

Moriarty, F., *The Extraordinary Absolution from Censures*, The Catholic University of America Canon Law Studies, n. 113, Washington, D. C.: The Catholic University of America, 1938.

Morinus, Joannes, *Commentaria Historica de Disciplina in Administratione Sacramenti Poenitentiae Tredecim Primis Saeculis in Ecclesia Occidentali, et huc usque in Orientali Observata*, Parisiis, 1651.

Mörsdorf, J., *Die Rechtssprache des Codex Iuris Canonici*, Bonn, 1933.

Noldin, H., et Schmitt, A., *Summa Theologiae Moralis Iuxta Codicem Iuris Canonici*, 22. ed., Oeniponte: Rauch, 1934.

Noval, I., *Commentarium Codicis Iuris Canonici, De Processibus,* 2 vols., Taurini: Marietti, 1920-1932.

O'Brien, Joseph, *The Exemption of Religious in Church Law,* Milwaukee: Bruce, 1943.

Ojetti, B., *Commentarium in Codicem Iuris Canonici,* 4 vols., Romae: Apud Aedes Universitatis Gregorianae, 1927-1931.

Ottaviani, Alaphridus, *Institutiones Iuris Publici Ecclesiastici,* 2. ed., 2 vols., Typis Polyglottis Vaticanis, 1936.

Panormitanus, Abbas (Nicolaus de Tudeschis), *Commentaria in Quinque Libros Decretalium,* 5 vols. in 7, Venetiis, 1588.

Pejška, J., *Ius Canonicum Religiosorum,* 3. ed., Friburgi in Brisg., 1932.

Pellé, P., *Le Droit Pénal de L'Eglise,* Paris, P. Lethielleux, 1939.

Perathoner, L., *Kirchliches Gerichtswesen und kirchliches Strafrecht,* Brixen, 1919.

Pesch, Christian, *Praelectiones Dogmaticae,* 2. ed., 9 vols., Romae, 1909.

Phillips, George, *Kirchenrecht,* 7 vols., Regensburg, 1845-1872.

Phillips, G., Vering, F. H., *Compendium Iuris Ecclesiastici,* 1. Latin version from 3. German edition, Ratisbonae, 1875.

Piatus, Montensis, *Praelectiones Iuris Regularis,* 3. ed., 3 vols., Tornaci, 1905.

Probst, Ferdinand, *Kirchliche Disciplin in den drei ersten christlichen Jahrhunderten,* Tübingen, 1873.

Putzer, Joseph, *Commentarium in Facultates Apostolicas,* 5. ed., New York, 1898.

Prümmer, Dominicus M., *Manuale Iuris Canonici,* 4. ed., Friburgi Brisgoviae: Herder, 1922.

Pyrrho, Carrado, *Praxis Dispensationum Apostolicarum,* Coloniae Agrippinae, 1698.

Rainer, Eligius, *Suspension of Clerics,* The Catholic University of America Canon Law Studies, n. 111, Washington, D. C.: The Catholic University of America, 1937.

Raus, Joannes, *Institutiones Canonicae iuxta Novum Codicem Iuris,* 2. ed., Lugduni, Parisiis: Vitte, 1931.

Rauschen, Gerhard, *Eucharist and Penance in the First Six Centuries of the Church,* authorized translation from 2. German edition, St. Louis: Herder, 1913.

Raymond of Penafort, *Summa S. Raymundi de Pennafort Barcinonensis de poenitentia et matrimonio,* 3 vols., Veronae, 1744.

Reiffenstuel, A., *Ius Canonicum Universum,* 5 vols. in 7, Parisiis, 1864-1870.

Reilly, E. M., *The General Norms of Dispensation,* The Catholic University of America Canon Law Studies, n. 119, Washington, D. C.: The Catholic University, 1939.

Reimarus, Petrus Blesensis, *Opusculum de distinctionibus in canonum interpretatione adhibendis, sive ut auctor voluit, speculum Iuris canonici,* Berlin, 1837.

Reintjes, Gulielmus, *De Absolutione Censurae,* Dissertatio ad obtinendum gradum Doctoratus in Facultate Iuris Canonici in Pontificio Collegio "Angelico" de Urbe Elaborata, 1925.

Richter, Aemilius, *Lehrbuch des katholischen und evangelischen Kirchenrechts,* 8. ed., 1 vol. in 2, Leipzig, 1886.

Riegger, J., *De Poenitentiis et Poenis Ecclesiasticis,* 4 vols., Vindobonae, 1772.

Ripoll, T., *Novisimas Instituciones de Derecho Canónico,* 2 vols., Madrid, 1920.

Roberti, Franciscus, *De Delictis et Poenis,* Romae, 1930.

Ryan, G., *Principles of Episcopal Jurisdiction,* The Catholic University of America Canon Law Studies, n. 120, Washington, D. C.: The Catholic University of America, 1939.

Salucci, Raffaele, *Il Diritto Penale secondo il Codice di Diritto Canonico,* 2 vols., Subiaco: Tipografia dei Monasteri, 1926-1930.

Sanchez, Thomas, *De Sancto Matrimonii Sacramento,* Antwerpiae, 1626.

Santamaria, Pena F., *Comentarios al Código Canónico,* 6 vols., Madrid, 1919-1922.

Santi, Franciscus, *Praelectiones Iuris Canonici,* 2 vols., Ratisbonae, Neo Eboraci, et Cincinnati, 1886.

Schaefer, T., *Compendium de Religiosis ad Normam Codicis Iuris Canonici,* 3. ed., Romae, 1940.

Schmalzgrueber, Franciscus, *Ius Ecclesiasticum Universum,* 5 vols. in 12, Romae, 1843-1845.

Schmidt, J., *Thesaurus Iuris Ecclesiastici,* 2 vols., Heidelbergae, 1779.

Schmitz, Herman, *Die Bussbücher und die Bussdisciplin der Kirche,* Mainz, 1887.

Schroeder, H. J., *Disciplinary Decrees of the General Councils, Text, Translation, and Commentary,* St. Louis: B. Herder Book Co., 1937.

Singer, C., *Die Summa Decretorum des Magister Rufinus,* Paderborn, 1920.

Sipos, Stephanus, *Enchiridion Iuris Canonici,* Pécs: Typographia "Haladás R. T.," 1926.

Smith, S. B., *Elements of Ecclesiastical Law,* 6. ed., 3 vols., New York, 1887.

Smith, M., *The Penal Law for Religious,* The Catholic University of America Canon Law Studies, n. 98, Washington, D. C.: The Catholic University of America, 1935.

Soglia, A., *Institutiones Iuris publici Ecclesiastici,* Parisiis, 1842.

Sohm, J., *Das alt-katholische Kirchenrecht und das Decretum Gratiani,* Leipzig, 1892.

Sole, Iacobus, *Praelectiones in Lib. V Codicis Iuris Canonici, De Delictis et Poenis,* Romae, Pustet, 1920.

Stiegler, M. A., *Dispensation, Dispensationswesen und Dispensationsrecht im Kirchenrecht geschichtliche dargestellt,* 3 vols., Mainz, 1901.

Suarez, Franciscus, *Opera Omnia,* ed. Ludovicus Vives, 26 vols., Parisiis, 1861; Vol. XXIII, *De Censuris in Communi.*

Tarquini, Camillus, *Iuris Publici Ecclesiastici Institutiones,* Romae, 1862.

Teetaert, Amedee, *La Confession aux Laïques dans l'Eglise Latine depuis le VIIIe jusqu' au XIVe Siècle,* Universitas Catholica Lovaniensis, Dissertationes ad gradum magistri in Facultate Theologiae consequendum conscriptae, Series II, Tomus 17, Wetteren, J. De Meester, Bruges: Beyaert, Paris: Gabalda, 1926.

Thesaurus, J., *De Poenis Ecclesiasticis Praxis Absoluta et Universalis,* Romae, 1760.

Thomassinus, Ludovicus, *Vetus et Nova Ecclesiasticae Disciplinae circa Beneficia et Beneficiarios,* Moguntiaci, 1753.

Toso, Albertus, *Ad Codicem Iuris Canonici Commentaria Minora,* 5 vols., Romae: Marietti, 1920-1934.

Van Espen, Zegerus B., *Ius Ecclesiasticum Universum,* 4 vols., Lovanii, 1753.

———, *Tractatus Historico-Canonicus de Censuris Ecclesiasticis,* Lovanii, 1753.

Van Hove, A., *Commentarium Lovaniense in Codicem Iuris Canonici,* Vol. I, 5 toms., Mechlinae-Romae: H. Dessain, 1928-1939.

Vermeersch, A., *Theologiae Moralis Principia, Responsa, Consilia,* 2. ed., 3 vols., Brugis: Beyaert, 1927.

———, *De Religiosis Institutis et Personis,* 4. ed., 2 vols., Brugis, 1907.

Vermeersch, A., et Creusen, J., *Epitome Iuris Canonici,* 3. ed., 3 vols., Mechlinae et Romae: Dessain, 1927-1928.

Von Kienitz, J., *Generalvikar und Offizial auf Grund des Codex Iuris Canonici,* Freiburg im Breisgau: Herder, 1931.

Vromant, G., *Ius Missionariorum, Introductio et Normae Generales,* Louvain, 1934.

Watkins, Oscar, *A History of Penance,* 2. vols., London: Longmans, Green & Co., 1920.

Wernz, Franciscus, *Ius Decretalium,* 6 vols., Romae et Prati, 1906-1913.

Wernz, F., et Vidal, P., *Ius Canonicum ad Normam Codicis Exactum,* 7 toms. in 8 vols., Romae: Apud Aedes Universitatis Gregorianae, 1923-1938.

Winslow, F., *Vicars and Prefects Apostolic,* The Catholic University of America Canon Law Studies, n. 24, Washington, D. C.: The Catholic University of America, 1924.

Wouters, Ludovicus, *Manuale Theologiae Moralis,* 2. ed., 2 vols., Brugis: Beyaert, 1927.

Woywod, Stanislaus, *A Practical Commentary on the Code of Canon Law,* 4. ed., 2 vols., New York: Wagner, 1929.

Zollinger, B., *Institutiones Iuris Naturalis et Ecclesiastici Publici,* Romae, 1823.

Periodicals

Apollinaris, Romae, 1928—

Archiv für katholisches Kirchenrecht, Innsbruck, 1857-1861; Mainz, 1862—

Collationes Brugenses, Bruges, 1896—

Commentarium pro Religiosis (later [1935] *Commentarium pro Religiosis et Missionariis*), Romae, 1920—

Ecclesiastical Review, The (originally *The American Ecclesiastical Review*), Philadelphia, 1889—

Ephemerides Theologicae Lovanienses, Brugis, 1924—

Irish Ecclesiastical Record, The, Dublin, 1864—

Jurist, The, Washington, 1941—

Jus Pontificium, Romae, 1921—

Monitore Ecclesiastico, Il, Romae, 1876—

Nouvelle Revue Théologique, Tournai, 1869—

Perfice Munus, Torino, 1926—

Theologisch-praktische Quartelschrift, Linz, 1832—

ARTICLES

Brys, J., "De potestate Episcoporum dispensandi in legibus Ecclesiae generalibus," *Collationes Brugenses,* XXIX (1929), 144-164.

Cappello, Felix, "De absolutione a censuris 'ab homine' ac de metu relate ad censuras," *Nouvelle Revue Théologique,* XLVII (1920), 525-531.

Crisci, F., "Evolutio historica delegationis a iure," *Apollinaris,* IX (1936), 270-299.

———, "De Delegatione a iure in iure canonico vigenti," *Apollinaris,* X (1937), 513-535.

Gillman, F., "Des Petrus Hispanus Glosse zur Compilatio I," *Archiv für katholisches Kirchenrecht,* CII (1922), 70-81.

Hilling, N., "Begriff und Umfang der potestas iurisdictionis ordinaria et delegata," *Archiv für katholisches Kirchenrecht,* CIV (1924), 192-195.

Kinane, J., "The Reservation of Censures 'Latae Sententiae' Imposed by a Particular Precept," *Irish Ecclesiastical Record,* XL (1932), 528-534.

Larraona, A., "Commentarium Codicis: Canon 488," *Commentarium pro Religiosis,* IV (1923), 39-46.

Meurer, Christian, "Die rechtliche Natur der Pönitenzen der katholischen Kirche in historischer Entwicklung," *Archiv für katholisches Kirchenrecht,* XLIX (1883), 177-218.

Michiels, Gommarus, "De reservatione censurae latae sententiae praecepto peculiari adnexae," *Ephemerides Theologicae Lovanienses,* IV (1927), 180-194; 613-619.

Pistocchi, L., "De Superiore Potestatem Coactivam Habente," *Il Monitore Ecclesiastico,* IX (1937), 10-22.

Pugliese, A., "De Vicario Delegato in territoriis missionum," *Apollinaris,* VI (1933), 196-217.

Raus, Joannes B., "Absolution von Zensuren l.s. ab homine," *Theologisch-praktische Quartelschrift,* LXXXIII (1930), 585-588.

Roberti, Franciscus, "An censura latae sententiae per praeceptum constituta sit reservata," *Apollinaris,* VI (1933), 341-348.

Roelker, Edward, "The Vicar General and the Special Mandate," *The Jurist,* II (1942), 346-362.

Rossi, Joseph, "De sacerdotibus qui matrimonium etiam civile tantum contrahere praesumpserint, quoad absolutionem a censura de qua in can. 2388, § 1," *Perfice Munus,* XI (1936), 346-350.

Schaaf, Valentine T., "The Seal of Confession: New Precautions," *Ecclesiastical Review,* XCII (1935), 540-541.

Tabera, A., "Nocion de la pena 'ab homine,'" *Illustracion del Clero,* XXIV (1931), 195-198; 227-230.

Toso, Albertus, "Iurisdictio quando ab Ecclesia suppleatur," *Jus Pontificium,* XVII (1937), 98-105.

ABBREVIATIONS

AAS—Acta Apostolicae Sedis.
AKKR—Archiv für katholisches Kirchenrecht.
ASS—Acta Sanctae Sedis.
CpRM—Commentarium pro Religiosis et Missionariis.
CSEL—Corpus Scriptorum Ecclesiasticorum Latinorum.
ETL—Ephemerides Theologicae Lovanienses.
JE—Jaffé, *Regesta Pontificium Romanorum*—ed. P. Ewald.
JK—Jaffé, *Regesta Pontificum Romanorum*—ed. F. Kaltenbrunner.
JL—Jaffé, *Regesta Pontificum Romanorum*—ed. S. Loewenfeld.
MGH—Monumenta Germaniae Historica.
MPG—Migne, *Patrologia, Series Graeca.*
MPL—Migne, *Patrologia, Series Latina.*
NRT—Nouvelle Revue Théologique.
TPQ—Theologisch-praktische Quartelschrift.

ALPHABETICAL INDEX

BIOGRAPHICAL NOTE

JOSEPH JAMES CHRIST was born on November 15, 1914, at Chicago, Illinois. After receiving his primary education in Saint Edward's School in the same city, he attended Quigley Preparatory Seminary in Chicago, from which he graduated in June, 1932. He then pursued his seminary studies at the Seminary of Saint Mary of the Lake, at Mundelein, Illinois, where he received the degrees of Bachelor of Arts in 1934, and of Master of Arts in 1935. In 1937 he received the degree of Bachelor of Sacred Theology. He was ordained to the priesthood by His Eminence, George Cardinal Mundelein, on April 23, 1938. In September, 1941, he entered the Catholic University of America, at Washington, D. C., where he received the degree of the Baccalaureate in Canon Law in June, 1941, and the degree of the Licentiate in Canon Law in May, 1942.

CANON LAW STUDIES *

1. Freriks, Rev. Celestine A., C.PP.S., J.C.D., Religious Congregations in Their External Relations, 121 pp., 1916.
2. Galliher, Rev. Daniel M., O.P., J.C.D., Canonical Elections, 117 pp., 1917.
3. Borkowski, Rev. Aurelius L., O.F.M., J.C.D., De Confraternitatibus Ecclesiasticis, 136 pp., 1918.
4. Castillo, Rev. Cayo, J.C.D., Disertacion Historico-Canonica sobre la Potestad del Cabildo en Sede Vacante ó Impedida del Vicario Capitular, 99 pp., 1919 (1918).
5. Kubelbeck, Rev. William J., S.T.B., J.C.D., The Sacred Penitentiaria and Its Relation to Faculties of Ordinaries and Priests, 129 pp., 1918.
6. Petrovits, Rev. Joseph, J.C., S.T.D., J.C.D., The New Church Law on Matrimony, X-461 pp., 1919.
7. Hickey, Rev. John J., S.T.B., J.C.D., Irregularities and Simple Impediments in the New Code of Canon Law, 100 pp., 1920.
8. Klekotka, Rev. Peter J., S.T.B., J.C.D., Diocesan Consultors, 179 pp., 1920.
9. Wanenmacher, Rev. Francis, J.C.D., The Evidence in Ecclesiastical Procedure Affecting the Marriage Bond, 1920 (Printed 1935).
10. Golden, Rev. Henry Francis, J.C.D., Parochial Benefices in the New Code, IV-119 pp., 1921 (Printed 1925).
11. Koudelka, Rev. Charles J., J.C.D., Pastors, Their Rights and Duties According to the New Code of Canon Law, 211 pp., 1921.
12. Melo, Rev. Antonius, O.F.M., J.C.D., De Exemptione Regularium, X-188 pp., 1921.
13. Schaaf, Rev. Valentine Theodore, O.F.M., S.T.B., J.C.D., The Cloister, X-180 pp., 1921.
14. Burke, Rev. Thomas Joseph, S.T.D., J.C.D., Competence in Ecclesiastical Tribunals, IV-117 pp., 1922.
15. Leech, Rev. George Leo, J.C.D., A Comparative Study of the Constitution "Apostolicae Sedis" and the "Codex Juris Canonici," 179 pp., 1922.
16. Motry, Rev. Hubert Louis, S.T.D., J.C.D., Diocesan Faculties According to the Code of Canon Law, II-167 pp., 1922.
17. Murphy, Rev. George Lawrence, J.C.D., Delinquencies and Penalties in the Administration and the Reception of the Sacraments, IV-121 pp., 1923.
18. O'Reilly, Rev. John Anthony, S.T.B., J.C.D., Ecclesiastical Sepulture in the New Code of Canon Law, II-129 pp., 1923.

* Below n. 100 only the following numbers are still available: Nn. 3, 4, 9, 25, 34, 57 and 75. Beginning with n. 100 only the following are unavailable: Nn. 100, 101, 102, 103, 104, 105, 106, 107, 108, 109, 110, 111 and 113.

19. Michalicka, Rev. Wenceslas Cyrill, O.S.B., J.C.D., Judicial Procedure in Dismissal of Clerical Exempt Religious, 107 pp., 1923.
20. Dargin, Rev. Edward Vincent, S.T.B., J.C.D., Reserved Cases According to the Code of Canon Law, IV-103 pp., 1924.
21. Godfrey, Rev. John A., S.T.B., J.C.D., The Right of Patronage According to the Code of Canon Law, 153 pp., 1924.
22. Hagedorn, Rev. Francis Edward, J.C.D., General Legislation on Indulgences, II-154 pp., 1924.
23. King, Rev. James Ignatius, J.C.D., The Administration of the Sacraments to Dying Non-Catholics, V-141 pp., 1924.
24. Winslow, Rev. Francis Joseph, O.F.M., J.C.D., Vicars and Prefects Apostolic, IV-149 pp., 1924.
25. Correa, Rev. Jose Servelion, S.T.L., J.C.D., La Potestad Legislativa de la Iglesia Catolica, IV-127 pp., 1925.
26. Dugan, Rev. Henry Francis, A.M., J.C.D., The Judiciary Department of the Diocesan Curia, 87 pp., 1925.
27. Keller, Rev. Charles Frederick, S.T.B., J.C.D., Mass Stipends, 167 pp., 1925.
28. Paschang, Rev. John Linus, J.C.D., The Sacramentals According to the Code of Canon Law, 129 pp., 1925.
29. Piontek, Rev. Cyrillus, O.F.M., S.T.B., J.C.D., De Indulto Exclaustrationis necnon Saecularizationis, XIII-289 pp., 1925.
30. Kearney, Rev. Richard Joseph, S.T.B., J.C.D., Sponsors at Baptism According to the Code of Canon Law, IV-127 pp., 1925.
31. Bartlett, Rev. Chester Joseph, A.M., LL.B., J.C.D., The Tenure of Parochial Property in the United States of America, V-108 pp., 1926.
32. Kilker, Rev. Adrian Jerome, J.C.D., Extreme Unction, V-425 pp., 1926.
33. McCormick, Rev. Robert Emmett, J.C.D., Confessors of Religious, VIII-266 pp., 1926.
34. Miller, Rev. Newton Thomas, J.C.D., Founded Masses According to the Code of Canon Law, VII-93 pp., 1926.
35. Roelker, Rev. Edward G., S.T.D., J.C.D., Principles of Privilege According to the Code of Canon Law, XI-166 pp., 1926.
36. Bakalarczyk, Rev. Richardus, M.I.C., J.U.D., De Novitiatu, VIII-208 pp., 1927.
37. Pizzuti, Rev. Lawrence, O.F.M., J.U.L., De Parochis Religiosis, 1927. (Not Printed.)
38. Bliley, Rev. Nicholas Martin, O.S.B., J.C.D., Altars According to the Code of Canon Law, XIX-132 pp., 1927.
39. Brown, Mr. Brendan Francis, A.B., LL.M., J.U.D., The Canonical Juristic Personality with Special Reference to its Status in the United States of America, V-212 pp., 1927.
40. Cavanaugh, Rev. William Thomas, C.P., J.U.D., The Reservation of the Blessed Sacrament, VIII-101 pp., 1927.

41. DOHENY, REV. WILLIAM J., C.S.C., A.B., J.U.D., Church Property: Modes of Acquisition, X-118 pp., 1927.
42. FELDHAUS, REV. ALOYSIUS H., C.PP.S., J.C.D., Oratories, IX-141 pp., 1927.
43. KELLY, REV. JAMES PATRICK, A.B., J.C.D., The Jurisdiction of the Simple Confessor, X-208 pp., 1927.
44. NEUBERGER, REV. NICHOLAS J., J.C.D., Canon 6 or the Relation of the Codex Juris Canonici to the Preceding Legislation, V-95 pp., 1927.
45. O'KEEFFE, REV. GERALD MICHAEL, J.C.D., Matrimonial Dispensations, Powers of Bishops, Priests, and Confessors, VIII-232 pp., 1927.
46. QUIGLEY, REV. JOSEPH A. M., A.B., J.C.D., Condemned Societies, 139 pp., 1927.
47. ZAPLOTNIK, REV. JOHANNES LEO, J.C.D., De Vicariis Foraneis, X-142 pp., 1927.
48. DUSKIE, REV. JOHN ALOYSIUS, A.B., J.C.D., The Canonical Status of the Orientals in the United States, VIII-196 pp., 1928.
49. HYLAND, REV. FRANCIS EDWARD, J.C.D., Excommunication, Its Nature, Historical Development and Effects, VIII-181 pp., 1928.
50. REINMANN, REV. GERALD JOSEPH, O.M.C., J.C.D., The Third Order Secular of Saint Francis, 201 pp., 1928.
51. SCHENK, REV. FRANCIS J., J.C.D., The Matrimonial Impediments of Mixed Religion and Disparity of Cult, XVI-318 pp., 1929.
52. COADY, REV. JOHN JOSEPH, S.T.D., J.U.D., A.M., The Appointment of Pastors, VIII-150 pp., 1929.
53. KAY, REV. THOMAS HENRY, J.C.D., Competence in Matrimonial Procedure, VIII-164 pp., 1929.
54. TURNER, REV. SIDNEY JOSEPH, C.P., J.U.D., The Vow of Poverty, XLIX-217 pp., 1929.
55. KEARNEY, REV. RAYMOND A., A.B., S.T.D., J.C.D., The Principles of Delegation, VII-149 pp., 1929.
56. CONRAN, REV. EDWARD JAMES, A.B., J.C.D., The Interdict,, V-163 pp., 1930.
57. O'NEILL, REV. WILLIAM H., J.C.D., Papal Rescripts of Favor, VII-218 pp., 1930.
58. BASTNAGEL, REV. CLEMENT VINCENT, J.U.D., The Appointment of Parochial Adjutants and Assistants, XV-257 pp., 1930.
59. FERRY, REV. WILLIAM A., A.B., J.C.D., Stole Fees, V-136 pp., 1930.
60. COSTELLO, REV. JOHN MICHAEL, A.B., J.C.D., Domicile and Quasi-Domicile, VII-201 pp., 1930.
61. KREMER, REV. MICHAEL NICHOLAS, A.B., S.T.B., J.C.D., Church Support in the United States, VI-136 pp., 1930.
62. ANGULO, REV. LUIS, C.M., J.C.D., Legislation de la Iglesia sobre la intencion en la application de la Santa Misa, VII-104 pp., 1931.
63. FREY, REV. WOLFGANG NORBERT, O.S.B., A.B., J.C.D., The Act of Religious Profession, VIII-174 pp., 1931.

64. ROBERTS, REV. JAMES BRENDAN, A.B., J.C.D., The Banns of Marriage, XIV-140 pp., 1931.
65. RYDER, REV. RAYMOND ALOYSIUS, A.B., J.C.D., Simony, IX-151 pp., 1931.
66. CAMPAGNA, REV. ANGELO, PH.D., J.U.D., Il Vicario Generale del Vescovo, VII-205 pp., 1931.
67. COX, REV. JOSEPH GODFREY, A.B., J.C.D., The Administration of Seminaries, VI-124 pp., 1931.
68. GREGORY, REV. DONALD J., J.U.D., The Pauline Privilege, XV-165 pp., 1931.
69. DONOHUE, REV. JOHN F., J.C.D., The Impediment of Crime, VII-110 pp., 1931.
70. DOOLEY, REV. EUGENE A., O.M.I., J.C.D., Church Law on Sacred Relics, IX-143 pp., 1931.
71. ORTH, REV. CLEMENT RAYMOND, O.M.C., J.C.D., The Approbation of Religious Institutes, 171 pp., 1931.
72. PERNICONE, REV. JOSEPH M., A.B., J.C.D., The Ecclesiastical Prohibition of Books, XII-267 pp., 1932.
73. CLINTON, REV. CONNELL, A.B., J.C.D., The Paschal Precept, IX-108 pp., 1932.
74. DONNELLY, REV. FRANCIS B., A.M., S.T.L., J.C.D., The Diocesan Synod, VIII-125 pp., 1932.
75. TORRENTE, REV. CAMILO, C.M.F., J.C.D., Las Procesiones Sagradas, V-145 pp., 1932.
76. MURPHY, REV. EDWIN J., C.PP.S., J.C.D., Suspension Ex Informata Conscientia, XI-122 pp., 1932.
77. MACKENZIE, REV. ERIC F., A.M., S.T.L., J.C.D., The Delict of Heresy in its Commission, Penalization, Absolution, VII-124 pp., 1932.
78. LYONS, REV. AVITUS E., S.T.B., J.C.D., The Collegiate Tribunal of First Instance, XI-147 pp., 1932.
79. CONNOLLY, REV. THOMAS A., J.C.D., Appeals, XI-195 pp., 1932.
80. SANGMEISTER, REV. JOSEPH V., A.B., J.C.D., Force and Fear as Precluding Matrimonial Consent, V-211 pp., 1932.
81. JAEGER, REV. LEO A., A.B., J.C.D., The Administration of Vacant and Quasi-Vacant Episcopal Sees in the United States, IX-229 pp., 1932.
82. RIMLINGER, REV. HERBERT T., J.C.D., Error Invalidating Matrimonial Consent, VII-79 pp., 1932.
83. BARRETT, REV. JOHN D. M., S.S., J.C.D., A Comparative Study of the Third Plenary Council of Baltimore and the Code, IX-221 pp., 1932.
84. CARBERRY, REV. JOHN J., PH.D., S.T.D., J.C.D., The Juridical Form of Marriage, X-177 pp., 1934.
85. DOLAN, REV. JOHN L., A.B., J.C.D., The Defensor Vinculi, XII-157 pp., 1934.
86. HANNAN, REV. JEROME D., A.M., S.T.D., LL.B., J.C.D., The Canon Law of Wills, IX-517 pp., 1934.

87. LEMIEUX, REV. DELISE A., A.M., J.C.D., The Sentence in Ecclesiastical Procedure, IX-131 pp., 1934.
88. O'ROURKE, REV. JAMES J., A.B., J.C.D., Parish Registers, VII-109 pp., 1934.
89. TIMLIN, REV. BARTHOLOMEW, O.F.M., A.M., J.C.D., Conditional Matrimonial Consent, X-381 pp., 1934.
90. WAHL, REV. FRANCIS X., A.B., J.C.D., The Matrimonial Impediments of Consanguinity and Affinity, VI-125 pp., 1934.
91. WHITE, REV. ROBERT J., A.B., LL.B., S.T.B., J.C.D., Canonical Ante-Nuptial Promises and the Civil Law, VI-152 pp., 1934.
92. HERRERA, REV. ANTONIO PARRA, O.C.D., J.C.D., Legislacion Ecclesiastica sobra el Ayuno y la Abstinencia, XI-191 pp., 1935.
93. KENNEDY, REV. EDWIN J., J.C.D., The Special Matrimonial Process in Cases of Evident Nullity, X-165 pp., 1935.
94. MANNING, REV. JOHN J., A.B., J.C.D., Presumption of Law in Matrimonial Procedure, XI-111 pp., 1935.
95. MOEDER, REV. JOHN M., J.C.D., The Proper Bishop for Ordination and Dimissorial Letters, VII-135 pp., 1935.
96. O'MARA, REV. WILLIAM A., A.B., J.C.D., Canonical Causes for Matrimonial Dispensations, IX-155 pp., 1935.
97. REILLY, REV. PETER, J.C.D., Residence of Pastors, IX-81 pp., 1935.
98. SMITH, REV. MARINER T., O.P., S.T.Lr., J.C.D., The Penal Law for Religious, VIII-169 pp., 1935.
99. WHALEN, REV. DONALD W., A.M., J.C.D., The Value of Testimonial Evidence in Matrimonial Procedure, XIII-297 pp., 1935.
100. CLEARY, REV. JOSEPH F., J.C.D., Canonical Limitations on the Alienation of Church Property, VIII-141 pp., 1936.
101. GLYNN, REV. JOHN C., J.C.D., The Promoter of Justice, XX-337 pp., 1936.
102. BRENNAN, REV. JAMES H., S.S., M.A., S.T.B., J.C.D., The Simple Convalidation of Marriage, VI-135 pp., 1937.
103. BRUNINI, REV. JOSEPH BERNARD, J.C.D., The Clerical Obligations of Canons 139 and 142, X-121 pp., 137.
104. CONNOR, REV. MAURICE, A.B., J.C.D., The Administrative Removal of Pastors, VIII-159 pp., 1937.
105. GUILFOYLE, REV. MERLIN JOSEPH, J.C.D., Custom, XI-144 pp., 1937.
106. HUGHES, REV. JAMES AUSTIN, A.B., A.M., J.C.D., Witnesses in Criminal Trials of Clerics, IX-140 pp., 1937.
107. JANSEN, REV. RAYMOND J., A.B., S.T.L., J.C.D., Canonical Provisions for Catechetical Instruction, VII-153 pp., 1937.
108. KEALY, REV. JOHN JAMES, A.B., J.C.D., The Introductory Libellus in Church Court Procedure, XI-121 pp., 1937.
109. MCMANUS, REV. JAMES EDWARD, C.SS.R., J.C.D., The Administration of Temporal Goods in Religious Institutes, XVI-196 pp., 1937.

110. MORIARTY, REV. EUGENE JAMES, J.C.D., Oaths in Ecclesiastical Courts, X-115 pp., 1937.
111. RAINER, REV. ELIGIUS GEORGE, C.SS.R., J.C.D., Suspension of Clerics, XVII-249 pp., 1937.
112. REILLY, REV. THOMAS F., C.SS.R., J.C.D., Visitation of Religious, VI-195 pp., 1938.
113. MORIARTY, REV. FRANCIS E., C.SS.R., J.C.D., The Extraordinary Absolution from Censures, XV-334 pp., 1938.
114. CONNOLLY, REV. NICHOLAS P., J.C.D., The Canonical Erection of Parishes, X-132 pp., 1938.
115. DONOVAN, REV. JAMES JOSEPH, J.C.D., The Pastor's Obligation in Prenuptial Investigation, XII-322 pp., 1938.
116. HARRIGAN, REV. ROBERT J., M.A., S.T.B., J.C.D., The Radical Sanation of Invalid Marriages, VIII-208 pp., 1938.
117. BOFFA, REV. CONRAD HUMBERT, J.C.D., Canonical Provisions for Catholic Schools, VII-211 pp., 1939.
118. PARSONS, REV. ANSCAR JOHN, O.M.Cap., J.C.D., Canonical Elections, XII-236 pp., 1939.
119. REILLY, REV. EDWARD MICHAEL, A.B., J.C.D., The General Norms of Dispensation, XII-156 pp., 1939.
120. RYAN, REV. GERALD ALOYSIUS, A.B., J.C.D., Principles of Episcopal Jurisdiction, XII-172 pp., 1939.
121. BURTON, REV. FRANCIS JAMES, C.S.C., A.B., J.C.D., A Commentary on Canon 1125, X-222 pp., 1940.
122. MIASKIEWICZ, REV. FRANCIS SIGISMUND, J.C.D., Supplied Jurisdiction According to Canon 209, XII-340 pp., 1940.
123. RICE, REV. PATRICK WILLIAM, A.B., J.C.D., Proof of Death in Prenuptial Investigation, VIII-156 pp., 1940.
124. ANGLIN, REV. THOMAS FRANCIS, M.S., J.C.D., The Eucharistic Fast, VIII-183 pp., 1941.
125. COLEMAN, REV. JOHN JEROME, J.C.D., The Minister of Confirmation, VI-153 pp., 1941.
126. DOWNS, REV. JOHN EMMANUEL, A.B., J.C.D., The Concept of Clerical Immunity, XI-163 pp., 1941.
127. ESSWEIN, REV. ANTHONY ALBERT, J.C.D., Extrajudicial Penal Powers of Ecclesiastical Superiors, X-144 pp., 1941.
128. FARRELL, REV. BENJAMIN FRANCIS, M.A., S.T.L., J.C.D., The Rights and Duties of the Local Ordinary Regarding Congregations of Women Religious of Pontifical Approval, V-195 pp., 1941.
129. FEENEY, REV. THOMAS JOHN, A.B., S.T.L., J.C.D., Restitutio in Integrum, VI-169 pp., 1941.
130. FINDLAY, REV. STEPHEN WILLIAM, O.S.B., A.B., J.C.D., Canonical Norms Governing the Deposition and Degradation of Clerics, XVII-279 pp., 1941.

131. Goodwine, Rev. John, A.B., S.T.L., J.C.D., The Right of the Church to Acquire Property, VIII-119 pp., 1941.
132. Heston, Rev. Edward Louis, C.S.C., Ph.D., S.T.D., J.C.D., The Alienation of Church Property in the United States, XII-222 pp., 1941.
133. Hogan, Rev. James John, A.B., S.T.L., J.C.D., Judicial Advocates and Procurators, XIII-200 pp., 1941.
134. Kealy, Rev. Thomas M., A.B., Litt.B., J.C.D., Dowry of Women Religious, IX-152 pp., 1941.
135. Keene, Rev. Michael James, O.S.B., J.C.D., Religious Ordinaries and Canon 198, V-164 pp., 1942.
136. Kerin, Rev. Charles A., S.S., M.A., S.T.B., J.C.D., The Privation of Christian Burial, XVI-279 pp., 1941.
137. Louis, Rev. William Francis, M.A., J.C.D., Diocesan Archives, X-101 pp., 1941.
138. McDevitt, Rev. Gilbert Joseph, A.B., J.C.D., Legitimacy and Legitimation, X-247 pp., 1941.
139. McDonough, Rev. Thomas Joseph, A.B., J.C.D., Apostolic Administrators, X-217 pp., 1941.
140. Meier, Rev. Carl Anthony, A.B., J.C.D., Penal Administrative Procedure Against Negligent Pastors, XI-240 pp., 1941.
141. Schmidt, Rev. John Rogg, A.B., J.C.D., The Principles of Authentic Interpretation in Canon 17 of the Code of Canon Law, XII-331 pp., 1941.
142. Slafkosky, Rev. Andrew Leonard, A.B., J.C.D., The Canonical Episcopal Visitation of the Diocese, X-197 pp., 1941.
143. Swoboda, Rev. Innocent Robert, O.F.M., J.C.D., Ignorance in Relation to the Imputability of Delicts, IX-271 pp., 1941.
144. Dubé, Rev. Arthur Joseph, A.B., J.C.D., The General Principles for the Reckoning of Time in Canon Law, VIII-299 pp., 1941.
145. McBride, Rev. James T., A.B., J.C.D., Incardination and Excardination of Seculars, XX-585 pp., 1941.
146. Król, Rev. John T., J.C.D., The Defendant in Ecclesiastical Trials, XII-207 pp., 1942.
147. Comyns, Rev. Joseph J., C.SS.R., A.B., J.C.D., Papal and Episcopal Administration of Church Property, XIV-155 pp., 1942.
148. Barry, Rev. Garrett Francis, O.M.I., J.C.D., Violation of the Cloister, XII-260 pp., 1942.
149. Bolduc, Rev. Gatien, C.S.V., A.B., S.T.L., J.C.D., Les Études dans les Religions Cléricales, VIII-155 pp., 1942.
150. Boyle, Rev. David John, M.A., J.C.D., The Juridic Effects of Moral Certitude on Pre-Nuptial Guarantees, XII-188 pp., 1942.
151. Canavan, Rev. Walter Joseph, M.A., Litt.D., J.C.D., The Profession of Faith, XII-143 pp., 1942.
152. Desrochers, Rev. Bruno, A.B., Ph.L., S.T.B., J.C.D., Le Premier Concile Plénier de Québec et le Code de Droit Canonique, XIV-186 pp., 1942.

153. Dillon, Rev. Robert Edward, A.B., J.C.D., Common Law Marriage, X-148 pp., 1942.
154. Dodwell, Rev. Edward John, Ph.D., S.T.B., J.C.D., The Time and Place for the Celebration of Marriage, X-156 pp., 1942.
155. Donnellan, Rev. Thomas Andrew, A.B., J.C.D., The Obligation of the Missa pro Populo, VII-131 pp., 1942.
156. Eltz, Rev. Louis Anthony, A.B., J.C.L., Cooperation in Crime.
157. Gass, Rev. Sylvester Francis, M.A., J.C.D., Ecclesiastical Pensions, XI-206 pp., 1942.
158. Guiniven, Rev. John Joseph, C.SS.R., J.C.D., The Precept of Hearing Mass, XIV-188 pp., 1942.
159. Gulczynski, Rev. John Theophilus, J.C.D., The Desecration and Violation of Churches, X-126 pp., 1942.
160. Hammill, Rev. John Leo, M.A., J.C.D., The Obligations of the Traveler According to Canon 14, VIII-204 pp., 1942.
161. Haydt, Rev. John Joseph, A.B., J.C.D., Reserved Benefices, XI-148 pp., 1942.
162. Huser, Rev. Roger John, O.F.M., A.B., J.C.D., The Crime of Abortion in Canon Law, XII-187 pp., 1942.
163. Kearney, Rev. Francis Patrick, A.B., S.T.L., J.C.L., The Principles of Canon 1127.
164. Linahen, Rev. Leo James, S.T.L., J.C.D., De Absolutione Complicis In Peccato Turpi, 114 pp., 1942.
165. McCloskey, Rev. Joseph Aloysius, A.B., J.C.D., The Subject of Ecclesiastical Law According to Canon 12, XVII-246 pp., 1942.
166. O'Neill, Rev. Francis Joseph, C.SS.R., J.C.D., The Dismissal of Religious in Temporary Vows, XIII-220 pp., 1942.
167. Prince, Rev. John Edward, A.B., S.T.B., J.C.D., The Diocesan Chancellor, X-136 pp., 1942.
168. Riesner, Rev. Albert Joseph, C.SS.R., J.C.D., Apostates and Fugitives from Religious Institutes, IX-168 pp., 1942.
169. Stenger, Rev. Joseph Bernard, J.C.D., The Mortgaging of Church Property, 186 pp., 1942.
170. Waldron, Rev. Joseph Francis, A.B., J.C.D., The Minister of Baptism, XII-197 pp., 1942.
171. Willett, Rev. Robert Albert, J.C.D., The Probative Value of Documents in Ecclesiastical Trials, X-124 pp., 1942.
172. Woeber, Rev. Edward Martin, M.A., J.C.D., The Interpellations, XII-161 pp., 1942.
173. Benko, Rev. Matthew Aloysius, O.S.B., M.A., J.C.L., The Abbot *Nullius*.
174. Christ, Rev. Joseph James, M.A., S.T.L., J.C.L., Dispensation from Vindicative Penalties.
175. Clancy, Rev. Patrick M. J., O.P., A.B., S.T.Lr., J.C.D., The Local Religious Superior, X-229 pp., 1943.

176. Clarke, Rev. Thomas James, J.C.D., Parish Societies, XII-147 pp., 1943.
177. Connolly, Rev. John Patrick, S.T.L., J.C.D., Synodal Examiners and Parish Priest Consultors, X-223 pp., 1943.
178. Drumm, Rev. William Martin, A.B., J.C.L., Hospital Chaplains.
179. Flanagan, Rev. Bernard Joseph, A.B., S.T.L., J.C.D., The Canonical Erection of Religious Houses, X-147 pp., 1943.
180. Kelleher, Rev. Stephen Joseph, A.B., S.T.B., J.C.D., Discussions with Non-Catholics: Canonical Legislation, X-93 pp., 1943.
181. Lewis, Rev. Gordian, C.P., J.C.D., Chapters in Religious Institutes, XII-169 pp., 1943.
182. Marx, Rev. Adolph, J.C.D., The Declaration of Nullity of Marriages Contracted Outside the Church, X-151 pp., 1943.
183. Matulenas, Rev. Raymond Anthony, O.S.B., A.B., J.C.L., Communication, a Source of Privileges.
184. O'Leary, Rev. Charles Gerard, C.SS.R., J.C.L., Religious Dismissed After Perpetual Profession.
185. Power, Rev. Cornelius Michael, J.C.L., The Blessing of Cemeteries.
186. Shuhler, Rev. Ralph Vincent, O.S.A., J.C.D., Privileges of Religious to Absolve and Dispense, XII-195 pp., 1943.
187. Ziolkowski, Rev. Thaddeus Stanislaus, A.B., J.C.D., The Consecration and Blessing of Churches, XII-151 pp., 1943.
188. Heneghan, Rev. John Joseph, S.T.D., J.C.L., The Marriages of Unworthy Catholics: Canons 1065 and 1066.

www.ingramcontent.com/pod-product-compliance
Lightning Source LLC
LaVergne TN
LVHW050256080826
844660LV00012B/644

* 9 7 8 0 8 1 3 2 2 3 6 3 6 *